CRITICAL THINKING

CRITICAL THINKING

Evaluating Claims and Arguments in Everyday Life SECOND EDITION

Brooke Noel Moore ❑ **Richard Parker**
CALIFORNIA STATE UNIVERSITY, CHICO

 Mayfield Publishing Company

Library of Congress Cataloging-in-Publication Data

Moore, Brooke Noel.
Critical thinking.

Includes index.
1. Thought and thinking.   I. Parker,
Richard.   II. Title.
B105.T54M66   1989   160   88-7962
ISBN 0-87484-841-5

Manufactured in the United States of America

10 9 8 7 6 5 4 3 2 1

Mayfield Publishing Company
1240 Villa Street
Mountain View, CA 94041

Sponsoring editor, James Bull; production manager, Gwen Larson; copy editor, Toni Haskell; text designer, Andrew Zutis; cover designer, Charles Kaplan; cover photo, THE IMAGE BANK West/Michel Tcherevkoff; illustrator, Kevin Opstedahl. The text was set in 11/12 Berkeley Old Style Book by Waldman Graphics and printed on 50# Finch Opaque by R.R. Donnelley & Sons Co.

Text Credits

Page 44   *An American Rhetoric*, 5th ed., by William W. Watt. Copyright © 1980 by Holt, Rinehart and Winston. Reprinted by permission.

Page 47   "Residential Lease-Rental Agreement and Deposit Receipt" reprinted by permission of Professional Publishing Corporation.

Pages 49, 225   Copyright by *Sacramento Bee*, 1985.

Page 55   Copyright 1985 by Time, Inc. All rights reserved. Reprinted by permission from TIME.

Page 56   Copyright 1988 by Time, Inc. All rights reserved. Reprinted by permission from TIME.

Page 56   Reprinted from *Newsweek*, February 1, 1988. Copyright © 1988 by Newsweek, Inc. All rights reserved.

(*Credits continue on page 470*)

To Alexander,
Bill,
and Sherry

Contents

Preface   xiii

Part One Claims

1 *What Is Critical Thinking?*   2
   Claims and Critical Thinking   3
   Claims and Reasons   4
   The Purposes Behind Claims   6
   Supported and Unsupported Claims   8
   The Issue   10
   Critical Thinking and Clear Writing   12
   Recap   12
   Exercises 1-1 through 1-6   13

2 *Understanding Claims*   21
   Sources of Unclarity: Ambiguity   22
   Exercises 2-1 and 2-2   25
   Vagueness   27
   Exercises 2-3 through 2-6   29
   Unfamiliar Words   31
   Exercise 2-7   32
   Meaning and Definition   32
   Exercises 2-8 through 2-10   35
   Analytically True Claims   38

Exercise 2-11   39
Complexity   40
Exercises 2-12 through 2-14   45
Understanding Spoken Claims   47
Exercise 2-15   49
Recap   50
Exercises 2-16 through 2-24   50

3 **Evaluating Informative Claims**   58
Conflicting Claims   59
Exercises 3-1 and 3-2   60
Conflicts with Personal Observations   61
Exercises 3-3 through 3-7   63
Conflicts with Background Knowledge   65
Exercise 3-8   66
Assessing Credibility   67
   Expertise   67
   Observer Credibility   73
   Reference Works   74
   Government Publications   75
   The News Media   75
Recap   76
Exercises 3-9 through 3-14   77

4 **Explanations**   83
Explanations and Arguments   83
Explanations and Justifications   85
Kinds of Explanations   86
   Physical Explanations   87
   Psychological Explanations   92
   Functional Explanations   94
Evaluating Explanations   95
   Testability   96
   Noncircularity   96
   Relevance   97
   Freedom from Excessive Vagueness   97
   Reliability   98
   Explanatory Power   98
   Freedom from Unnecessary Assumptions   99
   Consistency with Well-Established Theory   100
   Consideration of a Common Cause   100
Explanatory Comparisons (Analogies)   101
Recap   103
Exercises 4-1 through 4-9   104

5   Nonargumentative Persuasion   116

   Slanters   117
      Euphemisms   117
      Innuendo   119
      Loaded Questions   119
      Weaslers   120
      Downplayers   122
      Proof Surrogates   123
      Stereotypes   123
      Hyperbole   124
      Persuasive Definitions, Explanations, and Comparisons   126
   Exercises 5-1 through 5-5   128
   Information Tailoring and the News   132
      Who Makes the News?   132
      Who Brings Us the News?   134
      And Who's Paying Attention?   135
   Exercises 5-6 through 5-8   136
   Advertising   137
   Exercises 5-9 and 5-10   141
   Recap   142
   Exercises 5-11 through 5-15   142

6   Pseudoreasoning I   146

   The Subjectivist Fallacy   148
   Appeal to Belief   150
   Appeal to the Consequences of Belief   152
   Scare Tactics   154
   Appeal to Pity   155
   Peer Pressure (the Bandwagon)   157
   Apple Polishing   158
   The Horse Laugh   159
   Appeal to Spite or Indignation   161
   Two Wrongs Make a Right   162
   Recap   164
   Exercises 6-1 through 6-13   164

7   Pseudoreasoning II   177

   Ad Hominem   178
   Selfish Rationalizing   181
   Burden of Proof   182
   Straw Man   184
   False Dilemma   186
   Slippery Slope   188
   Recap   189
   Exercises 7-1 through 7-8   190

Part Two Arguments

8 Understanding and Evaluating Arguments   202
The Anatomy of Arguments   202
Exercises 8-1 through 8-5   205
Deduction and Induction 209
Exercises 8-6 through 8-9   213
Unstated Premises   215
Exercises 8-10 through 8-13   216
Techniques for Understanding Arguments   218
  Clarifying an Argument's Structure   218
  Distinguishing Arguments from Window Dressing   221
Evaluating Arguments   222
  Are the Premises Acceptable?   222
  Do the Premises Support the Conclusion?   223
Recap   223
Exercises 8-14 through 8-19   223

9 Common Patterns of Deductive Arguments   232
Arguments and Argument Patterns   233
Argument Patterns: Set One   234
  Modus Ponens   234
  Affirming the Consequent   235
Exercise 9-1   237
  Modus Tollens   238
  Denying the Antecedent   238
Exercise 9-2   240
  Chain Argument   240
  Reverse Chain Argument   241
Exercises 9-3 and 9-4   242
Argument Patterns: Set Two   243
  Valid Conversions   244
  Invalid Conversions   245
Exercises 9-5 and 9-6   246
  Valid Syllogisms   247
  Invalid Syllogisms   248
Exercises 9-7 and 9-8   250
Indirect Proof   252
Begging the Question   255
Recap   257
Exercises 9-9 through 9-11   258

10 *Generalization and Related Inductive Reasoning*　　262

General Claims　262
Exercises 10-1 and 10-2　265
Comparative General Claims　266
Exercises 10-3 through 10-5　269
Inductive Generalizations: From a Sample to a Class　271
　Statistical Inductive Generalizations　274
　Sample Size　278
　Summary　279
　Fallacies of Inductive Generalizations　280
Exercises 10-6 through 10-15　281
Inductive Analogical Arguments　286
　Sample Size　287
Exercises 10-16 through 10-20　288
Statistical Syllogisms　293
　Appeals to Authority　294
Exercises 10-21 and 10-22　296
Recap　298

11 *Causal Arguments*　　300

Causation Among Specific Events　300
　Summary　306
Exercises 11-1 through 11-3　307
Causation in Populations　310
　Controlled Cause-to-Effect Experiments　311
　Nonexperimental Cause-to-Effect Studies　315
　Nonexperimental Effect-to-Cause Studies　317
Recap　318
Exercises 11-4 through 11-7　320

12 *Moral Reasoning*　　328

Descriptive and Prescriptive Claims　328
Exercises 12-1 and 12-2　330
Getting an *Ought* from an *Is*　331
Exercises 12-3 and 12-4　334
A Principle of Morality and Reason　335
Exercises 12-5 and 12-6　338
Evaluating Moral Reasoning　341
Recap　346
Exercises 12-7 and 12-8　348

Appendices

1   *Categorical Logic*   353

2   *Truth-Functional Logic*   368

3   *Writing an Argumentative Essay*   388

Glossary   396
Answers, Suggestions, and Tips for Starred Exercises   406
Index   465

Preface

The first edition of this book appeared early in 1986. *Glastnost* lay in the future and no one outside New England had heard of Michael Dukakis. We were younger in '86, but so were you.

Since then we've also changed a bit in our views on the best way to help students develop critical thinking skills; hence, this new edition.

We should say right away that we haven't altered our thoughts on the basics. Critical thinking, we still maintain, includes a wide variety of deliberative processes aimed at making wise decisions about what to believe and do. Critical thinking is more than just the evaluation of arguments; it includes both the inclination and the ability to search out considerations that are relevant to an issue. The trick to teaching critical thinking, we still believe, is to integrate logic—both formal and informal—with a variety of skills and topics useful in making sound decisions about beliefs and actions, and to make it all palatable by presenting it in the context of real-life situations. This is what we try to do in this book, aiming our efforts at undergraduates and especially those in their first year or two of college. The book remains informal in tone and presents illustrations, examples, and exercises taken from or designed to resemble material that these students will find familiar.

Organization

The basic organization of the book is unchanged. The book has two parts, the first devoted to claims and the second devoted to arguments. Students find the distinction between supported and unsupported claims natural, and the two-part organization allows us, in Part One, to treat many features of claims and to discuss the variety of nonargumentative ways they are urged upon us, without becoming too deeply involved in the principles of argumentation.

This edition also contains a new appendix (Appendix 3) that offers guidance on constructing an argumentative essay. And we have added exercises to the two appendices retained from the first edition, which give compact but fairly complete treatments of categorical and truth-functional logic.

Alternative Approaches

The book is designed to offer the instructor great flexibility of approach and emphasis. For example, instructors who wish to teach a more traditional course in elementary logic will find the book adaptable to their needs. By emphasizing the first two appendices plus Chapters 8, 10, and 11, an instructor can use this book to teach a traditional inductive/deductive argument course while still taking advantage of the book's other features. One such feature is Chapter 5, which treats nonargumentative persuasion. Once upon a time we were baffled by the difficulty of applying the principles of logic to letters to editors, family discussions, articles in opinion magazines, and the like. Then it became clear to us that a large proportion of real-life attempts to win acceptance for claims doesn't involve principles of logic but consists in nonargumentative techniques. Hence, in Chapter 5 we treat a wide variety of nonargumentative persuasion devices. Our experience has shown that this component can help turn even the most traditional elementary logic course into a powerful tool for developing students' critical skills.

Instructors especially concerned with developing students' writing skills will probably wish to assign the new Appendix 3, Writing an Argumentative Essay, and may also prefer to stress the material in Chapters 1–7, placing less emphasis on the techniques of argument appraisal and analysis in Chapters 8–11. These instructors will find that Chapter 12, Moral Reasoning, is a good source of issues for extended treatment in essays, in addition to the topics suggested at the end of Appendix 3. Further, in every chapter we have added an exercise that calls for the writing of an essay.

Chapters on Pseudoreasoning

We should also draw attention to Chapters 6 and 7, which deal with what we call pseudoreasoning. Those familiar with the first edition will see that our thought about this notion has evolved some over the past few years, partly in response to suggestions from reviewers and correspondents. Pseudoreasoning is a fairly large and diversified inventory of irrelevancies, emotional appeals, and persuasive devices that all too often induce people to accept or reject a claim when they have no good reason for doing so. These chapters should help students distinguish between weak reasons and irrelevant considerations, a distinction that is subtle but real. Instructors can treat what we've called types of pseudoreasoning as informal fallacies; we've included many of the traditional fallacy names in our scheme. In this edition we have added several types of pseudoreasoning—for instance, Burden of Proof and Slippery Slope—that were not explicitly mentioned in the first edition.

In these chapters the emphasis is not on the usual classification of feelings or emotions to which appeals are made but on the relevance of the appeal to the issue at hand. Energy is finite, and we think it better for students to spend theirs on determining the relevance of an appeal rather than on deciding whether the appeal is to prejudice, patriotism, pride, or what have you.

Exercises

The exercises in this book do considerable work. There are more than a thousand in the text and many more in the accompanying resource guide, *The Logical Accessory*. An instructor's decision about how to use the exercises will help determine the nature of the course. Some of the exercises can serve as assignments that can be quickly graded; others are better used as the basis for classroom discussion. Still others might be used for short quizzes. The answers to starred questions often point out further details and extend some of the material in the text. Instructors may find the answer section useful as a direct teaching aid or as a foil for their own comments.

The Logical Accessory: Instructors' Resources

The Logical Accessory is an invaluable supplement for instructors. Like many instructor's guides, it contains answers to exercises not answered in the text. It also contains some important comments about the material in the text and some suggestions for teaching this material. Further, *The Logical Accessory* contains quizzes for each chapter, a pre- and post-course examination, and a bank of hundreds of additional exercise/examination questions—all with answers. Finding and inventing exercises is seldom fun; we hope those we have provided will help relieve the instructor of as much drudgery as possible.

Additional Features

Among the other features of the book that we have found useful in our own classes are the following:

- A glossary at the end of the book that provides students with definitions of key terms.
- A treatment of statistical studies designed for individuals more likely to encounter media reports of such studies than the studies themselves.
- An account of value-laden claims and moral reasoning that acknowledges the crucial importance of reason in moral matters.
- A serious treatment of causal arguments that avoids tedious discussion of Mill's methods but recasts what is important in them in accessible language.
- An account of analogies used as explanations as well as in arguments.
- A clear argument-diagramming technique, easily customized by the individual instructor.
- A treatment of credibility, authority, and expertise.
- A *short* treatment of definition and meaning.

Not everyone will wish to cover all the topics presented in the book. Topics can be selected to accommodate the situation of each instructor. There are about as many ways to combine the topics as there are creative instructors of critical thinking.

Specific Changes in the Second Edition

The second edition incorporates several improvements in addition to a routine cleaning up of first-edition corrigenda and updating of exercises and examples. The changes have been made, however, so that instructors accustomed to the first edition can use the second edition without revising their courses or (with one or two possible exceptions) their handouts or overheads.

One of our major objectives for this edition was to arrange things as much as possible so that students will not be frustrated by the difficulties that are involved in thinking critically. For example, as in the first edition there are some truly difficult problems scattered among the exercise sets, but in this edition we've tried to warn readers about the nastier items, and we've provided more preparatory problems of lesser difficulty. Instructors will especially appreciate these modifications to the exercises in Chapter 9, we think. We have also tried to indicate those topics about which reasonable people may disagree and to indicate those exercises for which there may not be such a thing as *the* correct answer. And we've moved the distinction between arguments and explanations from the first chapter to the fourth, making it easier to grasp. It is a subtle distinction, and the learning of it invites frustration; it inhabits the fourth chapter more comfortably than it did Chapter 1. In the new edition, instructors who think the distinction isn't worth the trouble it takes to teach can easily skip that part (or even all) of Chapter 4. In any case, it is no longer in a position to confront students on the first day of the term.

Among the other changes are these:

In Chapter 1 we explain the concept of the *issue,* which is fundamental to thinking critically and writing well. Readers will be better served, we think, by learning this concept at the outset.

In Chapter 2 we've incorporated several excellent suggestions we received from correspondents to strengthen and clarify our treatment of vagueness and ambiguity.

We haven't done much to Chapter 3, though a student who wrote and upbraided us for our skepticism about Bigfoot will be happy to see that Bigfoot has departed from this revision. We haven't changed our opinions about Bigfoot; we just haven't heard as much about him lately, and we're trying to keep current.

In Chapter 4 you'll now find a discussion of justifications and an explanation of how justifications often employ explanations. We've also added a section on explanatory power and have made a few minor revisions in terminology.

Chapter 5 (formerly Chapter 7) on nonargumentative persuasion has been moved ahead of the two chapters on pseudoreasoning (6 and 7). This change moves the section on slanting devices closer to the section on emotive language, and the relocation of the pseudoreasoning chapters helps smooth the transition from Part One to Part Two.

As for Chapter 8, judging from our mailbag, exactly half of those who teach critical thinking like argument diagrams and the other half detest them. However, most correspondents who use diagrams prefer the "standard" (Beardsly) tree-diagrams to our supposedly simpler version, so the diagramming technique you will now find in Chapter 8 is the standard version.

In Chapter 8 we also clear up a peculiar consequence of some of our definitions that seemed to make it theoretically possible for an instance of modus ponens to be invalid. None of our own students had spotted this problem; but then, neither had we.

The changes in Chapter 9 are all intended to make it easier for students to recognize the common patterns of deductive inference when they see them.

In Chapter 10 of this edition we have replaced the term *confidence interval* with the more popular term, *error margin.* Chapter 11 benefits, we think, from a simpler classification of causal arguments. The improvements in Chapter 12 are chiefly stylistic.

Finally, although many illustrations and examples relate to events current in the news, we've tried not to place students who are not up-to-date on these things at a great disadvantage. Granted, in real life you do pay penalties for having your head in the sand, and we've emphasized this in the text. But we don't want our explanations of basic principles of critical thinking to be incomprehensible to those who are unfamiliar with the subtleties of some current event.

Acknowledgements

If this book contains errors, it is in spite of the assistance we've received from the many people who have helped us with suggestions, commentary, encouragement, and advice. Those who have assisted us, in either this or our previous edition or both, and to whom we are very grateful, include J. Anthony Blair, University of Windsor; Linda Bomstad, California State University, Sacramento; David Conway, University of Missouri, St. Louis; Richard Double, Indiana University-Purdue University; Gunar Freibergs, Los Angeles Valley College; George Hammerbacher, King's College; Donald A. Henson, Wilkes College; Peter Horban, Simon Fraser University; Charles F. Kielkopf, The Ohio State University; Lenore Langsdorf, University of Texas, Arlington; John D. May, University of Queensland; Lorraine Viscardi Murray, Georgia State University; Robert Mutti, San Francisco State University; Paul Newberry, California State University, Bakersfield; John E. Parks-Clifford, University of Missouri, St. Louis (to whom we are indebted for the modifications in diagramming that are found in this edition); Anita Silvers, San Francisco State University; Deborah Hansen Soles, Wichita State University; Douglas F. Stalker, University of Delaware; Dan Turner, East Tennessee State University; Arnold Wilson, University of Cincinnati; and Perry Weddle, California State University, Sacramento.

We would also like to thank for their help our fellow workers at California State University, Chico, including Dan Barnett, Judy Collins, Esther Gallagher, Alexandra Kiriakis, Cindy Davidson, Frank Ficarra, Becky Lessley, Scott Mahood, Greg Maxwell, Anne Morrissey, Jack Safarik, Neil Schwertman, Joanna Tauscher, Robin Wilson, and an unknown predecessor at Chico State, whose abandoned classroom materials contained the idea for the cartoon that appears on page 210; and our families and friends, especially Patricia Edleman, Aaron Edlin, Dorothy Edlin, Ted Edlin, Maureen Hernandez, Rose Kraiss, Linda Moore, Ralph J. Moore, Sr., and Ralph J. Moore, Jr. Finally, we especially want to express our gratitude to the magnificently helpful and supportive staff at Mayfield Publishing Company, who know their business and do things right: Jan Beatty, Gwen Larson, Kirstan Price, Pamela Trainer, Jil Wood, and, above all, Jim Bull, who made it all happen.

B.N.M.
R.P.
October, 1988
Chico, California

CRITICAL THINKING

PART ONE

Claims

1 *What Is Critical Thinking?*

Now if we set about to find out what . . . [a] statement means and to determine whether to accept or reject it, we would be engaged in thinking which, for lack of a better term, we shall call critical thinking.

—B. OTHANEL SMITH

Think critically? That's what others don't do, isn't it?

—KIRK MONFORT

A newspaper editorial tries to convince you that you and your town would be better off if all the incumbents in the city council were defeated in the next municipal election. A magazine advertisement tries to sell you on a new brand of toothpaste, paper towels, or kitty litter. A friend tries to get you to go skiing next weekend. You are wondering whether you can afford to buy a car.

Unless you are camped out on some remote mountain peak, you are probably bombarded every day by requests, arguments, and exhortations to believe this or that or to do this or that. And making wise decisions about what to believe and what to do is not always an easy task. We would have liked to begin this book by telling you that it presents a neat and easy method for determining how to make such wise decisions, but unfortunately it does no such thing. However, certain methods, techniques, and precautions can make wise decisions easier and more likely. This book, when combined with some effort and careful reflection on your part, is intended to help you consider issues carefully and come to the best decisions you can. In short, it is designed to help you learn how to *think critically*.

Claims and Critical Thinking

What is critical thinking? We'll offer a definition of sorts, but first let's consider the idea of a claim. A **claim** is a statement that is either true or false. Now, many of the things we say are neither true nor false, as when we ask a question ("What time is it?"), greet a friend ("Hello, Theresa!"), or give an order ("Shut the door"). Such questions, greetings, and orders, as well as lots of other things we say and write, may be appropriate or inappropriate and clever or stupid, but we do not ordinarily think of them as true or false. Thus, none of these remarks counts as a claim in our sense of the word, because a claim must always have a truth value—that is, it must be true or false (although we do not have to *know* whether it is true or false).

Decisions such as the ones called for in the first paragraph of this chapter can be put in the form of claims we may accept or reject. The first example confronts you with the claim "You (or your town) will be better off if the current members of the city council are replaced by other candidates." The second example presents the claim "You should buy Brand X toothpaste (or paper towels, or kitty litter, or whatever)." The other two examples, respectively, present claims like these: "You ought to go skiing with your friend next weekend," and "You can afford to buy a car."

When we are confronted with a claim, we can accept it (that is, believe it), reject it (believe that it is false), or suspend judgment about it, possibly because we don't have enough information at the time to accept or reject it. **Critical thinking** is the careful and deliberate determination of whether to accept, reject, or suspend judgment about a claim. The ability to think critically is vitally important. In fact, our lives depend on it, since the way we conduct our lives depends on what claims we believe—on what claims we accept. The more carefully we evaluate a claim, and the more fully we separate issues that are relevant to it from those that are not, the more critical is our thinking. We'll spend a good bit of time discussing how this is done as we go along.

We do not do our critical thinking in a vacuum, of course. When we are confronted with a claim like those above, usually we already have a certain amount of information relevant to the issue, and we can generally figure out where to find more if we need it. Having both the desire and the ability to bring such information to bear on our decisions is part of the critical-thinking process. So critical thinking involves a lot of skills, including the abilities to listen and read carefully, to evaluate arguments, to look for and find hidden assumptions, and to trace the consequences of a claim.

If you are beginning to sense that there is no simple way of deciding when to accept a claim, then you are on the right track. We could say, of course,

A Word of Wisdom

There's one thing worse than making mistakes in your thinking: That's letting somebody else make them for you.

—ANTHONY BORD

that we should accept a claim only when we have a good reason for doing so, but this wouldn't help much, since there is no short-cut method for determining what constitutes a good reason for accepting a claim. People learn what a good reason is through example, illustration, and informed guidance. And that's where this book comes in. In these pages we'll give you examples of good reasons, and bad ones too, and help you to see the difference. We'll explain many of the principles that distinguish good reasoning from bad, and, most important, we'll try to guide you to an understanding of good reasoning and allow you to practice and develop your own skills as a critical thinker.

If you are to improve these skills, you will have to practice. Like playing tennis or the piano, critical thinking is a skill that you simply cannot become good at without practicing. Fortunately, there is plenty of opportunity for such practice. We have supplied lots of exercises throughout the book, and you'll find that examples of the material we cover will turn up regularly in your everyday life. Put what you learn into practice—critical thinking is not just a classroom activity.

In the remainder of this chapter we'll briefly explain how critical thinking includes traditional logic but is somewhat broader in scope. Then we'll discuss the variety of purposes people have for making claims and the various functions those claims serve. As you'll see, it is often helpful in evaluating a claim to know something about why the person making it is doing so. We'll also discuss a point on which we base a major division of this book: the difference between claims that are supported by stated reasons and those that are not. After that, we'll talk about the crucial problem of identifying issues. Unless you are able to identify the issue that's at stake in a discussion, you will not be able to put a lot of what you learn from this book to good use. We'll end the chapter with a short commercial for critical thinking and good writing and then get on with some exercises.

Claims and Reasons

When someone offers a claim for your consideration, how do you decide whether to accept it? If other claims—reasons—are presented in support of the claim, then you must determine whether those reasons really do justify accepting it. **Logic** is that branch of philosophy concerned with whether the reasons presented for a claim, if those reasons were true, would justify the claim's acceptance. Let's look at an example. Suppose Theresa, whom we'll hear from now and then throughout this book, tells you the following:

> It would be a good thing if Senator Leghorn were not reelected next November. He is known to take bribes, and nobody who does that ought to represent the people of this state.

Theresa has given reasons that, if true, do in fact support the claim that Leghorn ought not be reelected. But the task of critical thinking is not *just* to discover whether Theresa's claim is supported by its stated reasons. A critical thinker must assess the reasons themselves, determine whether there are other reasons for accepting the claim should the given reasons be defective, and weigh the result against any reasons there may be for rejecting the claim.

The claim in the above example—that the senator should not be re-elected—is important enough for a person to have an opinion about it. If Theresa had been unable to supply reasons for it, or if the reasons she supplied turned out to be false, then a critically thinking person would make a reasonable attempt to determine whether good reasons actually existed for accepting or rejecting the claim.

Traditional logic is an ancient and well-developed field of study, and there is a remarkable amount to be learned from it. But the main concern in logic is not the actual truth of claims but rather whether reasons, *if* true, would support the claims they are alleged to support. Logic is less concerned about the actual truth of either the reasons or the claims they are supposed to support

Claims, Their Reasons, and Logic

Logic is not especially interested in whether the reasons for a claim are in fact true. It is concerned only with the logical relationships between claims and their reasons: If the reasons were true, would the conclusion have to be true? The following hypothetical arithmetic problem is concerned with relationships in much the same way:

If gasoline costs 10 cents per gallon, then how much would 20 gallons cost?

Such problems have mathematically correct answers. Here the answer is based on the assumption of 10 cent-per-gallon gasoline, even though nobody has been able to buy gasoline at that price for years. Logic evaluates logical correctness in a similar way. Here's an example:

All Irish people have red hair. Kelly is Irish. So Kelly must have red hair.

This argument is logically correct even though we all know that not all Irish are redheads. It is irrelevant to logic that one of the reasons—all Irish people have red hair—happens to be false.

than about the relationship of the reasons to those claims. So, when we as critical thinkers try to decide whether or not to accept a claim, we must go beyond the traditional scope of logic to consider, among other things, whether the reasons offered for the claim are themselves worth believing.

Frequently people advance claims without presenting any reasons at all for accepting them. We are told that things go better with Coke, that Dodge builds better trucks, that Socrates died in 399 B.C., and that pear trees are not susceptible to oak root fungus. In most cases like these we are not given any real reasons to support what has been said. And traditional logic doesn't have much to say about such unsupported claims aside from analyzing their structures. But in the context of critical thinking we will look rather closely at such claims. After all, the fact that no reasons for accepting them have been presented does not mean that no reasons exist. (And, in an occasional rare case, it is unwise to wait for a reason before accepting a claim: When you hear "The building is on fire!" it is best to act first and reason later.)

The Purposes Behind Claims

In assessing the acceptability of a claim, especially one offered without supporting reasons, we have an advantage if we have some idea of the speaker's or writer's purpose. Before considering why this is so, however, let's ask what looks like an obvious question: Why do people make claims? It seems a truism to say that the making of a claim is intended to communicate information. But that is only the first of several reasons why people make claims. For example, we make claims to excuse ourselves ("It's getting late; I've got to be going"), to justify our actions ("I was too far away to help her"), to make promises ("I'll be there by five o'clock; you can count on it"), to express admiration ("The Capetown sunset is breathtaking!"), to get assistance ("I need help!"), to show disapproval ("I certainly wouldn't wear anything like that"), to elicit sympathy ("I've got a headache and I lost forty dollars in a poker game last night"), and so on. It is true that we communicate information in making some of these claims, but communicating information is not our principal objective: It is the means by which we achieve our primary objective, whatever that may be.

Thinking that people make claims only to communicate information can lead to misunderstandings. Here Theresa is talking to her friend Daniel:

THERESA: I hope I've made my point sufficiently clear!
DANIEL: Oh. That's interesting.

Daniel apparently thinks that Theresa is only trying to communicate information. Though most of us can see that Theresa is trying to emphasize the importance of some point she has already made, he believes that she is only stating a claim about her hopes and, given that belief, he is answering appropriately. Because he misunderstands the purpose of her remark, Daniel probably won't think carefully about the point itself.

Of course, people are not usually as dense as we've portrayed Daniel in this conversation. Or are they? The advertisers of Dewar's Scotch whiskey print handsome photographs of accomplished people—poets, architects, executives, and the like—together with biographical claims about their ages, the books they read, their hobbies, and so forth. Each sketch includes the fact that the person in question favors Dewar's Scotch. If we believe that the real point of these advertisements is to acquaint us with some interesting people who just

Put-Downs from Campaign '88

Notice the subtly different purposes of each of these nasties from '88:

"The only difference between Dan Quayle and Jane Fonda is that Fonda went to Vietnam."

—1988 presidential campaign joke

"Clint Eastwood says to criminals, 'Go ahead, make my day.' The governor of Massachusetts says, 'Go ahead, have a nice weekend.' "
—GEORGE BUSH, about the prisoner furlough program of Massachusetts

"I called Dan Quayle this morning to congratulate him (on being named George Bush's vice-presidential candidate) but he was shaving. First time."
—Senator ROBERT DOLE

"I wouldn't want to know."
—SEKA, a star of pornographic movies, when asked by columnist Mike Royko if she thought Bush would be "good in bed"

"After listening to Dan Quayle for 90 minutes I can understand why he kept talking about job training."
—Senator LLOYD BENTSEN, after his debate with Senator Dan Quayle

"I wouldn't be surprised if he thought a naval exercise is something you find in a Jane Fonda workout book."
—GEORGE BUSH, about Michael Dukakis

"He has got a tremendous problem. He cannot get elected unless things get worse, and things aren't going to get worse unless he gets elected."
—GEORGE BUSH, about Michael Dukakis

"QUESTION: What were the toughest three years in Dan Quayle's life? ANSWER: Second grade."

—1988 presidential campaign joke

happen to keep a supply of Dewar's on hand, we are uncritical readers indeed. The advertisers couldn't care less whether we remember anything about the individuals portrayed in the ads. They want us to buy their product, so they link it with people whose life-styles they think we will admire or envy. The hidden suggestion is that buying this brand of scotch will make us more like them. Unless we remember that, after all, these ads are designed purely and simply to sell a certain brand of scotch, we may forget that our choice of whiskey is going to contribute very little to our chances of attaining success. The advertisers, of course, hope that we will focus on the apparent purpose of their claims (i.e., to familiarize us with interesting people) and *overlook* the fact that their real purpose for these claims is to sell Dewar's.

The ostensible purpose behind a claim, then, is not always the most important one. In this book we will be concerned with claims that serve one or more of three basic purposes:

1. To convey information
2. To affect our attitudes about someone or something
3. To influence our behavior

Of course, our attitudes affect our behavior. Thus, people can seek to influence our attitudes *in order to* influence our behavior. And, as we saw with the Dewar's advertisements, although claims can provide information, their principal function *can* still be to influence our attitudes and behavior. Knowing that the apparent function or purpose of a claim is not always its real function makes us more careful readers and listeners.

Supported and Unsupported Claims

When Theresa claimed that Senator Leghorn shouldn't be reelected because he had taken bribes, she was giving us an argument. An **argument** is a set of claims, one of which (the **principal claim** or **conclusion**) is supposed to be supported by the rest (the *reasons* or **premises**).

Someone might say to you, for example, that we're in for a wet winter. You might ask why you should believe such a claim. If your informant then replies, "Because the folks at Scripps Institute of Oceanography say so, and they've never been wrong," he or she has given you an argument—reasons for accepting the claim that we'll have a wet winter. (These may not be *good* reasons for accepting it, but we didn't say that you were given a *good* argument. We'll get to that.) Had your informant simply said that we were in for a wet winter, you would have received not an argument but only an unsupported claim.

Similarly, one who makes a claim intended to influence your attitude or behavior may or may not give an argument in its support. For instance, Sandy might seek to diminish your respect for Alphonse by telling you that he is a habitual liar. Or you might try to get Scott to close the window by ordering him to do so. In neither case has an argument been given. But arguments *might* have been given. Sandy might have said that she checked up on the last several statements Alphonse made to her and discovered that they were all false. And you might have mentioned that the heating bill has been too high lately, and that Scott should close the window to keep the heat in. You and Sandy would then have supplied reasons for believing what was said about Alphonse and the window, respectively. Of course, it is not clear that, on the basis of those reasons alone, you ought to be convinced that Alphonse is a liar or that Scott should close the window. The point to remember here is simply that a claim, whether intended to inform or to affect someone's attitudes or behavior, may or may not come with supporting reasons.

An important distinction exists between *verbally* presenting reasons for a claim and giving someone reasons for it through nonverbal, nonlinguistic methods. If you're playing golf and somebody bounds out onto the fairway just as you're about to tee off, you have a good reason for waiting before making your shot—that is, for accepting the claim "I should wait before I shoot." Similarly, if a masked bandit waves a gun at you and tells you to lie down on the floor, you have a good reason for obeying—that is, for accepting the claim "I'd better lie down." In neither case have reasons been presented verbally.

In this book, to qualify as an argument a claim must be supported by at least one verbal reason—a reason stated either through speech or writing. Thus, the masked man did not offer an argument, under our definition. But if he had said, "Lie down or I'll blow your head off," he would have presented an argument, because he would have stated a reason for your compliance ("I'll blow your head off if you don't").

Sometimes claims come to us with no accompanying reasons, and it becomes our job to look about and see whether there are reasons for accepting or rejecting them. There are also times when our feelings motivate us to believe a claim or to act. Feelings can supply good reasons for an action, but they can also move us in ways we come to regret. A second serving of dessert or another beer might be tempting, but sometimes there are good reasons to resist such temptations.

If It Feels Good . . .

The popular slogan "If it feels good, do it!" is naive. There's certainly nothing wrong with doing something because it feels good. In fact, that's a reason for doing it. But, obviously not everything that feels good is wise. The critical thinker's version of this slogan might be put this way:

If it feels good, and there's no good reason *not* to do it, then do it!

The Issue

In the broadest sense of the word, an issue is simply a matter that is in dispute between two or more parties. If we said to you, "All in all, Reagan was a pretty good president," and you replied, "And I suppose you think the Edsel was a pretty good car," then there is an issue that divides us: whether or not Reagan was a good president. In this book you will get a lot of practice in recognizing issues, because if we can't identify issues, we certainly can't hope to resolve differences in our opinions and beliefs.

If you wish to settle an issue rationally, you use an argument, or a bunch of them. An argument always addresses or speaks to an issue. **The issue is the question the argument tries to settle.** To identify what's at issue in an argument, just ask what the conclusion of the argument is; that will tell you what the question is that the argument tries to settle. For example, consider this argument:

> John is opening up a law practice next month; apparently, **he passed the bar examination.**

The conclusion of the argument is the highlighted claim, "he passed the bar examination." The question the argument tries to settle, therefore, is *whether John passed the bar examination.* And that is the issue. One standard way of stating the issue an argument addresses is by placing the word *whether* in front of the claim made in the conclusion. Here's another example:

> **You should never lie to your roommate.** He or she is bound to find out about it and will never trust you again.

The conclusion of this argument is the claim, "You should never lie to your roommate." The issue, accordingly, is *whether you should never lie to your roommate.*

To find the issue addressed by an argument, therefore, you must be able to identify the conclusion of the argument. Later, in Part Two, where we deal at some length with arguments, we'll help you learn how to identify an argument's conclusion in difficult cases. Being able to identify an argument's conclusion, though not always easy, is always important, for doing so enables you to know what's at issue in the argument, and knowing that is knowing what the argument is about.

The settlement of one issue, incidentally, may bear on the settlement of another. For example, the issue of whether nuclear power plants are susceptible to dangerous accidents is closely related to the issue of whether we ought to build more of them. But it may be possible to settle the first issue and still leave the other in doubt. This is because there are other issues that also bear on whether to build more plants. If, for example, other forms of energy are nearly exhausted and there is no way to cut back on the consumption of energy, then it might be advisable to build more nuclear power plants even though they are dangerous.

Confusion results when two or more parties think they're addressing the same issue when in fact they're talking about different ones. Let's say that Daniel persists in offering arguments to the effect that nuclear power plants are dangerous. Theresa believes that, indeed, they are dangerous, but nonetheless they are worth the risk if we are to maintain our current standard of living. In this case, Daniel may be doomed to frustration unless he sees that the point he's making is not the one that is required to change Theresa's mind.

Being able to identify issues is an important part of critical thinking. Equally important is being able to determine what considerations bear on, that is, are relevant to, an issue. Whether nuclear power plants are dangerous is relevant to the issue of whether they should be built, but whether they should be built is not relevant to the issue of whether they are dangerous. You will get a lot of practice in this book in determining what is relevant to what.

Maybe kids don't boast about their fathers' being good at understanding issues, but it's an important skill to have.

Critical Thinking and Clear Writing

The importance of being able to write clearly is difficult to overestimate, and writing skills go hand in hand with critical-thinking skills. Generally speaking, clear writers are adept at critical thinking, and vice versa. Still, an ability to write clearly and an ability to think critically may be distinct. We might think of writing and speaking as "output" skills and critical thinking as a "processing" skill. (To continue the computer metaphor, we could call reading and listening "input" skills.) Currently the question of the relationship between these skills is controversial, and many would question whether they are distinct in the first place.

That being said, it is clear, we think, that an ability to think critically—an ability to know whether to accept, reject, or suspend judgment about a claim—can be an important and useful asset for anyone who desires to be a clear and effective writer or speaker. However, if this book is to help you with your writing skills, you must practice applying what you learn to your own claims. Since many of the exercises in this book call for written responses, you'll have ample opportunity for this practice. And remember: It is usually our own claims that are the most difficult to evaluate critically and therefore need the most careful scrutiny. Keeping this simple fact in mind is an important first step toward critically appraising your own thoughts, and applying what you learn here to the words you put on paper is an equally important step toward becoming a better writer.

Recap

Critical thinking is the careful and deliberate determination of whether to accept, reject, or suspend judgment about a claim. Though claims are made for any number of reasons, in this book we are especially concerned with those intended to convey information, affect our attitudes, or influence our behavior. If such claims are presented without stated reasons for their acceptance—that is, without supporting arguments—then we, as critical thinkers, must consider whether there are any credible reasons for accepting them. If they come to us with reasons, we must be able to tell whether those reasons are credible and whether they do in fact warrant acceptance of the claim. If the reasons are not credible or do not warrant acceptance of the claim, then we must consider whether there are any other reasons for accepting it.

Identifying the issue that's at stake in a discussion is crucial if we are to avoid talking at cross-purposes. The issue can often be expressed as a claim beginning with the word *whether*. Arguments are designed to help settle issues. If we think of an issue as a question, we can think of the conclusion of an argument as the answer to that question. Finally, we note that critical thinking and good, clear writing go hand in hand; nearly every improvement in your critical-thinking skills will be reflected in what you write.

Exercises

The exercises in this book are designed to provide practice in critical thinking. Some can be answered directly from the pages of the text, but some will require careful consideration. For many exercises in this book there is no such thing as *the* correct answer, just as there is no such thing as *the* correct way to serve a tennis ball or to write an essay. But some answers, like tennis serves and essays, are better than others. So, for many exercises it's not that your instructor's answers are "correct" and your answers, if they are not the same as your instructor's, are "incorrect." Still, your instructor's answers generally will be rational and sound, and worth paying attention to. Most university teachers have passed through a rigorous process that eliminates those who are not particularly good at thinking critically. Of course, like even the best umpire, your instructor may miss a few calls now and then. But generally, his or her judgment will be very reliable. The more you can bring your perceptions of what counts as a good answer into agreement with your instructor's perceptions, the better you will be at those skills that are central to the ability to think critically.

Starred exercises are answered in an answer section at the back of the book.

EXERCISE 1-1

Answer the questions based on your reading of the text.

★1. According to the text, what is critical thinking?
2. How does critical thinking differ from logic?
★3. Should a claim be rejected because no reasons have been given for its acceptance?
★4. Should a claim be accepted if no reasons have been given for its rejection?
5. Is there such a thing as an unstated argument?
6. Is it true that the purpose of making a claim is to communicate information?

★ 7. Where would you be most likely to encounter language that is used only to inform?

★ 8. Someone can try to inform you in order to influence your behavior. Can someone try to influence your behavior in order to inform you?

★ 9. Could someone try to influence your behavior without trying to inform you?

★ 10. Could someone try to influence your behavior in order to affect your attitudes about something?

★ 11. Could someone want to influence your attitude without wishing to affect your behavior?

★ 12. Could someone be interested only in influencing your behavior without caring about your attitude?

13. A reason for a claim can justify acceptance of that claim only if the reason itself is true. Do you agree with this statement? Why or why not?

14. What is an argument?

★ 15. Construct an argument that sixteen-year-olds should not be allowed to drink.

★ 16. A fast buildup of thunderclouds is a good reason to go inside or get a raincoat. Is it an argument?

17. "The weather report calls for rain today. You'd better take your raincoat." Is this an argument?

18. Suppose that you are trying to persuade your friend to miss his or her math class and go for a walk in the park with you. Can you think of a *non*argumentative method you might use?

★ 19. Is it ever reasonable to allow our feelings to influence our actions?

★ 20. What is the relationship between an issue and an argument?

EXERCISE 1-2

Although very little context information is provided to help you, try to determine the main purpose of each of the following claims. It may help to consider the speaker's identity and relationship to the subject of the claim. Ask yourself what the speaker would have accomplished (besides simply getting the claim accepted) if the claim were believed. After you have identified what you think is the speaker or writer's main purpose, try to come up with a claim that directly expresses that purpose.

EXAMPLE: At the end of the Iranian hostage crisis in 1980–81, Ronald Reagan stated, "We hear it said that we live in an era of limits to our powers. Well, let it also be understood, there are limits to our patience."

ANSWER: Reagan's purpose here was twofold: to warn terrorists and to reassure the American people that he would react strongly to the taking of hostages and other terrorist activity in the future. He might well have said: "Rest assured that this administration will take strong action against any terrorist activity directed toward Americans."

★1. "I was out of the loop."
　　　　　—GEORGE BUSH, when asked why he did not know about a proposal to sell arms to Iran in exchange for American hostages

2. "It is unfair that it remain empty and unspoiled."
　　　　　—HUGH STONE, developer of a proposed subdivision near Jordan Lake in North Carolina, commenting on official delays in approving his construction plans

★3. "Nothing makes a woman more beautiful than the belief that she's beautiful."
　　　　　—Actress SOPHIA LOREN

4. "Frankly, I think the fact that it has proven unworkable is ground for us to quit wasting money on it."
　　　　　—Senator BARRY GOLDWATER, speaking about the United Nations

★5. "Coke is it!"
　　　　　—From an advertisement for Coca-Cola

6. "I now pronounce you husband and wife."
　　　　　—A minister, speaking to the groom and bride

★7. "I once discovered a student cheating. He came to regret it."
　　　　　—A teacher, speaking to a class about to take a test

8. "I've already had three offers for this car and I'm considering a couple of them very seriously."
　　　　　—A seller, speaking to a potential buyer

★9. "It's okay for Alan Alda and Jane Fonda to be pro-abortion and for unilateral disarmament. But if conservatives speak out, they're labeled fanatics, bigots, or wackos—and they don't work anymore. The media tends to paint us with a swastika."
　　　　　—Singer PAT BOONE

10. "Experienced drivers buckle up."
　　　　　—A mother, speaking to a newly licensed teenage driver

★11. "Everything that anyone has done since I came along has been because of me. The Beatles, Michael, everybody. Whenever there's been a beat in the music and everyone starts to dance, it's because of me."
　　　　　—CHUBBY CHECKER, rock 'n' roll singer

12. "Scientists think that the llama and the alpaca came from the original guanaco. The . . . species do not breed with each other, in either their domestic or their wild state. Left to themselves, they may herd in the same areas but never mix."
　　　　　—GLADYS CONKLIN, *The Llamas of South America*

★13. "Presenting Sterling. It's only a cigarette like Porsche is only a car."
　　　　　—From an advertisement for Sterling cigarettes

14. "That nut's a genius!"
　　　　　—Conductor GEORGE SZELL, speaking about pianist Glenn Gould

★15. "The National Cancer Institute reports that research may suggest eating the right foods may reduce your risk of some kinds of cancer. Here are their recommendations. Eat high fiber foods . . ."
　　　　　—From the Kellogg's Cracklin' Oat Bran package

16. "Tomorrow's not promised to anybody."
>   —Chicago Bears running back WALTER PAYTON, before a championship game against a heavily favored team

★17. "They weren't watching babies die."
>   —DR. LEONARD BAILEY, who replaced "Baby Fae's" heart with that of a baboon, speaking about his critics

18. "I'm a conservative, but I'm not a nut about it."
>   —GEORGE BUSH

★19. "[People who sleep over grates in the street] are homeless, you might say, by choice."
>   —RONALD REAGAN

20. "Notice you didn't get a flat no."
>   —WALTER CRONKITE, when asked by Robert MacNeil if he might run for president

★21. "A lot of people didn't expect our relationship to last, but we've just celebrated our two months' anniversary."
>   —Actress BRITT EKLAND

22. "His [Michael Jackson's] music is characteristic of that ill-famed American lifestyle which the U.S.A. is trying to foist on the world. This film, *Thriller,* is really fascist, because it forces you to appreciate it like a drug. You were all sitting around obsessed with it—you couldn't even talk to each other."
>   —*Sovietskaya Kultura,* official Soviet cultural newspaper

★23. "What does she need to win for? Her father has millions."
>   —HANA MANDLIKOVA, after being defeated in the U.S. Tennis Open by Carling Bassett (who was recovering from mononucleosis)

24. "AIDS may give us an opportunity to discourage it, and that would be a good thing."
>   —Former Education Secretary WILLIAM BENNETT, speaking about teen sex

★25. "Yes, waking up. I always feel I should wake up the morning of the game. It's very important. If I do that, I feel I have an excellent chance of playing well that day."
>   —Ex-Forty-Niner RUSS FRANCIS, on being asked whether he had any superstitions or rituals he performed before important football games

EXERCISE 1-3

This exercise is somewhat more difficult. A complete critical evaluation of material of the following sort involves principles of critical thinking that we will discuss as we proceed in this book. For now, we want you to identify only (1) claims for which *no* supporting reasons are given, and (2) claims for which supporting reasons *are* given. Then, in each case, state in your own words the author's main purpose. We've numbered the paragraphs and lettered the sentences to make it easier to refer to them. (Check your work against ours in the answer section at the back of the book.)

Selection 1

★1. (a) The lead that is added to gasoline appears in the air in the form of lead compounds emitted from auto exhaust. (b) These compounds are breathed by all of us, including our children. (c) Although the peelings of lead-based paint are also a threat to our children, the major harm from lead comes from automobile emissions. (d) Therefore, every sane person should welcome a federal Environmental Protection Agency order to remove half the lead in leaded gasoline before July 1, 1985, and 91 percent of the deadly stuff by January 1, 1986.

★2. (a) The EPA began removing lead from gasoline in 1973, primarily because lead ruins catalytic converters that are used to control other automobile pollutants. (b) Unleaded gasoline was introduced primarily for this reason.

★3. (a) Now, however, the lead poisoning of children has become the main reason for removing the lead. (b) Studies show a clear correlation between childhood lead poisoning, with attendant brain damage, and lead levels in gasoline. (c) Other studies indicate that even small quantities of lead may cause high blood pressure. (d) The agency should not hesitate to require an eventual ban on lead altogether.

Selection 2

★1. Letter to the editor: (a) Pornography is harmful. (b) According to public records, the majority of molesters of boys and girls have admitted their acts were induced by pornography.

★2. (a) Further, pornography is morally shameful. (b) It sees people as things to abuse and manipulate. (c) Sex, which should be private between men and women, is translated into an object to sell and exploit. (d) Pornography teaches that sex is a game without morality, love, commitment, or responsibility.

★3. (a) Pornography is also psychologically damaging. (b) It places sex on a comparison and performance basis. (c) Many marriage counselors would agree that the majority of cases of sexual incompatibility are caused by the fear of failure resulting from a high emphasis on sexual performance.

★4. (a) Outlawing pornography is not prohibited by the First Amendment any more than is outlawing libel, slander, or yelling "fire" in a crowded theater. (b) District Attorney Joan Masterson is correct and proper in prosecuting the owners of the Pleasureland Bookstore. (c) I call on others in the Springfield area to express their concern in an orderly and responsible manner.

EXERCISE 1-4

Identify the main issue in each of the following passages.

EXAMPLE: Preston didn't come to class today. That fact makes it clear that he does not deserve to pass this course.

The issue is whether Preston deserves to pass this course.

★1. You're much better off buying a live Christmas tree than one that's been cut. For one thing, live trees are fresher and smell better. For another, they cost less, at least if you use the same tree for two or three Christmas seasons. And finally, you can give them to a nonprofit organization when you are finished using them and deduct their cost from your taxes.

2. "NORTH FOR PRESIDENT. HE'S GOT THE GUTS IT TAKES."

—Bumper sticker

★3. Letter to the editor: "They're at it again! Fall has arrived and it's time for the rice farmers to start polluting the air with smoke from the burning fields. This summer saw the worst forest fires in history and the smoke was nothing compared to what we get every fall day, courtesy of the friendly rice farmer. Yes, we know, the alternatives to burning are too expensive, but Mr. Rice Farmer, shouldn't your own conscience tell you to get out of a business that requires you to poison the air we breathe? Do you really have the right to make bucks at the expense of so many people?"

—*Tehama County Tribune*

4. "Turkeys may be the most popular holiday bird, but they are definitely not the smartest. Young turkeys aren't allowed outside of the brooding house because they will peer into the sky if it begins to rain. While admiring their first rainstorm, the young turkeys drown."

—*Homeowners* (real estate newsletter)

5. It is unusual for Republicans to support liberal candidates, and when they do, that is a sure sign that the candidate is not as liberal as he or she may seem. That's why it's likely that Senator Baldwin is a conservative despite the fact that she is a Democrat. She has received more contributions from Republicans than the Republican candidate has received himself.

6. Should I ask Brigitte out again? She doesn't seem crazy about me . . . but then who does? She probably wouldn't say "no," and we might have a good time . . . just as long as we don't have to talk about anything. Oh, I don't know. Maybe I'd better sleep on it.

★7. "The defeat of Judge [Robert] Bork's confirmation [to the Supreme Court] was healthy for our judicial system because it focused attention on the process of constitutional interpretation and the need for social consensus upon which the legitimacy of law so vitally depends. It was also a reminder that the process of seating a justice on the Supreme Court is an explicitly political one in which the legislative and the executive branches of government can and should play co-equal parts."

—JOHN B. OAKLEY, Sacramento Bee

8. "Your story about leadership is an exercise in unreflective scaremongering. The stock market is correcting itself, but the economy is still fundamentally sound, chugging along at 3.8% in GNP growth last quarter. Ronald Reagan's leadership style and free-market principles have left America an economic legacy of high growth, low inflation, rising incomes and expanding job creation. It is a record of tangible accomplishment."

—Letter to Time (November 30, 1987), ROBERT W. KASTEN, JR.,
U.S. Senator, Wisconsin

9. The cookbook says to cook it for 17–20 minutes a pound for rare. But seems like you're supposed to cook it longer the smaller it is, for some reason. So . . . what's a small roast, I wonder? Let's see—this was one of the smallest packages I could find, so I guess it's probably pretty small. I'll try 19 minutes a pound. That ought to be safe.

★ 10. "I have a simple logic. Socialism is bound to be good, and what is good is bound to be socialism. Our goals are a strong country, a wealthy people and an open society. Anything that helps us achieve these goals is socialism."

—An official in the Chinese Communist party, quoted in an article
by Andrew J. Nathan

★EXERCISE 1-5

The following editorial appeared in the *Sacramento Bee* in June of 1988. Read through the piece; then go back and identify the main issue, restating it in your own words. Ask yourself "Just exactly what is this writer trying to convince me of?" Then identify the reasons the writer uses to support his or her opinion on the main issue. (Check your version against ours in the back of the book.)

FSLIC's Popgun War

M. Danny Wall, chairman of the Federal Home Loan Bank Board, says the closing of two insolvent Southern California savings and loan institutions is the opening of a "second front" in federal regulators' war against the industry's problems. Unfortunately, to back up those brave words, Wall is armed only with a regulatory popgun. Until savings regulators are given more financial firepower, the best they will manage on their second front is a few guerrilla raids.

Federal regulators say they are attempting to close insolvent thrifts that drive up the costs at healthy institutions by paying above-average interest rates to attract depositors. That makes good sense. The two closed California thrifts had been operating under federal management because of losses stemming from what the government charges were fraudulent and imprudent loans. But to stay alive, they had been soliciting large depositors, most of them other financial institutions, by advertising interest rates more than a point above the going market. In so doing, they were only deepening their losses while cutting into the profits of the rest of the industry. Although it will cost the Federal Savings and Loan Insurance Corp. $1.35 billion to pay off the depositors at the two institutions, closing the thrifts protects the government deposit insurance fund from even larger future payments.

By the same logic, it would also make sense to close hundreds of other failing savings and loans. According to the General Accounting Office, almost one in six of the nation's federally insured thrifts is insolvent. But the price tag for paying off the depositors at those institutions would be $26 billion to $36 billion, says the GAO, and perhaps as much as $50 billion, say private analysts. By contrast, after closing the two south state thrifts, FSLIC has less than $2 billion in its cash account.

As a result, most industry analysts expect that, despite Wall's brave words, regulators will have to continue doing what they've done for most of the decade: muddle along by merging sick thrifts with healthy ones and by putting new cash and management into failing operations. As it has for the last several years, that will only increase the insurance fund's future liabilities and protect the industry's failed high-flying institutions at the expense of prudent and well-managed thrifts. Until Congress gets serious about adequately capitalizing FSLIC, the regulators will have to wage popgun war and hope that time and luck will turn the tide of S&L red ink.

EXERCISE 1-6 (ESSAY)

Every chapter has at least one opportunity to write an essay at the end of the exercises. You'll find some suggestions on how to write argumentative essays in Appendix 3, in the back of this book.

1. Fill in the blank in the following expression; then write a two- or three-page argumentative essay on the topic: "Whether there is a serious need for more critical thinking in the area of _____ ."
2. In a brief essay, explain the difference between critical thinking and pure logic.

2 *Understanding Claims*

Words, like eyeglasses, blur everything that they do not make clear.
—JOSEPH JOUBERT

Unless one is a genius, it is best to aim at being intelligible.
—ANTHONY HOPE

Before we can decide whether to accept a claim, we must be sure we really understand it. Consider these examples:

> Consciousness is a being such that in its being, its being is in question insofar as this being implies a being other than itself.
>
> —JEAN-PAUL SARTRE

> "When I was in the Marine Corps, I was plainly told that many good men died in the uniform that was issued to me."
>
> —From a letter to the editor

> Not every framistan has gussets.

To the typical reader, the first of these claims is hopelessly obscure, the second does not mean what it first appears to mean, and the third can be understood only by those familiar with framistans, whatever those are.

When we can't tell what is being claimed or asserted, and when the problem stems from the claim itself rather than from our dozing off or becoming distracted, there is a good chance the reason is that:

1. the claim is ambiguous;
2. the claim is too vague;
3. the claim contains words with unfamiliar meanings;
4. several of the above.

Our main chore in this chapter is to examine these three sources of unclarity—ambiguity, vagueness, and unfamiliar meanings.

Sources of Unclarity: Ambiguity

A claim is **ambiguous** if it can be assigned more than one meaning but the particular meaning it should be assigned is not made clear by context. If an accountant rises from her desk on Friday afternoon and says, "My work here is finished," she might mean that she has finished the account she was working on, that her whole week's work is done and she's leaving for the weekend, or that she is fed up with her job and is leaving the company. Similarly, the claim "his tongue has been cut off" could mean either that the tongue of his shoe has been cut off or, a more unpleasant alternative, that the tongue in his mouth has suffered that fate. Unless the context makes clear which meaning is intended, the claim is ambiguous.

MAYBE HOWIE'S CRITICAL, BUT HE'S STILL THINKING. GUESS THAT MAKES HIM A CRITICAL THINKER.

A claim can be ambiguous for different reasons. Consider these claims:

1. He always lines up on the right side.
2. She is cold.
3. I know a little Greek.
4. She disputed his claim.
5. My brother doesn't use glasses.

The meanings of these claims are unclear because each claim contains an ambiguous word or phrase. For example, *claim* in number 4 could mean either a statement or a claim to a gold mine; *glasses* in number 5 could mean either eyeglasses or drinking glasses. When the ambiguity of a claim is due to the ambiguity of a particular word or phrase, it is called **semantical ambiguity.** Semantical ambiguity can be eliminated by substituting an unambiguous word or phrase for the troublemaking one (e.g., *eyeglasses* for *glasses* in number 5).

Now consider these examples:

1. He saw the farmer with binoculars.
2. The waitress will bring a side order of sauce and he will put it on himself.
3. People who protest often get arrested.
4. He chased the girl in his car.
5. She likes candy more than her husband.

In contrast with those in the first list, these claims are ambiguous because of their structures. Even though we understand the meaning of the phrase *with binoculars,* for example, it is unclear whether it pertains to the farmer or to the subject of claim 1. Ambiguity of this sort is called **syntactical ambiguity.** The only way to eliminate syntactical ambiguity is to rewrite the claim.

A peculiar kind of semantical ambiguity, which we'll call **grouping ambiguity**, is illustrated by this claim:

Secretaries make more money than physicians.

Momma

By Mell Lazarus

Is this claim true or false? We can't say, because we don't know *what* the claim is. The reason for that is we don't know exactly what *secretaries* and *physicians* refer to. If the claim is that secretaries *as a group* make more money than physicians *as a group,* then the claim is true, since there are so many more secretaries than physicians. But if the claim is that secretaries individually make more money than physicians individually, then the claim is of course false. Whenever someone refers to a collection of individuals, we must determine whether the reference is to the collection as a group or as individuals before we can understand the claim.

Usually, but not always, the context of a claim will make clear which possible meaning a speaker or writer intends. If a mechanic said, "Your trouble is in a cylinder," it might be unclear at first whether he meant a wheel cylinder or an engine cylinder. His meaning would probably become clear, though, as you listened to what else he said and considered the entire context in which he spoke.

AT FIRST, OZZIE WAS PLEASED TO LEARN THAT DINNER WOULD BE ON THE HOUSE...

Although ambiguous claims can be a fine source of amusement, they can also furnish clever ways of duping people. In advertising, for example, a claim might make wild promises for a product when interpreted one way. But, under another interpretation, it may say very little, thus giving the manufacturer a loophole against the charge of false advertising. You'll find some examples of such claims in the exercises that follow.

We should note that a claim can be semantically ambiguous and syntactically ambiguous at the same time. You'll find an example or two of this "double" ambiguity in the exercises as well.

EXERCISE 2-1

Determine which of these claims are semantically ambiguous (ambiguous because of an ambiguous word or phrase), which are syntactically ambiguous (ambiguous because of structure), which have grouping ambiguities, and which are free from ambiguity.

EXAMPLE: "A former professional football player was accused of assaulting a thirty-three-year-old woman with a female accomplice."

ANSWER: This claim is syntactically ambiguous, since it isn't clear what the phrase "with a female accomplice" modifies—the attacker, the woman who was attacked, or, however bizarre it might be, the attack itself (he might have thrown the accomplice at the woman). In order to make it clear that the accused attacker had the accomplice, the phrase *with a female accomplice* should have come right after the word *player* in the original claim.

★1. We were invited to go to the movies yesterday.
  2. The biggest Forty-Niner fans come from Marin County.
  3. Did he inform you of what he said in his letter?
★4. "HOW THERAPY CAN HELP TORTURE VICTIMS"
    —*San Francisco Chronicle,* August 1, 1988
  5. "All my life I wanted to run for president in the worst possible way—and I did."
    —WALTER MONDALE
  6. They were both exposed to someone who was ill a week ago.
★7. Digital computing began the first time a person counted on his fingers.
  8. Scandinavians eat tons of cheese every year.
  9. An ad for formal wear: "Tuxedos Cut Ridiculously!"
    —Quoted by Herb Caen, *San Francisco Chronicle*
★10. Newspaper headline: "Police Kill 6 Coyotes After Mauling of Girl."
  11. Everybody knows that giraffes are dumb.
  12. Former governor Pat Brown of California, viewing an area struck by a flood, is said to have remarked, "This is the greatest disaster since I was elected governor."
    —Quoted by Lou Cannon, *The Washington Post*

★13. "The *Dartmouth Review* is in the process of beating down a suit by a disconsolate professor of music, who thought his injured ego required several million, and now is being sued on frivolous grounds by an assistant chaplain, who objects to publicity about his leftist and downright peculiar opinions."

—*The National Review*

14. Horatio plays the trumpet by ear.
15. Volunteer help requested: Come prepared to lift heavy equipment with construction helmet and work overalls.
★16. "GE: We bring good things to life."

—Television commercial

17. "Tropicana 100% Pure Florida Squeezed Orange Juice. You can't pick a better juice."

—Magazine advertisement

18. "It's biodegradable! So remember, Arm and Hammer laundry detergent gets your wash as clean as can be [pause] without polluting our waters."

—Television commercial

★19. If you crave the taste of a real German beer, nothing is better than Dunkelbrau.
20. Independent laboratory tests prove that Houndstooth cleanser gets your bathroom cleaner than any other product.

EXERCISE 2-2

Determine whether the italicized expressions in the following claims are more likely to refer to the members of the class taken as a group or taken individually. The claims may or may not be ambiguous in the sense defined in the text.

EXAMPLE: *Narcotics* are habit forming.

ANSWER: In this claim, *narcotics* refers to individual members of the class, since it is specific narcotics that are habit forming. (One does not ordinarily become addicted to the entire class of narcotics.)

★1. *Swedes* eat millions of quarts of yogurt every day.
2. *College professors* make millions of dollars a year.
3. *Our CB radios* can be heard all across the country.
★4. *Students at Pleasant Valley High School* enroll in hundreds of courses each year.
5. *Cowboys* die with their boots on.
6. *The angles of a triangle* add up to 180 degrees.
★7. *The New York Giants* played mediocre football last year.
8. On our airline, *passengers* have their choice of three different meals.
9. On our airline, *passengers* flew fourteen million miles last month without incident.
★10. *Hundreds of people* have ridden in that taxi.
11. *All our cars* are on sale for $200 over factory invoice.

12. Chicagoans drink more beer than New Yorkers.
*13. An invasion of *fruit flies* threatened the Florida fruit industry.
14. *The Baltimore Orioles* may make it to the playoffs by 1994.
15. *People* are getting older.

Vagueness

A claim is **vague** if it lacks sufficient precision to convey the information appropriate to its use. For example, if someone asks what time the movie begins, the reply "In a little while" is probably too vague to be useful—that is, the information it conveys is too imprecise to be helpful in that context.

Claims fall on a scale ranging from very precise to hopelessly vague. For example, the claim "579,102 people died in the United States in the 1918 influenza epidemic" is about as precise a statement as one would ordinarily require. "Several hundred thousand people died in the U.S. in the 1918 influenza epidemic" is more vague but would probably suffice in many circumstances. Only in a casual conversation would it be appropriate to make such a vague claim as "Lots of people died in the 1918 influenza epidemic."

Some vague claims permit a number of borderline cases to which they might apply. The claim "He is rich," for example, is clearly true of Donald Trump and is clearly not true of someone whose annual income is six thousand dollars. But in between are a host of cases where it is unclear whether the claim applies. Is a person who is worth a half-million dollars rich? One worth a quarter-million? Where does *rich* end and *well-off* begin?

Claims that are vague because they employ imprecise concepts with lots of borderline cases (as *tall* or *bald* do) are **properly vague.** Such claims would be vague in any context, although not necessarily too vague to be useful. Another kind of vague claim, which we'll call **contextually vague,** may be sufficiently precise in one context but not so in another. For example, "Mary plans to bring her sibling to class on Friday" is probably clear enough, depending on the kind of class we're talking about. But "Mary plans to bring her sibling to the slumber party Friday night" probably isn't (especially if it's your teenage daughter who is having the slumber party). Notice that *sibling* is not a vague word—it has a precise definition—but it's the wrong choice for the second of these contexts; it conveys too little information.

It makes little sense, however, to insist that a claim be *totally* free of vagueness. If we had to be absolutely precise whenever we made a claim, very little would get said or written. What matters is that a claim be sufficiently free of vagueness for the purpose at hand. If you want to know why you shouldn't walk any farther down 23rd Street, for instance, the remark "There are people shooting at each other down there" would be precise enough to tell you all

Malice Aforethought

The penal codes of many states define murder in the first degree as murder committed "with malice aforethought." If we investigate what the codes mean by *malice*, we find that some give this definition: "with an abandoned and malignant heart." Does this definition clarify the concept for you? Can you think of a reason why a legislature might *purposely* leave the concept of malice vague?

you need to know. That same statement, though, would be much too vague to serve as a police report of the incident. The appropriate criticism of a claim is not that it is too vague, but that it is too vague relative to what you wish to know.

Even if within a given context a claim is more vague than is desirable, it may still do the job. My description of my automobile's problem ("it makes weird noises when it's cold") might be annoyingly vague to my mechanic, and he may wish that it were less so, but it may be the best description I can give, and it's much better than no description at all. Remember: We should always strive for precision when we can—it is better for a claim to be a little more precise than necessary than a little too vague to be useful.

So clarity and precision are always desirable, but they are not qualities that a claim either has completely or entirely fails to have. What matters is whether or not a claim is clear *enough*. Remember too that the trouble it takes to understand a claim is not necessarily directly related to obscurity—a claim can be clear and still require considerable attention to be understood.

Advice from the Firmament

PISCES (Feb. 19–Mar. 19): Time alone is necessary. Avoid attractive nuisances for a while. Spend some time pulling yourself together. Leo, Aquarius can offer support.

—Horoscope for February 23, 1989

Horoscopes are notoriously ambiguous and vague. In this one, "time alone" was probably intended to mean time by oneself, but it could also mean time and nothing else—that is, nothing but time is necessary. What might "attractive nuisance" mean? The phrase is vague enough for nearly any of us to think of an application in his or her life. Does the fact that a friend is a Leo or an Aquarius mean that we should seek support from that friend? What if he or she is the wrong Leo or Aquarius? Or will just any do?

A horoscope could give precise information or advice to a Pisces only if all Pisces were in exactly the same circumstances and faced exactly the same problems. Since they aren't, horoscopes have to be vague enough for lots of people to "read into" them whatever they want.

EXERCISE 2-3

The lettered words and phrases that follow each of the following fragments vary in their precision. In each instance, determine which is the most vague and which is the most precise; then rank the remainder in order of vagueness between the two extremes. You will discover, when you discuss these exercises in class, that they leave some room for disagreement. Further class discussion with input from your instructor will help you and your classmates reach closer agreement about items that prove especially difficult to rank.

EXAMPLE: Over the past ten years, the median income of wage earners in St. Paul
(a) nearly doubled
(b) increased substantially
(c) increased by 85.5 percent
(d) increased by more than 85 percent

ANSWER: Choice (b) is the most vague, since it provides the least information; (c) is the most precise, since it provides the most detailed figure. In between, (a) is the second most vague, followed by (d).

★1. Eli and Sarah
(a) decided to sell their house and move
(b) made plans for the future
(c) considered moving
(d) talked
(e) discussed their future
(f) discussed selling their house

2. Manuel
(a) worked in the yard
(b) spent the afternoon planting flowers
(c) was outside all afternoon
(d) spent the afternoon planting *salvia* alongside his front sidewalk
(e) spent half the day grubbing about in the yard

3. The hurricane that struck South Carolina
(a) caused more than $20 million in property damage
(b) destroyed dozens of homes and other buildings
(c) was the worst storm of the year
(d) miraculously did not result in any fatalities
(e) produced no fatalities but caused $25 million in property damage

★4. The president's new income tax proposal
(a) will substantially reduce the taxes of those making more than $80,000 per year
(b) will lower the tax bracket for people making more than $80,000 per year from 50 percent to 35 percent and will give them other benefits
(c) makes important changes
(d) favors the rich

(e) will lower the tax bracket for singles making more than $80,000 per year from 50 percent to 35 percent, will reduce the tax on capital gains from 30 percent to 17.5 percent, and will double the investment credit

5. Smedley is absent because
    (a) he's not feeling well
    (b) he's under the weather
    (c) he has an upset stomach and a fever
    (d) he's nauseated and has a fever of over 103°
    (e) he has Type A flu virus and the usual symptoms

EXERCISE 2-4

Like many words, *serve* has some uses that are more vague than others. Of the ten uses of *serve* in the following examples, identify the four that seem to you to be the most vague. For our opinion see the answer section at the back of the book.

EXAMPLE: (1) The trees served to make shade for the patio. (2) He served his country proudly.

ANSWER: The use of *served* in (2) is much more vague than that in (1). We know exactly what the trees did; we don't know what he did.

1. Watson-Baker served six years as an officer in the Royal Fusiliers.
2. Alfredo served her a dinner of Kowloon chicken and curried rice.
3. The lawsuit served its purpose.
4. Horace served time in San Quentin.
5. Rodney's tennis serve is impossible to return.
6. Rooney served the church his entire life.
7. The spare tire served me very well.
8. Through his medical research Steiner served all of mankind.
9. The window also serves as an escape hatch.
10. His wife had him served with papers.

EXERCISE 2-5

Distinguish those uses of *turn* that are more vague from those that are less vague. (We find five of them in each category—see the answer section at the back of the book.)

1. As Minta neared the bottom of the slope, she cried out in pain. She had turned her ankle.
2. Without his wife, Arnold became hopelessly depressed. Finally, in his sorrow, he turned to religion.
3. Fenner's executive secretary turned viciously on the helpless stockboy.
4. These scales will turn on the weight of a hair.

5. Call the children—the roast is done to a turn.
6. They had just enough time left to take a quick turn around the park.
7. According to the president's press secretary, we've turned the corner on inflation.
8. Alas! The milk has turned sour!
9. Ah, spring. Time to turn the garden.
10. "Hey!" Blanchard screamed. "Turn the hot water back on!"

EXERCISE 2-6

This exercise is not easy, and is best suited to class discussion. Read the following passage and pay particular attention to the italicized and numbered words and phrases. All these expressions would be too vague for use in *some* contexts; determine which are and are not too vague in *this* context.

> According to *administration officials*,[1] considerable progress has been made in the *war on drugs*[2] during the past year. A spokesperson for the Drug Enforcement Agency (DEA) said yesterday that "We have definitely *turned the corner*[3] on drug addiction in this country." Much of the good news has come as the result of a *massive clean-up*[4] in the *Miami area*,[5] the official said. Federal agents from the DEA in cooperation with local police departments have more than *twice as many arrests*[6] during this past year as compared with the previous year.

Unfamiliar Words

No matter how large and varied one's vocabulary might be, new or unfamiliar words will turn up now and then. Unless we are prepared to track down meanings and seek clarifications, such unfamiliar words can paralyze our ability to think critically—or even to think at all. Since most of us have at least a passing familiarity with the use of dictionaries and encyclopedias, and all of us know how to ask speakers what they mean by particular words, the principal obstacle to making an unfamiliar word a familiar one is simple lack of motivation. Whether we automatically look up a word we don't know or simply let it slide by and hope the context will suggest its meaning is largely a matter of habit. Needless to say, the first alternative is a good habit and the second is a bad one.

Looking up a word's meaning not only helps us understand the claim in which it occurs, but also helps to enlarge our vocabularies a bit each time we do it. Since language is the main tool of the trade for critical thinkers, the larger our vocabularies are and the more comfortable we are with them, the better prepared we will be regardless of the subject at hand. So, here is an important suggestion: Work on developing the habit of looking up unfamiliar words—right away or, after making a note, at your first opportunity. And don't be afraid to ask for clarification from a speaker—the alternative is to succumb to intimidation and remain in ignorance.

EXERCISE 2-7

How many of the words in the list below do you know? For each word that is unfamiliar to you, make a *guess* about its meaning based on its appearance or sound, and create your own definition. Then look up each word and find out how close you were. In the answer section at the back of the book, you'll find two morals that can be drawn from this exercise.

1. Meretricious
2. Parvenu
3. Pursy
4. Besotted
5. Trenchant
6. Mettle
7. Noisome
8. Ursine
9. Pervicacious
10. Adjuration

Meaning and Definition

When you seek clarification of a word, phrase, or statement, whether from a speaker or a dictionary, and whether the unclarity is due to vagueness, ambiguity, or unfamiliar language, what you are looking for is the intended meaning. When you ask what such and such means, what are you asking for? You could be asking for one of several kinds of meaning. For most purposes, two of these kinds are most important.

First, the **denotation**, or denotative meaning, of a term is simply all those things to which the term correctly applies. For example, the denotative meaning of the term *taxpayer* is all those people who pay taxes: you, the authors, Richard Nixon, Julia Child, etc. The denotation of *city* is simply all cities: San Francisco, Detroit, Hartford, etc.

Second, the **sense** of a term is the set of characteristics a thing must have for the term to correctly apply to it. The sense of the word *taxpayer,* in most circumstances, can be given as "a person who is assessed and pays a pecuniary charge or duty to the government." Anybody who fits this description qualifies as a taxpayer. In another example, the phrases *creature with a heart* and *creature with a lung* turn out to have the same denotative meaning, because, as it happens, every creature that has one of these organs has the other. But these phrases have very different senses, since the characteristic a thing must have to be a creature with a heart is quite different from the one it must have to be a creature with a lung.

Clearly akin to a term's meaning, its **emotive force** is its tendency to elicit certain feelings, attitudes, or emotions. The terms *elderly lady* and *old crone* have the same denotative meaning and sense, but they differ in the attitudes they convey about an older woman. The former term conveys a favorable attitude, the latter an unfavorable one. The emotive force of terms, which is subjective, is usually not taken to be a part of their "literal" meanings. (Literal meanings encompass denotation and sense.)

The emotive force of many terms varies considerably from one person to another. The term *Communist,* for example, is a term of praise for some people, a term of condemnation for others, and is perfectly neutral for still others. Bertrand Russell was changing only the emotive force of his remark when he said that "I am firm, you are stubborn, and he is pig-headed." The three terms, *firm, stubborn,* and *pig-headed* all have about the same sense; they differ only in the fact that you would use *firm* for someone you wished to praise, *pig-headed* for someone you wished to criticize, and *stubborn* for someone about whom you were more or less neutral.

When the purpose of a claim is to convey information, then it should be as free of words with highly charged emotive force as you can make it. Such language distracts from the information the claim conveys. The presence of emotionally charged terminology in what one might have expected to be purely informational discourse is an indication that the speaker or writer has some purpose in mind in addition to (or other than) the plain and simple communication of information. Emotionally charged language is generally used to influence someone's attitudes or behavior and should be minimized in speech and writing whose purpose is simply to convey information.

Somber News

The somber news from the White House today was that once again the administration will abrogate its responsibility to all Americans for the sake of the privileged few. A presidential spokesman announced this morning that, despite the President's campaign pledge not to reduce the ballooning federal deficit by attacking safety net programs, the administration is currently considering ways of reducing expenditures on Social Security. This disheartening development . . .

Any "news report" that began this way would obviously be intended not merely to inform the reader of some White House announcement but also to influence the reader's attitude toward that announcement through the use of emotionally charged language. (Such nonargumentative attempts to affect attitudes are discussed at some length in Chapter 5.)

However, those who seek to communicate information effectively do try to keep the interests of their audience in mind. When striving to communicate information to students, good teachers, for example, will seek to make a presentation arresting, even if the effort requires extra words and colorful language. In general, however, a claim or set of claims put forth solely or primarily for the purpose of communicating information should be clear, concise, and objective.

When appraising attempts to change your attitudes or influence your behavior, you must pay particular attention to the emotive force of terms, as will be emphasized in Chapter 5.

When a claim is unclear because you do not know the meaning of one or more of its words, what you need is a definition. These come in several forms, some of which are much more common than the others. Below, we briefly explain three kinds of definition—example, synonym, and analytical. Then we describe two frequent *uses* of definitions—uses that are sometimes erroneously treated as further kinds of definitions: precising and persuasive.

1. **Definition by example.** We define a term by example by pointing to, naming, or describing one or more examples of something to which the term applies. "Franklin Roosevelt is what I mean by a *liberal*." "This [waving a bottle of Kentucky Sludge] is what I mean by *good bourbon*." This kind of definition is sometimes known as ostensive definition.

2. **Definition by synonym.** We define a term by synonym by giving another

word or phrase that means the same thing. "*Pulsatile* means the same as *throbbing*"; "to be *lubricous* is to be slippery." This method of definition can be very efficient provided a close synonym exists for the word needing definition and that one's audience is familiar with that synonym—conditions that one cannot always depend upon.

3. *Analytical definition.* An analytical definition, also called a genus and species definition, defines a term by specifying (a) the type of thing the term applies to and (b) the differences between the things the term applies to and other things of the same type. The resulting definition in effect gives the sense of the term. "The *thrust bearing* is the main engine bearing that has thrust faces to prevent excessive end play of the crankshaft." "A *sepoy* was a native of India employed as a soldier by a European power, usually Great Britain."

Definitions can serve a variety of purposes besides the obvious one of introducing new or unfamiliar terms. One that is used to reduce the vagueness of a term, for example, is called a *precising definition* (or a stipulative definition). Such a definition limits the applicability of a term whose usual meaning is too vague for the use in question: "Throughout this contract, the term *money* will mean only United States dollars." "For our purposes, *death* may be said to have occurred at the time of irrevocable cessation of all brain processes as monitored on an electroencephalograph." Notice that, of the three types of definition mentioned, only an analytical definition is useful as a precising definition.

Definitions are used not only to clarify language but also to convey or evoke an attitude about the defined term and its denotation. These are *persuasive definitions* (although they sometimes do very little to actually define a term, since they may not specify much of its actual meaning). Persuasive definitions can take any of the three forms of definition we have covered. "That," one might say after having seen a particularly obnoxious and spoiled child coddled by its parent, "is what I mean when I talk about *progressive child-raising*" (definition by example). "*Communism* is but dictatorship under another name" (definition by synonym). "A *liberal* is a person who wants to waste taxpayers' money supporting people who are too lazy to go out and find jobs" (analytical definition). Persuasive definitions are often used to convince the listener or reader to feel a certain way about something without giving any solid reasons for feeling that way. For example, if you allow *abortion* to be defined as "the murder of an unborn person," no reasoning will be necessary to establish that abortion is wrong.

Remember, both precising (or stipulative) and persuasive definitions are not kinds of definitions; they are *uses* of definitions.

EXERCISE 2-8

Give definitions by example for as many of the following words as you can. You may use the name or a description of an example that you can't point to directly (e.g., the name Mars will do for the first one). You will have trouble

Definitions, Soviet Style

The most prestigious dictionary of the English language, the *Oxford English Dictionary*, has recently been adapted in two forms by Soviet lexicographers. The results are the *Oxford Learner's Dictionary of Current English* and the *Oxford Student's Dictionary of Current English*. Sanctioned for use by the Kremlin, these works contain some definitions that are somewhat less neutral and objective than we've come to expect. A couple of examples:

- *Marxism* is defined as "teaching on the main laws of development of nature and society."
- *Capitalism* is defined as "the last antagonistic social and economic system in human history, based on the exploitation of man by man, replacing feudalism and preceding communism."
- *Zionism* is defined as "the ideology and policy of the bourgeoisie in Israel, supported by certain imperialists."

We recommend that you compare these definitions with those found in any standard dictionary of English, including the original *Oxford English Dictionary*.

with some items, since some words are very difficult or impossible to define by example. (For example, the number four and the concept of grammar are things we would have trouble pointing to, either directly or by means of words. How could you give someone an example of grammar that would convey what you were giving an example *of*?) Explain the difficulty in any troublesome cases.

★1. Planet
★2. Dictator
3. Tall item
★4. Thing
5. Abstraction
6. Genius
★7. World Series winner
8. Expensive gift
9. Unicorn
★10. Charity

11. Ambiguous claim
12. Education
★13. Immoral act
14. Toothache
15. The color red
★16. Classification system
17. Industrial health hazard
18. Reasoning
★19. Concept
20. Problem

EXERCISE 2-9

For each of the following, indicate the kind of meaning that is probably intended: denotation, sense, or neither.

EXAMPLE: *Citrus fruit* means oranges, lemons, limes, etc.

ANSWER: This gives the denotation of the term.

EXAMPLE: The raise in pay means I can buy a new automobile.

ANSWER: This gives neither denotation nor sense; it is an entirely different use of the word *means*.

★1. *Free country* means places like the United States, Canada, and France.
2. *Epistemologist* means "someone who studies the nature of knowledge."
3. *Widow* refers to a woman whose husband has died.
★4. What I mean by setting a good example is not putting your feet on the table.
5. *Poltroonery* means the same thing as *cowardice*.
6. Honor means being willing to lay down your life for a just cause.
★7. Towering clouds mean that it's going to rain.
8. Happiness means having your own VCR.
9. Being a soldier means being able to tolerate the sight of blood.
★10. A word means anything you want it to.

EXERCISE 2-10

Classify each of the following as definition by example, definition by synonym, or analytical definition. If you run across items that do not seem to fit comfortably in any one category, explain in your own words how the word or concept is being defined.

★1. *Congenial* means companionable.
2. Mayonnaise is a thick sauce of egg yolk beaten together with vegetable oil and seasonings.
3. Meat that contains larval tapeworms is said to be *measly*.
★4. "Hit me" means you want another card.
5. A diode is a solid-state electronic device that allows the passage of an electric current in only one direction.
6. *Either* is a disjunctive correlative used before two or more words, phrases, or clauses that are joined by *or*.
★7. The differential is the gear assembly between axles that permits one wheel to turn at a different speed from the other while transmitting power from the drive shaft to both axles.
8. "Character consists of what you do on the third and fourth tries."
—JAMES MICHENER
9. A professional bureaucrat is anyone like our present governor.
★10. " 'Mother' has always been a generic term synonymous with life, devotion, and sacrifice."
—ERMA BOMBECK
11. Interest is an amount paid for the use of borrowed money.
12. Real property is land and anything that is erected on, growing on, or attached to the land. Your house and lot, for instance, are real property.

⋆ 13. When you bunt, you slide your hands apart on the bat and then tap the ball.

14. "Oyez" is what the bailiff calls out to quiet everybody when the judge enters the courtroom.

⋆ 15. "Eternity is two people and a turkey."

—JAMES DENT

Analytically True Claims

Some claims are true simply because of the definitions of the words in them. For example, the claim "A female fox is a vixen" is true by virtue of the meanings of *female fox* and *vixen*. The claim "Either today is Thursday or it is not" is true by virtue of the meanings of the logical words *or* and *not*. (Appendix 2 explains in some detail how such words work.) Since such claims are "true by definition," they are impossible to refute.

Analytic truths are intrinsically uninteresting to anyone who understands what they say: They may reflect something about language, but they tell us nothing about anything else. Occasionally, however, you may run across a claim that seems profound or insightful and yet appears as impossible to refute as an analytic truth. For example, someone might offer the following claim:

Every deliberate human action is based on a selfish motive.

On the face of it, this claim certainly seems to be more interesting and profound than "Either today is Thursday or it is not" and "Every female fox is a vixen." But when we challenge this claim, it might seem as irrefutable as an analytic truth, since any action can be explained by a selfish motive no matter how selfless that action appears. One might object that Mother Theresa, who received a Nobel Prize for her humanitarian efforts in behalf of India's poor, is surely an exception to the claim. But we can reply that she works for the poor because it makes her feel better to do so, and doing something to make oneself feel better is acting in one's own self-interest. Did you contribute some of your paycheck to charity? Well, doing so must have made you pleased or happy, since otherwise you wouldn't have done it. And, once again, acting to make yourself pleased or happy (or even just to avoid guilt later) is acting in your own self-interest.

Notice that something suspicious has happened. In general, enjoying what you're doing does not automatically make what you're doing an act of selfishness. That isn't what the word *selfish* means. However, if we expand the meaning of *selfish* to include every action that a person might want to perform for any reason—in other words, if we *redefine* the term—then of course it is true

Analytic Truths(?)

> It's not over 'til it's over.
> —YOGI BERRA, former manager of the New York Yankees
>
> To beat the Forty-Niners, you've got to outscore them.
> —JOHN MADDEN, former coach of the Oakland Raiders,
> now a TV sports commentator
>
> These remarks were probably not intended to be analytically true, but they turned out that way. They might sound profound (you can't argue with an analytic truth), but they don't tell us very much. Can you figure out the *non-analytic* messages that these individuals were probably trying to convey?

that every human action is a selfish one. Then the claim in question becomes true by virtue of our new definition of *selfish*, and is thus analytic. However, in making the claim true by making it analytic, we have made the claim much less interesting, and it certainly is not the profound statement it seemed to be at first. A direct analogy would be redefining the word *elderly* to make it refer to everybody over the age of twelve and then going on to claim that "all teenagers are elderly." The claim would be true, given our redefinition. But though it might *sound* important or profound, it would be neither.

EXERCISE 2-11

Determine whether the following express analytic truths. Explain why or why not. (Numbers nine through fifteen may require careful discussion.)

EXAMPLE: Squares have four sides.

ANSWER: This is an analytic truth, since it's true by definition of the word *square*.

★1. All thieves are criminals.
2. It is fun to be rich.
3. It is uncomfortable to live in a hot climate without air conditioning.
★4. If you've written a book, then you're an author.
5. Adultery is a sin.
6. Eighteen is a smaller number than twenty.
★7. All citizens of the United States are Americans.
8. If nobody can get into the concert without a ticket, then anybody without a ticket can't get in.
9. Matter occupies space.
★10. Normal people act like the majority of people.
11. You can't see what doesn't exist.

12. You can't hate and love a person at the same time.
★13. Nobody could ever build a machine that would take a person back in time.
14. Everyone is getting older.
15. I exist.

Complexity

Besides ambiguous, vague, emotional, and undefined language, one major source of befuddlement for listeners and readers is complexity. In general, claims are most informative and easiest to understand if they are highly concise and focused. They should say what needs to be said in as few words as possible (although *clarity* should never be sacrificed to save words). The reason writers of instruction manuals don't tell jokes is not because they have no sense of humor, but because jokes would impede the purpose at hand—to inform the reader how to do something.

Here is an example of a claim that is unnecessarily windy:

They expressed their belief that at that point in time it would accord with their desire not to delay their departure.

There is obviously a much less convoluted way of saying the same thing:

They said they wanted to leave.

The first claim requires the reader to work very hard to understand its meaning; its complexity distracts from the information it contains.

Unfortunately, inexperienced writers often make the mistake of overcomplicating their work in an attempt to appear more sophisticated than they really are. The results often resemble the first version of the above claim. Sometimes, in attempts to write "over their heads," such writers say things they simply don't mean. They forget that complex language should be saved for complex uses—as we'll see in a moment—and that they should be careful to stay within their own limitations. If you are not comfortable with the language you are using, your reader will probably notice your discomfort. Even worse, you might confuse or misinform your reader by misusing language that you are uncomfortable or unfamiliar with.

Comfortable and familiar language can produce greater clarity for a wider audience even though more of it might be required than more complex language. If the shortest way of making a point requires words that are likely to be unfamiliar to the listener or reader (never mind the speaker or writer!), then the speaker or writer should avoid those words in favor of more familiar ones, even if it takes more of the latter to express the information. Compare these two claims:

1. His remarks were obfuscatory and dilatory.
2. His remarks confused the issue and were unnecessarily time consuming.

The second claim, though longer than the first, will be clearer to most readers. It is also the safer of the two, unless the writer is certain that he is using *obfuscatory* and *dilatory* correctly. Unfortunately, writers and speakers often forget these principles, and when they do, it may be difficult to understand their claims, let alone evaluate them.

Sometimes complex claims, though confusing, are not really unclear. One of the authors' insurance policies contains the following, immediately above the place for signature:

> To the extent permitted by statute, I hereby expressly waive, on behalf of myself and of any person who shall have or claim any interest in this insurance, all provisions of law forbidding any licensed physician, surgeon, medical practitioner, hospital, clinic, insurance company, or other organization, institute or person from disclosing any knowledge or information about the spouse of the applicant acquired through any legitimate means and hereby authorize them to make such disclosures.

This is a *long* claim, and a moderately complex one, but it is not really unclear. Indeed, this passage is long and complex in order to *achieve* clarity. Let's have a look at it again, but with certain parts of it placed in brackets:

> To the extent permitted by statute, I hereby expressly waive [on behalf of myself and of any person who shall have or claim any interest in this insur-

Want Clarification? How's This??

George Bush has a way with words, though maybe not always the best way. When asked what his greatest fault was, Bush reflected, "I guess maybe my weakest attribute is that sometimes I trust people too long."

If that leaves you wondering, you have company. Pressed to clarify what that meant, Bush explained, "I dunno. I guess it means I don't always believe that people are out to get me. And that doesn't make me as suspicious as sometimes I should be. But that doesn't mean it's a bad quality at all."

So now you know.

Of course, for pure unadulterated obscurity, nothing tops Vice President Dan Quayle's classic, speaking in favor of the Strategic Defense Initiative during the 1988 presidential campaign:

"Bobby Knight told me this: 'There is nothing that a good defense cannot beat a better offense.'"

ance,] all provisions of law forbidding any [licensed physician, surgeon, medical practitioner, hospital, clinic, or other organization, institute or] person from disclosing any [knowledge or] information about the spouse of the applicant [acquired through any legitimate means] and hereby authorize them to make such disclosures.

What we've bracketed is most of the language not directly related to the main point of the passage. Let's look at it with the bracketed portions removed:

To the extent permitted by statute, I hereby expressly waive all provisions of law forbidding any person from disclosing any information about the spouse of the applicant and hereby authorize them to make such disclosures.

It is now much simpler to determine what is going on in this passage: The applicant will allow disclosure of information about his or her spouse. There are laws that would disallow such disclosures, but the applicant is waiving all rights under those laws. The bracketed information that was removed simply specifies more precisely who is waiving rights (the applicant and others with an interest in the policy), who is being allowed to disclose information (physicians, surgeons, etc.), and what kind of information may be disclosed (any acquired legitimately). These bracketed portions of the passage may make the original more difficult to read and understand the first time through, but they make the document *more* clear rather than *less* clear because they indicate exactly to whom and what the document applies.

It is often important that the provisions of a document be clear no matter what circumstances arise, but it can be a complicated matter to spell out these provisions with respect to all foreseeable circumstances. Wills are another common example. If you make a will, you might want to leave your entire estate to one beneficiary. But what if that beneficiary were to die at the same time you did? The document must provide for that circumstance if no confusion is to result. When *all* the reasonably foreseeable circumstances are covered, you will have a moderately complicated document, but not necessarily a confusing or unclear one. Once again, the complexity will be necessary in order to avoid confusion.

In short, we sometimes have to live with complexity; the world is a rather complicated place, and the language we use to describe it often has to be correspondingly complicated. But complicated language can be understood. Remember that patience and a systematic approach are what is called for: Look for what seems to be the main point in a complex passage. Usually a key phrase or two will help you determine what that point is—in the above example, the first thing to notice is that somebody is waiving rights to something. Everything else in the paragraph hinges on that. Next, skip over words, phrases, or even whole sentences that do not seem to bear directly on the main point. Keep simplifying in this way until you understand the basic message of the passage. (Sometimes you can simplify further, or make the claim more understandable, by paraphrasing the boiled-down passage.) When you are certain you understand the basic point, go back and add the removed language, a bit at a time, in order to get the full meaning of the passage.

Let's apply this method to one more example:

> The problem that Plato and his conversants were concerned about, quite naturally given the intellectual atmosphere of their time, is one to which the label *the One and the Many* has become permanently attached—the question of whether in the final analysis the world consists of a single, ultimate, undifferentiated entity (the One), as Parmenides believed, or whether it consists of an indefinite multiplicity of entities (the Many), the position Plato took to be that of Heraclitus.

First, we'll go through the passage and bracket all those portions that do not seem to bear directly on whatever the main point might be. (Remember: we're presuming that the main point is not clear from the outset.) Here is the result:

> The problem [that Plato and his conversants were concerned about, quite naturally given the intellectual atmosphere of their time] is [one to which the label *the One and the Many* has become permanently attached]—the question of whether [in the final analysis] the world consists of a single, ultimate, undifferentiated entity [(the One), as Parmenides believed] or whether it consists of an indefinite multiplicity of entities [(the Many), the position Plato took to be that of Heraclitus].

Leaving out the bracketed portions, we get this:

> The problem is the question of whether the world consists of a single, ultimate, undifferentiated entity or whether it consists of an indefinite multiplicity of entities.

This version is much more manageable than the original. We might even venture a paraphrase of what this claim states: "The problem is whether there is only one thing or whether there are many things." If we consider the material that we earlier omitted, we learn that this problem was one that Plato and some of his contemporaries were concerned about, that Parmenides adopted the first alternative, that Heraclitus seems to have adopted the second, and so forth.

If you are worried that, despite our work on this passage, you still don't have much of a grasp of the problem of the One and the Many, we can relieve your concern: The original passage doesn't do much to explain the details of that problem either. It would take a considerably longer passage than the original, never mind our simplified version, to explain this subject in any satisfactory detail.

The point is that we *were* able to give a version that conveyed the meaning of the original without serious distortion. The method used, eliminating the unnecessary and paraphrasing the remainder, is not foolproof, but it can be very helpful when you're faced with complex writing.

Gobbledygook

Gobbledygook is a term coined in 1944 by writer Maury Maverick for near-gibberish of all sorts. Gobbledygook comes in many forms; here are just a few, with translations given in brackets.

Obscure or unnecessary phrases

Economically disadvantaged people
[The poor]

Personnel ceiling reduction
[Layoff]

Open to everyone regardless of age, race, creed, sex, color, national origin, etc.
[Open to everyone]

At this point in time
[Now]

In the event that
[If]

Because of the fact that
[Because]

Mixed (up) metaphors

They better get it in gear because they have a long row to hoe.
[They should start because they have a difficult task.]
The United States can no longer use atomic power as an ace in the hole to hold over the heads of other world powers.
[The United States can no longer threaten other countries with atomic power.]
—WILLIAM W. WATT, *An American Rhetoric*, 5th ed.

They give you the ball and let you run with it. Of course, the only thorn in your side is that there's always a fly in the ointment.

[You're allowed to use your own judgment, but there's always a problem. (We're guessing at this one.)]

Unnecessary abstractions

Two important factors constitute the grounds for the uniqueness of supervision as educational method: First, the content of social case work and its training goals for the worker; and second, the learning situation composed of two people, a supervisor and a student, instead of a class situation.
—WILLIAM W. WATT, *An American Rhetoric*, 5th ed.

[One-on-one supervision is different from classroom instruction because of the subject matter and because there's no class. (Trying to translate this shows us how little it actually says.)]

Talk for talk's sake

This category constitutes much of what passes for commentary on television. The following conversation took place between commentators Don Meredith and Joe Theisman during the American Broadcasting Company's broadcast of the 1985 Superbowl football game:

MEREDITH: Joe, do you see anything different in [Miami Dolphin quarterback Dan Marino's] delivery? Does he look like he's hesitating a little bit?

THEISMAN: He was hit—I think that as young as he is and with the arm he has, sometimes you see the receiver and then you let the ball go. He's pretty much done it all year. But in this kind of football game, the working mechanism of the delivery doesn't necessarily come exactly the way you want it to.

We think Theisman means that Marino is not passing very well.

Colorful self-contradictions

Translations of these are either unnecessary or impossible:

Include me out!

—SAM GOLDWYN

Okay, youse guys, line up in alphabetical order according to height.

—CASEY STENGEL

Although gobbledygook is usually not genuinely indecipherable gibberish, it takes work to understand it. Unless you believe that it might contain something you need to know, our advice is not to bother.

EXERCISE 2-12

Simplify the following passage from sections of the California State Insurance Code. The idea here is to identify the main point or points in the paragraph. Use the bracketing method described in the text if you find it helpful to do so.

No bank, or bank holding company, subsidiary, or affiliate thereof, or any officer or employee of a bank, bank holding company, subsidiary, or affiliate, may be licensed as an insurance agent or broker or act as an agent or broker for insurance, in this state, or control a licensed insurance agent or broker, except that a bank or a bank holding company subsidiary, or affiliate of a bank, may be issued a license to act as a life and disability agent limited to the transaction of credit life and disability insurance, or an agent limited to the transaction of insurance which is limited solely to assuring repayment of the outstanding balance due on a specific event of the involuntary unemployment of the debtor, or both. A commercial bank may be licensed to sell insurance or act as an insurance broker as provided in Section 1208 of the Financial Code. This section shall not apply to any bank or bank holding company which, under the authorization of the Federal Reserve Board, had prior to January 1, 1976, a subsidiary or affiliate licensed to sell insurance (except that subsequent authorization to expand such activities shall be subject to this section), or to any bank holding company owning a state/chartered bank which had, prior to January 1, 1976, a subsidiary or affiliate licensed to sell insurance.

EXERCISE 2-13

Simplify the following passage from a residential lease agreement. Use the method described in the text (bracketing and eliminating extraneous or repetitious material; see the section on complexity) or any other method you find useful (even rereading the passage several times counts as a method). To make sure you understand the salient points of the passage, we'll ask you some questions at the end.

Tenant shall, at his own expense, and at all times, maintain the premises in a clean and sanitary manner including all equipment, appliances, furniture, and furnishing therein and shall surrender the same, at termination thereof, in as good condition as received, normal wear and tear excepted. Tenant shall be responsible for damages caused by his negligence and that of his family or invitees and guests. Tenant shall not paint, paper, or otherwise redecorate or make alterations to the premises without the prior written consent of the Owner. Tenant shall irrigate and maintain any surrounding grounds, including lawns, shrubbery, trees, and keep the same clear of rubbish or weeds if such grounds are a part of the premises and are exclusively for the use of the Tenant. Tenant shall not commit any waste upon said premises, or any nuisance or act which may disturb the quiet enjoyment of any tenant in the building.

Questions
1. May the tenant wallpaper a room?
2. Is the tenant responsible for keeping all grounds weed-free?
3. If the house comes equipped with a working refrigerator that later breaks down, who is responsible for repairing it?
4. Who is responsible for unclogging clogged drains?

EXERCISE 2-14

Simplify the following passage from a residential lease agreement. Use the method described in the text (bracketing and eliminating extraneous or repetitious material; see the section on complexity) or any other method you find useful (even rereading the passage several times counts as a method). To make sure you understand the salient points of the passage, we'll ask you some questions at the end.

> *Default:* If Tenant shall fail to pay rent when due, or perform any term hereof, after not less than three days written notice of such default given in the manner required by law, the Owner, at his option, may terminate all rights of Tenant hereunder, unless Tenant, within said time, shall cure such default. In the event of a default by Tenant, Owner may elect to (a) continue the lease in effect and enforce all his rights and remedies hereunder, including the right to recover the rent as it becomes due, or (b) at any time, terminate all of Tenant's rights hereunder and recover from Tenant all damages he may incur by reason of the breach of the lease, including the cost of recovering the premises, and including the worth at the time of such termination, or at the time of an award if suit be instituted to enforce this provision, of the amount by which the unpaid rent for the balance of the term exceeds the amount of such rental loss which the Tenant proves could be reasonably avoided."

Questions

1. Suppose the tenant is five days late in his rent. What, if anything, is the owner entitled to do?
2. Suppose rent is due on the first of the month. On the fourth of the month the owner notifies the tenant in writing that he has not paid his rent. On the sixth the tenant pays the rent. What, if anything, is the owner entitled to do?
3. If the tenant fails to pay rent within three days of having received written notification by the owner that he is in default, is the lease cancelled?
4. Suppose the owner has correctly terminated the tenant's rights in accordance with the provisions of the document. Suppose further that there are six months remaining on the lease. Is the owner entitled to the six months' unpaid rent?
5. Suppose there are six months remaining on the lease, and the tenant has vacated the premises. Does the owner have a right to the unpaid rent if she chooses not to terminate the lease?

Understanding Spoken Claims

Spoken presentations present special problems that written discourse does not. Probably the two most common difficulties are, first, that spoken language is presented at a speed determined by the speaker rather than the listener, and, second, that we often have only one opportunity to catch what is being said.

In some circumstances, of course, dealing with spoken material is an advantage. If the presentation is not a formal lecture or a broadcast, then we may be in a position simply to ask the speaker to slow down or to repeat a point. We can also ask for clarification or additional information, and we can follow up on interesting or obscure points. It is important to take advantage of such situations. We'll have occasion more than once to note that your thinking is only as good as the information you have, and one way to enhance that information is to ask questions. People often let their fear of speaking up and appearing more dull-witted than their peers interfere with their understanding. It's true, of course, that nobody likes to hear or answer irrelevant or dumb questions. But if you're careful to think about what you need to know before you ask, and if you don't ask questions merely to hear your own voice, this needn't be a problem. If you fail to catch a point because a speaker is speeding along faster than you can follow, the chances are excellent that other listeners are straining too. Everybody, and this usually includes the speaker, profits from good questions. (Most experienced professors can make a fairly accurate guess at a student's overall performance in a class based only on the number and quality of the questions that student asks during lectures—provided the student asks some, of course.)

But those are the easy cases, ones in which we can participate in the discussion. When the presentation is a formal lecture or a broadcast of a speech or discussion, we have to take it pretty much as it comes (although recorders, which are fast becoming ubiquitous, can eliminate much of the burden if we are prepared to make use of them).

Fortunately, when we are not in a position to ask questions or make requests we can usually make use of pencil and paper. It's a good habit to jot down important points of a talk, since good speeches are apt to contain much material that is there just for color or humor, material that helps keep an audience's attention but that can distract from the main focus of the speech.

Good note taking is an art. It results from knowing what *not* to write down as much as knowing what *to* write down. If we are determined to write down every point just as it was stated, we may still be scribbling one while a more important one is offered. So be selective—note only points that are crucial to the presentation. And, unless you are practiced at shorthand, jot down just the heart of each remark—a few key words will usually do—so you'll be ready for the next one.

Organize your notes as you go along. You don't want to wind up with merely a list of points and no indication of their interrelationships. Keep points on a single topic together on a page and indicate how they fit together. One of the authors uses a system of arrows to indicate which points support others: An arrow drawn from A to B indicates that point A supports point B. Unless the speaker is very well organized indeed, she will not always cover topics in a logical order. Therefore, you might wind up with arrows snaking around the page. Still, the arrow system will help you figure out the speech later.

Neither note taking nor tape recording is an efficient substitute for careful listening. The key to careful listening is the ability to pay close attention to what is being said while still being able to follow the general flow of the speech. Concrete details are more easily remembered than general or abstract points. The former will come to you without much effort, so you must concentrate on the latter, using whatever devices are necessary to help you remember and understand.

It is impossible to teach the ability to listen carefully in the space permitted here—and it's difficult enough to teach it from the pages of a book no matter how much space is available. But it is true that practice can improve your listening skills. Classrooms are excellent places to practice, but news and discussion programs on television and radio also provide ample opportunity to practice. Just *hearing* someone talk ensures nothing, but if you practice enough you'll find that you are *listening* as well as hearing.

EXERCISE 2-15

This exercise is intended to enhance your ability to understand spoken claims. Your instructor may use it as a model in constructing other, similar exercises. Ask someone to read the following article aloud twice. Then answer as many of the questions that appear at the end of the article as you can. If you wish, you may take notes as you listen.

> To Tijuana shopkeeper Luis Montoya, there's no reason for the Navy's 3-month-old curfew that prohibits U.S. service personnel from making nighttime visits to the Mexican border city.
>
> "There was no problem, no reason for putting Tijuana off-limits at night. If I come to San Diego and drink and fight, I'll be arrested the same as here. There is no difference," Montoya said.
>
> But Navy officials said there has been a problem—reports of extortion and abuse of sailors and Marines by Mexican police. Despite pleas from shopkeepers and the appointment of a new police chief, Tijuana remains off-limits for service personnel from 8 P.M. to 5 A.M.
>
> The curfew was imposed Oct. 5 by Commodore E. Inman Carmichael, commander of Naval Base San Diego. The Navy said for 18 months before the curfew, U.S. service personnel reported mistreatment and threats by Tijuana police officers with arrest and impoundment of their automobiles unless bribes were paid to the officers.
>
> There had followed months of discussion about the reported incidents between Navy and Tijuana officials, but no resolution to the problem. So Carmichael imposed the curfew.
>
> Luis Manuel Serrano, spokesman for Tijuana Mayor Rene Trevino, said: "The tourists are still coming. . . . Maybe the curfew is good for Tijuana during those hours (8 P.M. to 5 A.M.) to keep out servicemen who get drunk and ask for trouble."
>
> —JAMES WRIGHTSON, "Navy Keeps Curfew for Tijuana," *Sacramento Bee*

Questions
1. To whom does the curfew apply?
2. Who set it?
3. What are the hours of the curfew?
4. As of the time the article was written, how long had the curfew been in effect?
5. Why was the curfew begun?
6. What does the Tijuana mayor think of the curfew?
7. According to the article, what do Tijuana shopkeepers think of it?
8. How long were threats, etc., reported before the curfew was initiated?
9. How long will the curfew be in effect?
10. What was the result of discussions between Navy and Tijuana officials?

Recap

In this chapter we considered several ways in which claims can lack clarity and defeat understanding. The message a person intends to communicate in a claim can be obscured by ambiguity, vagueness, or unfamiliar language. You can eliminate ambiguity and reduce vagueness by recasting a claim and by providing definitions of the proper type. We identified several types of definitions and looked at some of their best uses. But we also showed that even certain definitions—those of the "persuasive" type—can be used to hinder understanding if they are distorted. As with vagueness, a certain amount of complexity is sometimes necessary. But careful reading and the use of a simplifying technique can make a complex claim understandable as long as it suffers from no other defect. Finally, we considered some tips designed to help you become a better listener, since the spoken word is the means by which we learn much of what we know. We pointed out that there are no hard and fast rules that can guarantee clarity and understanding but we also showed that the clear-headed application of common sense combined with the suggestions made here can make a difference.

Additional Exercises

EXERCISES 2-16

Some people believe that you can know a person's character and attitude toward food merely by learning his or her astrological sign. Read each of the twelve descriptions of character traits and attitudes toward food, and then determine which fits you (and any aquaintances you choose). Then check in the answers section at the back of the book to see whether you selected the "correct" description for people with your birthdate. If you did, you shouldn't immediately decide that the astrologers have you figured out—ask your instructor to survey the class to see how many of your classmates selected the descriptions associated with their birthdates and signs.

1. You are interested in people, known for tact and fairness, and dislike being alone. You go to great lengths to keep a relationship together. You have a sweet tooth, preferring cake to vegetables.

2. People born under your sign are nurturers. You are generous, easygoing, and like to parent and protect people. You have great patience, rely more on intuition than intellect, and relate well to children. People see you as tough, but underneath you are a sensitive and creative person. You love to eat and are probably a good cook. You turn to food when you're upset.

3. You do not make friends easily but value the few you make. You have great patience, and are well organized. You prefer the familiar and are fond of routine. You're a builder, not a pioneer. Dieting comes hard for you, since you really enjoy fine food.

4. You have a sparkling personality and a sunny disposition. People love to be with you, and you enjoy the company of others. You sometimes act first and consider consequences later. You dare to be different and are always looking for something new. You eat too fast and often skip meals.

5. People of your sign are passionate. You are sexy, but your main passion is for knowledge: You love to learn. You have an active social life. You're a great pretender; you appear calm and detached even when you're not. You're very secretive and possess great willpower. You tend to overdo it when it comes to rich, spicy food and good wine.

6. You're interested in progress. You're a nonconformist, and nobody knows what to predict about you. You want to help people any way you can. You're an excellent friend, but probably won't get involved in a serious emotional relationship until later in life. You can gain weight without even knowing it until someone tells you.

7. You are truly individualistic and believe that rules were made to be broken. You don't like being told what to do. You have good luck and an infectious optimism. You don't ask for commitments, because you hate being tied down. You're always searching for a new experience and sometimes are too foolhardy for your own good. If you gain weight, you always vow to start dieting tomorrow, but it's never easy for you.

8. Those with your sign are the mystics of the zodiac. You are benevolent and tenderhearted, but possess ideals, inspiration, vision, and imagination. You are quiet, unpretentious, and gentle. You identify with others. You hate violence of all kinds. You are very artistic. You make serving food an art; you gain and lose weight in cycles.

9. Your sign represents honors, career, authority, and public recognition. You are the most disciplined sign in the zodiac. You seem wiser and more mature than others. You are very practical; chance never enters into your scheme of things. You're a hard worker and are loyal, trustworthy, and dependable. Appearances are important to you. When eating alone, you're frugal, but when you entertain, only the best will do. You're a conservative cook.

10. You are quick-witted and able to judge the moods of others with uncanny accuracy. You can do more than one thing at once; you can adapt yourself to nearly any situation or environment. You analyze things and are not very emotional. You believe life is a game. You are highly unlikely to experience any weight problems, but you are so busy you often bolt down your food.

11. You are pragmatic and practical. You love for things to be orderly and are fairly predictable. You have good organizational skills. You're diligent and take on responsibility well. You set high standards and can be critical of those who don't measure up. You know about health foods and consume them, but tension is your diet's biggest enemy: You eat when you're overstressed.

12. There's never a dull moment in the life of a person with your sign. You are sure of who you are and what you want. You are a natural leader, but you do not abuse your authority. You're a soft touch—you believe the best about everybody. You need love more than any other sign. You love children, but you want to play with them, not protect them. You enjoy good food just as you enjoy all of life. You are the best host or hostess in the zodiac.

EXERCISE 2-17

This is the same kind of exercise as 2-4, but this time the word in question is *round*. Which uses of this word are the most vague? (We find three of them more vague than the others. They are identified in the answer section at the back of the book.)

1. Round off your answer to two decimal places.
2. When his daughter got home after midnight, he scolded her roundly.
3. The guards fired more than a hundred rounds at the escapees.
4. Jim's bride-to-be is joining him in Seattle, but she bought a round-trip ticket.
5. The kids were looking for round rocks to use in their slingshots.
6. When the talk was finished, the speaker received a round of applause.
7. Parnelli was knocked out in the second round.
8. After the argument, Ben and Maria rounded up their children and left.
9. The marathon runners set a round pace from the beginning of the race.
10. J. S. Bach could compose a round as fast as you could write it down.

EXERCISE 2-18

Define these words by providing synonyms. Refer to a dictionary if necessary.

★1. Capsize
2. Classmate
3. Litigate
★4. Awkward
5. Fool

6. Pensive
★7. Buddy
8. Teacher
9. Help
★10. Miser

EXERCISE 2-19

Define each of the following by synonyms, using one synonym that carries a complimentary meaning and one that carries a derogatory emotive meaning.

EXAMPLE: For *thin person* you might give either *slender person* or *svelte person*, both of which are complimentary; or you might give *skinny person*, which is derogatory.

★1. Overweight
2. Thrifty
3. Proud
★4. Display
5. Farmer

6. Public servant
★7. Drinker
8. Humble
9. Decayed
★10. Intellectual (noun)

EXERCISE 2-20

For each of the following, give an analytic definition that is flattering.

EXAMPLE: Doctor—a person who is dedicated to alleviating the pain and suffering of others.

★1. Conservative (noun)
2. Politician
3. Feminist
★4. Liberal
5. Educator

EXERCISE 2-21

For these words, give an analytic definition that is *unflattering*.

EXAMPLE: Doctors—men who prescribe medicines of which they know little, to cure diseases of which they know less, in human beings of whom they know nothing.

—Attributed to VOLTAIRE

　★1. Playboy
　 2. Hunter
　 3. Teenager
　★4. Philosopher
　 5. Educator

EXERCISE 2-22

Make a judgment about the writer's purpose in each of the following definitions. Determine whether the primary purpose is to eliminate ambiguity, to
reduce vagueness, to introduce or explain a new or unusual word, or to evoke
an attitude about something (persuasive definition). If the purpose seems to
be none of these, try to explain it in your own words.

EXAMPLE: The sinciput is the forehead.

PURPOSE: To introduce or explain an unusual word.

　★1. A memory buffer is a temporary storage facility for information in a
computing system.
　 2. For the purposes of this article, the elderly are that class of people who
are sixty-five or older.
　 3. When I talk about my "better students," I mean those who get As and
Bs on their exams.
　★4. "An idealist is one who, on noticing that a rose smells better than a
cabbage, concludes that it will also make a better soup."
　　　　　　　　　　　　　　　　　　　　　　　　　—H. L. MENCKEN
　 5. No, no. I'm not talking about *Catholic* sisters; I'm talking about your
mother's daughters!
　 6. "Conscience is an inner voice that warns us somebody is looking."
　　　　　　　　　　　　　　　　　　　　　　　　　—H. L. MENCKEN
　★7. When I told you to root for him I meant cheer for him, not dig a hole
in the ground!
　 8. A tax shelter is a government-approved arrangement that enables a taxpayer to avoid, reduce, or postpone paying income taxes.
　 9. Atomic clock—an electronic clock the frequency of which is supplied or
governed by the natural resonance frequencies of atoms or molecules of
suitable substances.
　★10. "Conservative, *n*. A statesman who is enamored of existing evils, as distinguished from the Liberal, who wishes to replace them with others."
　　　　　　　　　　　　　　　　　　　　　　　　　—AMBROSE BIERCE
　 11. "What is a committee? A group of the unwilling, picked from the unfit,
to do the unnecessary."
　　　　　　　　　　　　　　　　　　　　　　　　　—RICHARD HARKNESS
　 12. "Cold Duck—A carbonated wine foisted upon Americans (who else

would drink it?) by winery ad agencies as a way of getting rid of inferior champagne by mixing it with inferior sparkling burgundy."

—JOHN CIARDI

★13. " 'Classic.' A book which people praise and don't read."

—MARK TWAIN

14. "The interior decorator is simply an inferior desecrator of the work of an artist."

—FRANK LLOYD WRIGHT

15. *Disinterested,* which is quite different from *uninterested,* means impartial or unbiased.

★16. A halyard is a line used for raising and lowering sails.

17. "Logic is neither a science nor an art, but a dodge."

—Ascribed to BENJAMIN JOWETT

18. The spine is that part of the human anatomy that was intended to support the shoulders, the head, and the chiropractor.

★19. "Socialist—a man suffering from an overwhelming compulsion to believe what is not true."

—H. L. MENCKEN

20. "A good teacher is one who drives the students to think."

—HERM ALBRIGHT

EXERCISE 2-23

Distill the "hard" news from the following passages from news magazines. Eliminate whatever background material, coloration, phrases designed to maintain interest, emotion-laden language, and other extraneous material you find imbedded in them. In short, reduce these passages to the facts. Number 1 is condensed in the answer section.

★1. "Since 1945, millions of Americans have looked in their mailboxes for those familiar green, punch-card checks that have been Uncle Sam's way of sending money. The Government now issues 600 million of the checks annually for everything from Social Security to income tax refunds.

"Last week the Treasury announced that it was time to give Government spending a new hue. Over the next three years the green check will be phased out and replaced by a version that features a spectrum of pastel colors, beginning with pale blue on the left, shading to light green and then peach. The new checks will be decorated with drawings of the Statue of Liberty. The first will go into the mail next month.

"Treasury officials have practical as well as aesthetic reasons for making the switch. For one thing, the multicolored checks will be harder to counterfeit than the green ones. In addition, Miss Liberty checks will be cheaper to produce because they will be printed on lightweight paper and will not need to have holes punched in them. The Treasury will be using processing equipment that will scan symbols printed on the checks rather than read patterns of holes. The change to Miss Liberty is expected to save Uncle Sam $6 million a year."

—*Time*, January 21, 1985

2. "Long ago, no doubt in a top-secret Swiss lab, a cosmetic-company researcher discovered a revolutionary skin-care ingredient: mumbo jumbo. This, of course, transformed ordinary cold cream into an exotic "anti-aging formula." Unsupported claims have multiplied ever since. But last week science finally overtook pseudoscience. According to a study published in the *Journal of the American Medical Association,* Retin-A, a prescription cream used against severe acne, can diminish fine wrinkles and other defects caused by exposure to the sun.

"Retin-A, which contains a chemical, retinoic acid, related to vitamin A, won Food and Drug Administration approval as an acne treatment in 1971. Doctors soon observed that on certain older patients who used it, some wrinkling and blotchiness faded. Tests in 1986 by Albert Kligman of the University of Pennsylvania confirmed the drug's anti-wrinkle potential, but skeptics awaited research showing that Retin-A worked *better* than, say, plain moisturizer. Dermatologist John Voorhees and co-workers at the University of Michigan Medical Center have done just that. In the journal's editorial, Barbara Gilchrest, a dermatologist at the Boston University School of Medicine, cautioned that relatively few subjects were tested, but she also said that 'a new age has dawned.'

"In the Michigan study, 30 subjects, aged 35 to 70, daily applied Retin-A to one forearm and a dummy cream to the other. After four months all of the drug-treated forearms had fewer fine wrinkles and most were smoother; in contrast none of the placebo-treated forearms showed improvement. Also, 14 of the 15 patients who applied Retin-A to their faces showed fewer fine wrinkles, while none of the 15 who used placebo cream showed any change. In six patients there was 'slight improvement' in course wrinkles. Microscopic analysis revealed that the treated skin grew new tissue to replace dead or sun-damaged cells; this, explains Voorhees, ruled out the possibility that, say, the skin merely absorbed more water to puff out the wrinkles."

—*Newsweek,* February 1, 1988

3. "A tacky mural of the Lower Manhattan skyline served as backdrop. The band's version of *Theme from New York, New York* compensated in decibels for what it lacked in finesse. The ballroom of the thoroughly lived-in Omni Park Central Hotel was too small and too warm for the hundreds crammed together like rush-hour commuters on the A train. But the atmospherics last Tuesday night mattered not at all. Chants of 'Duke! Duke! Duke!' alternated with cries of 'Let's go, Mike!' And when Michael Dukakis paused before speaking, his usually constricted smile was as broad and welcoming as New York harbor. Campaign workers cheered ecstatically at the Duke's

every prosaic line. 'I love New York!' brought hurrahs. 'Friends, if we can make it here, we can make it anywhere.' Delirious applause."

—*Time*, May 2, 1988

EXERCISE 2-24 (ESSAY)

Write a brief essay in which you describe the consequences of a term's being used ambiguously or too vaguely. The first part should be narrative; this is where you describe what happens (either fact or fiction—use your imagination). The second part should be analytical—what clarification would have prevented the problem?

3 Evaluating Informative Claims

It isn't what's said that counts, it's who says it.
> —Old saying [In truth, this adage is half right: What counts is not *only* what gets said, but who says it.]

It's one thing to understand a claim; it's another to decide whether or not to accept it. The central task of critical thinking, you'll recall, is determining whether to accept a claim. In this chapter we consider some general factors that bear on the acceptability of claims used to convey information. We concentrate here on claims that are presented without explicit supporting argumentation. The second half of the book is devoted to claims offered along with their support—that is, to arguments.

It is important to understand that the person communicating information may be performing any of several specific functions in the process. That person may be reporting, explaining, generalizing, predicting, drawing an analogy, making a statistical claim, describing, classifying, or giving instructions—and who knows what else, including combinations of several such activities.

But regardless of what form the communication might take, generally speaking *it is reasonable to accept an unsupported informative claim if it issues from a credible source and does not conflict with (1) what you have observed, (2) your background information, or (3) other creditable claims.* We will examine several aspects of this general principle, beginning with what it means for two claims to conflict with each other.

Conflicting Claims

Two conflicting claims cannot both be correct. If a given claim conflicts with another, a critical thinker will be wary of both of them until he or she can determine which claim, if either, is correct. Such conflict can be resolved only through the acquisition of further information.

Claims can conflict in two ways: they can be contradictories or they can be contraries. Two claims are **contradictories** if they are exact opposites—they cannot both be true at the same time and they cannot both be false at the same time.

Here are Theresa and Daniel making contradictory claims:

THERESA: Silas Marner hot dogs are at least 30 percent pork.
DANIEL: No, their pork content is less than 30 percent.

If Theresa is right then Daniel is wrong, and if she is wrong then he is right. Their two remarks cannot both be true and they cannot both be false.

But consider the following two claims. You will see that, although they conflict, they are not exact opposites:

1. Silas Marner hot dogs are made entirely of pork.
2. Silas Marner hot dogs contain no pork at all.

These two claims cannot both be true, but they are not *exact* opposites, because it is possible for both of them to be false—if, for example, the hot dogs in question were part pork and part something else. Two claims are **contraries,** then, if they cannot both be true at the same time but can both be false at the same time.

Frequently a pair of claims will seem to conflict when in fact they do not. For example,

3. Silas Marner hot dogs are at least 30 percent pork.
4. Silas Marner hot dogs are at most 30 percent pork.

These two claims do not conflict, because the hot dogs may be exactly 30 percent pork, in which case both claims are true.

5. Silas Marner hot dogs are at least 30 percent pork.
6. Silas Marner hot dogs are at least 20 percent pork.

These two claims do not conflict because, if the hot dogs are 30 percent or more pork, both the claims are true. Before you reject a factual claim for conflicting with other factual claims, make sure it really *does* conflict.

An Enigmatic Agreement

Both of these statements appear in a collective bargaining agreement between a hospital and a nurses' association:

1. If an employee is required to work on a holiday, that employee will receive straight time for the actual hours worked in addition to the holiday pay.
2. An employee who works on a holiday has the option of being paid the straight-time rate for hours worked on the holiday and taking a compensatory day off with pay or being paid at the rate of time and one-half for hours worked on the holiday in addition to holiday pay.

If you were the payroll clerk for the hospital, would you be able to identify the conflict?

EXERCISE 3-1

Determine whether the pairs of claims are contradictories, contraries, or not in conflict at all.

★1. (a) A drink or two a day won't hurt anyone's health.
    (b) Heart patients absolutely should not drink at all.

2. (a) None of the legal staff showed up for work today.
    (b) Some of the legal staff showed up for work today.

3. (a) The temperature was over 90 degrees by three o'clock.
    (b) The temperature was over 85 degrees by three o'clock.

★4. (a) It's unpleasantly cool today.
    (b) It's over 90 degrees today.

5. (a) Duluth is bigger than Terre Haute.
    (b) Terre Haute is at least as big as Duluth.

6. (a) Eisenhower was the president who first remarked that "the future lies ahead."
    (b) Hoover was the president who first remarked that "the future lies ahead."

★7. (a) Canseco hit no home runs in the 1988 World Series.
    (b) Canseco hit three home runs in the 1988 World Series.

8. (a) The rate of inflation in 1988 was 5 percent or more.
    (b) The inflation rate in 1988 was less than 5 percent.

9. (a) Digital communications will require fiber optics by 1990.
    (b) Fiber optics will not be necessary for digital communications by 1990.

★10. (a) Winthrop, South Carolina, is the only town in the country that has a law against carrying an ice cream cone in one's pocket.
    (b) Monfort, Florida, has a law against carrying an ice cream cone in one's pocket.

EXERCISE 3-2

Determine whether these pairs of claims are contradictories, contraries, or not conflicting. If there are assumptions that would make a difference in the relationship between the claims, make that assumption explicit.

★1. (a) Friday is payday.
(b) No, I'm sorry; Monday is payday.

2. (a) Helgren is going to fail his logic course.
(b) Helgren is going to pass his logic course.

3. (a) Everybody in Helgren's class passed the exam.
(b) George is in Helgren's class, and he did not pass the exam.

★4. (a) Everybody in Helgren's class passed the exam.
(b) No, at least one person in Helgren's class did not pass the exam.

5. (a) Since the stock market crash of October 1987, investors have not had as much confidence in stocks.
(b) Some investors have regained as much confidence in stocks as they had before the crash of October 1987.

6. (a) All good paper has at least forty percent rag content.
(b) No good paper has at least forty percent rag content.

★7. (a) All good paper has at least forty percent rag content.
(b) Some good paper has no more than thirty percent rag content.

8. (a) All good paper has at least forty percent rag content.
(b) Some good paper has at least fifty percent rag content.

9. (a) The odds against you in roulette are so bad that nobody can win in the long run.
(b) Harry played roulette in Atlantic City and won a huge amount of money.

★10. (a) The sentence after this one is true.
(b) The sentence before this one is false.

Now that you understand how claims can conflict with one another, let's return to our principle that it is reasonable to accept a claim from a credible source as long as it does not conflict with one's observations, one's background knowledge, and other creditable claims. To make this principle clear we'll discuss in turn personal observations, background knowledge, and the credibility of sources.

Conflicts with Personal Observations ———————————

Our most reliable source of information is our own observations. But observations are not infallible, a fact that critical thinkers recognize. Observations may not be reliable if made when the lighting is poor or the room is noisy;

when we are distracted, emotionally upset, or mentally fatigued; when our senses are impaired; or when our measuring instruments are inexact, temperamental, or inaccurate.

In addition, critical thinkers recognize that people vary in their powers of observation. Some people see and hear better than others and for this reason may be better at making observations than those whose vision or hearing is less acute. But this is not necessarily so. Customs agents and professional counselors, even those who wear glasses or hearing aids, are better able than most of us to detect signs of nervousness or discomfort in people they observe. Laboratory scientists accustomed to noticing subtle changes in the properties of substances they are investigating are doubtless better than you or I at certain sorts of observations. But they may not be better at others: Some professional magicians actually prefer an audience of scientists, believing that such a group is particularly easy to fool.

Our beliefs, hopes, fears, and expectations also affect our observations. Tell someone that a house is infested with rats and he is likely to believe he sees evidence of rats. Inform someone who believes in ghosts that a house is haunted and she may well believe she sees evidence of ghosts. Observers at seances staged by the Society for Psychical Research to test the observational powers of people under seance conditions insist that they "see" numerous phenomena that simply do not exist. Teachers who are told that the students in a particular class are brighter than usual are very likely to believe that the work those students produce is better than average even when it is not.

Our biases also affect our perceptions. We overlook many of the mean and selfish actions of the people we like or love—and when we are infatuated with

When Is Seeing Believing?

On a segment of her program "Not for Women Only," Barbara Walters watched psychic Uri Geller bend spoons (allegedly through psychic power) and perform other psychic feats. Reportedly Walters was convinced that Geller accomplished the feats through nonphysical psychic methods. The videotape of the program, however, revealed that Geller simply bent the spoons with his hands, a fact that Walters just failed to notice even though she watched him very closely.

On a later program three magicians performed the rest of Geller's tricks, using perfectly standard magician's chicanery and sleight of hand.

Like Walters, we cannot always depend on what we *believe* we see turning out to be what we *actually* see. She was doubtless influenced the first time around by being told that Geller would bend the spoons with psychic powers alone; hence she didn't *notice* that he had used his hands until she watched the videotape. Our expectations, desires, and beliefs have a lot to do with what information our senses pass along to us.

someone, everything that person does seems wonderful. On the other hand, people we detest can hardly do anything that we don't perceive as mean and selfish.

Further, the reliability of our observations is no better than the reliability of our memories, except in those cases where we have the means at our disposal to record our observations. And memory, as most of us know, can be deceptive. Critical thinkers are always alert to the possibility that what they remember having observed may not be what they did observe.

But even though first-hand observations are not infallible, they are still the best source of information we have. Any factual report that conflicts with your own direct observations is subject to serious doubt.

EXERCISE 3-3

Let's compare your powers of observation with those of your classmates. Answer the following sets of questions about your instructor and your classroom. Answer both sets at home, and bring the results to class for checking and comparison with the observations and recollections of others.

Observations of Your Instructor from Your Most Recent Class Meeting
1. Note the following, based on your observations and estimations:
   - a. Approximate height _____
   - b. Approximate weight _____
   - c. Hair color _____
   - d. Eye color _____
2. Was he or she wearing . . . ?
   - a. a belt _____
   - b. a tie _____
   - c. glasses _____
   - d. rings _____
   - e. a watch _____
   - f. a hat _____
3. Did he or she . . . ?
   - a. bring a coat to class _____
   - b. bring a briefcase _____
   - c. arrive early at the classroom _____
   - d. speak from notes _____
4. State in a sentence the main topic of discussion in the most recent class meeting:
   _____

Observations of Your Classroom
1. Your classroom has how many . . . ?
   - a. windows _____
   - b. doors _____
   - c. chairs or desks _____
   - d. clocks _____
2. What color are the . . . ?
   - a. walls _____
   - b. ceiling _____
3. What kind of floor does the classroom have (e.g., tile, wood, carpeted, concrete, etc.)? _____
4. Approximately how high is the ceiling? _____

5. Does the room contain . . . ?
   a. a lectern _____
   b. an overhead projector _____
   c. a chalkboard _____
   d. a movie screen _____
   e. pictures on the walls _____
   f. blinds or curtains _____
6. As you sit facing the front of the room, which direction of the compass are you facing? _____

EXERCISE 3-4

To illustrate how widely our powers of recall vary, your instructor will make up and recite a sequence of eight numbers. Beginning only after you have heard the *last* number, write down as much of the sequence as you can remember. Compare your list with those of your classmates.

EXERCISE 3-5

This time your instructor will read eight items from a typical grocery list. Beginning after you have heard the *last* item, write down as much of the sequence as you can remember. Compare your list with those of your classmates.

★EXERCISE 3-6

List at least eight factors that may reduce the reliability of a person's observations.

EXERCISE 3-7

Without referring to the text, supply the proper words or phrases for as many of the blanks as you can. See the answer section at the back of the book for answers to all the items in this exercise.

1. According to the text, it is reasonable to accept an unsupported claim if it comes from a _____ source and does not conflict with _____ , _____ , and _____ .
2. Our most reliable source of information is _____ .
3. The reliability of our observations is no better than the reliability of _____ .
4. Two conflicting claims that are exact opposites are called _____ .
5. Two conflicting claims that are not exact opposites are called _____ . Such claims could both be _____ .

Conflicts with Background Knowledge

Factual claims must always be evaluated against our background knowledge—that immense body of true and justified beliefs that consists of facts we learn from our own direct observations and facts we learn from others. Such knowledge is "background" because we may not be able to specify where we learned it, which is different from something we know because we witnessed it this morning. Much of our background knowledge is well confirmed by a variety of sources, although we may not be able to recall any particular one at the moment. Factual claims that conflict with this store of knowledge are quite properly dismissed, even if we cannot disprove them through direct observation. We immediately reject the claim "Palm trees grow in abundance near the North Pole" even though we are not in a position to confirm or disprove the statement by direct observation. If we had little in the way of reliable background information, we would be forced to evaluate each new claim in isolation—an enormous chore if possible at all.

How do we know that we can depend on our background knowledge? Of any person's stock of beliefs, some are going to be false—not everything we *believe* turns out to be something we *know*. You cannot simply survey your stock of beliefs and identify those that may be false, for you would not hold a belief in the first place if you had serious doubts about it. Nevertheless, though you cannot learn which of your beliefs might be false solely by reviewing what you think you know, you ought not accept a new factual claim that stands in conflict with one you already believe (or dismiss the old one) until you have weighed the two against each other and against further data. For example, if you receive word that you are overdrawn by a thousand dollars in your checking account, and you are unaware of any recent financial activity that might have resulted in such a negative balance, you will not accept such a claim at face value. Either the bank has made an error, you might decide, or someone is trying to pull a joke on you. But you do have reason to do some investigating in order to determine just what, if anything, is going on with your bank account. As in most other cases, nothing can take the place of such further investigation and the gathering of more information—no neat formula can resolve a conflict between what you already believe and a new piece of information.

Clearly you are handicapped in evaluating a factual report on a subject in which you have no background knowledge. This means that the broader your background knowledge is the more likely you are to be able to evaluate any given report effectively—without some rudimentary knowledge of economics, for example, one is in no position to evaluate claims about the dangers of a large federal deficit. The single most effective means of increasing your ability as a critical thinker, regardless of the subject, is to increase what you know: Read widely, converse freely, and develop an inquiring attitude! There is simply no substitute for broad, general knowledge.

EXERCISE 3-8

List fifteen statements that you believe to be true about the United States government or about specific government officials. When you are finished, trade your list for that of a classmate. Place each item from your classmate's list into one of three categories: (1) those you believe to be true, (2) those you believe to be false, and (3) those you are uncertain about.

Next, explain to each other why you assigned the items as you did.

Finally, based on this discussion, compile a third list that contains only those items from the original lists that you and the other person both know to be true. Submit this list to your instructor for any comments he or she might have.

Sensational!!! (But False)

WW2 BOMBER FOUND ON MOON. Perfectly preserved warplane sitting in crater, say experts.

—*Weekly World News*

KILLER SEA MONSTER STILL AT LARGE

—*The Examiner*

600 HITLERS CLONED BY RUSSIANS

—*Weekly World News*

INJURED UFO CREW IN SOVIET HOSPITAL

—*Weekly World News*

MERMAIDS DO EXIST!

—*National Enquirer*

BABY BORN WEARING 3,000-YEAR-OLD ANKLET. "This child has lived before," says expert.

—*Weekly World News*

MIRACLE OF THE LIQUEFYING BLOOD: Several times yearly in Naples, Italy, blood of the fourth-century martyr bubbles and foams.

—*Fate*

BABY TALKS AT BIRTH AND GIVES DAD WINNING LOTTERY NUMBER

—*National Enquirer*

Assessing Credibility

Our guiding principle in evaluating unsupported informational claims requires that they come from credible sources. But how do you determine whether a source is credible?

In general, the more knowledgeable a person is about a given subject, the more reason there is to accept what the person says about it. If Parker knows more about automobile mechanics than Moore, for example, you have that much more reason to accept Parker's diagnosis of your car's problem than Moore's.

It is sometimes said that observation reports are an exception to this general rule. Observation reports are eyewitness records (or recollections) of events, and that's just what many informative claims are, or are based upon. Although it may at first appear that one person's observation reports are as acceptable as the next person's, we have seen that this is not true. Even if two people are both making eyewitness reports, there is more reason to accept the claims of the one who knows most about the subject, since that person is in general more apt to make accurate and reliable observations about occurrences within his or her sphere of expertise than will a lay person. A musician will generally make more accurate observations than the rest of us about the intonation of the wind instruments in last Friday's concert; a carpenter will be more reliable in reporting on the house being built down the street.

When considering the credibility of the person who asserts a claim, then, an important factor is that person's relevant background knowledge.

Expertise

Even if Parker knows more about engines than Moore, he may still not be an expert in the subject. An **expert** is one who, through education, training, or experience, has special knowledge or ability in a subject. The informational claims made by experts are the most reliable of such claims, provided they fall into the expert's area of expertise. This is true even if two conflicting claims are both reports of first-hand observations: If one of the claims is made by an expert and the other by a lay person, there is more reason to accept the claim of the former.

We have to consider the claims of experts carefully, however. We sometimes make the mistake of thinking that whatever qualifies someone as an expert in one field automatically qualifies that person in other areas. Even if the intelligence and skill required to become an expert in one field *could* enable

High Stakes Make a Difference

The principle with which we began this chapter, you'll recall, is that, *generally speaking,* it's reasonable to accept an unsupported informative claim if it comes from a credible source and does not conflict with your observations, your background knowledge, or other creditable claims. We've included the words "generally speaking" because there are exceptions to the principle when there is something very important at stake.

Consider: What if you go to your doctor and he tells you that the lump on your knee is cancerous and it will be necessary to amputate the leg? Our principle is dependable in most cases, but not in this one. The stakes are high in this case—you could lose a leg—and that makes a big difference. Even though the source is credible (your physician), and unless you're an oncologist, the claim probably doesn't conflict with your background knowledge, your observations, or other creditable claims. Still, because the consequences of accepting the doctor's claims are so serious, no reasonable decision can be made without at least a second (and, better, a third) opinion. In short, the principle doesn't always hold when the stakes are high; in such cases the reasonable alternative is to subject the claim to the most stringent tests you can—in the case described, the opinions of other physicians.

I GRANT THAT HE IS A WELL-INFORMED, UNBIASED, CLEAR-THINKING, HIGHLY-RESPECTED UNOPINIONATED EXPERT——BUT WHY SHOULD I BELIEVE HIM?

someone to become an expert in any field—an assumption that is itself doubtful—it is one thing to possess the ability to become an expert and an entirely different thing actually to *be* an expert. Thus, informational claims put forth by experts about subjects outside their fields are not automatically more acceptable than claims put forth by nonexperts.

Five main factors serve to establish someone as an expert: (1) education and (2) experience are often the most important factors, followed by (3) accomplishments, (4) reputation, and (5) position, in no particular order. It is not always easy to evaluate the credentials of an expert, and credentials vary considerably from one field to another. Still, there are some useful guidelines that are worth mentioning.

Education includes but is not strictly limited to formal education—the possession of degrees from established institutions of learning. (Some "doctors" of this and that received their diplomas from mail-order houses that advertise on matchbook covers. The title *doctor* is not automatically a qualification.)

Experience is an important factor in expertise both in terms of the kind and the amount of experience. Experience is important if it is relevant to the issue at hand, but the mere fact that someone has been on the job for a long time does not automatically make him or her good at it.

Accomplishments are an important indicator of someone's expertise, but, once again, only when those accomplishments are directly related to the question at hand. A Nobel Prize winner in physics is not necessarily qualified to speak publicly about the state of the economy, public school education (even in science), or nuclear disarmament. The last issue may involve physics, it's true, but the political issues are the crucial ones, and they are not taught in physics labs.

The "Authority" of Experience

. . . a farmer never laid an egg, but he knows more about the process than hens do.

—HENRY DARCY CURWEN

No one knows more about this mountain than Harry. And it don't dare blow up on him. This goddamned mountain won't blow.
   —HARRY TRUMAN, 83-year-old owner of a lodge near Mt. St. Helens in Washington, commenting on geologists' predictions that the volcano would erupt. (A few days later it did erupt, killing Harry Truman.)

Through their "observations" the hen and Harry know well enough what it's like to lay an egg or live near a volcano, but these observations are obviously not enough to qualify them as reliable sources about the biological and geological processes involved in egg laying and volcanic eruptions.

A person's reputation always exists only among a particular contingent of people. You may have a strong reputation as a pool player at your local billiards emporium, but that doesn't necessarily put you in the same league with Minnesota Fats. And your friend may consider his friend Mr. Klein the greatest living expert on some particular subject, and he may be right. But you must ask yourself if your friend is in a position to evaluate Mr. Klein's credentials.

The Experts Aren't Always Right

If excessive smoking actually plays a role in the production of lung cancer, it seems to be a minor one.
—DR. W. C. HEUPER, National Cancer Institute, 1954

There is not the slightest indication that (nuclear) energy will ever be obtainable. It would mean that the atom would have to be shattered at will.
—ALBERT EINSTEIN, 1932

With over 50 foreign cars already on sale here, the Japanese auto industry isn't likely to carve out a big slice of the U.S. market for itself.
—*Business Week,* August 2, 1968

The end of the decline of the Stock Market will . . . probably not be long, only a few more days at most.
—IRVING FISHER, professor of economics at Yale University, November 14, 1929 (The decline actually continued for about three years, by which time an estimated $50 billion had been wiped out.)

When the U.S. government stops wasting our resources by trying to maintain the price of gold, its price will sink to . . . $6 an ounce rather than the current $35 dollars an ounce.
—HENRY REUSS, chair of the Joint Economic Committee of Congress, 1967 (In 1971 the United States stopped buying gold; the price of gold then rose until at one time it stood at over $800 an ounce.)

I would like to suggest that Ronald Reagan is politically dead.
—TOM PETIT, political correspondent for NBC, January 22, 1980

[T]he aeroplane . . . is not capable of unlimited magnification. It is not likely that it will ever carry more than five or seven passengers.
—WALDEMAR KAEMPFERT, managing editor of *Scientific American* and author of *The New Art of Flying,* June 28, 1913

There is no reason for any individual to have a computer in their home.
—KEN OLSON, president of Digital Equipment Corporation, 1977 (Digital, second only to IBM as a computer manufacturer, began selling its own line of microcomputers in 1982.)

As much fun as it is to read these mistaken expert opinions, keep in mind that, even if they turn out to be wrong, expert opinions are still the best we've got.

Most of us have met people who were recommended as experts in some field but who turned out to know little more about that field than we ourselves knew. (Presumably in such cases those doing the recommending knew even less about the subject, or they would not have been so quickly impressed.) By and large, the kind of reputation that counts most is the one a person has among other experts in his or her field of endeavor.

The positions people hold provide an indication of how well *somebody* thinks of them. The director of an important scientific laboratory, the head of an academic department at Harvard, the author of a work consulted by other experts—in each case the position itself is substantial evidence that the individual's opinion on a relevant subject warrants serious attention.

But expertise can be bought. And sometimes a person's position is an indication of what his or her opinion, expert or not, is likely to be. The opinion

Presidential Expertise

Presidents of the United States have access to professional expertise in nearly any area they want to learn about. But their own personal expertise may fall short in many areas; after all, they must demonstrate only an ability to get elected in order to win the job. And sometimes they find themselves in situations where they make claims about subjects they know nothing about. Here are some examples:

Gentlemen, you have come sixty days too late. The depression is over.
— HERBERT HOOVER, responding to a delegation requesting a public works program to help speed the recovery, June 1930

By 1980 we will be self-sufficient and will not need to rely on foreign enemies . . . uh, energy.
— RICHARD NIXON, 1973

Because of the greatness of the Shah, Iran is an island of stability in the Middle East.
— JIMMY CARTER, 1977

Approximately eighty percent of our air pollution stems from hydrocarbons released by vegetation. So let's not go overboard in setting and enforcing tough emissions standards for man-made sources.
— RONALD REAGAN, 1980

[A] drastic reduction in the deficit . . . will take place in the fiscal year '82.
— RONALD REAGAN, March 6, 1981 (The 1982 budget deficit was larger than any previous one, well over twice the size of the previous record.)

Alaska . . . has a greater oil reserve than Saudi Arabia.
— RONALD REAGAN, 1980 (U.S. Geological Survey and Department of Energy figures show this claim wrong by a very large margin.)

of the chief engineer for the Wyoming Gas and Electric Company, offered at a hearing on the safety of nuclear power plants, should be scrutinized much more carefully (or at least viewed with more skepticism) than that of a witness from an independent firm or agency that has no stake in the outcome of the hearings. It is too easy to lose objectivity where one's interests and concerns are at stake, and this is true even if one is *trying* to be objective.

Experts sometimes disagree, especially when the issue is complicated and many different interests are at stake. In these cases a critical thinker is obliged to suspend judgment about which expert to endorse, unless one expert clearly represents a majority viewpoint among experts in the field, or one expert can be established as more authoritative or less biased than the other.

Of course, majority opinions sometimes turn out to be incorrect, and even the most authoritative experts occasionally make mistakes. Thus, a claim that you accept because it represents the majority viewpoint or the most authoritative expert may turn out to be thoroughly wrong. Nevertheless, take heart: At the time you were rationally justified in accepting the majority viewpoint as the most authoritative claim. The reasonable position is one that agrees with the most authoritative opinion but allows for enough open-mindedness to change if the evidence changes.

Finally, and do keep in mind that, as noted above, it is sometimes wisest to form no opinion at all. If we are suspicious of our sources and the evidence

Position, Bias, and Credibility

Notice the positions held by the people making these claims. It is often difficult to determine whether individuals are doing their best to state objective facts as they know them or simply defending a personal or, as in these cases, institutional position.

There is growing evidence that smoking has pharmacological . . . effects that are of real value to smokers.
> —JOSEPH F. CULLMAN III, president of Philip Morris, Inc., 1962 annual report to stockholders

We have firmly established the safety, dosage and usefulness of Kevadon [a brand name for thalidomide] by both foreign and U.S. laboratory and clinical studies.
> —William S. Merrell Company executive, October 1960

There is no major health problem in Niagara Falls.
> —BRUCE G. DAVIS, executive vice president of Hooker Chemical Company, which had been using the Love Canal area of Niagara Falls as a chemical dump site, 1978

Oh, no radiation was released. You don't have to worry about that.
> —Spokesman for Metropolitan Edison Company, in reference to the malfunctioning reactor at Three Mile Island, March 29, 1979

with which we've been presented, the best course may be to suspend judgment about a claim rather than to accept or reject it prematurely.

Observer Credibility

Many eyewitness reports are made by nonexperts. Most of the observational claims made by your friends, for instance, will be made by nonexperts. Even if your friends are experts in certain subjects, then, unless they are very boring

Experts Disagree and Disagree, and Disagree, and Disagree . . .

When John Hinckley, Jr., was tried for attempting to assassinate Ronald Reagan, expert witnesses gave the following testimony about Hinckley. We'll bet you can identify which experts were testifying for the prosecution and which for the defense.

[Hinckley suffers from] process schizophrenia.
> —DR. WILLIAM CARPENTER, psychiatrist

Hinckley does not suffer from schizophrenia.
> —DR. PARK E. DIETZ, psychiatrist

[Hinckley was suffering from] a very severe depressive disorder.
> —DR. ERNST PRELINGER, psychologist

There is little to suggest that he was seriously depressed.
> —DR. PARK E. DIETZ

[CAT scans] were absolutely essential [to my diagnosis of schizophrenia].
> —DR. DAVID M. BEAR, psychiatrist

[CAT scans revealed] no evidence of any significant abnormality whatsoever.
> —DR. MARJORIE LeMAY, radiologist

There's no possible way that you can predict people's behavior or whether they're schizophrenic or not schizophrenic, from a CAT scan, period.
> —DR. DAVID DAVIS, radiologist

[I]t is a psychiatric fact that Mr. Hinckley was psychotic.
> —DR. DAVID M. BEAR

Mr. Hinckley has not been psychotic at any time.
> —DR. PARK E. DIETZ

Besides conflicts among expert opinions, these excerpts bring up another point: the vagueness of such terms as *schizophrenia, depressive,* etc. Disagreement is much more likely when the issue involves terms without precise, agreed-upon criteria.

conversationalists, most of what they say to you about what they've seen and heard will not pertain to their specialties.

It is reasonable to regard an eyewitness as credible unless there is some specific reason for challenging his or her credibility. The kinds of reasons for making such a challenge include precisely those we must be cautious about with regard to our own observations: (1) bad physical conditions for making observations (bad lighting, excessive noise, many distractions, peculiar circumstances, etc.); (2) sensory impairment (e.g., poor vision); (3) poor condition of the observer (fatigue, emotional distress, intoxication, etc.); (4) dubious equipment (unreliable instruments); (5) failure of memory, if, that is, the observations were not recorded at the time they were made or if they were not drawn from very recent memory; and (6) bias on the part of the observer. Even the observations of an expert within his or her field of specialization must be challenged if they are defective in one or more of these ways.

Before leaving the subjects of expertise and observer credibility, one last principle needs to be stated. The more extraordinary a claim is—that is, the more unusual or surprising its content—the greater is the need to establish its source as credible. You ought to be willing to accept the authority of any friend or acquaintance, for example, for a claim such as "I called the theater and found that the play begins at 8:15." (We presume, of course, that you have no reason to suspect that the friend would want to sabotage your evening.) But for a claim such as "Clyde's eighty-seven-year-old grandmother swam all the way across Lake Michigan last winter," you are going to want more credible authority than merely your friend's conviction.

Reference Works

Reference works fall into two categories: general works, which include encyclopedias, bibliographies, dictionaries, and indexes, and works for special subjects (e.g., history, philosophy, mathematics, applied science), which include encyclopedias, bibliographies, dictionaries, indexes, guides, manuals, abstracts, handbooks, and other materials.

Many reference works are credible sources of information, of course, but not all are considered authoritative on every aspect of the material they cover. (Author and critic Dwight MacDonald takes the third edition of *Webster's International Dictionary* to task in "The String Untuned," in *Against the American Grain* [New York: Random House, 1983], and philosopher W.V.O. Quine had to correct the *Random House Dictionary* about the size of Monaco—the dictionary had it larger than it actually is.) A possible exception, fortunately, is the *Guide to Reference Books*, in its current edition by Eugene P. Sheehy, published by the American Library Association and updated frequently. This work contains guidelines (for librarians and other interested parties) for appraising reference works, and, in addition, provides a comprehensive list of them. These

Two Kinds of Knowledge

> Knowledge is of two kinds. We know a subject, or we know where we can find information upon it.
>
> —SAMUEL JOHNSON

listings are annotated, so the *Guide* is an excellent work to consult when your informational needs lead to the reference library.

Government Publications

Some government publications are considered authoritative sources of information; others are not. It depends on who produces them and for what uses they are intended. We recommend two guides to such publications: Joe Morehead's *Introduction to United States Public Documents* (Littleton, Colorado: Libraries Unlimited, Inc., 1983) and Laurence Frederick Schmeckebier and Ray B. Easton's *Governmental Publications and Their Uses,* 2nd ed. (Washington, D.C.: The Brookings Institution, 1969).

The News Media

Our best and most common sources of information about current events are newspapers, news magazines, and the electronic media, radio and television. Newspapers offer the broadest coverage of general news, the electronic media the most severely edited and least detailed (with the exception of certain extended-coverage programs and of some Public Broadcasting System programs); news magazines fall somewhere in the middle, although they usually offer extended coverage in their feature stories. Most news reports, especially those that appear in major metropolitan newspapers (tabloids excepted), national news magazines, and television and radio news programs are credible sources of information, although this claim is subject to qualification, as noted below and in Chapter 5.

The breadth of coverage from such news sources is restricted by space, by their audience's interests, and by the concerns of advertisers, pressure groups, and government officials. The accessibility of reliable reports also restricts coverage, since governments, corporations, and individuals often simply withhold information.

The location, structure, and headline of a news story in both print and electronic media can be misleading as to what is important or essential in the story. Finally, opinion sometimes gets blended with fact. When an item is

One Person's Thoughts

And what a person thinks on his own without being stimulated by the thoughts and experiences of other people is even in the best case rather paltry and monotonous.

—ALBERT EINSTEIN

labeled "editorial," "opinion," "commentary," "essay," or "analysis," we expect an element of subjectivity. But we also find opinion leaking into straight news in what we expect to be straightforward reporting. This happens in weekly news magazines rather often, but you will also find it in front-page newspaper stories.

Nevertheless, reports from these sources can usually be counted on to be accurate, though their importance, relevance, and completeness may be different from what is stated or implied. Thus it is reasonable to accept the factual claims found in these reports unless they conflict with what you have observed or otherwise know, or with informative claims from other sources.

Recap

Informative claims should be relatively clear, concise, and free from emotionally charged language, as we saw in Chapter 2. Most important, however, they must be correct. It is generally reasonable to accept an unsupported claim if it is either an analytic truth or issues from a credible source and does not conflict with what you have observed or otherwise know or with other creditable claims. You can regard as credible a person who reports an observation unless there is some specific reason for believing otherwise. The more extraordinary a claim is, the greater should be the credibility of its source. In general, the more knowledgeable someone is in a given field, the more credible that person is—that is, the more reason there is to accept an informational claim the person makes relative to that field. Informational claims put forth by experts—those with special knowledge in a subject—are the most reliable, but they must pertain to the expert's specialty, they must not conflict with claims made by other experts in the same subject, and there must be no reason to question the expert's ability to make a sound and objective judgment in the case at issue. Print and electronic media are credible sources in general, but it is necessary to keep an open mind about what we learn from them.

Additional Exercises

EXERCISE 3-9

For each of the following numbered items, rank the listed observers as best you can in order of their credibility, beginning with the one you think would be most credible. Base your judgment on both expertise and the likelihood of bias.

1. The Surgical Practices Committee of Grantville Hospital has documented an unusually high number of problems in connection with tonsillectomies performed by a Dr. Choker. The committee is reviewing her surgical practices. All those present during a tonsillectomy are
   (a) Dr. Choker
   (b) The surgical proctor from the Surgical Practices Committee
   (c) An anesthesiologist
   (d) A nurse
   (e) A technician

★2. The mechanical condition of the used car you are thinking of buying.
   (a) The used-car salesperson
   (b) The former owner (whom we assume is different from the salesperson)
   (c) The former owner's mechanic
   (d) You
   (e) A mechanic from an independent garage

3. A demonstration of "psychokinesis" (the ability to move objects at a distance by nonphysical means).
   (a) A newspaper reporter
   (b) A psychologist
   (c) A police detective
   (d) Another psychic
   (e) A physicist
   (f) A customs agent
   (g) A magician

★4. American ice skater Brian Boitano's performance at the 1988 Olympics.
   (a) An American ice hockey coach
   (b) An American swimming coach
   (c) Brian's mother
   (d) A Russian ice-skating coach
   (e) A Canadian ice skater

5. The Dukakis-Bush presidential debates. (If the following sources are un-

familiar to you, do some investigation. They are all significant publications.)
(a) The *New Republic*
(b) The *New York Times*
(c) *The National Review*
(d) *The Nation*
(e) *Newsweek*
(f) The *Times* (London)

EXERCISE 3-10

For each of the items below, discuss the credibility and authority of each source relative to the issue in question. Whom would you trust as most reliable on the subject?

★1. Issue: Is DMSO an effective anticancer agent?
   (a) *Consumer Reports*
   (b) Life Extension Products (the firm that markets DMSO as a cancer cure)
   (c) The owner of your local health food store
   (d) The U.S. Food and Drug Administration
   (e) Your local pharmacist

★2. Issue: Should possession of handguns be outlawed?
   (a) A lawyer
   (b) A representative of the National Rifle Association
   (c) A chief of police
   (d) A United States senator
   (e) The father of a murder victim

★3. Issue: What was the original intention of the Second Amendment to the United States Constitution, and does it include permission for every citizen to possess handguns?
   (a) A representative of the National Rifle Association
   (b) A justice of the United States Supreme Court
   (c) A constitutional historian
   (d) A United States senator
   (e) The president of the United States

4. Issue: Is decreasing your intake of dietary fat and cholesterol likely to reduce the level of cholesterol in your blood?
   (a) *Time* magazine
   (b) *Runner's World* magazine
   (c) Your physician
   (d) The National Institutes of Health
   (e) The *New England Journal of Medicine*

5. Issue: When does a human life begin?
   (a) A lawyer

(b) A physician
(c) A philosopher
(d) A minister
(e) You

EXERCISE 3-11

Each of these items consists of a brief biography of a real or imagined person followed by a list of topics. On the basis of the information in the biography, discuss the credibility and authority of the person described on each of the topics listed.

★1. John Fellowstone teaches sociology at the University of Illinois and is the director of its Population Studies Center. He is a graduate of Harvard College, where he received a B.A. in 1965, and of Harvard University, which granted him a Ph.D. in economics in 1968. He taught courses in demography as an assistant professor at UCLA until 1972; then he moved to the sociology department of the University of Nebraska, where he was associate professor and then professor. From 1977 through 1979 he served as acting chief of the Population Trends and Structure Section of the United Nations Population Division. He joined the faculty at the University of Illinois in 1979. He has written books on patterns of world urbanization, the effects of cigarette smoking on international mortality, and demographic trends in India. He is president of the Population Association of America.

Topics
(a) The effects of acid rain on humans
(b) The possible beneficial effects of requiring sociology courses for all students at the University of Illinois
(c) The possible effects of nuclear war on global climate patterns
(d) The incidence of poverty among various ethnic groups in the United States
(e) The effects of the melting of glaciers on global sea levels
(f) The change in death rate for various age groups in all Third World countries between 1960 and 1980
(g) The feasibility of a laser-based nuclear defense system
(h) Voter participation among religious sects in India
(i) Whether the winters are worse in Illinois than in Nebraska

2. John Calhoun graduated *cum laude* from Cornell University with a B.S. in biology in 1963. After two years in the Peace Corps, during which he worked on public health projects in Venezuela, he joined John D. Dacus, a mechanical engineer, and the pair developed a water pump and purification system that is now used in many parts of the world both for regular water supplies and emergency use in disaster-struck areas. Calhoun and

Dacus formed a company to manufacture the water systems, and it prospered as they developed smaller versions of the system for private use on boats and motor homes. In 1971, Calhoun bought out his partner and expanded research and development in hydraulic systems for forcing oil out of old wells. Under contract with the federal government and several oil firms, Calhoun's company was a principal designer and contractor for the Alaskan oil pipeline. He is now a consultant in numerous developing countries as well as chief executive officer and chairman of the board of his own company, and he sits on the boards of directors of several other companies.

Topics
(a) The image of the United States in Latin America
(b) The long-range effects of the Cuban revolution on South America
(c) Fixing a leaky faucet
(d) Technology in Third World countries
(e) The ecological effects of the Alaskan pipeline
(f) Negotiating a contract with the federal government
(g) Careers in biology

EXERCISE 3-12

You are sitting on a jury in a trial in which the plaintiff is suing the defendant, a physician, for malpractice. The judge instructs the jury that the question it must decide is whether the plaintiff received the kind of care that one could expect given the practices of physicians in that community. The defendant's attorney presents testimony from two expert witnesses (both physicians, one of them the defendant himself) who testify that the defendant did exercise proper care relative to the practices of physicians in the community. The plaintiff's attorney also produces two physicians who testify that the defendant did not exercise proper care relative to those standards. The credentials of all the physicians who testified are explained to the jury. No other expert witnesses are produced by either side.

In a brief essay, discuss the kinds of considerations regarding the credentials of the testifying physicians that are relevant to the question the judge has instructed you to decide.

EXERCISE 3-13

Consider each of the following informative claims and its source. From what you know about the nature of the claim and the source, and given your general knowledge, assess the claim as probably true, probably false, or requiring further documentation before a judgment can be made. The last category would be appropriate for any claim that was hopelessly vague, an expression of purely subjective opinion (e.g., "Paul Newman is extremely handsome"), ambiguous, nonsensical, and so on. Explain your answer.

★1. There was a conspiracy at the highest levels of American military intelligence to underreport enemy troop strength in Vietnam in order to deceive Lyndon Johnson and the American people into believing that the United States was winning the Vietnam War.

—Paraphrased from "The Uncounted Enemy," broadcast by CBS

★2. "Former Israeli Defense Minister Ariel Sharon and other Israeli military officials shared an indirect responsibility for the massacre by Lebanese Phalangist soldiers of hundreds of civilian Palestinian refugees in Lebanon two days after the assassination of Lebanese President-elect Bashir Gemayel."

—*Time* magazine

★3. "Maps, files and compasses were hidden in Monopoly sets and smuggled into World War II German prison camps by MI-5, Britain's counterintelligence agency, to help British prisoners escape, according to the British manufacturer of the game."

—Associated Press

★4. "Tancredo Neves became Brazil's first civilian president in 21 years yesterday. He was chosen on a 480–180 electoral college vote and is scheduled to take office in two months."

—Associated Press

5. "For the majority of people, smoking has a beneficial effect."

—Dr. Ian G. MacDonald, a Los Angeles surgeon quoted in *Newsweek,* November 18, 1963

6. "Cats that live indoors and use a litter box can live four to five years longer."

—From an advertisement for Jonny Cat litter

7. "A case reported by Borderland Sciences Research Foundation, Vista, California, tells of a man who had attended many of the meetings where a great variety of 'dead' people came and spoke through the body mechanism of Mark Probert to the group of interested persons on a great variety of subjects with questions and answers from 'both sides.' Then this man who had attended meetings while he was in a body, did what is called 'die.' Presumably he had learned 'while in the body' what he might expect at the change of awareness called death, about which organized religion seems to know little or nothing."

—George Robinson, *Exploring the Riddle of Reincarnation,* undated, no publisher cited

★8. "Because of cartilage that begins to accumulate after age thirty, by the time . . . [a] man is seventy his nose has grown a half inch wider and another half inch longer, his earlobes have fattened, and his ears themselves have grown a quarter inch longer. Overall, his head's circumference increases a quarter inch every decade, and not because of his brain, which is shrinking. His head is fatter apparently because, unlike most other bones in the body, the skull seems to thicken with age."

　　　　　　—JOHN TIERNEY (a staff writer for *Science '82* magazine), *Esquire*

9. "Gardenias . . . need ample warmth, ample water, and steady feeding. Though hardy to 20°F or even lower, plants fail to grow and bloom well without summer heat."

　　　　　　—*The Sunset New Western Garden Book* (a best-selling gardening reference in the West)

10. ". . . Victor Reuther of the United Auto Workers . . . urged Attorney General Robert Kennedy to use federal agencies, including the IRS, to silence conservative critics of the Kennedy administration, like Senators Barry Goldwater and Strom Thurmond and Dr. Fred Schwarz's Christian Anti-Communism Crusade."

　　　　　　—RICHARD VIGUERIE, *The New Right: We're Ready to Lead*

★11. "As a nation we commit over 224 million tons of food and drink to our garbage dumps and sewers over the course of a year."

　　　　　　—ANITA BORGHESE, quoted in Gordon Edlin (professor of biology at the University of California, Davis) and Eric Golanty, *Health and Wellness* (Boston: Science Books International, 1982)

12. "A generation ago, the college experience touched only a small proportion of the American people. In 1960, less than a quarter of the nation's high school graduates were enrolled in an institution of higher education. In all of the United States that year, there were 100 million people age 25 or over. Only eight million of them had a college degree."

　　　　　　—"A Profile of Higher Education," *The NEA* [*National Education Association*] *1984 Almanac of Higher Education*

13. "Soviet scientists have stunned their colleagues with a shocking discovery—Mars is bristling with missiles and they're aimed at our planet."

　　　　　　—BEATRICE DEXTER, *Weekly World News*

★14. "Got a nasty puddle under your car every morning? If it appears to be coming from the area where the engine bolts to the trans it could be either a worn-out flywheel seal or a crack in your case. Either way, the engine's got to come out."

　　　　　　—JON KENNEDY, "How to Do It," *Dune Buggies and Hot VWs*

15. "Exercise will make you feel fitter, but there's no good evidence that it will make you live longer."

　　　　　　—DR. JORDAN TOBIN, National Institute on Aging

EXERCISE 3-14 (ESSAY)

Choose an issue on which experts are currently in disagreement (consider science, politics, world affairs), and write an essay in which you decide that one side has a better case *or* that the most reasonable position for a nonexpert to take is to suspend judgment for the time being.

4 Explanations

I wish you would explain his explanation.

— LORD BYRON

If we go on explaining, we shall cease to understand one another.

— TALLEYRAND

"Are you lost, Daddy?" I asked tenderly. "Shut up," he explained.

— RING LARDNER

Explanations aim to convey information or knowledge, and thus fall under the general heading of informational claims. But explanations are a bit different from most informational discourse. They must meet the same standards as other claims when it comes to precision, clarity, credibility, and so on, but they must also bear an appropriate relationship to the phenomenon being explained. This chapter is largely devoted to an examination of this relationship.

Explanations and Arguments

Explanations are not primarily designed to provide reasons for believing *that* the thing being explained exists, happened, or is true. Arguments do that.

83

Explanations are usually designed to show *how* or *why* the phenomenon in question exists, happened, or is true. For example, let's start with the claim,

(1) Bill hasn't shown up for work.

And let's say that Phil makes the further claims

(2) Bill is out with a cold.

and

(3) He spent last Tuesday with Theresa and she was very sick at the time.

In this case Bill's absence is being *explained* by claim (2) that he has a cold. Notice that the truth of claim (1) is not *at issue;* you and Phil both know that Bill isn't at work today, so attempts to convince you of that fact are unnecessary. On the other hand, claims (2) and (3) constitute an argument: By offering claim (3), Phil has provided you with a reason for believing claim (2), that Bill is out with a cold.

In general, when a claim is not at issue — when it is accepted by the parties concerned — then we are more likely to find the claim the subject of an explanation. If the claim is at issue, however, we are more likely to find it as the conclusion of an argument. Clearly, then, the context in which a discussion occurs can be important in determining whether it contains an explanation or an argument. We need to know whether one party is trying to convince another that some claim is in fact true. Oftentimes the language a speaker or writer uses is sufficient to allow us to make this decision, but this is not always the case.

Although it complicates the issue a bit more, we must point out that the two categories of argument and explanation do overlap — that is, there are cases where a passage *both* offers reasons for believing a claim *and* explains how it came to be true. Consider the following:

You won't be able to see the comet from here tonight. The reason is that we're too close to the lights of the city to see anything that faint in the sky.

This passage does indeed supply a reason for believing that you won't be able to see the comet, which indicates the presence of an argument; but it also tells us why this is (or will be) so. Whether it would be better to call this an argument or an explanation will depend upon the context and the interests of the parties concerned. It may suffice to say that it is both an argument *and* an explanation.

If it cannot always be clear whether a passage contains an argument or an explanation or both, you might wonder why we make the distinction between them at all. Well, one part of a critical thinker's job is to understand what a speaker or writer is most likely trying to accomplish in a passage, and another part is to get quite clear in her mind what she is about in her own thinking. Furthermore, notice that if you are addressing an audience who does not believe that X is true, then you may be wasting your time trying to explain how it probably came to be true. For example, it may be useless to explain to a person how he came to get a disease if in fact he does not believe he has it. You might *argue* that he has it by pointing out symptoms; you might *explain* how he got it by talking about how the disease is contracted and referring to his recent history. It may be that pointing out how he may have contracted it will count not just as an explanation but as an argument as well.

There are often alternative ways of explaining the same phenomenon, and arguments are frequently used to show that one explanation of the phenomenon is better than another. Is the air full of smoke because lots of people have built fires in their fireplaces or because the rice farmers are burning the stubble in their fields? When more than one explanation is available, we bring arguments to bear on the issue of which one (or ones) are best. Later in this chapter you'll find a list of criteria helpful in evaluating explanations. These criteria are relevant, as no doubt is obvious, to an evaluation of arguments about explanations.

Explanations and Justifications

It is especially important to see the difference between the function of an explanation and that of a particular kind of argument—a justification. A *justification* of an action is an argument given in defense of it, an attempt to show that it is just, proper, appropriate, lawful, or morally acceptable. Although we usually use explanations and justifications for different purposes (just as the purposes of explanations and arguments in general differ), we do sometimes employ explanations when we try to justify something. For example, in attempting to justify his theft of a loaf of bread, a person might explain his motives (e.g., to feed his hungry family).

It is nonetheless important to notice when an explanation is *not* an attempt to justify. For example, someone may try to explain why many Germans adopted the vicious anti-Semitic views of the Nazi party during the 1930s. He may point out that the German economy was in a mess and that the country still suffered from terms imposed on it at the end of World War I, and he may also note that people often look for scapegoats on which they can blame their troubles. These remarks may help us understand why the German people were easily led into anti-Semitism, but it can sometimes seem to an uncritical listener that there is an attempt going on to muster sympathy for those people and their actions. It does not follow, of course, that the person doing the explaining has any sympathy at all for such views or the actions taken by those who held them.

So, explanations themselves can be entirely neutral with regard to approval or disapproval of X, even though we might include an explanation of X as part of an attempt to justify it.

It is important that we see the difference between explaining an event and justifying it, for otherwise we may find ourselves stifling attempts to explain bad behavior. And unless we are able to explain and understand such behavior, we will be hampered in our attempts to discourage it.

We'll turn next to the identification of three different kinds of explanations and examine how they work and why they are useful. Then we'll look at criteria on which we evaluate explanations, for it's important to be able to distinguish between good and bad explanations, since a bad explanation is usually worse than no explanation at all. The last portion of the chapter is devoted to explanatory comparisons, which, although they are generally used to accomplish the same goals as other kinds of explanations, are different enough to warrant their own separate treatment.

Kinds of Explanations

So many kinds of things require explaining at one time or another that it shouldn't be surprising that many different kinds of explanations exist. Consider the following requests for explanations:

How did we get this flat tire?

What does a carburetor do?

Why did Pete leave early last night?

How does a bill get through Congress?

Can you explain what that lecture was all about?

How did you know I would choose the seven of diamonds?

How is the game of football played?

What's it like to play football?

How do you register for this course?

No single kind of explanation will do for such a variety of requests. Fortunately, though, we have at our disposal a variety of kinds of explanations. Although there are other types of explanations, in this section we'll identify and concentrate on three important and common types: (1) physical (or causal) explanations, which explain phenomena in terms of causes and effects; (2) psychological explanations, which explain phenomena in terms of reasons or motives; and (3) functional explanations, which explain phenomena in terms of their functions or purposes.

Physical Explanations

How did we get this flat tire?

Why did the rocket explode just after lift-off?

Why did the system crash the minute I logged on to the computer?

Each of these questions asks for a **physical** or **causal explanation.** Such explanations tell us how or why something happens in terms of the *physics* of the event by giving us its causal background. This background includes the general conditions under which the event occurred—such as the ambient temperature, atmospheric pressure, relative humidity, presence or absence of electrical fields, and so on. These conditions are often left unstated if they are normal for the situation; we simply take them for granted. For example, if there is nothing unusual about the temperature on a day when we have a tire blowout, we would not be inclined to list temperature among the possible causal factors of the tire's failure. On the other hand, had we been driving on a blisteringly hot day, that fact might turn out to be important and thus worth an explicit note as part of the event's causal background.

More important, the causal background of an event includes whatever events we determine to be the *direct cause* of the phenomenon in question. The direct cause is generally given in terms of *causal chains* made up of links, each of which is the cause of the next link in the chain. In constructing an explanation, we identify the links in the chain by proceeding backward from the event we wish to explain. If we want to explain, say, Z, we identify the event that immediately precedes and causes it, Y, as the next link up the chain; then Y's cause, X, becomes the next link, and so forth, with the chain always going backward in time.

More than one causal chain can contribute to the cause of an event. For the phenomenon of a baseball's flight from the bat to the right-field fence, we can trace back two causal chains, one accounting for the bat's arrival at the point of impact and the other accounting for the ball's arrival at the fence. If we choose, we can interpret the causal history of the event in terms of a single direct cause, relegating the other chain to a place further in the background. Whether we do that, and which causal chain we focus on, will be determined by our knowledge and interests. A person studying batting technique would probably think of the pitch as a less critical part of the picture than the batter's swing, naming the latter as the crucial direct cause of the hit. We would expect the opposite view from a student of pitching. Whether we say the home run's direct cause was a good swing, a bad pitch, or both depends on our interests; each way of putting it can be useful for different purposes.

Tracking Down a Physical Explanation: Some Things That Go Bump in the Night

A few years ago one of the authors of this text wrote a book on the possibilities of immortality. He had just finished examining reports of ghosts, hauntings, apparitions, specters, and other supposedly supernatural indications of the existence of spirits when strange and suggestive occurrences intruded into his own life. Four separate incidents haunted him.

First, he was awakened one night by a loud crash in what seemed to be the bedroom. Assuming that he must have been dreaming, he went back to sleep. The next morning he discovered that a heavy oak drawer had been removed from a dresser by his bed and transported several feet away to the middle of the room.

A few mornings later, he awakened to find that a stemmed goblet left on his nightstand the evening before was now broken cleanly at the stem; the bowl was still on the nightstand and the rest of the glass was on a chest on the other side of the room.

The third incident occurred a few nights later. He and his wife awakened to find the foot of their mattress soaked with water.

Your author was puzzled by all the explanations he could think of: practical jokes by his children, a sleepwalker perhaps? But these two notions were dispelled a few nights later when the children were away and he and his wife sat in bed reading. A loud clanging from the direction of the kitchen startled them into apprehensive watchfulness—you could also say it scared the living daylights out of them. When they heard the clanging a second time, he was forced to investigate, but could find nothing in the kitchen that would even have made the right kind of clanging sound. Returning to bed, he and his wife eventually slept, but none too well.

The next morning he resolved to find the explanation for these unwelcome occurrences. Thinking as critically as he could, he sifted through the possibilities until he began to get a picture of what had been going on.

Have you a clue to his thinking? He is not inclined to favor ghosts, aliens, or creatures from other realms, incidentally. (Check the next box to see if your thinking matched his.)

Interests also determine which link in a causal chain we identify as *the* cause of an event. Imagine for a moment the danger of an outbreak of bubonic plague. Plague is caused by a bacillus, *Yersinia pestis,* which is carried by fleas that in turn are carried by rats, ground squirrels, and other mammals, and that, in medieval Europe, infested the matting used for floor coverings. A medical researcher would properly think of the bacillus as *the* cause of the disease, but a public health official more interested in preventing the spread of the disease than in its biology might profit more from thinking of rat infestations or the presence of a medium in which fleas flourish—the reed matting in the Middle Ages, for example. In such a case, each individual's knowledge and background determine his or her interest and focus. The medical researcher might view inoculation against plague as a contribution to the fight against it; hence, the bacillus itself would be the focus of interest. The public health official would focus on that part of the causal chain that calls for his or her own expertise. Because of their different perspectives on the eradication or prevention of the disease, the two would focus on these different links, identifying them correctly as the most important for their different purposes. What they would have in common would be an interest in breaking the chain at *some* point or other. Causal chains, like other chains, are only as strong as their weakest links, and breaking whatever link turns out to be the weakest can be said to be eliminating *the* cause of the phenomenon.

Let's return now to one of the questions we listed earlier: "How did we get this flat tire?" Ordinarily, this question will elicit a short explanation: "The tire has a nail in it" would be enough. While this answer explains the phenomenon sufficiently under normal circumstances by supplying its direct cause, it may not be sufficient under unusual circumstances. If the tire had been in the garage rather than on an automobile, we might require another link in the causal chain, one that would tell us how the nail got in the tire. This event might be explained by the claim that the tire fell off the garage wall and onto the nail. We might or might not be satisfied with stopping there—we might want to find a further link in the chain—the cause of the tire's falling. We might run out of requests for further links when we learn that the hook on which the tire hung pulled out of the garage wall, or that an earthquake shook the whole town and caused the tire to fall.

Pushing a line of questioning in this way can lead to the first of three general kinds of mistakes that we can make regarding physical, or causal, explanations.

If we continue to require that a causal chain be traced further and further back, we eventually find ourselves being unreasonable, much like four-year-olds, who sometimes ask "Why?" until they become exasperating. Eventually, we must reach a point where we require no further links, since, theoretically at least, every causal chain extends indefinitely far into the past—unless it makes a shift into another kind of explanation, which we'll discuss in a moment. But it is not easy to identify the precise point at which a demand to extend a causal chain becomes unreasonable. Sometimes, when the causal chain has taken us far afield from the original phenomenon, we have grounds for bringing the search for further links to a halt. (The apricots fell from the tree early because the tree was irrigated too heavily late in the season; the heavy irrigation was due to a faulty meter on the irrigation system pump; the faulty meter was the result of a solder joint that came loose, . . . etc. We are now a good bit away from falling apricots.) At other times, the causal chain can become so complex that sorting it out would make the explanation more complex than the original phenomenon justifies. (A person needn't learn what causes earthquakes in order to explain why the tire is flat.) Sometimes we bring a causal chain to a stop when a human decision intervenes: The numbers of fish are down because of contaminated coastal waters; the waters are contaminated because of toxic chemicals flowing from rivers into the sea; the toxic chemicals are dumped by chemical and manufacturing plants upriver. If we then ask why the plants dump chemicals or why they were built there in the first place, we are asking why people made certain decisions. That takes us out of the realm of physical or causal explanation and into a type we'll be getting to soon. For the moment, we can note that we're asking a different kind of question when we ask why particular people made particular decisions.

Fortunately, our needs and curiosity being what they are, we generally *do* reach a point at which we are satisfied and stop searching for further links in the chain. Four-year-olds, who sometimes fail to reach such a point, may have to be threatened, ignored, or pacified by some means other than answers to their endless questions.

A second mistake we can make when dealing with physical explanations is to expect a reason or motive behind a causal chain. For example, we can legitimately ask why electrons take up certain orbits around an atom's nucleus if we are asking for the physical cause of the phenomenon only. But physical accounts cannot help us if we mean by our question, "What is the *point* of the electrons' behavior?" The vocabulary of physics does not officially include references to the *point* or *purpose* of an event, or to desires, intentions, goals, and the like. Physical explanations can work in concert with psychological explanations, as we'll see. But physical or causal explanations do not refer to intentions or motives. They explain what happens in terms of the descriptive laws of physics; they do not attribute intelligent design to those laws.

The Solution: Why Things Went Bump in the Night

Only one explanation accounting for the strange occurrences detailed in the last box made sense to the author. It came to him as soon as he realized that *the occurrences did not have to have a cause common to them all.* Looking more closely into the clanging in the kitchen, he discovered three metal folding trays stacked in the garage against the *outside* of the kitchen wall. The trays were stacked so that the slightest pressure against the bottom of the leg of one table levered the trays into a clanging action, the source of which seemed to be within the kitchen itself. Peering closely around the bottom of the trays he discovered evidence of mice.

This account meant that all the remaining events could be covered by the hypothesis that someone in the household was sleepwalking. In fact, this was confirmed when one night he stayed awake and observed his wife sleepwalk, something no member of the household had ever suspected before these episodes.

A third kind of mistake we can make in giving a physical explanation is to give it at the wrong technical level for our audience. Usually in discourse, a commonsense explanation suffices. If we wish to know why the water in a pan is boiling, we are ordinarily satisfied by learning that the pan is sitting on an electric burner. Occasionally, however—say, in an elementary physics class—a more detailed explanation, involving the movement of excited molecules in the burner, pan, and water, may be appropriate. Even though both explanations are equally *correct*, each can be *inappropriate* in the wrong context. A good explanation is always given at a level that is appropriate to the context in which it is given.

Physical explanations are mainly of two types, those that explain specific events (why there is a puddle on the kitchen floor) and those that explain regular occurrences in nature (why apples always fall to the ground when they're released).

Specific Events

An explanation of a specific event has two parts. One part must make reference to certain other specific events (earlier links in the causal chain), and the other part must refer to a law of nature that governs such events. For example, one might explain a puddle on the kitchen floor by noting

1. Bill spilled water from a glass when he walked through the room.
2. Spilled (or dropped or released) things fall to the floor.

Part 2 of the explanation states a law of nature that governs events such as the one mentioned in part 1. (When the law is as much a matter of common knowledge as the one cited here, it is usually taken for granted and simply left unstated.) Notice that knowing the law in part 2 and learning about the event in part 1 lead us to *expect* the event that is explained. It is one mark of a successful explanation of this kind that, given the explanation, we could have *predicted* that the event in question would have occurred.

Regular Occurrences

How do we explain regular occurrences—for example, the fact that gases expand when heated? Ordinarily we have to explain regular occurrences by reference to a theory. For example, the general claim that objects dropped in the proximity of the earth always fall to its surface can be explained only by reference to the theory of gravitation. That oil floats on water is explained by the respective specific gravities of the two substances and, finally, by reference to molecular theory.

Occasionally, we don't go back to a general physical theory to explain a regularity. For example, in explaining why oak trees lose their leaves in the autumn, we can usually cite climatic changes and their effects on the circulatory systems of trees. We do this as if we were explaining why a specific oak tree drops its leaves (or just a single, typical leaf) in the same way we would explain any other specific event. What counts as an explanation for that typical oak tree will count as an explanation for every other oak tree. However, if we mean to give a thorough account of the phenomenon, we will have to explain a number of general statements that state regularities (having to do with chemical changes, capillary action, and so on), and we will eventually find ourselves referring to molecular theory again.

Psychological Explanations

A second kind of explanation is called for by questions like these:

> Why did Pete leave early last night?
>
> Why did the union vote to approve the contract?
>
> Why is the president asking Congress to fund the MX missile?

In each of these cases, the question calls not so much for a cause as for a reason or motive. (Within some contexts it would be appropriate to distinguish between reasons and motives, but for purposes of this discussion we need not do so.) The first and third questions ask for an individual's reasons or motives for doing what he did, while the second is probably best answered with whatever reasons or motives were most prevalent among union members. An explanation for an occurrence in terms of someone's reasons or motives is a **psychological explanation.**

Note that there is often a difference between *a* reason for somebody's actions and *that person's* reason. There might be some good reasons, for example, for a political leader's request for aid for the Nicaraguan Contras, but those reasons may not have included *his* reason or reasons; he might ignore, disbelieve, or be ignorant of the good reasons and go ahead with his request for some bad reason. We have to be careful, both in requesting and in giving this kind of explanation, to make clear whether we are requesting or giving the *best* reasons we can think of or some person or persons' *actual* reasons. If we are doing the former we are constructing an argument; if we are doing the latter we are constructing an explanation.

A difference between psychological and physical explanations emerges when we begin to analyze them a bit. Earlier we said that we give physical explanations for specific events by referring to earlier specific events in conjunction with a law of nature (remember the example of the puddle on the floor). If we mean to explain the event in terms of a person's reasons or motives, however, we have to use a somewhat different explanatory scheme. In particular, we must supply the following:

1. Some antecedent event or situation
2. A dependable psychological generality

You Know Your Own Reasons Best

Unlike most informational claims, some explanations are not easily measured against the usual standards. The words *true, false,* and, to some extent, *correct* and *incorrect* do not always apply to explanations very well. A case in point: Suppose someone says to you, "The reason we don't want you to smoke in our house is that it makes the house smell bad." If you were to reply, "That's true," your answer would be taken to apply to the causal connection between smoking in the house and the bad smell, and not to the entire explanation. That is, you would *not* be understood as saying, "That's true, that's your reason all right." Ordinarily, we do not second-guess a person's stated reason. The exceptions, when we might actually say, "That's not correct," after a person gives a reason, are when we suspect the person is lying or suffering from self-deception.

We speak of dependable psychological generalities rather than laws, because general statements about human behavior and decision making tend to allow for more exceptions than do the laws of physics.* For example, if we wish to explain why a union voted down a proposed contract, we might say

1. The contract contained provisions that were not in the interest of the union members.
2. People will not in general support what is not in their self-interest.

Item 2 is hardly a law of nature; people do occasionally support measures that are not in their self-interest. But item 2 is a generality dependable enough to be useful. If it is to be useful in this fashion we must be able to use it to make predictions. Since our claim in this example is dependable enough in this regard, we can use it in conjunction with item 1 and predict that the union would probably vote down the contract. Remember from our earlier discussion of physical explanations that the event in question should be predictable from our explanation. The same holds true in cases of psychological explanations. But psychological explanations seldom enable us to make predictions with the same degree of confidence that physical explanations allow.

Another difference between psychological and physical explanations emerges when we try to explain regularities of a psychological sort. If we are interested in the question of why people do not support what is not in their own interest, we must refer to a *psychological theory.* As with physical expla-

---

*Some physical laws, like those that describe the movements of electrons, are stated in terms of probabilities and do admit exceptions. Most of our everyday physical explanations, however, rely on laws that do not allow exceptions and that have a high degree of reliability. For example, an exception to the law stating that pure water under standard pressure boils at 212° F would startle us—we would sooner expect an experimental error than an exception to this law. Because of the different nature of the subject, such laws are seldom claimed in psychology.

nations, our explanation can be only as good as our theory. And, because psychological theories—so far, anyway—tend to be less well confirmed than most accepted physical theories, we can claim less confidence in them than in the latter, and hence our explanations of psychological regularities are to that extent more tentative than those of the regularities of physics.

Functional Explanations

Physical explanations always point backward in time from the phenomenon being explained; **functional explanations**, on the other hand, are not bound by this restriction. Consider these requests for explanations:

What's a carburetor?

What do antibodies do?

Why do skunks smell so awful?

Each of these questions asks about the function of something, and its answer will explain that thing's function or purpose. Ordinarily, the explanation requires putting the thing to be explained in a wider context and indicating its role in that context. For example,

Carburetors mix fuel and air for combustion engines.

Antibodies attack foreign bodies and thus help prevent infection.

Skunks use a foul-smelling spray to ward off predators.

An object's actual function may be different from its originally intended function, if indeed any function was ever intended for it. More than one piece of sculpture winds up as a doorstop; people's noses serve very well as supports for eyeglasses while they keep the rain out of our breathing apparatuses. The last example reminds us that an item may have more than one function, and that the particular function relevant to a given discussion has to be clear for an explanation to be relevant. In other words, to be helpful a functional explanation must be given in terms of the correct context.

Functional explanations can be as simple as those in the preceding examples or they can be extremely complicated. An explanation of the Constitution of the United States will be relatively complex—just how complex, however, will depend, as in the case of levels of causal explanations, on the audience and the circumstances in which the explanation is called for.

To give a good account of a phenomenon, we must sometimes use more than one kind of explanation. For example, if the nail in the tire had got there not because the tire fell on it but because a neighbor pounded it in with a hammer, a thorough account of the event would have to include mention of whatever reason was behind the neighbor's action. Similarly, if a functional explanation needs detailed elaboration, some amount of physical explanation may be required; it may be appropriate to explain not only *what* a carburetor does but also *how* it does it as well. So, even though we understand the differences between different kinds of explanations, we need not be at pains to avoid using them in combination if that is what will produce the best understanding of the phenomenon for our audience.

Evaluating Explanations

Having examined several different kinds of explanations, we turn now to some criteria on which they can be evaluated. Remember that the point of an explanation is not just to say something correct about the phenomenon being explained, but rather to say as economically as possible those things that will help the listener or reader understand as much as possible. The following nine criteria are useful for evaluating an explanation with which you are presented, but they are also intended as aids in constructing good explanations of your own.

You should be suspicious of any explanation that is defective with respect to one or more of these criteria, including those you discover coming out of your own mouth. At the same time, please keep in mind that an explanation that is not defective with respect to any of these criteria might still be inadequate

Who has the better explanation?

or unsound or unacceptable for other reasons. For example, it might just simply be incorrect. There is no finite list of hard and fast rules that can be applied automatically and unthinkingly in the appraisal of explanations. Suffice it to say that the nine criteria that follow are some of the more important points to consider when you encounter an explanation; doing so will certainly help protect you from accepting (or proposing) explanations of doubtful validity.

Testability

An explanation must be subject to testing; if there is no way to test it for correctness, then there is no way to know whether it is in fact correct. An account that could not be verified or refuted under any circumstances is one that should be viewed with plenty of suspicion. Some explanations are not testable in that they are "rubber" explanations (or "ad hoc hypotheses," as some prefer to call them): They can stretch around any objection. The only reason offered for believing an untestable explanation is the presence of the phenomenon it was produced to explain; no other evidence can be brought to bear on it. An example:

> Daniel explains why his pocket watch works by telling you that a very small gremlin lives inside it and cranks away at the movement, thus causing motion in the gears. If you want to see this wonderful thing, he explains that it is invisible. It also cannot be felt; neither does it show up in x-rays; and if you listen closely you'll find it is absolutely silent.

The point here is that if Daniel modifies the account so that it is consistent with any test you might propose, he modifies it out of existence. However, the fact that an explanation is difficult—even very difficult—to test does not mean it is not a good one. Some perfectly good scientific hypotheses are enormously difficult to test. But we are justified in being suspicious when there seem to be *no* means to test the explanatory claim, or when new, less vulnerable versions of it are produced when a previous one becomes endangered. Another example:

> Poor Horace! Why did he die at such a young age? I guess it was due to fate.

Is there any conceivable way we could test to see whether Horace's death was due to fate?

Noncircularity

An explanation is circular if it merely restates the phenomenon it was intended to explain. Such an explanation only *looks* like an explanation, because it describes the phenomenon in different words. Notice that with untestable or ad hoc explanations the phenomenon explained is the only evidence for the explanation, but in a circular explanation the explanation and the thing explained are the same thing. Example:

> He sits at the typewriter but he simply cannot think of a thing to write. It's because he has writer's block.

We may as well say that he can't write because he can't write.

Relevance

Obviously, an explanation has to connect somehow with the thing or event being explained. But how do we characterize what is relevant and what is not? We noted in an earlier section that a good physical or psychological explanation would allow us to predict the phenomenon it explains with some degree of confidence. We can say that such explanations are relevant to the extent that they enable us to make such predictions. Example:

> Daniel's car misses, sputters, and backfires. He explains this by saying that the battery is weak.

It's true that weak batteries can cause trouble, but they cannot make an engine miss and backfire. So, having a weak battery does not allow us to predict the phenomena we need to explain. The explanation is not relevant to the phenomena. A second example:

> Daniel wishes to explain why Theresa always orders peppermint at the ice cream shop, and he says that she is allergic to chocolate.

Daniel's explanation does explain why Theresa doesn't order chocolate, but it fails to account for her favoring peppermint. On the basis of knowing about her allergy alone, we cannot predict her selection with any confidence at all. (Note: If there were only two selections available, chocolate and peppermint, it would be a strange ice cream shop but the explanation would be a good one.)

Freedom from Excessive Vagueness

Like any other claim or set of claims, an explanation can suffer from vagueness (see the section on vagueness in Chapter 2). Notice how little explaining is accomplished in this example:

> Daniel is rude and snappish on the telephone, and Theresa asks another acquaintance why. She is told that Daniel is out of sorts today.

This does tell Theresa something, but not very much, since *out of sorts* is a vague phrase and could apply to Daniel in a great number of circumstances.

An Explanation That Doesn't Explain Much

When an earthquake occurred in California in the spring of 1987, it registered 4.3 on the Richter Scale at the UC Seismographic Station at Berkeley, but the US Geological Survey in Menlo Park recorded it at 3.5 magnitude. The difference in readings, according to an official of the USGS, is "not a question of accuracy as much as it is a combination of factors."

—From an Associated Press story

Reliability

If an explanation leads to predictions that turn out to be false, then it is unreliable. Example:

> The lights go out all over your house. Someone offers the claim that the utility company has suffered a power failure. Looking out the window, however, you notice that lights are on in other houses in your neighborhood.

We cannot tell if the explanation in this example is bad until we come to the last sentence of the passage, where we find that the explanation leads to a false prediction—namely, that the neighbors' lights should be out. Notice that reliability cannot be tested at first glance as can some of the other criteria. We must first make predictions based on the explanation; the reliability of the explanation will hinge on whether such predictions turn out to be true. In effect, we are testing the explanation. In the example above, the account failed the test because, had it been true, there would have been no lights in other houses in the neighborhood.

Explanatory Power

Other things being equal, the more phenomena an explanation explains, the better. This is especially important when the explanation comes in the form of a scientific theory.

For example, let's say that, according to the archeological evidence, there were two tribes of people living in southern Mexico hundreds of years ago, and that they seem to have disappeared at about the same time. Anthropologist A comes up with a theory that explains what may have happened to one tribe, but his theory is irrelevant to the other tribe. Anthropologist B comes up with a theory that explains what may have happened to both tribes. Even if both theories are equal on all other grounds, and both are equally supported by the physical evidence, the explanation offered by anthropologist B has the edge over that of anthropologist A on the grounds of greater explanatory power— it simply explains more.

Another example:

> Bill plants a new variety of tulip in his garden, and it comes up earlier than is usual. The earlier development may indeed be due to the characteristics of the new variety. But Bill notices that nearly every one of his flowers is up earlier than usual this year. Then he remembers that January and February have been much warmer than usual.

In this case, the warm weather provides a better explanation for the early blooming tulips than do their genetic characteristics, since the weather accounts for the early development of the other plants as well. (Notice that the tulips' genetic features may contribute to their early development; these two explanations are not incompatible.)

Freedom from Unnecessary Assumptions

One explanation is generally considered better than another if it requires fewer assumptions than the second. Such assumptions can be about the existence of dubious entities or of especially unusual events involving familiar entities. (A dubious entity is one that we have reason to be skeptical about because it is not part of our background knowledge.) Example:

> A medium (or "psychic") comes up with surprising information about the sitters at a seance—family nicknames, facts about friends and relatives, and so on. Aside from "natural" explanations about how this is done (e.g., subconscious cuing), observers might come up with these two explanations: (1) the medium acquired the information telepathically from the people at the table, or (2) the medium acquired the information through telepathic communication with spirits of deceased people.

The second of these explanations is more complicated; it requires that we assume the existence of departed spirits. Both explanations require unusual

How to Tell If You're Possessed

reads the headline on the *Weekly World News* for March 1, 1988. Inside, a "top psychologist" estimates that about 80 percent of her patients are suffering from problems brought on by possession by spirits of the dead.

To tell if you are among the possessed, she advises that you look for certain telltale symptoms, including "low energy levels," "character shifts or mood swings," "impulsive behavior," "memory problems," "poor concentration," "a sudden onset of anxiety or bouts of depression (especially after hospitalization or any other trauma)," and "weight gain with no obvious cause."

If possession is the only explanation for these problems, then we're surprised that only 80 percent of her patients are possessed.

and even dubious activities—telepathic communication—but the first requires *only* this assumption. (One reason natural explanations are generally preferable is that they require fewer such assumptions.)

Consistency with Well-Established Theory

Sometimes a time-tested theory turns out to be defective. (Newtonian physics was well established before Einstein and other twentieth-century physicists discovered its limitations.) Still, though, we cannot take such theories lightly; it takes very powerful evidence before we consider giving them up. So, if an explanation conflicts with such a theory, we have good reason to look for an alternative account. Example:

> Ian Stevenson is both one of America's foremost psychical researchers and a strong believer in reincarnation. But he admits that reincarnation challenges standard biological theory on certain fundamental details.

If Stevenson is right in allowing this conflict, then we should be suspicious of reincarnation as an explanation for anything, since standard biology is widely confirmed and accepted.

Consideration of a Common Cause

Sometimes we accept one thing as an explanation for another, when in fact some third item is the cause of the other two. Example:

> Daniel loses his appetite one day and explains that it is the result of a bad headache.

It may be, however, that both Daniel's loss of appetite and his headache are the result of some further cause—he might have celebrated a bit too much the night before, or he might be coming down with the flu.

Pseudoexplanations

Q: Mommy, why does my leg hurt so much?
A: Because you're just trying to get attention, that's why.

Q: All right, then, why do *you* think the federal deficit is so high?
A: Because if it weren't, you liberals wouldn't have anything to complain about.

Irrelevance is what makes these "explanations" so perfectly unhelpful.

Explanatory Comparisons (Analogies)

When we compare two or more objects, events, or other phenomena, we can have any of several purposes in mind. One of these is explanation. If X is more familiar than Y, then we may be able to communicate information about the latter by comparing it to X, provided the two have significant features in common. For example, we might explain to a European what the climate is like in California by comparing it with that of the Mediterranean region of Europe.

Comparisons (or analogies, as they are often called) that are used to explain are interesting in that we sometimes find it hard to label them "true" or "correct." If we try to explain to an English person what American football is like, for example, we might compare it to a game with which our listener is familiar, rugby, since this game resembles football more than, say, soccer or darts. But it is neither "true" to say that football is like rugby nor "false" to say that it is like soccer (or even darts—it isn't *much* like darts, but there may be *something* useful in making such a comparison). What we are trying to do in making such statements is to enlighten, to be helpful. And we succeed to one degree or another when we do this, or we fail entirely if, for example, our listener understands no more when we're finished than when we began.

The goal of the comparison mentioned in the last paragraph is to explain how the game of football is played. This is a relatively complicated matter, and the term chosen to compare to football will be most helpful if it resembles it in as many aspects as possible. This, of course, is what makes rugby a better candidate than darts. But notice that the two items do not have to resemble one another in some precise number of respects in order for the comparison to be "correct." Nor do the resemblances themselves have to be exact. Since it is unclear just what will be most helpful in getting across the idea we want to communicate, we opt for the comparison that will give us the greatest number of close resemblances and the shortest list of important differences. In the example at hand, we begin with the game of rugby, assuming for the moment that football is just like it, and then we point out differences between the two. Rugby is going to have a greater chance of success than darts precisely because the list of differences between football and the latter is so much longer.

In general, our success in getting the idea across to our audience is more important than whether our comparison is in some sense "correct." This is especially true when the features of the items that we compare are vague, complicated, or numerous, or when the comparison itself is metaphorical. When the features we identify as being in common in the items compared are clear, relatively simple, and few, and the comparison itself is literal, we can

An Explanatory Comparison

An electric current travels with lightning speed—20,000 miles per second along a copper wire—but individual electrons do not: They amble along at less than an inch per second. The current streaks through the wire because the electrons jostle each other all the way.

The phenomenon can best be understood by imagining a pipe completely filled with golf balls. If an additional ball is pushed in at one end of the pipe, a ball will pop out almost instantly at the other end. Similarly, when a distant power plant forces electrons into one end of a wire, other electrons almost immediately come out at the other end—to light a lamp, perhaps, or start the coffee.

—Editors of Time-Life Books, *How Things Work in Your Home*

evaluate the comparison with regard to correctness. In the statement "John's car is the same color as your hat," it is clear which features of the car and the hat are being compared—the comparison is between one definite color and another (in this case, the same color). Similarly, one can explain something of how a rocket engine works by comparing it with what happens when a balloon is blown up and released to fly around the room. In this case the balloon exemplifies Newton's third law of motion, a principle on which rocket engines work. In both cases the respect in which the two items are being compared is quite definite and literal.

The same is true of the comparison between football and rugby—if we select a certain narrow aspect of both for comparison. We can say, for example, that carrying the ball across the goal line counts as a score in football just as it does in rugby. This claim is either correct or it is not, for it is sufficiently precise and simple to admit of such evaluation. But if we are trying to communicate the general idea of football and do not mean to take a lifetime to do it, we are better off not identifying every possible feature of the game for comparison with some feature of rugby. The economy we gain by having rugby as a comparative of football is lost in such a scheme—we get more for our efforts by leaving the comparison rather vague and ignoring the standard of correctness. We can still hope for some degree of success with our explanation by giving our audience at least a general idea of what football is like.

We have a different situation if we consider the poet's comparison "My love is like a red, red rose." Now, his love is probably not *literally* like a red rose in any respect at all. This is not to say, though, that the poet has said something false. He may have told us something about his love, but he has done it in an indirect, nonliteral way that we call metaphorical. His intention was to get us to react in a certain way—to evoke a certain feeling, perhaps—and in that fashion give us a kind of understanding that we may not have had before. He might succeed or fail in this. One person may indeed understand something new as a result of the line of poetry; another may walk away puzzled about how his love could resemble a flower.

A point worth noticing here is that only a person who is familiar with both terms of an explanatory comparison is in a position to evaluate it. The individual for whom the comparison is made, since he or she is familiar with only one term, is in a position to determine only if his or her new understanding makes sense, not whether it is accurate with regard to the phenomenon at issue. Our English person may have a very clear picture in mind as a result of our comparison with rugby but might still be thoroughly surprised upon seeing a football game for the first time. The clarity of his or her mental image, which was all this individual was in a position to evaluate, is no guarantee of its accuracy or completeness.

Often a comparison is made not to explain but to illustrate a point that is not explicitly stated. Consider: "I'd rather beat my head against the wall than go jogging," or "James has about as much imagination as a bridge abutment." These are simply colorful ways of saying that the speaker has a distaste for jogging and that James has no imagination; in neither case is any explanation being offered. In such cases, the comparisons themselves are less important than the point that is implicit in them. In such cases as the football/rugby example, the comparison, and the terms being compared, are very important. But one could substitute barbells or any number of things for the bridge abutment in the other example; success or failure of the remark hinges on whether the listener takes notice of what the real point is (which is probably to influence the listener's attitude). In this case, the speaker is likening James to something with no imagination at all. These examples might be called **persuasive comparisons,** and could take a place beside persuasive definitions (see Chapter 2). Besides conveying information, they are intended to express or evoke an attitude by means of their colorful language.

Recap

A variety of kinds of explanation exist, and each type has its own uses. The three kinds we singled out for examination are especially important: physical (causal), psychological, and functional explanations. Physical explanations account for a phenomenon by providing cause-and-effect relationships among elements in its causal background. In particular, they establish causal chains that extend backward temporally. What we determine to be the important links in such chains is decided largely by our interest in the event explained. A psychological explanation accounts for an event in terms of an agent's reasons or motives. Both physical and psychological explanations account for specific events in terms of antecedent conditions and generalizations—either laws or dependable generalities. Both explain regular occurrences by reference to theories. A functional explanation places an object or event in a context and shows what role it plays there.

We can evaluate explanations on the basis of an assortment of criteria, including testability, relevance, reliability, explanatory power, and the lack of circularity, vagueness, unnecessary assumptions, conflict with well-established theory, and ignoring a common cause.

Explanatory comparisons make use of common features in a familiar and an unfamiliar item in order to explain the latter. We often evaluate such comparisons more in terms of their success in conveying a conception of an object or event than in terms of their correctness.

Although there are times when a set of claims will count as both an explanation and an argument, these are two separable functions. Explanations are designed to show *how* or *why* something is or was or will be so; arguments are designed to show *that* something is or was or will be so. One should be especially careful not to confuse explanations with justifications. While some justifying arguments do indeed contain explanations, to explain an event is not necessarily to justify it.

Exercises

EXERCISE 4-1

Determine whether the following passages contain arguments, explanations, or both. Determine also whether any argument present attempts to justify an action or practice. Identify what is being argued for, explained, or justified. (There may be some items that cannot be answered without knowing more about the context. Explain what you would need to know in such cases.)

★1. The dog is scratching again—I told you it had fleas.
2. The reason the dog is scratching is that it has fleas.
3. Harold must be rich. Just look at the car he's driving.
★4. I agree that the water contamination around here is getting worse and worse. It's because we've allowed people to install septic systems whenever and wherever they want.
5. "I could never endure to shake hands with Mr. Slope. A cold, clammy perspiration always exudes from him, the small drops are ever to be seen standing on his brow, and his friendly grasp is unpleasant."
—ANTHONY TROLLOPE, *Barchester Towers*
6. I know you think I wasted my vote by voting for Harold Stassen in the '88 election, but that isn't so. I didn't approve of either of the main

candidates, and if I'd voted for one of them and he had won, then my vote would have counted as an endorsement of him and his views. I don't want to add my endorsement to what I think are bad policies.

★7. It could be that you're unable to sleep because of all that coffee you drink in the evening.

8. The coffee I drink in the evening can't be why I'm not sleeping since I drink only decaffeinated coffee.

9. Of *course* the real estate industry depends on tax benefits. Just look at how hard the real estate lobby fought to preserve those benefits.

★10. Although the case of the computer is double-insulated, the pins in the cable connections are not insulated at all. In fact, they are connected directly to the logic board inside the machine. So, if you are carrying a charge of static electricity and you touch those connector pins, you can fry the logic circuits of your computer.

11. The orange is sour because it didn't have a chance to ripen properly.

12. "In 1970 Chrysler abandoned reverse-thread lug bolts on the left-hand side of its cars and trucks. One of those engineers must have realized, after about fifty years of close observation, that sure enough, none of the wheels were falling off the competition's cars, which had your ordinary, right-hand wheel fastenings."

—JOHN JEROME, *Truck*

★13. "Economically, women are substantially worse off than men. They do not receive any pay for the work that is done in the home. As members of the labor force their wages are significantly lower than those paid to men, even when they are engaged in similar work and have similar educational backgrounds."

—RICHARD WASSERSTROM, "On Racism and Sexism," in *Today's Moral Problems*

14. Some people think that Iowa has too much influence in determining who becomes a leading presidential candidate, but I don't agree. Having early caucuses in a relatively small state makes it possible for a person to begin a run at the presidency without spending millions and millions of dollars. And it may as well be Iowa as any other state.

15. "The handsome physical setting of Los Angeles is more threatened than the settings of most of the world's major cities. All the region's residents are affected by the ever-present threat of earthquakes, foul-smelling and chemical-laden tap water, and the potential for water shortages by the year 2000."

—CHARLES LOCKWOOD and CHRISTOPHER LEINBERGER, "Los Angeles Comes of Age," in *The Atlantic Monthly*

EXERCISE 4-2

Review: Answer the questions based on your reading of the text.

1. Fill in the blanks: A _____ explanation shows the purpose of an

object or event; a _____ explanation supplies reasons or motives; and a _____ explanation explains in terms of causes and effects.

★2. What is included in the causal background of an event?

3. Can more than one causal chain be important in explaining the cause of an event?

4. What determines our selection of the most important causal chain leading to an event and the most important links in that chain?

5. What are three mistakes that can be made in dealing with physical explanations?

★6. What are the two parts to a physical explanation of a specific event? Which one is more likely to be left unstated? Why?

7. What is the usual basis for explanations of regularities in nature?

8. What are the two parts to a psychological explanation of a specific event?

★9. We often have somewhat less confidence in psychological explanations than in physical explanations. What might the reason be?

10. Can an object have more than one function?

11. Does the current function of an object depend on the intentions of the creator or designer of that object?

12. Without going back to the section on evaluating explanations, list as many of the nine criteria for explanations as you can.

★13. If you want to explain what X is like to someone who is unfamiliar with it, how might you do so using a comparison or analogy?

14. What is the difference between a literal comparison and a metaphorical one?

★15. Why might we say that success is more important than correctness in an explanatory comparison?

EXERCISE 4-3

Identify any phenomena explained in the following passages and determine for each what kinds of explanations are employed.

★1. Why do women always open their mouths when they apply eye makeup? The reason is that it tightens the skin around the eyes.

2. In Southern California the grass turns brown in the summer because there is no rain.

3. Even though cold air sinks, refrigerators with freezers on the bottom cost more to run than models with their freezers on top. That's because the motor is on the bottom and it heats up the freezer compartment.

★4. That black rubber is around the tailgate to prevent water from leaking into the back of the stationwagon.

5. Bruce Weitz, who played a detective on NBC's "Hill Street Blues," explained the decline in the ratings of the series during its sixth year: "I think there's no reason in the sixth year of an episodic series that you

can't take some chances. And [the producers] are not taking any chances; they're being very conservative."

6. At the outbreak of World War I, [Charles Edward] Montague dyed his gray hair black in order to conceal his age and join the army. H. W. Nevinson remarked that Montague was the "only man on record whose hair turned black in a single night from fearlessness."

—CLIFTON FADIMAN

★7. This is why Hitchcock's movies are so scary. Near the very beginning Hitchcock has a single terrifying scene and after that he just sits back and lets viewers frighten themselves through anticipation of further terror.

8. The reason spring came so late this year is that people just forget how long winter really is around here.

9. Debi Thomas lost the gold medal in the '88 Olympics because she stumbled. But she stumbled because she didn't really want to win.

★10. "The trouble started a fortnight ago—and by last week thousands of people in five Midwestern states were suffering from abdominal pain, diarrhea, nausea and dehydration. Illinois reported most of the cases, and it didn't take local health officials long to discover the cause: *Salmonella typhimurium,* a bacterium sometimes found in meat and dairy products. By the weekend more than 3,600 cases had been confirmed in one of the worst outbreaks of food poisoning ever. The source of the salmonella was quickly traced to two brands of milk sold by the giant Jewel Food Stores chain—specifically, milk processed and packaged at the company's main processing plant in the Chicago suburb of Melrose Park. . . . What puzzles both the company and health officials is how the salmonella could possibly survive the pasteurization process, which heats raw milk to 160 degrees and should destroy pathogenic bacteria."

—*Newsweek*

11. "Question: Why is the use of two-way radios prohibited near construction sites where blasting is under way? Answer: Because explosives are detonated by radio signal, and the ban is a safety measure to prevent a stray signal on the detonation frequency from prematurely setting off the blast."

—The *New York Times*

12. The game of Pictionary placed second among hot-selling toys (behind the Nintendo Entertainment System) in 1987. The reason, according to Pictionary spokesman Tom McGuire, is that "it's a game the whole family can enjoy."

★13. The Supreme Court recently decided to allow a family to sue the United States government. A youngster in the family contracted a severe case of polio as a result of having been vaccinated against polio with a government-approved vaccine.

14. "Africa's next famine crisis is building in the southwest Saharan nation of Mali, where an acute drought has spawned an 80-percent decline in

livestock herds, a cholera epidemic, and grain shortages that affect at least a third of the nation's seven million people. Neighboring Senegal, Niger, Mauritania, and Bourkina Faso (formerly Upper Volta) also are suffering shrunken harvests that have doubled some food prices and forced emergency government relief efforts."

—*World Press Review*

15. "Question: I've driven past petroleum refineries and noticed flares of gas burning 24 hours a day. Why, considering these times of fuel shortages, isn't this gas used to make gasoline or some other useful product? Answer: Most refineries do recycle gaseous by-products of catalytic crackers, but it is neither physically possible nor economical to save 100 percent of the gas. Some of it is flared as unsalvageable."

—*New York Times*

★EXERCISE 4-4

The following selection contains a number of explanations. Note as many as you can identify, citing what phenomenon is being explained, what the explanation is, and whether it is physical (causal), psychological, or functional. Describe in your own words any explanations that do not fit neatly into one of these categories. This passage is discussed in the answer section.

Why do people drink? When queried in [a] Gallup poll, 54 percent said they did it for "social reasons," 18 percent drank for "relaxation," 16 percent because they "enjoy it," while 10 percent imbibed only "on special occasions." "You can't go to a party with a certain circle of friends and not have any drinks," said a California housewife. "It's mostly habit—we get together, we drink." An Illinois executive drinks "to unwind" after work. "With people screaming at you all day, you need a couple of whiskies to become civilized again."

Of those who drink for conviviality or relaxation, most feel they could give it up without ill effect. However, studies by the National Institute on Alcohol Abuse and Alcoholism indicate that 21 percent of even moderate drinkers become "psychologically dependent" on alcohol: They think they need it. Another 14 percent are "symptomatic drinkers," meaning they are physically dependent and have difficulty in controlling their drinking, suffer blackouts, skip meals while drinking, sneak drinks, etc.

In the 14-to-29-year-old group, many males drink heavily because they consider it macho or socially "in." Heavy drinking in high school and college is attributed to peer pressure and to the sudden release from parental restraint. "No matter what we start out to do, we always end up at a bar and get smashed," says a Maryland coed.

But people are drinking less, many for reasons of health. Medical findings show that, taken to excess, alcohol destroys brain cells, leading to mental deterioration. Heavy drinkers are more prone to cirrhosis of the liver, cancers of the digestive tract and heart disease. Particularly alarming to men is recent research confirming evidence that alcohol can reduce sex drive, fertility and potency. Women are generally aware that drinking can affect a fetus, causing birth defects, and with this in mind 24 percent abstain from alcohol during pregnancy.

For many Americans the most worrisome aspect of alcohol abuse is drunk driving. Drivers with blood-alcohol concentrations of .10 percent are up to 15 times more likely to have a fatal accident than nondrinking drivers—and it takes only five or six drinks in two hours for a 155-pound man to reach this level. Even three or four drinks will increase the risk of fatal accidents up to three times. The slaughter among young drivers is particularly horrendous, with alcohol present in about 50 percent of their fatal accidents.

Tough laws alone are unlikely to curb alcohol abuse—unless they are accompanied by a change in personal attitudes. Recent decreases in sales of distilled spirits and beer, and the decline in the proportion of Americans who consume them, indicate that such a change may already have begun.

—Excerpted from RONALD SCHILLER, "Why Americans Are Drinking Less," *Reader's Digest*

EXERCISE 4-5

Evaluate the following explanations using the criteria listed in the text. In cases where the criteria do not apply, explain in your own words what is wrong with the explanation.

★1. The reason he has blue eyes is that he acquired them in a previous incarnation.

2. The Kings did much better in the second half of the game. That's because they gained momentum.

3. "Men are biologically weaker than women and that's why they don't live as long, a leading expert declares."

—*Weekly World News*, February 23, 1988

★4. THERESA: Gad, there are a lot of lawyers in this country today.
DANIEL: That's because there are so many lawsuits there's a huge demand for lawyers.

5. Why did he come down with the flu? He's just prone to that sort of thing, I guess.

6. If God had meant for people to fly He'd have given them wings.

★7. Alcoholics find it so difficult to give up drinking because they have become physiologically and psychologically addicted to it.

8. Alcoholics find it so difficult to give up drinking because they have no willpower.

9. The reason *Real Genius* was a box-office hit is that Siskel and Ebert, two of the most influential movie critics, both gave it good reviews.

★10. According to some psychologists, we catch colds because we want to. Most of the time we are not aware of this desire, which may, therefore, be said to be subconscious. Viruses are present when we have a cold, but unless we desire to catch cold, the viruses do not affect us.

11. Why does she sleep so late? I guess she's just one of those people who have a hard time waking up in the morning.

12. I wonder what made me choose Budweiser. Maybe I've been subjected to subliminal advertising.

★13. The area along this part of the coast is especially subject to mudslides because of the type of soil that's found on the slopes and because there is not enough mature vegetation to provide stability with root systems.

14. How did he win the lottery twice? I'd have to say he's psychic.

15. Parapsychologist Susan Blackmore failed to find evidence of ESP in numerous experiments over more than a decade. *Fate* magazine's consulting editor D. Scott Rogo explained her negative results as follows: "In the course of my conversations with Blackmore I have come to suspect that she resists—at a deeply unconscious level—the idea that psychic phenomena exist. . . . *if* Blackmore is ever fortunate enough to witness a poltergeist or see some other striking display of psychic phenomena, I am willing to bet that her experimental results will be more positive."
—*The Skeptical Inquirer,* Winter, 1986–1987

★16. "American Airlines, United Airlines and TWA confirmed to the *Los Angeles Times* that some of their crews bypass passenger metal detectors.
"They said their current security procedures are effective and argued that switching to metal detectors would be costly and inefficient. Furthermore, they said, their security policies have been approved by the Federal Aviation Administration."
—*Los Angeles Times,* March 6, 1988

EXERCISE 4-6

Large-scale economic phenomena are notoriously difficult to explain. The following passage presents such a phenomenon and offers two explanations. Do the explanations compete? Are they compatible? What kind of information would help a person prefer one explanation over the other?

Between 1980 and 1988 the rate of inflation in the United States dropped from around twenty percent to about four or five percent. A variety of causes have been suggested for the drop. The most popular explanation among Republicans is that "Reagonomics," the "supply-side" economic policies instituted during Ronald Reagan's administration, were the primary cause. These policies consisted primarily in providing a number of tax breaks for businesses and investors. The idea was that this frees up more money for rebuilding plants, creating new jobs, and pepping up the economy in general.

Not surprisingly, most Democrats believe that the supply-side policies merely handed some extra money to those who already had the most. They think that the real reasons for the drop in inflation were the monetary policies of the Federal Reserve Board and the recession of the early eighties. The unemployment caused by the loss of jobs in the country's industrial belt left people without money to spend, say those unfriendly toward the Reagan legacy, and this is what brought inflation under control.

EXERCISE 4-7

The first paragraph below describes a phenomenon of recent interest to paleontologists and astronomers. Two possible explanations, (A) and (B), are given afterward. After reading about the phenomenon and both explanations, follow the directions for answering the questions at the end of the exercise.

The Phenomenon: The age of dinosaurs came to an end approximately sixty-five million years ago. Nearly every species of dinosaur, and countless other species as well, became extinct in a very short period of time. Recently, two scientists at the University of Chicago, John Sepkoski and David Raup, completed an exhaustive study of the earth's fossil record for the last 250 million years. Their study turned up evidence that mass extinctions like that of the dinosaurs have happened on a regular, cyclical basis every 26 million years.

Common Evidence: Two explanatory theories have been produced to explain these regular catastrophes, based in large part on Berkeley geologist Walter Alvarez's discovery of a layer of clay containing large amounts of the rare element iridium, which is often found in extraterrestrial bodies such as asteroids. This clay was laid down at about the time of the passing of the dinosaurs, giving Alvarez reason to think that the impact of asteroids on the planet and the consequent raising of massive dust clouds in the atmosphere caused the extinctions. This problem remained: What might cause the pelting of Earth by asteroids in twenty-six-million-year cycles?

Explanation A: One view holds that the sun, like many stars, has a smaller companion star in a binary orbit, one that brings it into the vicinity of the solar system and a nearby cloud of asteroids once every twenty-six million years. The star, nicknamed "Nemesis," is presumed to be quite small, which fact, in combination with its huge orbit, would make it very difficult to spot. But it is of sufficient size and gravitational attraction to dislodge asteroids from their ordinary paths and send them flying through the solar system, where some of them would fall into the earth's gravitational field and be pulled to the surface of the planet. Hence the impacts, the dust clouds, and the extinctions.

Explanation B: The second theory, from astronomer Daniel Whitmore, hypothesizes *not* an as yet undiscovered companion star but an undiscovered new planet, dubbed "Planet X." This planet, it is suggested, orbits the sun about once every one thousand Earth years in a region far beyond the farthest known planet, Pluto. The orbit of Planet X would bring it into proximity with the asteroid cloud every twenty-six million years, with the same result as suggested for the star, Nemesis. Planet X might also account for the mysterious wobbles that exist in the orbits of Pluto and Uranus.

Questions

★1. Do the two explanatory theories seem evenly matched to you, given the information supplied, or does one seem any more likely than the other?

★2. An orbit as large as that of Nemesis, some scientists believe, would be sufficiently unstable to prevent its being absolutely regular in a twenty-six-million-year cycle. How much damage, if any, does this do to explanation A?

★3. What effect, if any, would there be on explanation B if Pluto and Uranus did not wobble in their orbits?

★4. If no iridium had been found in the clay layer, would the likelihood of either A or B be affected?

★5. If the extinctions occurred in a less regular fashion, would either A or B be affected?

EXERCISE 4-8

Read the following passage and answer the questions at the end.

In March 1984 some unusual events occurred in the household of John and Joan Resch of Columbus, Ohio. They live in a two-story house with their twenty-five-year-old son John, their fourteen-year-old adopted daughter Tina, and four young foster children. The following are excerpts from a story that describes the incidents:

> [Joan] had turned off the lights in the empty dining room, but now they were on again. So were lights in the deserted and previously unlighted hallway. With no one upstairs, the shower began to run.
>
> Back in the kitchen, the washer and dryer sounded odd, and Joan could see by the dials that they were going through their cycles too fast. The hands on the electric clock raced wildly.
>
> John, a man of impressive girth and few words, listened to their story of household appliances apparently gone haywire. When he called an electrician, there was an odd noise on the phone—according to both men, "almost a howl."
>
> To veteran electrician Bruce Claggett, the Resches' problem sounded like a faulty main breaker-switch. But he found the switch in perfect working order. Maybe some electronic interference, he guessed. But individual lights still seemed to be controlled by their respective wall switches, which went from off to on by themselves. He went from room to room taping the switches down. But before he could make a full sweep through the house, the first lights were on again and the tape had disappeared.
>
> After three hours, Claggett gave up. "I had a strange feeling I never want to have again," he says. That evening, he called John Resch. "The lights

seem to be okay now," John told him. "But something worse is happening. Things are flying through the air."

Pictures tumbled from their hooks. A treasured set of stemware crashed, piece by piece, from its display shelf. Chairs seemed to move on their own, and couches upended themselves. Bewildered, the Resches called the police, and two officers arrived to hear their story. "You need help," one officer said, "but it's not the kind we can give." That night the family stayed together, some sleeping on convertible sofas in the family room and the others in sleeping bags on the floor.

The next day, the Resches thought they had a clue. John remembered that, on Saturday, there had been an hour of calm while Tina was out visiting a friend. On Sunday morning, the trouble started again when she awoke.

"I'm not making it happen," Tina insisted. "I'm not doing it on purpose." And they hadn't seen her do anything. Saturday, in fact, a candlestick had taken flight and hit Tina on the head.

Was it a poltergeist? "I don't believe in such things," Joan said, finding another name for it. "A force," she called it. "Maybe Tina can't control it, but that's what it is."

On Monday morning, Joan Resch called Mike Harden, a Columbus *Dispatch* columnist who had written about the family and their foster children. She hoped Harden would know where she could turn for help.

"I don't believe in the supernatural," Harden told Joan when he arrived at the house. For a while, he talked quietly with the family. Then a mug of hot coffee seemed to move on its own, spilling into Tina's lap. Magazines fell mysteriously from a table. Mike telephoned for a photographer.

Fred Shannon arrived for "the most bizarre assignment of my life." While Tina was perched on the arm of a chair, he saw a loveseat move toward her, "as if to attack her." When she shifted to the loveseat, an afghan rug flew up from the floor and draped itself over Tina's head. Fred snapped the picture. Tina was about four feet away from a tissue box when Fred saw it take off from a table and fly across the room.

Again and again a white phone seemed to hurl itself at Tina. Fred wanted a picture of the flying phone, but it apparently was camera-shy. To outwit "the force," he readied his camera, and then turned away, watching only out of the corner of his eye. At the first flash of movement, he clicked the shutter. The result was a photograph of the phone flying across Tina's body, "the picture of a lifetime," published in newspapers around the world.

The Columbus *Dispatch* story and picture of the flyng phone made other journalists clamor for access to the house, and Drew Hadwal, of WTVN-TV in Columbus, had his camera focused when a large lamp seemed to hurl itself to the floor. Triumphantly, Drew raced back to the studio.

Rolling the tape in slow motion, he found that the camera had caught what the human eye had missed. Tina, on tape, was looking around as if to check if anyone was watching. There was her hand, reaching up to tip the shade and knock over the lamp.

The next day, Tina explained. "I was tired and angry. I did it so the reporters could have what they came for and leave." The explanation seemed plausible. Still, if Tina played a trick once, had she done so other times?

The family invited a team from the Psychical Research Foundation of Chapel Hill, N.C. into their home. Director William Roll says that, of the "poltergeist" cases he has investigated, he's found about one-third to be trickery or natural phenomena (such as house settling), another third to be "inconclusive," and a final third to be "genuine." Roll does not, however, believe in poltergeists as "noisy spirits," in the literal meaning of the word. Phenomena attributed to poltergeist activity are, he says, the product of something he calls Recurrent Spontaneous Psychokinesis (RSPK), a power some individuals possess that causes objects to fly around by themselves.

According to Roll, RSPK is usually involuntary and is most often an affliction of teen-agers. He believes it's an energy that comes out of the turmoil so many teen-agers feel.

At the time of the disturbances in her house, Tina Resch had been feeling more stress than most teen-agers. Along with problems in school that had led to her staying home and working with a tutor, she had just broken up with her first boyfriend. And she was beginning to wonder about finding her birth mother, who had brought Tina to a hospital when she was ten months old and never returned for her.

Roll and an assistant lived with the Resches for a week, checking for natural causes and for wires and trick devices. They found nothing. All the while, Roll kept Tina under close observation. Objects still seemed to move on their own.

Investigators from the Committee for the Scientific Investigation of Claims of the Paranormal (CSICOP), with headquarters in Buffalo, N.Y., were turned away. "One group at a time is enough," Joan said.

The CSICOP team—two university scientists (an astronomer and an astrophysicist) and James Randi, a noted magician who has revealed trickery in many cases of claimed paranormal events—had to settle for interviews with witnesses. Their key question: "Did you see the phone or the glass or any other object actually take off and begin to fly?"

Again and again, witnesses admitted they'd missed the takeoff, the point at which a human hand might have started the object on its flight. Photographer Fred Shannon, however, insisted that he had seen a telephone and also a tissue box as they rose into the air and began to fly.

"The hand," says Prof. Steven Shore, the astrophysicist on the team, "is always quicker than the eye." He believes that's the explanation for all the recorded events.

Tina's is the most publicized case of suspected paranormal phenomena in recent years, and one of the best-documented. Yet the events are hard to prove or disprove. Odd things happened when Tina went with Roll to North Carolina—a door seemed to open by itself, a telephone flew from a desk and struck Tina in the back.

By the time she was back home, two months had passed since the curious events had begun. The house has remained calm since Tina's return.

It is *eerie* to think that a young girl might have the uncontrollable power to make objects fly through the air. But it is also hard to accept that an average teen-ager, with no special skill or knowledge or dexterity, could beguile and hoodwink so many adults.

Both skeptics and believers agree on one thing. Whether the events in the Resch household were paranormal or a prank, the energy for them came from the storms and stresses of being a teen-ager.

"There are things that can't be explained," their minister told the Resch family. One of them is poltergeists. Another is teen-agers.

—Excerpted from Claire Safran, "Poltergeist, Or Only a Teen-ager," *Reader's Digest*, December 1984

Questions

★1. How many different explanations were suggested by the people who appear in the story?

★2. Did the writer of the story seem to prefer one explanation over the rest?

3. Of the people who suggested explanations, who seems to you to be the most credible? Why?

★4. William Roll does not believe in poltergeists, it was said. He attributes the phenomena to "recurrent spontaneous psychokinesis." Does either of these accounts—poltergeists or RSPK—seem more credible than the other when measured against the criteria listed in the "Evaluating Explanations" section of the text?

5. Measured against the same criteria, how does the RSPK explanation compare with the "natural" explanation made by Professor Shore of the CSICOP team?

6. Look back to the third paragraph from the end. Are the two explanations given there *equally* hard to accept? Keep in mind your answer to the preceding question, here.

EXERCISE 4-9 (ESSAY)

Find an explanation in a newspaper or magazine and write a brief essay about it. Identify the phenomenon explained, describe the explanation given, and evaluate the explanation. If more than one explanation is given (or occurs to you), compare the two on the basis of the criteria given in the text.

5 *Nonargumentative Persuasion*

The person who uses language emotively is primarily concerned with the creation of a work of art.

—With apologies to A. J. Ayer

[Advertising is] the modern substitute for argument; its function is to make the worst appear better.

—GEORGE SANTAYANA

. . . the ads of our times are the richest and most faithful daily reflection that any society ever made of its entire range of activities.

—MARSHALL MCLUHAN

Besides simply conveying information to us, claims can affect our attitudes and beliefs about their subjects by other means. Some attempts (either explicit or implicit; conscious or unconscious) to encourage the acceptance of a claim or to influence our attitude about a subject do not involve anything that even resembles evidence or support. Instead of reasons, they rely on persuasive devices present in the claims themselves. We call such attempts **nonargumentative persuasion.**

Nonargumentative persuasion is often accomplished by the use of emotive language, to which we were introduced in Chapter 2, and we'll look at some of the ways this happens in the first section of this chapter. Besides emotive force, there are other devices that, when smuggled into a claim, can change its

116

meaning or affect us in ways that are sometimes subtle and easily overlooked—and often that's just what the author of the claim intends. We'll classify and discuss some of these devices as well.

In the second and third sections, we'll have a brief look first at the news media and then at advertising. Both news and advertising claim large chunks of our attention, and the more we know about how they work (and don't work!) the better prepared we are to evaluate critically what they have to tell us.

Slanters

The term **slanters** covers a wide range of linguistic devices that can affect what we feel or believe about a subject. Some of them make use of emotive language, some smuggle in unwarranted assumptions, and some exaggerate or distort in other ways. All of them attempt to achieve their ends without argumentation.

Euphemisms

Some subjects, such as war, disease, death, and torture, are simply unpleasant or offensive to think or talk about. A writer or speaker who does not wish to refer to such topics by their usual labels, which carry a lot of negative feelings with them, can use less offensive terms or even terms that replace those negative emotional associations with positive ones. This may allow the unpleasantness to be overlooked, or at least disguised. **Euphemisms** (literally, "good sounds") are the words or phrases used to accomplish such shifts. These substitutes for negatively charged language play an important role in language used to affect our attitudes. People may be less likely to disapprove of an assassination attempt on a foreign leader, for example, if it is referred to as *neutralization*. People fighting against the government of a country can be referred to neutrally as *rebels* or *guerillas,* but a person who wants to build support for them may refer to them by the euphemism *freedom fighters*. A government is likely to pay a price for initiating a *revenue enhancement,* but voters will be even quicker to respond negatively to a *tax hike*. The United States Department of Defense performs the same function it did when it was called the Department of War, but the current name makes for much better public relations.

The opposite of a euphemism is a **dysphemism**. Dysphemisms are used to produce a negative effect on a listener's or reader's attitude toward something or to tone down the positive associations it may have. While *freedom fighter* is a euphemism for *guerilla* or *rebel, terrorist* is a dysphemism.

It's All in the Name

According to an AP story by Gene Grabowski, some distillers and marketers of hard liquor have an idea they hope will increase their sales to the baby-boom generation: They believe that "light liquor," spirits with less alcohol and fewer calories than regular liquor, will sell better to younger people. Currently, these potential customers tend to avoid hard liquor, and the liquor industry has surely noticed the success of "light" beer.

Unfortunately for the industry, federal law requires that liquor that is less than 80 proof (40 percent alcohol) be labeled *diluted*. Those in the liquor industry who want to bring the new product to market have requested that *diluted* be replaced on the label by *light* or *mild*.

What difference do you think it would make in sales if the literally correct *diluted* appeared on the label instead of the euphemism *mild* or *light*? How would the word *diluted* affect the product's success?

We note that the Association of Tequila Producers is having none of this: "Diluted Tequila is not in character" with their product's "macho style and mystique." Who was it who said he always ordered industrial-strength Tequila?

Euphemisms and dysphemisms are often used in deceptive ways, or ways that at least hint at deception. All the examples in the preceding paragraphs are examples of such uses. But euphemisms can at times be helpful and constructive. By allowing us to approach a sensitive subject indirectly—or skirting it entirely—euphemisms can sometimes prevent hostility from bringing rational discussion to a halt. They can also be a matter of good manners: *Passed on* may be much more appropriate than *dead* if the person to whom you're speaking is a recent widow.

Staking a Claim on the P.M.

Many advertisements use words that, taken literally, have neither a positive nor negative effect and indeed say nothing at all. Consider, for instance:

"The night belongs to Michelob."

Taken by itself, this phrase isn't likely to affect a person one way or the other, or even to make much sense. But coupled with vivid imagery and upbeat music, it takes on a meaning, or at least an emotive force, of its own—one of pleasurable excitement (if you like that sort of imagery and music). This feeling, of course, makes you want to buy the product.

We've wondered why Yuban or Hills Brothers hasn't claimed the morning.

Innuendo

The use of **innuendo,** a form of suggestion, enables us to insinuate something deprecatory about something or someone without actually saying it. For example, if someone asks you if Ralph is telling the truth, you may reply, "Yes, this time," which would suggest that maybe Ralph doesn't *usually* tell the truth. Or you might say of someone, "She is competent—in many regards," which would insinuate that in some ways she is *not* competent.

Sometimes we condemn somebody with faint praise—that is, by praising a person a small amount where grander praise might be expected, we hint that praise may not really be due at all. This is a kind of innuendo. Imagine, for example, reading a letter of recommendation that says, "Ms. Flotsam has done good work for us, I suppose." Such a letter does not inspire one to want to hire Ms. Flotsam on the spot. Likewise, "She's proved to be useful so far," and "Surprisingly, she seems very astute," manage to speak more evil than good of Ms. Flotsam. Notice, though, that the literal information contained in these remarks is not negative in the least. Innuendo lies between the lines, so to speak.

Loaded Questions

If you overheard one person ask a second, "Have you always loved to gamble?" you would naturally assume that the second person did in fact love to gamble. This assumption is independent of whether the person answered *yes* or *no*, for it underlies the question itself. Now, every question rests on assumptions. An innocent question such as "What time is it?" depends on the assumptions that the hearer speaks English, has some means of finding out the time, and so on. A **loaded question** is less innocent, however. It rests on one or more *unwarranted* or *unjustified* assumptions. The world's oldest example, "Have you stopped beating your wife?", rests on the assumption that the person asked has in the past beaten his wife. If there is no reason to think that this assumption is true, then the question is a loaded one.

The loaded question is technically a form of innuendo, since it permits us to insinuate the assumption that underlies a question without coming right

An Example from a Master

I didn't say the meat was tough. I said I didn't see the horse that is usually outside.
—W. C. FIELDS

This is innuendo with a vengeance.

out and stating that assumption. But such questions have their own special form, and hence lend themselves to separate treatment.

Weaslers

The expressions that we call **weaslers** are linguistic methods of hedging a bet. When inserted into a claim, they help protect it from criticism by watering it down somewhat, weakening it, and giving the claim's author a way out in case the claim is challenged.

You have surely heard the advertisement for a brand of sugarless gum claiming that "three out of four dentists surveyed recommend sugarless gum for their patients who chew gum." This claim contains two weaseling expressions. The first is the word *surveyed*. Notice that the ad does not tell us the criteria for choosing the dentists who were surveyed. Were they picked at random or is there some reason to think that only dentists who might not be unfavorably disposed toward gum chewing were surveyed? Nothing indicates that the sample of dentists surveyed even remotely represents the general population of dentists. If 99 percent of the dentists in the country disagree with the ad's claim, its authors could still say truthfully that they spoke only about those dentists surveyed, not all dentists.

The second weasler in the advertisement appears in the last phrase of the claim, . . . *for their patients who chew gum*. Notice the ad does not claim that *any* dentist believes sugarless gum chewing is as good for a patient's teeth as no gum chewing at all. You can imagine that the actual question posed to the dentists was something like, "If a patient of yours insisted on chewing gum, would you prefer that he or she chew sugarless gum or gum with sugar in it?" If dentists had to answer that question, they would almost certainly be in favor of sugarless gum. But this is a far cry from recommending that any person chew any kind of gum at all. The weaslers allow the advertisement to get away with what *sounds* like an unqualified recommendation for sugarless gum, when in fact nothing in the ad supports such a recommendation.

Let's make up a statistic. Let's say that 98 percent of American doctors believe that aspirin is a contributing cause of Reye's syndrome in children, and that the other 2 percent are unconvinced. If we then claim that "some doctors are unconvinced that aspirin is related to Reye's syndrome," we cannot be held accountable for having said something false, even though our claim might be misleading to someone who did not know the complete story. The word *some* has allowed us to weasle the point.

Words that sometimes weasle—such as *perhaps, possibly,* and *maybe,* among others—can be used to produce innuendo, to plant a *suggestion* without actually making a claim that a person can be held to. We can suggest that Berriault is a liar without actually saying so (and thus making a claim that might be hard to defend) by saying that Berriault *may* be a liar. Or we can say that it is *possible* that Berriault is a liar (which is true of all of us, after all). "*Perhaps* Berriault is

One Picture Is Worth 1000 Votes

YES    NO

Which Way Chico?

This ad, which was distributed without comment by the people who wanted us to vote "yes" on the measure in question, is an example of *nonlinguistic* nonargumentative persuasion. The photographs are of spokespersons for the "yes" and "no" sides. The "yes" people, incidentally, lost in the election, perhaps demonstrating that one picture is *not* worth 1000 votes.

a liar" works nicely too. All these are examples of weaslers used to create innuendo, as discussed earlier.

Not every use of these words and phrases is a weaseling one, of course. Words that can weasel can also bring very important qualifications to bear on a claim. The very same claim in which one of the above words is a weasler can, in a different context, contain no weaseling at all. For example, if a detective is considering all the possible angles on a crime, and he has just heard Smith's account of events, he may say to an associate, "Of course, it is *possible* that Smith is lying." This need not be a case of weaseling. The detective may simply be exercising due care. Other words and phrases that are sometimes used to weasel can also be used legitimately. Qualifying phrases such as *It is arguable that . . . , It may well be that . . . ,* and so on have at least as many appropriate uses as weaseling ones. Others, such as *Some would say that . . . ,* are likely to be weaseling more often than not, but even they can be proper in the right context. Our warning, then, is to be watchful when qualifying phrases turn up. Is the speaker or writer adding a reasonable qualification, insinuating a bit of innuendo, or giving herself a way out? We can only warn; you need to assess the speaker, the context, and the subject to establish the grounds for the right judgment.

Downplayers

Downplayers are words used to downplay or undermine the importance of a claim. When you see or hear the words *nevertheless* or *however,* there is a chance that they are there to play down the claim that preceded them—it may be a claim the author does not want to call too much attention to. For example, a person who said, "Well, no, I didn't actually read the book; *nevertheless,* I know exactly what the author was trying to say," would not want you to dwell on the fact that he or she hadn't read the book: *Nevertheless* serves to downplay that fact.

We often set one claim out alongside another and have no interest in calling attention to one of them at the expense of the other. The conjunction *and* exhibits neutrality between such claims, as in "The new tax is fair, and half the revenue benefits education." But we cannot *always* limit ourselves to *and,* even when we mean to be evenhanded in our assertion of two claims. Most other conjunctions (including the one with which we began the preceding sentence) set claims against each other to one extent or another, and then there is a chance of favoritism coming through. Our purpose here is to warn you against the purposeful use of such downplaying expressions. Like those mentioned above, *still, but, though,* and the like can all be used to indicate that we should not attach so much importance to the *preceding* claim that we allow it to overshadow the one following. For instance:

> The leak at the Union Carbide plant in Bhopal, India, was a terrible tragedy; *however,* we must remember that such pesticide plants are an integral part of the "green revolution" that has helped to feed millions of people.

The word *although* operates similarly, downplaying the claim that comes right after it: "Although the leak at the Union Carbide plant was a tragedy, we must remember that . . . , etc."

Downplayers

As a journalist, I am sure I am not singular in being slightly schizophrenic about the press and, in general, the media. I believe, with some passion, in a free press, radio, and television; free, of course, from state interference or control. But I am appalled at the capacity of the free media to get things wrong or to mislead the public.

—BRIAN CROZIER, *National Review*

Notice the downplaying *but* at the beginning of the last sentence. Which point do you think the writer is going to develop and defend in the remainder of the article—the first point, that there should be a free press, or the second, that the media mislead the public? (If you said the first point, reread the chapter.)

Proof Surrogates

An expression used to suggest that there is evidence or authority for a claim without actually citing such evidence or authority is a **proof surrogate**. Sometimes we can't *prove* the claim that we're asserting, but we can hint that there *is* such proof available, or at least evidence or authority for it, without committing ourselves to that proof, evidence, or authority. Using *informed sources say* . . . is a favorite way of making a claim more authoritative. Who are the sources? How do we know they're informed? How does the person making the claim know they're informed? *It's obvious that* . . . sometimes precedes a claim that isn't obvious at all. But we may keep our objections to ourselves in the belief that it's obvious to everybody but us, and we don't want to appear more dense than the next guy. *Studies show* . . . crops up in advertising a lot. Note that this phrase tells us nothing about how many studies are involved, how good they are, who did them, or any other important information.

The thing to remember is that proof surrogates are just that, surrogates; they are not real proof or evidence. There may *be* such proof or evidence, but, until it has been presented, the claim at issue remains unsupported.

Stereotypes

When a writer or speaker lumps a group of individuals together under one name or description, especially one that begins with the word *the* (the liberals, the Communists, the right-wingers, the Jews, the Catholics, etc.), chances are that a stereotype is being offered. A **stereotype** is an oversimplified generalization about a class of individuals, one based on a presumption that every member of the class has some set of properties that is (probably erroneously)

Wartime Stereotypes

These offensive stereotypes are from a 1941 issue of *Time:*

- Chinese are not as hairy as the Japanese and seldom grow an impressive mustache . . . the Chinese expression is likely to be more placid, kindly, open; the Japanese more positive, dogmatic, arrogant. . . .
- Some aristocratic Japanese have thin, aquiline noses, narrow faces and, except for their eyes, look like Caucasians.
- Japanese are hesitant, nervous in conversation, laugh loudly at the wrong time.
- Japanese walk stiffly erect, hard-heeled. Chinese are more relaxed, have an easy gait, and sometimes shuffle.

—Reprinted courtesy of *Time* magazine

identified with the class. "The Catholics are behind the anti-abortion movement." (Although the Catholic Church officially opposes abortion, this position is not held by all Catholics.) "Women can't handle management-level decision making. They're too emotional." (Some women become emotional in the face of a difficult decision, just as some men do, but a great number do not.)

Our stereotypes come from a great many sources, many from popular literature, and they are often supported by a variety of prejudices and group interests. The American Indians of the Great Plains were considered noble people by most whites until just before the mid-nineteenth century. But as white people grew more interested in moving them off their lands and as white/ Indian conflicts escalated, popular literature increasingly described the Plains Indians as subhuman creatures. This stereotype supported the group interests of whites. Conflicts between nations usually produce derogatory stereotypes of the opposition: It is easier to destroy enemies without pangs of conscience if we think of them as less "human" than ourselves. Stereotyping becomes even easier when there are racial differences to exploit.

Hyperbole

Hyperbole is extravagant overstatement. A claim that goes beyond what is required to state a fact or judgment in neutral terms is on its way to becoming hyperbole. Whether it gets there depends on the strength of its language and the point being made. To describe a hangnail as a serious injury is hyperbole; so is using the word *fascist* to describe parents who insist that their teenager be home by midnight. Not all strong or colorful language is hyperbole, of course. "Oscar Peterson is an unbelievably inventive pianist" is a strong claim,

Nicknames

Several stories have come from the news services recently about a nationwide phenomenon known as *bum-busting,* a term that refers to physical assaults on homeless transients, usually but not always by teenagers. In one episode in 1984, for example, three young men hunted homeless "street people" in Santa Cruz, California, using a homemade bazooka, with which they shot a transient, severely wounding and nearly killing him. On Christmas Day 1984, in Sacramento, California, two teenagers were arrested for shooting and killing a transient for sport. Similar reports have come from across the nation.

Robert Hayes, who heads an organization called the Coalition for the Homeless, a national network of groups helping to house, feed, and fight legal battles for the needy, thinks that part of the problem is in the nicknames given the homeless. "Calling them trolls, tree people, and bums makes it easier to view them as some kind of subspecies and not as human beings," he observed.

but it is not hyperbolic—it isn't really extravagant. On the other hand, "Oscar Peterson is the most inventive musician who ever lived" has crossed over the line into hyperbole. When the claim clearly goes beyond what the speaker or writer is justified in saying, we can call the claim hyperbole. (How could one know that Oscar Peterson is more inventive than, say, Mozart?)

A claim can be hyperbolic without containing excessively emotive words or phrases. Neither the hangnail nor the Oscar Peterson examples contain such language; in fact, the word *unbelievably* is probably the most emotive word in the two claims about Peterson, and it occurs in the nonhyperbolic claim. But a claim can also be hyperbole as a result of the use of such language. "Parents who are strict about a curfew are fascists" is an example. If the word *mean* were substituted for *fascists,* we might find the claim strong or somewhat exaggerated but we would not call it hyperbole. It's when the colorfulness of language becomes *excessive*—a matter of judgment—that the claims in which it appears are likely to turn into hyperbole.

The ways in which hyperbole can be used as a slanting device are pretty obvious. People overstate in a positive way what they want to endorse, and they overstate in a negative way what they want to disparage. You may have no trouble identifying hyperbolic claims as exaggerated, but, in so doing, you can allow yourself to tacitly accept a less exaggerated version of the claim even while you are rejecting the excessive one. You may laugh off the claim "Negotiating with the Russians is the same as begging to be deceived," but, almost in the spirit of compromise, you may accept the milder version: "The Russians are commonly deceptive in negotiations." While the milder claim might be true, the fact that the exaggerated claim is false is not a reason for the milder version. Remember, a claim that is hyperbolic is not a reason, not even a bad one, for your accepting a less overstated version. A hyperbolic claim is pure persuasion.

We have discussed a wide variety of slanting devices in this section, but there are still others that would not fit comfortably in any of our categories. In a recent issue of the *National Review,* for example, the United States' departure from UNESCO (the United Nations Educational, Scientific, and Cultural Organization) was described this way: "There can be nothing cleaner than the air you breathe after walking out of a pig sty." Well, that certainly suggests that UNESCO is pretty awful indeed (notice that it does not argue the point—it gives nothing that resembles reasons). But this remark is not easily classified among any of the slanters we have discussed, with the possible exception of innuendo, though it's a little too straightforward even to be placed in that category. Remember that suggestion—hints, insinuations, emotive associations—comes in many forms, and not all of them fit neatly into our categories. And keep in mind that the incidental associations that language carries along are not evidence for a claim. In a 1950s television series, *Dragnet,* deadpan detective Joe Friday became famous for demanding "just the facts, ma'am, just the facts." Life needn't be as unembellished as Joe Friday might have wished, but the way in which a claim is stated is still no substitute for evidence.

The Closed State Cometh

In the hands of the generals and directors of the national security state, secrecy is a weapon of aggression as well as a device of defense. This Administration is obsessed with secrecy, and every time it mobilizes to staunch a leak, indict a spy, or shroud a space shot, it is also projecting police power and military might. The uses of secrecy are extending far into the political realm, beyond the necessity of self-protection.

—*The Nation* magazine

The article continues similarly. Notice the use of emotively powerful phrases—*national security state, obsessed with secrecy, weapons of aggression, police power,* etc. The net effect is to *suggest* that the administration has secretly and willfully set out to destroy the Bill of Rights; that it is dedicated to removing our ability to exchange ideas and information freely; and that we are moving inexorably toward the creation of a closed state in which the free exchange of information no longer exists. To conclude on the basis of a paragraph like this that the administration is trying to curtail the free exchange of ideas would be to succumb to the power of suggestion, not to follow the voice of reason.

Persuasive Definitions, Explanations, and Comparisons

We've discussed definitions, explanations, and comparisons in earlier chapters, and we'll have more to say about the last of these in Chapter 10. But we want to remind you here that all three can be fashioned as slanters. An example or two of each should suffice.

Persuasive definitions are phrased in emotive language intended to influence us (see Chapter 2). For example, to define a *liberal* as someone who "wants to sacrifice the rights of innocent victims for the rights of vicious criminals" is to seek to instill negative opinions toward liberals without arguing that such opinions are actually warranted.

A *persuasive explanation* is intended less to explain than to express one's attitude about something and, sometimes, to influence the attitudes of others. "She did it because she is egotistical, selfish, and childish" is a particularly overblown example.

The Three Boxes

In America, freedom and justice have always come from three sources—the ballot box, the jury box and, when those fail, the cartridge box.

—Sen. STEVEN SYMMS (R-Idaho)

Symms, a strong opponent of gun control, offers us here a persuasive comparison.

A Persuasive Explanation

Dear Editor:

... political experts are predicting that Michael Dukakis will never pick Jesse Jackson to be his vice president, and they may or may not be right. If it is a Dukakis-Jackson ticket it will be because of the liberals' fondness for wanting the absolutely least qualified individuals to run the country, which we see illustrated every four years ...

—*Pyramid Shield*

No question what this writer thinks of the Democrats. His explanation of a Dukakis-Jackson ticket expresses his own distaste for the ticket, and encourages the reader to have similar sentiments.

His Elevator Doesn't Go to the Top

The last presidential campaign was called the dirtiest in history (they say that every four years, don't they?). One of the main amusements of supporters of the Democratic ticket in '88 was attacking Dan Quayle, and often this came in the form of non-argumentative persuasion.

A notable example of non-argumentative Quayle-bashing was a column by Colin McEnroe, of the *Hartford Courant*. Though it happened years ago, wrote McEnroe, he could remember plain as day when his papa was looking out the window at the neighbor kid, little Danny Quayle. "Land sakes," McEnroe remembers his papa saying, "that boy doesn't have a whole lot of buckwheat in his pancake, does he?"

McEnroe then proceeded to "remember" the observations of little Danny Quayle made by the rest of his (McEnroe's) family. Included were these sturdy old persuasive comparisons:

"That boy is a few logs shy of a cord."

"He's kinda all bell and no clapper."

"I don't reckon he got quite enough mercury in his thermometer."

Then, to clinch his case against Quayle, McEnroe "remembered" visiting the Quayles', and spying a needlepoint on the Quayle wall which said, "Home is good."

When he (McEnroe) mentioned to the Quayles that he thought the customary saying was, "Home, Sweet Home," the Quayles, he remembered, were overwhelmed by the words:

"That's terrific," one Quayle said.

"Did you make that up?" asked another.

"Get a pencil and write that down, Mildred," another said.

"Home Sweet—how did that go again? Is there a comma in there some-place?" asked another.

You get the idea. Even a staunch Quayle supporter might feel uncomfortable defending Quayle's intelligence after this. Yet no argument was presented.

Persuasive comparisons are used to express or influence attitudes, as mentioned in Chapter 4. If you want to indicate that Beryl is a small person, you might compare her to an elf. But you might also compare her to a gnome or a Chihuahua, which would be considerably less flattering while conveying the same literal information. You might communicate the fairness of a person's skin by comparing it either to new-fallen snow or to whale blubber, but you'd be better off making the latter comparison out of the individual's hearing. Anyone who likens the current president of the United States either to Hitler or to a saint obviously wishes to convey or arouse strong feelings about the president.

EXERCISE 5-1

Identify and explain the use of any weaslers, downplayers, stereotypes, innuendos, and other slanting devices you find in the following selections and explain their functions in the passages.

★1. "Maybe somebody moved the files from where Harriet told you she put them. Surely she wouldn't have come right out and lied to you."

2. "Harvey tells me he won't be able to join us for the winter ski trip this year. He's had a negative-cash-flow problem since last August."

3. "During World War II, the United States government resettled many people of Japanese ancestry in internment camps."

★4. "Although it has always had a bad name in the United States, socialism is nothing more or less than democracy in the realm of economics."

5. "The fact that Janet B. Thompson's new book has slithered its way onto the best-seller lists provides one more reason, as if any more were required, that the American people's appetite for uncompromised sex and violence is insatiable."

6. "If the United States is to meet the technological challenge posed by Japan, Inc., education must expand beyond the classroom and into the corporate office and the industrial plant."

★7. "Maybe Professor Lankirshim's research hasn't appeared in the first-class journals as recently as that of some of the other professors in his department; that doesn't necessarily mean his work is going downhill. He's still a fine teacher, if the students I've talked to are to be believed."

8. "Even though its detractors like to paint pictures of robber barons exploiting the workers, capitalism is nothing but individual freedom in the realm of economics."

9. "Since they preside over the buying and selling of about half the world's oil, the independent traders who make up the spot market control the prices of oil like absolute monarchs of the sixteenth century."

★10. "The new Wingover driver's patented aerodynamic design can add up to *seven miles per hour* to clubhead speed at the crucial point-of-impact portion of your golf swing. University tests prove that this additional speed can translate into as much as *twenty extra yards off the tee added to your drives!"*

EXERCISE 5-2

Identify any slanting devices used in the following passages and explain their purposes.

★1. Former TV evangelist Pat Robertson ran for the Republican nomination for the presidency in 1988. *The New Republic* reviewed a debate featuring all the Republican candidates, and had this to say about Robertson:
"Pat Robertson did better than expected, mostly by chuckling a lot and going easy on the Bible-thumping. He invoked his friend God only in his closing statement, which was calculated to reassure. . . . Yet for all his attempts to seem normal, the Howdy Doody–faced evangelist did contribute the debate's one moment of transcendent lunacy. It came when Robertson advanced the theory that banning abortion is the solution to the problem of financing Social Security. . . ."

2. "*Fortune* magazine had just published a gooey cover story entitled, "What Managers Can Learn from Manager Reagan." It was full of choice nuggets such as: "Surround yourself with the best people you can find, delegate authority and don't interfere as long as the policy you've decided on is being carried out." And: "Picking competent people who are on his wavelength has also enabled Reagan to delegate more effectively than most Presidents." But tucked amid the fawning praise was a prescient warning: "Management experts caution corporate leaders against disdaining detail to the extent Reagan does."
—*Newsweek*, March 16, 1987

3. If there is to be any revitalization of populism in the next couple of years, it will center on trade policy, which has lately been discussed as a political abstraction framed on the one hand by the Republicans' "free trade" rhetoric and on the other by the dead hand of the labor movement's protectionism.

★4. Editorial comment: "Most scientists who have studied it regard the Star Wars premise of a technical defense against nuclear attack as a fraud. No technology imagined, let alone developed, holds a faint hope of providing safety to populations. The radical escalation in Star Wars research sought by President Reagan and rubber-stamped by Congress is a scam.
"Technological innovation has been crucial to the U.S. economy. Scientists who are bribed into devoting their lives to 'interesting' military problems, such as hardening computers to withstand the electromagnetic pulses in nuclear blasts, are not available to pioneer manufacturing techniques or robotics or biogenetics. The 'brain drain' affects the U.S. position in the world economy. . . ."
—*Boston Globe*

5. Editorial comment: "President P. W. Botha has declared open season on blacks. That, of course, is a too hard and inaccurate assessment of what

is happening in that strife-torn country. Nevertheless, it is a view that might include some degree of truth.

"South Africa has persistently pursued apartheid, the doctrine of separate development that denies blacks the right to vote, the right to travel freely, the right to work anywhere that work can be found and any of the ordinary freedoms people in much of the world accept without second thought.

"It is a morally bankrupt policy that can only be enforced and perpetuated by the force of arms.

"Sooner or later, the boiling caldron of racial strife will boil over again because Botha and his white cohorts refuse to bring their 19th century racist thinking into line with the realities of the late 20th century."

—*Salt Lake Tribune*

EXERCISE 5-3

Rewrite the following selections so that the informational content remains the same as in the original, but the language is as emotively neutral as you can make it.

1. Delwood is dumb as a stump—I don't think he can get out of bed in the morning without asking directions.

★2. Michael Hawkins, undersea explorer and award-winning maker of underwater films, wouldn't cast off without his hard-charging Zephyr 75 outboard engine from International Marine Corp. Smooth as silk when maneuvering around playful dolphins, the 75 can power Michael out of the hole and down the chute fast enough to leave bigger engines contemplating their macho images.

3. The bureaucrats at the Postal Service must have run out of slush funds— I see they're going to raise postal rates again.

★4. The sneak attack on Pearl Harbor in December 1942 horrified the sensibilities of most Americans.

5. Assembly-line work turns people into unthinking robots by requiring mindless repetition of menial tasks. Eventually, though, real robots will handle such work, liberating a large part of the country's work force for more stimulating, creative jobs.

★6. Our do-nothing government had had thirty years' advance warning that the killer bees that escaped in South America would eventually find their way to this country. Still, only a few university scientists have tried to do anything about the coming invasion, working on a way to breed some civilized genes from European bees into their killer cousins. Even though it knew about the efforts of these scientists, the government has turned its back on them. When the killer bees annihilate United States agriculture, we consumers will wind up paying for this head-in-the-sand attitude.

7. Announcing a Summertime Spectacular! Owens Motors in Clifton Heights is pleased to offer you spectacular savings during its midsummer super-sale! We have an incredible inventory of new Fords and Mercurys, and you simply won't believe our prices. We absolutely refuse to be undersold by any dealer in the state. So some on out and see tomorrow's cars at yesterday's prices—the twenty-minute drive to Clifton Heights can save you a bundle!

★8. Daryn Kaiser is a quiet, soft-spoken man. He keeps his opinions to himself most of the time, but when he does speak, you can depend on his having thought about his subject enough to make contradicting him a dangerous matter—he can make you wish you hadn't.

9. The recent massacre of six government officials and three innocent by-standers in El Salvador signals a vicious new turn in that country's con-tinuing civil struggle. In a letter to a San Salvadoran newspaper the Salvadoran Revolutionary Party (PRS) claimed "credit" for the slayings. "Every member of the current regime's government is an enemy of de-mocracy and of the El Salvadoran people, and they have now begun to fall," gloated the PRS letter. It went on to profess "profound regret" for the deaths of the three nongovernment civilians, saying that the deaths of innocents were an unfortunate by-product of ridding the country of what it alleged to be the current "people-oppressing regime."

10. Now you can afford it: The Art of Living. If you put off buying a new home because it cost too much to really move up, you can be glad you've waited. Forest Hills is the prize your patience has won. Exclusive country living that is more than just a home—it's a life-style all its own. Luxurious modern appointments throughout these two- and three-bedroom homes make coming home a pleasure. Best of all, innovative concepts in financing allow you to make Forest Hills your new address with the most modest of down payments and truly affordable monthly payments.

★EXERCISE 5-4

Explain the difference between a weasler and a downplayer. Find a clear ex-ample of each in a newspaper, magazine, or other source. Next find an example of a phrase that is sometimes used as a weasler or downplayer but that is used appropriately or neutrally in the context of your example.

★EXERCISE 5-5

Explain how persuasive definitions, persuasive comparisons, and persuasive explanations differ. Find an example of each in a newspaper, magazine, or other source.

Information Tailoring and the News

Brainwashing, drugs, and torture are three effective nonargumentative ways to influence a person's attitudes and behavior. But we're concerned with more subtle attempts to persuade, those that are purely linguistic. One powerful way to influence is to select the information a person receives, since our attitudes are shaped in large part by our information. It is extremely difficult to dictate *exactly* what information people receive, but if others wish to influence your attitude they can be selective in the information they give you and hope that no other sources of information counter theirs, or else that you will trust them sufficiently or for some other reason neglect to acquire other information.

The best safeguard against manipulation through the selective presentation of facts is to be well informed. Of course you cannot be better informed than your sources of information permit. But most of us are not nearly as well informed as we could be, given the available sources of information. Many of us simply do not avail ourselves of the best available sources of information.

Who Makes the News?

In general, at least as far as contemporary events are concerned, the best sources of information available to most of us are newspapers, news magazines, and the electronic media. But it pays to be careful even when using such sources as these, for there is no ironclad guarantee that they are presenting news in a thoroughly factual, unbiased fashion. Some of them wear their biases on their faces: Some magazines make no bones about their political slants, and editorial opinions in both the electronic and print media are usually labeled as such.

WE'LL Decide When We're Fed Up, Thank You

An editorial about news leaks in the *Indianapolis Star* began this way: "The public is fed up with Iran-Contra 'news' courtesy of the anonymous source, the unnamed high-level official, the unidentified spokesman, etc."

How does the *Star* know this? The public may prefer leaked news to no news. More likely, the public doesn't care very much rather than is fed up. Most likely is that somebody at the *Star* is fed up.

Re-creations

You behold the scene before you with horror: A tough, young boy is shown screaming threateningly at his mother, who cowers in fear. So caught up are you in this report on what drugs do to kids, you barely notice the commentator informing you that the scene is a "re-creation."

Such re-creations are common in TV news these days, and, while they are done for dramatic effect, their potential for use in slanting news stories is obvious.

But even the "objective" news found in the media is subject to shaping by the conscious and subconscious perspectives of those who write and control it. A brief look at a couple of reasons why this is so should serve as a warning.

First, we must remember that the popular notion of the hardworking investigative reporter who ferrets out facts, tracks down elusive sources, and badgers people for inside information is largely a creation of the movie makers. No news service can afford to devote more than a small portion of its resources to real investigative reporting. Occasionally, this kind of reporting pays off handsomely, as was the case with Bob Woodward and Carl Bernstein's reporting of the Watergate affair in the early seventies. *The Washington Post* won awards and sold newspapers at a remarkable rate as a result of that series of articles. But such cases are relatively rare. The great bulk of news is *given* to reporters, not dug up after weeks or days or even hours of investigation. Press conferences and press releases are the standard means of getting news from both government and private industry into the mass media. And, since spokespeople in neither government nor industry are especially stupid or self-destructive, they tend to produce news items that they and the people they represent *want* to see in the media.

Further, it is true that reporters depend on sources in governmental and private institutions to pass items along, and reporters who offend those sources are not likely to have them very long.

How's This for Straightforward Reporting?

And the genuineness of Paul Simon's dippy persona carried him into the semifinals, but there was no way that a political Mister Magoo was actually going to be nominated.

—*Time*

Nice, clear, objective reporting, right? (Paul Simon, remember, was a contender for the Democratic presidential nomination in 1988.)

It just occurs to us, incidentally, that this claim from *Time* sets forth an explanation. Check it out against the criteria in Chapter 4.

Who Brings Us the News?

It is important to remember that the news media in this country are private businesses. This situation has both good and bad sides. The good side is that the media are independent of the government, thus making it very difficult for government officials to dictate exactly what gets printed or broadcast. The bad side is that the media, as businesses, have to do whatever it takes to make a profit, even if this affects which items make the headlines and which are left out entirely.

Aside from the sources of news, the media must therefore be careful not to overly offend two other powerful constituencies: their advertisers and their audiences. The threat of canceled advertising is difficult to ignore when that is the source of the great bulk of a business's revenues. (This is true of newspapers, which receive more money from advertisers than from those of us who purchase the papers, and of the electronic media as well.) The other constituency, the news-reading and news-watching public, has its own unfortunate effects on the quality of the news that is generally available. The most important of these is the oversimplification of the information presented. Too many people would be bored by a competent explanation of the federal budget deficit or the latest crisis in Central America to allow the media to offer such accounts often or in much detail without fearing the loss of their audiences. And, in this context at least, it is not important whether American audiences are unwilling to pay attention to complicated issues or whether they are simply unable

More Conflicting Claims

LEADER OF RIGHT IN FRANCE BACKS CHIRAC INDIRECTLY
—*Wall Street Journal,* May 2, 1988

CHIRAC GETS SNUB FROM FAR RIGHTIST
—*Boston Globe,* May 2, 1988

Perhaps there are no such things as bare, uninterpreted facts, and the editors of these two newspapers seem to differ in their interpretations of the same event. It is clear, we assume, that the wording of newspaper headlines can influence readers' opinions and attitudes as well as reflect those of the paper's editors. But, just in case you don't believe us, consider these two headlines, both from the same issue of the *Sacramento Bee,* the first headline appearing on page 1, the second on page D1:

FOUR LOCAL DISTRICTS SCORE BELOW STATE SAT AVERAGE

CITY STUDENTS IMPROVE SCORES IN MATH ON SAT

These two headlines don't actually conflict, but notice how different are the expectations they create. They illustrate quite nicely how readers' opinions can be affected by the way a newspaper words its headlines.

Is It Sensationalism or Just the Hard Truth?

Letter to the editor: Your recent story about the execution that took place in Georgia was appalling ("Two jolts required to execute Georgia murderer," Dec. 12). I question your motives in presenting such graphic and sensationalistic details—are you reporting the news or trying to sway public opinion? Among other things, you stated that "Stephens trembled as he was strapped into the chair at 12:15 A.M. He watched intently, biting his lip." Later you say, ". . . his head rolled slowly and his chest heaved up and down . . . the electricity was shut down, but he was still breathing."

You are poking your nose into politics when you print a story like this, especially in view of the fact that the death penalty is undergoing judicial review in this state. Why don't you save your persuasive tactics and just stick to the facts? You might try reporting some good news for a change, too.

—*North-State Record*

What do *you* think?

to understand them. (In other contexts, however, this distinction is highly significant. Between a third and a half of all American adults would probably be unable to read and understand the page you're now reading.) Whatever the reason, it is clear that complicated issues are lost on a large percentage of American adults.

Notice the level at which television commercials and political advertisements are pitched. These products are made by highly skilled professionals, who are aware that the projection of an "image" for a candidate or a product goes much further than the coverage of facts and issues. A television network that devotes too much of its prime time to complex social issues in a nonsensationalist way will soon be looking for a new vice-president for programming.

And Who's Paying Attention?

We come now to another problem with relying on the mass media for a real understanding of events. Much of what goes on in the world, including many of the most important events, is not only complicated, it is not very exciting. If a television station advertised that its late news would offer extended coverage of several South American countries' threats to default on loans from United States banks, a considerable part of its audience would either go to bed early or watch reruns on another channel. And they would do so even though loans to other countries are currently having an enormous impact upon the American economy. (How many Americans could explain the connection between Brazil's loan-payment schedule and the unusually high finance charges Americans pay on their bank-card accounts?) The threatened defaults are apt to get only fifteen seconds so as not to shortchange the story of the fire at a local laundry accompanied by some exciting film. The point is that sensational, unusual, and easily understood subjects can be counted on to receive more attention than the unexciting, the usual, and the complicated, even if the latter are much more important in the long run.

The same kind of mass preference holds for people as well as issues and events. The number of show business people interviewed on talk shows far outweighs the effects that entertainers have on most of our lives. But they are entertaining in ways that, say, the chairman of the Federal Reserve Board is not.

In making this point we are not implying that there is anything wrong with entertainment and our desire to be entertained. What is wrong is the overindulgence of our desire to be entertained at the expense of our need to be informed. As long as this is the case, we can count on the media to indulge us; their business is primarily to give us what we will pay for. Like individuals, the media are selective in the information they pass along.

EXERCISE 5-6

Watch two network television news programs on the same day. Compare the two on the basis of (a) the news stories covered, (b) the amount of air time given to two or three of the major stories, and (c) any difference in the slant of the presentations of a controversial story.

From your reading of the chapter, how would you account for the similarities between the two in both the selection and content of the stories?

Television News and Crime

Although crime rates leveled off in the 1970s and decreased dramatically in the early 1980's, public opinion polls indicate that most Americans believe the crime rate is rising. Part of the problem may be television news. According to one source, 10 percent of network news time and 20 percent of local news time is devoted to crime reporting. Further, most TV news crime reports concern violent crime, though only 10 percent of crimes actually are violent (George Bennet, *TV Guide*). Heavy TV viewers, according to the Figgie Report on Fear of Crime, are those most likely to believe that crime is on the increase.

Clearly, what television news programs choose to broadcast can determine what a large number of Americans believe about a subject. Without saying that the crime rate is high and rising, they can unintentionally create that impression simply by devoting substantial attention to crime stories. But then they probably have reason to think that TV audiences prefer crime stories over stories on other subjects. The result is a vicious circle.

EXERCISE 5-7

Listen carefully to a radio or television news broadcast, or read through the national news section of a newspaper, and try to identify as many news items as you can that were supplied by the subjects of the stories rather than found or "dug up" by reporters. Look for phrases that identify the source as a news release, a spokesperson, a representative, and so on.

EXERCISE 5-8

Choose a news story of national importance and compare the treatment it gets in a national television news broadcast with the one it gets in a national newspaper (e.g., the *New York Times*). Consider the thoroughness of explanation, the amount of information given, and the expression of any alternative opinions.

Advertising

Advertising is used to sell many more products than merely toasters, television sets, and toilet tissue. Ads can encourage us to vote for a candidate, agree with a political proposal, take a tour, give up a bad habit, or join the army. They can also be used to make announcements—for instance, about job openings, lectures, concerts, or the recall of defective automobiles—and some ads are designed to create favorable climates of opinion—for example, toward labor unions or offshore oil drilling.

Advertising firms understand our fears and desires at least as well as we understand them ourselves, and they have at their disposal the expertise to exploit them. Such firms employ trained psychologists and some of the world's most creative artists, and they use the most sophisticated and well-researched theories about the motivation of human behavior. Maybe most important, they can afford to spend whatever is necessary to get each detail of an advertisement exactly right. (On a per-minute basis, television ads are the most expensively

Ads and Art

It is far easier to write ten passably effective sonnets, good enough to take in the not too inquiring critic, than one effective advertisement that will take in a few thousand of the uncritical buying public.

—ALDOUS HUXLEY, *On the Margin*

produced pieces that appear on your tube.) A good ad is a work of art, a masterful blend of word and image often composed in accordance with the exacting standards of artistic and scientific genius (and some ads, of course, are just plain silly). Can untrained lay people even hope to evaluate such psychological and artistic masterpieces intelligently?

Fortunately, it is not necessary to understand the deep psychology of an advertisement to evaluate it in the way that's most important to us. When confronted with an ad, we should ask simply: Does this ad give us a good reason to buy this product? And the answer, in general terms, can be simply put: Since the only good reason to buy anything in the first place is to improve our lives, the ad justifies a purchase only if it establishes that we'd be better off with the product than without it (or that we'd be better off with the product than with the money we would trade for it).

However, do we always know when we'll be better off with a product than without it? Do we really want, or need, a kerosene heater or a computer? Would we even recognize "better taste" in a cigarette? Advertisers spend vast sums creating within us new desires and fears—and hence a need to improve our lives by satisfying those desires or eliminating those fears through the purchase of advertised products. They are often successful, and we find ourselves needing something we might not have known existed before. That others can instill in us through word and image a desire for something we did not previously desire may be a lamentable fact, but it *is* clearly a fact.

Still, *we* decide what would make us better off, and *we* decide to part with our money. So it is only with reference to what in *our* view would make life better for us that we properly evaluate advertisements.

There are basically two kinds of ads: those that offer reasons and those that do not. Those that offer reasons for buying the advertised product almost always promise that certain hopes will be satisfied, certain needs met, or certain fears eliminated. (You'll be more accepted, have a better image, be a better parent, etc.)

Those ads that do not rely on reasons fall mainly into three categories: (1) those that bring out pleasurable *feelings* in us (e.g., through humor, glad tidings, pretty images, beautiful music, heartwarming scenes, etc.); (2) those that depict the product being used or endorsed by *people* we admire or think of ourselves as being like (sometimes these people are depicted by actors, sometimes not); and (3) those that depict the product being used in *situations* in which we would like to find ourselves. Of course, some ads go all out and incorporate elements from all three categories, and for good measure state a reason or two why we should buy the advertised item as well.

Buying a product (which includes joining a group, deciding how to vote, etc.) on the basis of reasonless ads is, with one minor exception that we'll explain shortly, never justified. Such ads tell you only that the product exists and what it looks like (and sometimes where it is available and how much it costs); if it tells you much more than this, then it begins to qualify as an ad that gives reasons for buying the product. Such ads do tell us what the adver-

Not All Ads Are for Beer, Cars, or Candidates

A recent antismoking message depicted a simulated fetus (actually a plastic puppet) puffing on a cigarette. ABC has said it considers the public service spot important and plans to broadcast it. Both NBC and CBS, however, have decided it is too graphic. The thirty-second spot from the American Cancer Society, which cost $25,000 to produce, has the narrator asking "Would you give a cigarette to your unborn child? . . . You do, every time you smoke when you're pregnant." At that point, the fetus brings the cigarette to its mouth, inhales, and blows out a puff of smoke.

—FRED ROTHENBERG, *Sacramento Bee*

Like some ads for beer, cars, or candidates, some public service announcements have trouble avoiding television censors.

tisers think of our values and sense of humor (not always a pleasant thing to notice, given that they have us pegged so well), but this information is irrelevant to the question of whether we should buy the product.

Ads that submit reasons for buying the product might have been treated in Part Two of this book, which is devoted to arguments. However, so little need be said about argumentative ads that we will discuss them here. Such "promise ads," as they have been called, usually tell us more than that a certain product exists—but not much more. The promise, with rare exception, comes with no guarantees, and it is usually extremely vague (Gilbey's gin promises "more gin taste," Kleenex is "softer").

Such ads are a source of information about what *the sellers of the product* are willing to claim about what the product will do, how well it will do it, how it works, what it contains, how well it compares with similar products, and how much more wonderful your life will be once you've got one. However, to make an informed decision on a purchase you almost always need to know more than the seller is willing to claim, particularly since no sellers will tell you what's wrong with their products or what's right with those of their competitors.

The Price of Pain . . .

Tylenol advertisements claim that more of its product is dispensed by hospitals than the next four most popular brands of pain medicine combined. What the ads don't tell you is that Tylenol drastically cuts its prices to hospitals and the other brands don't. Do you suppose it might be the price that hospitals find attractive rather than the product?

Further, the claims advertisers make are notorious not only for being vague, but also for being ambiguous, misleading, exaggerated, and sometimes just plain false. Even if a product existed that was so good that an honest, unexaggerated, and fair description of it would justify our buying it without considering competing items (or other reports on the same item), and even if an advertisement for this product consisted of just such a description, we would still not be justified in purchasing the product on the basis of that advertisement alone. For we would be unable to tell, simply by looking at the advertisement, that it was uninflated, honest, fair, and not misleading. Our suspicions about advertising in general should undercut our willingness to believe in the honesty of any particular advertisement.

Thus, even advertisements that present reasons for buying an item do not by themselves justify our purchase of the item. Sometimes, of course, an advertisement can provide you with information that can clinch your decision to make a purchase. Sometimes the mere existence, availability, or affordability of a product—all information that an ad can convey—is all you need to make a decision to buy. But if the purchase is justifiable, you must have some reasons apart from those offered in the ad for making it. If, for some reason, you already know that you want or need and can afford a particular kind of car with a rotary engine, then an ad that informs you that a firm has begun making such a thing would supply you with the information you needed to buy one. If you can already justify purchasing a particular brand of microwave oven but cannot find one anywhere in town, then an advertisement informing you that the local department store stocks them can clinch your decision to make the purchase.

For people on whom good fortune has smiled, those who don't care what kind of whatsit they buy, or those to whom mistaken purchases simply don't matter, all that is important is knowing that a product is available. Most of us, however, need more information than ads provide to make reasoned purchasing decisions. Of course, we all occasionally make purchases solely on the basis of advertisements, and sometimes we don't come to regret them. In such cases, though, the happy result is due as much to good luck as to the ad.

Won't Burn or Smoke

boldly announces Parkay Cookery margarine on its label, "when used as recommended," it adds in smaller letters. But if you're impressed with this advance in cooking chemistry, don't read Parkay's recommendation for usage (on the back label): "Reduce heat if margarine begins to smoke."

The Amazing Turnaround

In the span of three months before the 1988 presidential election George Bush went from around 17 points down in public opinion polls, relative to his opponent Michael Dukakis, to almost the same amount on the plus side. In the eyes of many Americans, Bush changed from an inept and unappealing wimp to a strong leader and nice guy, while Dukakis went from an efficient manager to a tax-and-spend, soft-on-crime, weak-on-defense, out-of-the-mainstream "liberal."

This turnaround was arguably in part the result of effective techniques of nonargumentative persuasion by Bush campaign directors, who used a two-pronged approach. First, Bush was made likeable by admitting and laughing at his own image problem. Second, Dukakis was hit with television ads that, although very simple, left viewers with indelible images: Massachusetts prisoners going through a revolving door; garbage floating in Boston harbor; tax bills streaming through a mail slot; and Dukakis peeping out of a tank, looking like a little gnome no one could take seriously.

Some argument accompanied these ads, but the images, we suspect, are what helped the Bush cause. And we think the Bush people would agree.

More Quayle-Bashing

One of the most blatant examples of non-argumentative Quayle-bashing during the 1988 presidential campaign (see the box on page 127 for another) was in a Michael Dukakis political ad. One thirty-second spot simply displayed a vacant chair at the president's desk while an announcer said:

"One in five American vice presidents has had to take on the responsibilities of the most powerful office in the world. For this job, after five months of reflection, George Bush made his personal choice: J. Danforth Quayle. Hopefully, we will never know how great a lapse of judgment that really was."

The ad *did* argue for voting against Bush. But the argument's *premise* (that Quayle was unqualified) was only insinuated, and not itself argued for.

EXERCISE 5-9

Find five advertisements that give no reasons for purchasing the products. Explain how each ad attempts to make the product seem attractive.

EXERCISE 5-10

Find five advertisements that give reasons for purchasing the products. Which of the reasons are promises to the purchaser? Exactly what is being promised? What is the likelihood that the product will fulfill that promise?

Recap

Speakers and writers sometimes win acceptance for a claim or influence a person's attitude or behavior without presenting reasons. We call this nonargumentative persuasion. A primary means of such persuasion is the use of slanters—words and phrases that suggest favorable or unfavorable images and associations. Persuasive definitions, explanations, and comparisons are slanters, as are euphemisms, innuendo, loaded questions, weaslers, downplayers, proof surrogates, stereotypes, and hyperbole. Such devices are often used deliberately, but subtle uses can creep into people's speech or writing even when they think they are being objective. Some such phrases, especially euphemisms and words that can be used to weasel, have both valuable, nonprejudicial uses and slanting ones. Only by speaking, writing, listening, and reading carefully can we use and distinguish between prejudicial and nonprejudicial uses of these devices.

Our beliefs, attitudes, and behavior depend heavily upon what information we receive. A primary source of such information is the news media. Despite even the best efforts of people in the news business, we cannot be sure that the stories presented are complete and unbiased. We must listen critically even to the evening news.

Advertising assaults us at every turn with nonargumentative persuasion, attempting to sell us goods, services, beliefs, and attitudes. Substantial talent and resources are employed in this effort, making it necessary for us to constantly ask ourselves whether the products in question will really make the differences in our lives that their advertising claims or hints they will make.

Additional Exercises

EXERCISE 5-11

Identify any slanting devices used in these passages and explain their purposes. State the claim you think the author is trying to persuade you to accept by use of the slanter.

★1. "How can the major media be so wrong so often? The answer is obvious: They are profoundly out of sympathy with the ideals and goals of the American people. Of course, there are sound and honest journalists in all parts of the country. But the elite media—and you know who they are—are overwhelmingly produced by men and women who, if they do not hate America first, certainly have a smug contempt for American ideals and principles."

—Senator JESSE HELMS, quoted by James Kilpatrick,
"A Conservative View"

2. "New York's Daniel Patrick Moynihan, the Senate's most gifted huffer and puffer, does not agree. 'There is a word for ideological tests of the judiciary,' he says. 'That word is corruption.' Well, there also is a word for Moynihan's posturing. The word is baloney."

—JAMES J. KILPATRICK, "A Conservative View"

3. "The race is on to beef up the public schools' sex education curricula, the better to prevent AIDS, my dear . . .

"Well, we face a 'crisis,' don't we? Yes—a crisis unheard of in the days when our benighted Puritan ancestors had to struggle through life without singles bars. We now have AIDS, abortion and acrimony . . .

"Liberals think the AIDS 'crisis' is serious enough to justify violating traditional proprieties to the extent of teaching 10-year-olds how to use condoms, but not serious enough to warrant abandoning their own inhibitions against teaching traditional morals in public schools. Some things are still sacred—including the liberal version of the First Amendment."

—JOSEPH SOBRAN

4. "The vast majority of Americans no doubt conceive of 'political repression' as something which only occurs in foreign lands. . . . As one would expect, the built-in ideological bias of the major media results in the quick exploitation of alleged human rights abuses in communist societies, particularly the Soviet Union. Repression in friendly sub-fascist dictatorships within America's Free World empire receives considerably less media attention, sometimes being ignored altogether. Nevertheless, this right-wing terror used to preserve economic and political stability is so blatantly excessive that even our ostrich-like mainstream newspeople must on occasion recognize its existence."

—SCOTT SUNESON, *Third World Forum*

★5. "Somalia is one of those countries noticed by the U.S. press only when it seems possible that imperial interest might be affected. . . . The usual pattern is that an itinerant U.S. journalist (a) visits the country, (b) confers with the local U.S. ambassador or C.I.A. head or station, (c) files a dispatch that either (d) muses on 'Timeless Rhythms of Peasant Life Unchanged' or (e) alerts the American people of trouble.

"Just such was Sheila Rule's report from Somalia in the *New York Times* for July 20 . . ."

—*The Nation*

EXERCISE 5-12

"By the time this election is over, Willie Horton will be a household name," said Republican campaign strategist Lee Atwater.

"The only question is whether we depict Willie Horton with a knife in his hand or without," said Roger Ailes, the chief Republican media consultant.

These two remarks were made about a television advertisement run by the Republicans during the 1988 presidential election that was generally agreed by many experts to be the single most powerful piece of political advertising anyone had produced in years. The advertisement showed a photo of Willie Horton, a convicted felon who murdered a woman while out on a furlough program from a Massachusetts prison. The point of the ad was to associate the governor of Massachusetts, Michael Dukakis, with being "soft" on dangerous criminals.

Discuss this advertisement with your class, identifying any element of nonargumentative persuasion you find. (If a videotape of the ad is available it can be helpful to view it with other members of the class.)

In particular, what is it that made *this* ad more powerful than other political advertisements? How much of the difference was due to the information conveyed and how much to the *way* it was conveyed?

EXERCISE 5-13

Discuss this question in class or in a group.

One of the most controversial films of recent years was *The Silent Scream*, a twenty-eight-minute documentary that shows ultrasound images of a twelve-week-old fetus being aborted. In the film, the fetus reportedly appears to shrink from the probes of the abortionist's suction tube and to open its mouth in a "chilling silent scream," according to the narration, which also describes the "child being torn apart . . . by the unfeeling steel instruments of the abortionist."

Does this film qualify as nonargumentative persuasion?

EXERCISE 5-14

The following is a list of poll questions that, according to the *Conservative Digest,* have a proliberal bias. If there is a slant to the questions, you would expect to find slanters of some sort used in them. Examine the questions, decide whether they are slanted, and, if they are, identify the type of slanting device used. Can *you* state the questions neutrally?

1. "When a badly deformed baby, who could live only a few years, was born at a Midwest hospital, the parents asked the doctors not to keep the baby alive. Would you take the same position as the parents did or not?"

   —Gallup Poll

2. "In your opinion, which of the following increased the chances of nuclear war more—a continuation of the nuclear arms buildup here and in the Soviet Union, or the U.S. falling behind the Soviet Union in nuclear weaponry?"

   —Gallup Poll

3. "As you may know, the United States through the CIA is supporting rebels in Nicaragua. Would you say you approve or disapprove of the United States being involved in trying to overthrow the government?"

—*ABC/Washington Post*

4. "Do you think [former President] Reagan cares or doesn't care if his program results in hardship for many blacks?"

—*ABC/Washington Post*

5. The final item is somewhat longer. According to the *Conservative Digest*, Lou Harris ran a poll in April 1984 on the question of whether then presidential counselor Ed Meese should be confirmed as attorney general. Those polled were furnished with the following statement and asked to register whether they agreed or disagreed with it. Read the statement and identify whatever slanting devices, if any, you find there.

"Since federal law says that high officials must report all loans they receive, it looks as though Meese violated the law by not reporting a fifteen thousand dollar loan from a couple who were close friends, both of whom later got federal jobs paying a combined total of close to one hundred thousand dollars a year.

By taking personal loans from people who later received appointments to jobs in the Reagan Administration, it sounds as though Meese was just selling jobs for his own personal gain."

EXERCISE 5-15 (ESSAY)

Write an essay in which you address the issue of whether advertising is a useful tool for making consumer decisions. Include at least a short discussion of advertising and the costs of products.

6 Pseudoreasoning I

*It is not right to pervert the judge by moving him to anger or pity—
one might as well warp a carpenter's rule before using it.*

—ARISTOTLE

Since Chapter 1 we've been concentrating primarily on claims that stand alone, claims that we encounter or make ourselves without any accompanying support. In Part Two we'll turn our attention to several varieties of arguments, focusing on the evaluation of reasoning from one or more supporting claims (premises) to another claim (the conclusion). The subject of this chapter and the next is a kind of middle ground—a large and varied catalog of emotional appeals, factual irrelevancies, and persuasive devices that sometimes move people to accept or reject claims when they have no good grounds for doing so. In some such cases, people accept or reject claims because of misplaced or misdirected feelings; in others, they do so because they are presented with (or they invent themselves) something that at least approximates an argument (although a bad one). We'll sort out and provide labels for many of these ways of going wrong as we proceed through these two chapters. In the meantime let's lump them into one general class and call them all **pseudoreasoning.**

Our notion of pseudoreasoning includes many of what are known as "fallacies." (A fallacy is any bad argument, one in which the reasons advanced for a claim fail to warrant its acceptance.) But it also includes such things as plain old wishful thinking, which almost never occurs as anything resembling an argument but which can nevertheless be a powerful motivating force.

In most types of pseudoreasoning, including all those covered in this chapter, the inducement that erroneously leads one to accept or reject a claim is in fact irrelevant to the truth of the claim. We'll refer to such inducements as **pseudoreasons.** Here's an example:

DANIEL: What do you think of nuclear power, Theresa? Do you think we ought to have more nuclear power plants?

THERESA: Well . . .

DANIEL: Well, we should develop nuclear power, and I'll tell you why. I'm sick and tired of these antinuclear environmentalists, always complaining about something or other. What a bunch of troublemakers. They find something wrong with everything.

THERESA: I hate to tell you, Daniel, but you haven't said anything about nuclear power plants.

Theresa is exactly right, of course. Daniel hasn't said anything relevant to the issue of whether nuclear power should be more widely developed. This sort of irrelevance is typical of most pseudoreasoning. What Daniel is doing is putting up a *smokescreen;* he's bringing in another topic—one that many people may think of when they consider the nuclear power issue, but one that is in fact a wholly separate matter. This irrelevant topic, the "antinuclear environmentalists," diverts our attention from the original issue. The latter can then get lost in the fog generated by the irrelevant topic, and hence the label *smokescreen.* (*Red herring* is another name for an irrelevant consideration brought into a discussion.) As you will probably notice, several of the types of pseudoreasoning described below can occur as smokescreens; in fact, they are frequently introduced intentionally to distract us from the original issue.

Here is an example from Senator Peckingham, who is dining with some fellow Democrats:

You know, there really is some merit in that "Star Wars" proposal that the administration is sponsoring. If we Democrats are going to survive as a party we've got to demonstrate we're as tough-minded about defense as the Republicans, since that's what the public wants.

Anyone who thinks Peckingham has given a reason for believing the Star Wars proposal has merit is sadly mistaken, of course. When he says Democrats need to get tough-minded about defense, he may be saying something true, but it is irrelevant to Star Wars' merits. Notice that a pseudoreason may actually give support to *some* claim, just not the one it is alleged to support. Peckingham's remark may well help support the claim that Democrats should develop a tougher defense policy, but it doesn't support claims about the merits of any particular proposal.

It would be difficult, and probably impossible, to list all the kinds of pseudoreasoning that people engage in. Still, some varieties are more common than others, and we'll describe several of these types below and in Chapter 7. Remember two things as you go along: First, something does not have to fall

Watt Was That Again . . . ?

Former Interior Secretary James Watt says he thinks Cuba's purported use of isolation camps for AIDS victims is a good idea, but he says the United States lacks the courage to do the same. Watt, who served under Reagan from 1980–83, spoke Thursday at Weber State College in Ogden, Utah. When asked whether such tactics would violate human rights, Watt responded, "Do you want an AIDS victim to sneeze on your salad when he's serving you at a local restaurant?" Experts say that acquired immune deficiency syndrome cannot be spread through casual contact. Watt said it was his statement describing his staff as "a black, a white, two Jews and a cripple" that forced him to quit his cabinet job. Watt said he now agrees it was an "insensitive statement," but feels the only offensive part was the word "cripple." "The new word is handicapable," he said. "I'm from Wyoming and didn't know that."

—*Sacramento Bee*, February 1988

Notice that, as far as the question about human rights is concerned, the former secretary's answer is a red herring—or, if you prefer, a smokescreen.

into one of our categories to be pseudoreasoning. As mentioned, we cannot hope to catalog every type, and listing too many categories leads to confusion. Besides, getting a piece of pseudoreasoning neatly classified is not as important as seeing that it *is* pseudoreasoning.

The second thing to remember is that not everything that *looks* like pseudoreasoning *is* pseudoreasoning. Many cases that resemble a category of pseudoreasoning are actually legitimate cases of reasoning. Don't get tunnel vision and think that everything that reminds you of a pseudoreasoning category automatically falls into that category. We'll warn you about this from time to time as we proceed.

The Subjectivist Fallacy

How many times have you heard someone say "Well, that may be true for you, but it isn't true for me" when they've been confronted with a claim that they don't want to accept? In almost every case, to make such a remark is not to present a reason for rejecting the claim; it is to commit the **subjectivist fallacy**. All one accomplishes by saying "true for you but not for me" is to say that maybe you accept the claim but I don't. That's quite a bit different, of course, from the claim's actually being true for someone else and its being false for you. Claims don't work that way, by and large: If they're true, they're true, period. What would it mean for the claim "The door is open" to be true for one person and false for another? It doesn't make any difference to the door whether anybody believes that it's open; the door is simply where it is, and it's either open or it's not.

Claims may be true *about* one person and false *about* another, which we can see in this example:

> THERESA: Look here, Daniel. I read, and I really believe, that people who don't sleep at least six hours each night tend to feel unhealthy.
>
> DANIEL: That may be true for you, Theresa, but it certainly isn't true for me.

Here Daniel makes the perfectly reasonable remark that, although Theresa may need six hours of sleep each night, he doesn't. He is not offering a reason for believing anything. Nor, in all likelihood, does he even think that he is. He is simply observing that he doesn't need at least six hours of sleep. But, in most cases, a person who says "true for you but not for me" is trying to insist that it's acceptable for you to believe the claim and equally acceptable for him or her to reject it. All they've managed to do, however, is to say that they disagree with you; they haven't given a reason for anything at all.

The view that underlies the subjectivist fallacy is sometimes called *relativism,* and it seems to be a common view among many students. In a nutshell, it is the position that truth is relative. Now, lots of things are relative among individuals (fear of going to the dentist, for example), and among cultures (e.g., the acceptability of going about without clothes). Some people argue that the truth of moral claims like "Murder is wrong" is relative. (This is a controversial point, and there are sophisticated arguments on both sides.) But most claims, given reasonable freedom from vagueness and ambiguity, are simply true or false independently of any particular person's acceptance of them.

Another version of the subjectivist fallacy is the "Just his (or her) opinion" syndrome. Opinions may differ, of course, and some of them may be wrong. But the fact that a claim is part of someone's opinion is hardly a reason for rejecting it. We can make a *reasonable* use of a remark like "That's just John's opinion" if we mean either (a) nobody holds this view except John, or (b) there is no reason to believe that John's claim is true. Notice, though, that neither of these is a reason for believing that his claim is *false.*

We suspect that people often make use of one or the other version of the subjectivist fallacy not because they somehow really deny the objectivity of truth, but because they simply want to put an end to rational discussion—they use the fallacy as a conversation stopper. In general, it would be better simply to admit that one doesn't wish to discuss a subject than to dress one's wish up in the subjectivist fallacy.

The Objectivity of Truth

Philosophers may differ as to the definition of "truth," but at any rate it is something objective, something which, in some sense, everybody ought to accept.

—BERTRAND RUSSELL

Appeal to Belief

Be ever alert to the possibility of pseudoreasoning when someone tries to establish a claim by citing common belief, like this:

X is true because everyone [lots of people, most societies, others, I, etc.] think that X is true.

Examples:

Free will? Of course people have free will. Everyone believes that. It hardly seems possible *not* to believe it.

A job in management is surely better than a job as, say, a bus driver. Just ask anybody. They'll tell you that it's better to get an education and go into management.

The fact that nearly everybody believes in free will—or even, were it true, that everybody without exception believes in it—does not assure us that there is any such thing. This pseudoreason is no more to the point than the argument in medieval times that, since everyone believed that the earth was the center of the universe, it had to be true.

Most people seem to assume that bus driving and similar jobs are somehow less desirable than white-collar jobs. The widespread acceptance of this assumption creates its own momentum—that is, we tend to accept it because everybody else does, and we don't stop to think about whether it actually has anything to recommend it. For a lot of people, a job driving a bus might make for a much happier life than a job as a manager.

In some instances, we should point out, what people think actually determines what is true. The meanings of most words, for example, are determined

A Principle Worth Remembering

Trying to prove a proposition by citing what everyone believes amounts to confessing that one has no proof.

—Philosopher's maxim

This principle was perhaps first articulated by John Stuart Mill, in connection with those who would try to establish the doctrine of immortality by an appeal to belief. (Be sure to note the qualifications to the principle discussed in the text.)

by popular usage. In addition, it would not be pseudoreasoning to conclude that the word *ain't* is out of place in polite speech because most speakers of English believe that it is out of place in polite speech.

There are other cases where what people think is an *indication* of what is true, even if it cannot *determine* truth. If several Bostonians of your acquaintance think that it is illegal to drink beer in their public parks, then you have some reason for thinking that it's true. And, if you are told by several Europeans that it is not gauche to eat with your fork in your left hand in Europe, then it is not pseudoreasoning to conclude that European manners allow eating with your fork in your left hand. The situation here is one of credibility, as was discussed in Chapter 3. Natives of Boston in the first case and Europeans in the second case can be expected to know more about the two claims in question, respectively, than others. In a kind of watered-down sense, they are "experts" on the subjects, at least in ways that many of us are not. In general, when the "everyone" who thinks that X is true are or include experts about X, then what they think is indeed a good reason to accept X.

Thus it would be incorrect to automatically label as pseudoreasoning any instance in which a person cites people's beliefs in order to establish a point. (No "argument" fitting a pattern in this chapter should *unthinkingly* be dismissed.) But it is important to view such references to people's beliefs as red alerts. These are cautionary signals that warn you to look closely for genuine reasons for the claim asserted.

Before we leave pseudoarguments that attempt to prove a point by referring to people's beliefs, it is worth noticing that a common pseudoreasoning technique is to induce others to accept a claim by "reporting" that people with whom they identify accept the claim. Assertions such as "RV drivers are concerned that X," "Conservatives believe Y," or "Educators think that Z" are simply remarks about what some people think. But if you happen to be an RV driver, a conservative, or an educator, you might find it easy to believe, when you read such a report, that X, Y, or Z is *true*. Thus writers for special-interest publications who are unable or too lazy to offer their readers *reasons* why they should accept X, Y, or Z will sometimes simply suggest that such claims are among those the reader's group accepts. It is sometimes easier to get a reader to accept a claim by means of this pseudoreasoning technique than by means of genuine argument. For example,

> Sarah is deeply concerned about environmental issues. When reading the latest copy of a conservationist magazine, she notices a letter to the editor about water in the Springfield area being treated with chlorine. She reads, "Environmentalists are concerned that the chlorination of drinking water in Springfield is a health hazard." She finds herself concerned that the water of yet another American city is health threatening.

Now, it may be true that some environmentalists are concerned that the chlorination of drinking water in Springfield poses a threat to health. And if these environmentalists are reputable (anyone can call him- or herself an environmentalist, remember), then there is a reason for Sarah to be concerned by what they say. So, before Sarah concludes that Springfield drinking water is dangerous, either she should take steps to ensure that at least some reputable environmentalists do indeed deem the water dangerous, or she should consider for herself the evidence for saying that it is. Otherwise she runs the risk of accepting some unknown person's belief on faith, without having any reason to accept that belief.

Still, we should not automatically conclude that anyone who says "Ys believe X" is trying to sucker us into believing without giving us reasons. One can report what Ys believe solely to inform readers of the fact. And, as noted in Sarah's case, in some instances the fact that Ys believe something is an excellent reason for everyone to believe it. But we should avoid concluding mechanically that a claim must be true just because someone says that people we identify with think it is true.

Appeal to the Consequences of Belief

Sometimes we try to "prove" a claim by making an **appeal to the consequences of belief** or disbelief in it. We say or think, in effect, something like this:

> *X is true [or acceptable, reasonable, creditable, okay, etc.] because, if we didn't believe that X were true, then there would be unpleasant consequences.*

Examples:

> God must exist, since if everyone believed there was no God, then we'd have no reason to treat anyone with kindness or respect. The world would be in utter chaos.

> I don't think there will ever be a nuclear war. If I believed that, I wouldn't be able to get up in the morning. I mean, how depressing!

The consequences of our beliefs about God and nuclear war are irrelevant to the questions at issue (whether God exists; whether there will be a nuclear war). However, consider the following passage, which, *although a genuine argument*, is very similar to the pseudoarguments found in the previous two examples:

> It's true that we should treat others justly, since if most people didn't believe this, life would be intolerable.

This is not really a case of pseudoreasoning. The fact that life would be intolerable if we didn't believe that we should treat others justly is a reason for *believing* that we should treat others justly, and a reason for *believing* that we should treat others justly is a reason for *treating* others justly.

However, the claim "we should treat others justly" is not a statement of fact as is "there will be a nuclear war" or "God exists." A statement such as "we should treat others justly" is a prescriptive statement, a statement about what we should do (see Chapter 12). And many claims about what we should do, according to some philosophers, *are* to be accepted or rejected on the basis of the consequences of our believing or disbelieving in their truth.

Thus, citing the consequences of our believing in a claim, X, is a case of pseudoreasoning only when X is not a statement about what should be done.

Closely related to the appeal to the consequences of belief is what might be called wishful thinking—believing that something is true because you want it to be true (or believing that it is false because you don't want it to be true). Some people, for example, so fervently hope there is an afterlife that they convince themselves there is. Or, in another example, a smoker might discount reports on smoking's ill effects precisely because they are so unpleasant to contemplate. Such thinking is related to the appeal to the consequences of belief, in that, in the first example, believing in life everlasting is comforting—that is, it produces comfort as its consequence. Likewise, believing the reports on smoking may have as its consequence, at least in the short run, much discomfort.

Regardless of what it is called or what it is related to, it is pseudoreasoning to think, in effect,

> *I wish fervently that X were true; therefore X is true.*

Such thinking underlies many empty philosophies of "positive thinking"—those that claim that "you are what you want to be." To believe in your dreams—that is, to believe they will come true for no better reason than that you hope they will—may be to solace the soul, but it is not to think critically.

Wishful Thinking from an Unexpected Source

Martin Gardner, the author of numerous books on science and mathematics who is famous for his hard-bitten criticism of the claims of psychics, parapsychologists, and other believers in the supernatural, defends his own belief in God in *The Whys of a Philosophical Scrivener:*

I am quite content to confess with Unamuno that I have no basis whatever for my belief in God other than a passionate longing that God exists and that I and others will not cease to exist.

This seems to be pseudoreasoning. One's longing for something's being true is no basis for believing that it is true. Gardner's wish that God exist is irrelevant to the question of whether He does exist.

Scare Tactics

Dear Professor Smith:

I'd like to make an appointment to see you tomorrow about my final grade. I think it was unfair and I should have gotten a better one. My telephone number is below, so please call me.

By the way, I believe you know my aunt. She's your dean.

Sincerely yours,
Mabel McThreat

In this example the student provides no reason for believing that she was misgraded, but she does manage to threaten Professor Smith with retaliation via her aunt, the dean. She's hoping to induce fear in her professor in order to get him to revise her grade.

The underlying structure of these examples, and of all pseudoreasoning based on psychological inducements, is the same. Something is said in connection with a claim that elicits or is intended to elicit a psychological response of some sort—a desire, a fear, some feeling or emotion—that may well induce acceptance of the claim. But neither what is said nor the psychological response elicited is a reason for accepting the claim, because neither is logically related to the claim. To accept a claim on the basis of such irrelevant psychological inducements is to fall victim to pseudoreasoning.

Mabel McThreat's attempt to induce fear in Professor Smith in the hope of getting her grade revised is a straightforward example of scare tactics. She says, in effect,

X is so because of Y [where Y is a fact that, it is hoped, induces fear in Professor Smith].

Here is a somewhat more subtle example:

You've been shopping for a house. You find one that comes close to suiting your needs, but the kitchen is much too small and the house needs more repairs than you would care to contend with. So you conclude that you really don't want this house. When you explain your concerns to the realtor, he observes that the seller already has four offers that he is considering and will probably sell very soon. This moves you to make an offer on the house after all. "The kitchen isn't that small," you think. "And there aren't really that many things that need repairing."

The realtor in this example is using a form of scare tactic to get you to make an offer. Let's identify the issues to which his assertion is relevant.

Legitimate Scare Tactics?

Your chances of surviving an accident are lowered by half if you're not wearing a seat belt!

—Public service announcement (radio)

So-called public service announcements frighten us with statistics about smoking, not using seat belts, drunk driving, and so forth. Are these service announcements mere scare tactics? Well, yes, they drive home their point with facts that are alarming to most people. But, no, as long as the facts are relevant to one's health and well-being, the ads are not instances of pseudoreasoning. It is not pseudoreasoning to try to avoid something you fear, and it is not irrational to fear a misfortune that you have been given reason to believe might happen. You can question the factual statements in such announcements with respect to clarity, credibility, and considerations treated later in this book, but the statements and the fears they elicit are, ordinarily at least, *relevant* to the course of action recommended in the ad. That's why, whatever else one might say of such ads, they don't count as pseudoreasoning.

Incidentally, some public service announcements rely on graphic photographs, rather than facts, to alarm viewers. Such announcements count less as pseudoreasoning than as *nonargumentative persuasion*, treated in Chapter 5.

What you have learned is that the value of the house as determined by what others might pay for it may be greater than you had previously believed. This new information is indeed a reason for considering whether to try to live with the defects you have identified in the house. It isn't a very good reason, of course, for you have no information on the amount that has been offered, if indeed anything has been offered (mentioning "other offers" is a common sales gimmick). Still, it is a reason for considering whether to try to live with the defects of the house. *But the new information is not a reason, not even a bad one, for changing your mind about the size of the kitchen or the need for repairs.* To avoid pseudoreasoning, it is important to recognize to which issues your feelings are relevant and to which they are not. Fear of the house being sold to someone else is not a reason for thinking that the kitchen is acceptably large or that the repairs are less serious than you first believed. Learning that the house *may* be more valuable than you thought is a reason for reconsidering whether you wish to put up with the problems of the house.

Appeal to Pity

Helen is running for a seat on the city council. Though you like her, you have doubts about her qualifications and in fact believe that an opposing candidate would make a better member of the council. When you communicate your concerns about her qualifications to a mutual friend, the friend counters by saying that Helen would be terribly hurt if she were to lose the election. After thinking this over, you conclude that maybe Helen's qualifications are not so bad after all.

The mutual friend has evoked compassion in you for Helen, but she has not given you a reason for changing your opinion of Helen's qualifications. Clearly the issue—whether her qualifications are sufficient—is unaffected by the fact that her feelings will be hurt if she loses the election.

Notice that even if the mutual friend had told you Helen would be terribly hurt to learn what you think of her credentials, she would still have failed to give you a reason for changing your evaluation of them, though she would have given you a reason for not sharing your opinion with Helen.

Does your compassion for Helen enter the picture at all? Certainly, but only in this way: You now have to weigh Helen's hurt at losing the election

Pseudoreasoning or Plain Pity?

Saying he is losing sleep over a $100,000 Proposition 36 campaign debt, tax crusader Howard Jarvis once again resorted to the mails to ask his supporters for money.

"The defeat of our Proposition 36 brings several words to mind . . . none of them printable," Jarvis said in a computerized mailing to the 315,000 people who have responded to his appeals in the past.

"Not only did we lose, we also ran up a substantial campaign debt," Jarvis wrote. "I authorized this debt when the polls were dead even near Election Day. It was too late to contact you."

Jarvis asks for contributions of "at least $15," saying: "I'm 82, with very modest assets and one small home. It isn't possible for me to shoulder this debt alone."

Proposition 36 would have invalidated court decisions that Jarvis claims have nullified important parts of Proposition 13, his famed 1978 property tax-cutting measure. Critics said Proposition 36 would have cost state and local government many millions in refunds to property owners.

"We owed around $300,000 after the campaign was over," Jarvis said in an interview. "It's now down to around $100,000. . . ."

—Associated Press

This is not a case of pseudoreasoning. Jarvis is indeed trying to capitalize on the compassion one might feel for an eighty-two-year-old man "with very modest assets" who needs money enough to lose sleep over it. But he *is*, after all, giving a reason for his past supporters to send money, though one might not think much of the reason. If Jarvis had tried to parlay his readers' sympathy for his circumstances into support for Proposition 36, or any other such measure, *that* would have been pseudoreasoning.

against the consequences of having her as a council member instead of the better-qualified candidate. Which, you have to decide, is more important?

Let's look at another example:

> ROOFER: I'm positive that my work will meet your requirements. I really need the money, what with my wife being sick and all.

The roofer seems to be giving a reason for thinking that his work will meet your requirements. But of course he is not: That issue is unaffected by the fact that he really needs the money. This fact is not a reason, not even a bad reason, for concluding anything at all about the quality of his work.

Notice, though, that actions performed out of concern for others are often rationally and ethically justified. Indeed, in some instances they count as among the noblest of human deeds. If the roofer is qualified and needs the money for his wife's illness, and you are willing to take a chance on his work, then by all means hire him! Just don't think that he has given you a reason for thinking that his work will meet your specifications; whether it will or not is something you must establish on other grounds.

Peer Pressure (The Bandwagon)

You're trying to decide whether you're a good enough skier to tackle the South Face. You're pretty sure that you are not, but then one of your friends changes your mind. "C'mon," he says, "you don't see any of the rest of us holding back, do you?" You decide that you're as good as your friends, and that they're going to tackle it, so you figure you're good enough to give it a try.

Daniel and some of his friends are discussing which brands of beer taste best. Daniel is pretty fond of Blitzkrieg, but when he mentions this some of his buddies laugh at him. "You're probably the only person in town who'll touch that stuff," they hoot. Daniel makes a note to hide his case of Blitzkrieg before anyone comes over on the weekend.

In the first of these examples, you have been given no reason at all for altering your initial assessment of your skiing abilities; you've been induced to alter them through **peer pressure**, which plays on a person's desire not to be disliked or disrespected or left off the "bandwagon." But your abilities are what they are, and what they are is not affected by what your friends think or do. (If your initial assessment of your skiing ability was right, and it's true that you ski as well as your friends, there may be a busy hour ahead for the ski patrol.)

In the second example Daniel *does* have a reason for *hiding* his Blitzkrieg,

Generic Red Herring

We found this unclassifiable irrelevancy disguised as an argument against a bond measure in the 1988 *California Ballot Pamphlet*:

"We admit that this measure is popular. But we also urge you to note that there are so many bond issues on this ballot that the whole concept is getting ridiculous."

The number of bond issues isn't the only ridiculous thing around here.

assuming he doesn't want his friends laughing at him again (though in fact he could well win some respect for independence if he sticks with his preference). But if Daniel is like many of us, he may do more than hide his beer; he may conclude that the beer doesn't taste that great after all. He may even start looking for reasons for thinking that it is inferior ("It *does* seem a bit raw, and bitter too"), though his friends haven't given him any reasons for that opinion. In this case, Daniel has been peer pressured. (And if Daniel is like a lot of people, he'll feel peer pressure on issues much more important than this.)

It may have occurred to you that one's sense of *loyalty* can also induce one to get on the bandwagon and do, think, or say what one's family, friends, school, club, or nation are doing, thinking, or saying. This is true. And, as is well known, our loyalties can at times induce us to embrace unthinkingly some claim or course of action. However, as with all the psychological responses that we discuss in this chapter, loyalty *is* a relevant consideration with respect to certain issues; loyalty results in pseudoreasoning only when we accept a claim on the basis of considerations that, though arousing our sense of loyalty, are irrelevant to the truth or falsity of the claim. As we have stressed, it is the sometimes difficult task of the critical thinker to identify those issues to which one's sentiments are relevant and those to which they are not.

Apple Polishing

Hannah, I'd be proud if you'd support me in my campaign for city council. People know they can trust you, and I know it too. I need an honest, reliable person on my side, and they don't come much better than you.

This is an old-fashioned case of **apple polishing** (there are more graphic names for it, too). We can hope that Hannah doesn't think she's been given a *reason* for supporting the speaker.

Apple Polishing in Ads

You've come a long way, baby.

—Virginia Slims

You've got what it takes.

—Salem Lights

What did *you* do to deserve Beefeater?

—Beefeater

Show your good taste.

—Blue Nun

Ads that give as "reasons" for purchasing the advertised products that you are discriminating, perspicacious, or sophisticated, or that you just plain "have what it takes" are pieces of advertising flattery (as if you didn't know).

Dear Professor Smith:

If it's not too much trouble, please send my final grade on the attached postcard and drop it in the mail. I've already addressed the card.

I certainly enjoyed your course. You are a wonderful instructor and did an excellent job of making the class interesting and useful. There is one thing, though: Would you mind taking another look at my grade on the second exam? With one more point I would have made an A.

Sincerely,
Sean O'Flattery

The issue, whether the student earned an A, is unaffected by the fact that he likes (or gives the appearance of liking) his professor. So that fact is no reason for changing his grade. Again, the attempted inducement is through an appeal to the instructor's vanity.

The Horse Laugh

X? Ha, Ha! You've got to be kidding.

Ridicule is a powerful rhetorical tool—most of us simply do not like being laughed at. But one who attempts to reject or refute a claim by laughing at it ("Send aid to Libya? Har, har, har!"), by laughing at some second claim that

That's a Lot of Syllogisms

One horse laugh is worth a thousand syllogisms.

—Attributed to H. L. MENCKEN

A syllogism is a form of argument. Laughter, unlike argumentation, cannot really refute our claims, but sometimes, alas, it silences us (as Mencken wryly points out). It shouldn't.

may or may not follow from it ("Support the Equal Rights Amendment? Sure, when the ladies start paying for the drinks! Ho, ho, ho!"), by telling an unrelated joke, or simply by laughing at the person who makes the claim has not really raised any objection to the claim itself. Nevertheless, it hurts our pride when others laugh at our serious proposals—nobody relishes the role of fool, whether or not it is deserved—and so it is very easy for us to abandon our own claims when others laugh at them.

The Subtle Touch

A survey sponsored by the House Aging Committee—did you know you pay for a House Aging Committee?—supports the claim of the House Aging Committee that Americans would like someone else to pay their health costs, along the lines suggested by the House Aging Committee.

—*National Review*

Translation: "The Aging Committee's survey and recommendations?—ho, ho; scoff, scoff. You've got to be kidding!" This is a subtle example of the horse laugh. The passage manages to insinuate derisively and without real argument that there is something amiss both with the committee's survey and its recommendations.

Note, though, that the passage could also be classified as an ad hominem (see Chapter 7). That it can be classified in more than one way illustrates a significant point: So very often, it's not as important that you are able to classify the pattern of pseudoreasoning displayed in a passage, as it is that you are able to spot lack of argument or irrelevancy of reasoning when you encounter it. In the case of the passage above, the most important thing to see is that you haven't been given a legitimate reason for discounting the committee's survey or recommendations.

Appeal to Spite or Indignation

You and your friend are discussing Loman, who is being considered for a promotion. Your personal view is that Loman handled the Byerly contract rather well, and you are inclined to write a letter of support for him. Your friend then reminds you that Loman did nothing to help you win a promotion three years ago. And you had almost forgotten! Becoming a bit angry, you decide that you won't write a letter after all. "When you think about it," you might mutter, "Loman didn't do *that* great a job on the Byerly contract."

Your friend's words have made you indignant; thus out of spite you decide not to support Loman. However, that Loman didn't help you, while a cause for anger on your part, is irrelevant to the question of how well he did on the Byerly contract. If you talk yourself into believing that he didn't do very well, you're pseudoreasoning.

Incidentally, suppose that your original position had been that Loman had *not* done an especially good job on the Byerly contract, and you were inclined *not* to support his promotion. Suppose that then your friend reminded you that Loman had written a strong letter in support of *your* promotion a while back. Under these circumstances might you not feel an inducement to support Loman? After all, Loman supported you; isn't it only fair to return the favor?

If you think it is only fair to return the favor, then it is not *irrational* for you to do so (though we hope you find some way of supporting Loman that does not require you to be dishonest). However, don't talk yourself into *changing your opinion of Loman's work on the Byerly contract* on the basis of what your friend has said, for what has been said does not relate to his work on the contract, though it *is* relevant to what you choose to say about his work.

It may have occurred to you by now that we are inclined to require exceptional performance from people we don't like before we give them praise, but our friends win our admiration for being merely competent. It takes careful thinking to keep our general feelings about others from coloring our evaluation of some specific accomplishment or action on their part. But realizing that we are subject to these natural inclinations is a big step in the right direction.

Of course, people we don't know and have no feeling about one way or another frequently do things that arouse our pleasure or displeasure. Furthermore, because we have no general feeling about these strangers, our reactions to what they do are often more objective than our reactions to the activities of people we know. In any case it is important to realize that there is nothing illogical in condemning an action that makes us angry or indignant (or in praising an action we like), regardless of whether the action is taken by an acquaintance or someone we know nothing about. But it is illogical to let the pleasure or displeasure we feel as the result of one action influence our evaluation of another action. It is also illogical to consider a person's action wrong simply *because* it makes us angry: Presumably, we are angry because it is wrong; it isn't wrong because we are angry.

Two Wrongs Make a Right

"Two wrongs make a right" is a form of pseudoreasoning that is intended to justify the claim that it is all right for A to do something harmful to B. Specifically, the pseudoreason supplied to justify this claim is that B would do the same to A. That is,

> *It's acceptable for A to do X to B, because B would do X to A.*

Examples:

> After leaving the local supermarket, Serena notices that the sales clerk has given her too much change. "Oh well," she rationalizes, "if I had given him too much money, he wouldn't have returned it to me."

> Smith and Jones are discussing a Vietnamese attack on a Kampuchean refugee camp that was the headquarters of Khmer Rouge resistance fighters. Smith is horrified by the attack, which took the lives of hundreds of Kampuchean civilians. Jones takes a different view. "I find it difficult to condemn such actions," he says, "when the Khmer Rouge themselves engage in such savage and brutal acts of violence."

Serena is indeed rationalizing. She is trying to excuse her dishonesty with a pseudoreason. Even assuming that the clerk wouldn't have returned the money to her had the situation been reversed, that fact does not justify a similar action by another person, herself included. Similar comments hold true for the second case. Even assuming that the Khmer Rouge do engage in savage attacks on civilian populations, that fact does not justify similar attacks by anyone else. The Golden Rule is to do to others as you would *have them* do to you—not as they *would* do to you.

   Notice, though, that another scheme that is very similar to this pattern of pseudoreasoning is not pseudoreasoning, but is, rather, quite acceptable. It is *not* wrong for A to do X to B *if doing so is necessary to prevent B from doing X to A.* Thus, for instance, most people would agree that it is not wrong for you to injure a mugger if doing so is necessary to prevent that person from injuring you.

Furthermore, according to some moralists at least, acts done for the sake of revenge or retribution are in some instances morally acceptable. "An eye for an eye, a tooth for a tooth" succinctly expresses this view. In this view, the fact that B wrongfully *did* X to A would justify A's doing X to B. But in the first example above, the clerk did not wrongfully take any of Serena's money. In the other example, what Jones is excusing and what Smith is horrified by is, presumably, that the Vietnamese attack killed civilians, individuals who had not themselves attacked the Vietnamese.

A variation of "two-wrongs" pseudoreasoning consists of trying to defend a wrong action by explaining that it is **common practice.** Example:

> During the Watergate scandal of the early seventies, Richard Nixon's practice of secretly tape recording conversations with White House guests was excused by Nixon apologists on the grounds that several former U.S. presidents had done the same thing.

By the same token, one might defend driving over the speed limit on the grounds that everyone else is doing it. Or one might argue that it is all right to cheat, since everyone else is doing it and there is no way to stop them from doing so. However, valid justification for these actions would not be simply that everyone else is doing it, but rather that because everyone else is doing it it is necessary to do the thing oneself for the safety or well-being of oneself or others. Driving much more slowly than surrounding traffic can sometimes create a hazard; not cheating when *everyone* else is doing it with impunity subjects one to an unreasonable disadvantage. Situations involving one's own self-interest must be scrutinized very carefully indeed—it is very easy to mistake a pseudoreason for a real one in such instances.

Appeal to Common Practice

That seven soldiers and Marines should be jailed for trying to smuggle home automatic weapons captured in Grenada, while an admiral who attempted to bring in 24 of them went free, is obviously wrong. But then the question arises: Was the Navy too soft on Admiral Joseph Metcalf III, who pleads ignorance of the regulations governing personal pre-emption of captured weapons, or were the Army and the Marine Corps too harsh in their treatment of the captain and six NCOs who tried to hang on to their war trophies? Probably the latter, when you consider the rusting Japanese, German, Chinese, and North Korean guns and swords this generation of American servicemen has seen at home, souvenirs of the wars their fathers fought, and also won.

—*National Review*

Recap

Sometimes something happens or someone says something that awakens feelings of fear, compassion, pride, guilt, loyalty, or any of a host of others in us. Frequently these feelings and emotions, or whatever has aroused them, seem to be reasons for accepting or rejecting a claim to which they are in fact unrelated. To take these feelings or other irrelevant matters as grounds for accepting or rejecting the claim is to fall prey to pseudoreasoning.

In this chapter we examined the following categories of pseudoreasoning:

Subjectivist fallacy
Appeal to belief
Appeal to the consequences of belief
Scare tactics
Appeal to pity
Peer pressure
    Bandwagon
    Appeal to loyalty

Apple polishing
    Appeal to vanity
Horse laugh
Appeal to spite or indignation
Two wrongs make a right
    Common practice

Exercises

In daily life it is not terribly important that you be able to label a case of pseudoreasoning as, say, "subjectivist fallacy" or "appeal to belief." What is important is being able to identify pseudoreasoning wherever it occurs, and to have an idea of why the would-be reasons are irrelevant to the point at issue. Nevertheless, in the exercises that follow, we will ask you to name patterns of pseudoreasoning, and your instructor may do the same on an exam. The objective is to help you become familiar with and remember these common patterns so that you will be alert to pseudoreasoning when it occurs in daily life.

EXERCISE 6-1

Identify any instances of pseudoreasoning that occur in the following passages, either by naming them or, where you think they do not conform to any of the patterns we have described, by explaining in one or two sentences why the pseudoreasons are irrelevant to the point at issue.

★1. The tax system in this country is unfair and ridiculous! Just ask anyone!

2. SHE: I think it was exceedingly boorish of you to finish off the last of their expensive scotch like that.

   HE: Bosh. They certainly would have drunk ours, if given the chance.

3. Overheard: "Hmmmm. Nice day. Think I'll go catch some rays."

   "Says here in this magazine that doing that sort of thing is guaranteed to get you a case of skin cancer."

   "Yeah, I've heard that, too. I think it's a bunch of baloney, personally. If that were true you wouldn't be able to do anything—no tubing, skiing, nothing. You wouldn't even be able to just plain lay out! Ugh!"

★4. I've come before you to ask that you rehire Professor Johnson. I realize that Mr. Johnson does not have a Ph.D., and I am aware that he has yet to publish his first article. But Mr. Johnson is over forty now, and he has a wife and two high-school-aged children to support. It will be very difficult for him to find another teaching job at his age, I'm sure you will agree.

5. JUAN: But, Dad, I like Horace. Why shouldn't I room with him, anyway?

   JUAN'S DAD: Because I'll cut off your allowance, that's why!

6. "Hey! Don't pick up that toad—they cause warts! Everyone knows that!"

★7. RALPH: He may have done it, but I don't hold him responsible. I'm a determinist, you know.

   SHARON: What's that?

   RALPH: A determinist? Someone who doesn't believe in free will. There's no free will.

   SHARON: Oh. Well, I disagree.

   RALPH: Why's that?

   SHARON: Because. Maybe that's your view, but it's not mine.

8. WINIFRED: Hey, read this! It says they can actually teach gorillas sign language!

   ELDRIGE: Uh huh, sure. And next they'll make them presidents of universities.

9. HE: Tell you what. Let's get some ice cream for a change. Sunrise Creamery has the best—let's go there.

   SHE: Not that old dump! What makes you think their ice cream is so good, anyway?

   HE: Because it is. Besides, that old guy that owns it never gets any business any more. Every time I go by the place I see him in there all alone, just staring out the window, waiting for a customer. He can't help it that he's in such an awful location. I'm sure he couldn't afford to move.

★10. Student speaker: "Why, student fees have jumped by more than 300 percent in just two years! This is outrageous! The governor is working for a balanced budget, but it'll be on the backs of us students, the people who have the very least to spend! It seems pretty clear that these increased student fees are undermining higher education in this state."

EXERCISE 6-2

Answer the following questions and, where relevant, explain your answers.

★1. Is the fact that a brand of toothpaste is advertised as a best-seller relevant to the issue of whether to buy that brand?

2. Is the fact that a brand of toothpaste *is* best-selling relevant to the issue of whether to buy that brand?

★3. Is the fact that an automobile is a best-seller in its class relevant to the issue of whether to buy that kind of automobile?

4. Is the fact that a movie is a smash hit relevant to the issue of whether to see it?

5. Is the fact that a movie is a smash hit a reason for liking it?

6. Is the fact that your friends like a movie relevant to the issue of whether to see it?

★7. Is the fact that your friends like a movie a reason for liking it?

8. Is the fact that your friends like a movie relevant to the issue of whether to say that you like it?

9. Is the fact that movie critics like a movie relevant to the issue of whether to see it?

★10. Is it peer pressure (bandwagon) pseudoreasoning to advertise a product as best-selling?

EXERCISE 6-3

Sharon is considering whether to participate in a public demonstration against the administration's foreign policy. Her father is opposed to her doing so. "Given our position in this community," he says, "it would be very embarrassing to your mother and me for you to be seen doing something like that."

★1. What emotion or other psychological response, if any (e.g., fear, pity, anger, etc.), is Sharon's father trying to evoke? Be as specific as possible.

2. Is what he has said relevant to the issue of whether Sharon should participate in the demonstration?

★3. Is it relevant to what Sharon should think of the administration's foreign policy?

4. Is it relevant to the question of whether the administration's foreign policy is meritorious?

★5. Is Sharon's father trying to influence Sharon's opinion on the merits of the administration's foreign policy? (Base your answer on the situation as here described.)

EXERCISE 6-4

After the Grenada military rescue of 1983, the media complained that the Reagan administration had denied them access to the operation. However, according to public opinion polls, there was much popular support for the president's policy regarding the media. Here's an excerpt from a letter to the editor at the time:

> . . . I say, let them [the media] complain! These people distort the news for their own ends, and have no respect for even basic human courtesies, like leaving people alone who have just lost a loved one. If there is even the slightest suspicion that a public official has done something wrong, they'll hound him to death, and if there isn't any suspicion, they'll invent a reason for some.

★1. What emotion or other psychological reaction (i.e., fear, pity, guilt, etc.) is the writer expressing?

2. Do you think the writer is trying to establish or prove something? If so, what?

★3. Is the excerpt relevant to the issue of whether the media had been denied access to the rescue operation?

4. Is the excerpt relevant to the issue of whether the media *should* have been denied access to the rescue operation?

★5. Is the excerpt a case of pseudoreasoning?

EXERCISE 6-5

An advertisement shows attractive and trim young people using a home exercise machine. Nothing is stated in the ad except the name of the manufacturer of the device.

★1. Is the ad intended to arouse *fears* (of becoming old, overweight, etc.) or *desires* (of becoming trim, fit, etc.) or both?

2. On the basis of the ad, would one have a reason for thinking that a home exercise device would help make one trim and fit or avoid becoming overweight and out-of-shape?

★3. Is there anything in the ad relevant to the issue of which exercise device to buy, assuming that one wishes to make such a purchase?

4. Is the ad an instance of pseudoreasoning?

★5. Is it conceivable that the ad might be pseudoreasoning to one person but not to another?

EXERCISE 6-6

A commercial for a carpet spray shows a woman sniffing the air with an expression of distaste. Apparently she finds some odor offensive.

★1. What psychological response, if any, is the ad intended to arouse?

2. Does the ad give someone who has a carpet a reason for thinking that the carpet might have an unpleasant odor?

★3. Does the ad give someone who owns a carpet a reason for checking to see if it has an unpleasant odor?

4. Does the ad give someone who owns a carpet a reason for purchasing a carpet spray?

★5. Does the ad give someone who owns a carpet a reason for favoring one carpet spray over another?

EXERCISE 6-7

You can easily see yourself in the scene the salesman is describing. You're alone beside your broken-down car on a desolate desert highway; few pass by and no one stops to help. "Me, I'd never travel without my CB," the salesman concludes.

★1. What feeling is the salesman trying to elicit, if any?

2. Is his little story relevant to the issue of whether you should buy a CB?

★3. Is it relevant to the issue of which brand of CB to buy, assuming that you decide you want one?

4. Is it relevant to the issue of whether you can afford to buy a CB?

★5. Is it relevant to the issue of whether you might break down on a desert highway?

EXERCISE 6-8

"In the family, we all drive Fords. We always have and we always will. Henry T. gave your grandfather his first job, and he worked for him for forty-five years. Don't even think of buying some other car."

★1. What feeling or sentiment is the speaker attempting to elicit, if any?

2. Is his statement relevant to the issue of whether to buy a car?

★3. Is it relevant to the issue of which make of car to buy?

4. Is it relevant to the issue of which make of car is best mechanically?

★5. Is it pseudoreasoning?

EXERCISE 6-9

For each of the following passages, (a) briefly state the main issue—that is, the claim in question, if any; (b) identify the feeling or sentiment (e.g., fear, pity, anger, etc.), if any, the speaker or writer is trying to express or elicit; and (c) state whether that feeling or sentiment, or any claim made in the effort to elicit it, is relevant to the main issue. In addition, (d) if the passage illustrates a kind of pseudoreasoning that has a name, give the name.

EXAMPLE: "It *is* my turn to deal. Or shall I take my cards and go home?"

ANSWER:
(a) *Issue:* Whether it is my turn to deal
(b) *Feeling or sentiment:* Fear of my taking my cards away

(c) *Is the feeling or are the claims that elicit it relevant to the issue?* My threat is not relevant to the issue. It is, of course, relevant to the issue of whether I should be *allowed* to deal, my turn or not.

(d) *Name:* Scare tactics

★1. Overheard: "Why is it so important to halt production of nuclear weapons? Well, did you see that TV movie, *The Day After?* If you did you know what a horrible thing nuclear war would be. Millions would be incinerated instantly. Poof! Gone! Those who weren't would die in terror and agony. Disease, starvation, radiation sickness, and violence would prevail. The world would be dark and cold, a nightmare. We must stop producing these insane weapons now!"

 2. Mother: "I think he has earned an increase in his allowance. He doesn't have any spending money at all, and he's always having to make excuses about not being able to go out with the rest of his friends because of that."

 3. Advertising blurb: "Don't let anyone ever tell you that beauty comes with birth. Successful models have learned that any woman can be beautiful, if she matches her makeup with her natural skin tones. Limelight Blush blends naturally with your basic skin colors to enhance and highlight your natural radiance."

★4. Aw, c'mon, Ralph, let's get some beer and go over to Harry's for a little poker. Worry about the wife later; she'll forgive you. You know, the one thing I really like about you is that in your family *you* wear the pants!

 5. You know what's going to happen if you continue to jog like that? For one thing, it's probably ruining your joints. How about your knees—have they started to hurt yet? For another, just look at you! You look just awful, skinny and run-down like that! You really ought to give it up, if you don't want to end up an invalid.

 6. During the Lebanese hostage crisis of midsummer 1985, the captors of the American hostages demanded, as a condition of the hostages' release, that Israel free seven hundred Lebanese prisoners. The United States government reportedly did not ask Israel to release the prisoners. Instead, administration sources made such statements as this: "We figure that [Israel's Prime Minister] Peres can read our minds. . . . Certainly there are enough people over here of the Jewish faith . . . who must be telling people over there [in Israel], 'for God's sake, look what you're doing to American public opinion.' "

—Reported by George F. Will, *Washington Post*

★7. "During the same crisis, hostage Allyn Conwell, the spokesman for the hostages, expressed 'genuine sympathy' for the captors. Another hostage, Peter Hill, stated later that Conwell had been 'sucked in,' and said indignantly: 'I asked him if he was going to carry the Koran and Islamic prayer beads with him to the White House.' "

—*Time* magazine

8. Overheard: "You're telling me that you actually believe that this battery will last twenty-five years? Well, I've got some nice ocean-front property in Nebraska that you might like to buy, too."

9. Overheard: "I'll tell you what I'd do about those people that hijacked that TWA flight and are holding all those hostages. I'd go in and kidnap some of the leaders of Lebanon and Iran and hold *them* hostage. Two can play that game!"

★10. Either God exists or He does not. If we believe that He does and we are wrong, then nothing is lost. But if we are right, eternal salvation and happiness will be our reward. Since there is nothing lost by believing that He exists and much to be gained, it is reasonable to believe that He exists.

—A version of Pascal's Wager

EXERCISE 6-10

For each of the following passages, (a) briefly state the main issue; (b) identify the feeling or sentiment, if any, the speaker or writer is trying to express or elicit; and (c) state whether that feeling or sentiment, or any claim made in the effort to elicit it, is relevant to the main issue. In addition, (d) if the passage illustrates a type of pseudoreasoning that has a name, give the name.

★1. "Grocers are concerned about *sanitation problems* from beverage residue that Proposition 11 could create. Filthy returned cans and bottles—*over 11 billion a year*—don't belong in grocery stores, where our food is stored and sold. . . . Sanitation problems in other states with similar laws have caused increased use of *chemical sprays* in grocery stores to combat rodents and insects. Vote no on 11."

—Argument against Proposition 11, California Ballot Pamphlet, November 1982

2. Overheard: "I'm not going to vote for Tomley for governor and you shouldn't either. I lived in L.A. when Tomley was mayor, and the crime was so bad we had to leave. You couldn't walk around alone, for fear of your life, and I mean this was in the middle of the day!"

3. STUDENT: I think I deserve a better grade than this on the second question.
PROF: Could be. Why do you think so?
STUDENT: You think my answer's wrong.
PROF: Well, your answer *is* wrong.
STUDENT: Maybe you think so, but I don't. You can't mark me wrong just because my answer doesn't fit your opinion.

★4. C'mon, George, the river's waiting and everyone's going to be there. You want me to tell 'em you're gonna worry on Saturday about a test you don't take 'till Tuesday? What're people going to think?

5. ATTENDANT: I'm sorry, sir, but we don't allow people to top off their gas at this station. There's a state law against it, you know.

RICHARD: What? You've got to be kidding! I've never heard of a place that stopped people from doing that!

6. HE: Hey, don't go that way! Here, over behind the elephant cage we can slip in without paying.

SHE: Isn't that dishonest?

HE: Oh, what's the difference? Lots of people get in that way.

★7. That, in sum, is my proposal, ladies and gentlemen. You know that I trust and value your judgment; and I am aware I could not find a more astute panel of experts to evaluate my suggestion. Thank you.

8. Letter to the editor: "So Joanne Edwards wishes that the Army Reserves would not use Walnut Park for exercises, does she? Well, Ms. Edwards, pardon me, but I hardly think that the Reserves disturb the solitude of the park. After all, we should be proud of our armed forces who stand ever-prepared to defend flag, nation, and American honor."

—*Tri-County Observer*

9. HAROLD: I think what we should do is buy a new Chevy Blazer and call it a business expense so that we can write it off.

ETHEL: I don't know, Harold. That sounds a little like cheating to me. We wouldn't really use the car much in the business, you know.

HAROLD: Oh, don't worry about it. Just about everyone fudges a little on their taxes, after all.

★10. Overheard: "I tell you, it's disgusting. These college students come up here and live for four years—and ruin the town—and then vote on issues that will affect us long after they've gone somewhere else. This has got to stop! I say, let only those who have a genuine stake in the future of this town vote here! Transient kids shouldn't determine what's going to happen to local residents. Most of these kids come from Philadelphia . . . let them vote there."

EXERCISE 6-11

For each of the following passages, (a) briefly state the main issue; (b) identify the feeling or sentiment, if any, the speaker or writer is trying to express or elicit; and (c) state whether that feeling or sentiment, or any claim made in the effort to elicit it, is relevant to the main issue. In addition, (d) if the passage illustrates a type of pseudoreasoning that has a name, give it.

★1. Chair, Department of Rhetoric (to department faculty): "If you think about it I'm certain you'll agree with me that Mary Smith is the best candidate for department secretary. I urge you to join with me in recommending her to the administration. Concerning another matter, I'm presently setting up next semester's schedule and I hope that I'll be able to give you all the classes you have requested."

2. NELLIE: I really don't see anything special about Sunquist grapefruit. They taste the same as any other grapefruit to me.

NELLIE'S MOM: Hardly! Don't forget that your Uncle Henry owns Sunquist. If everyone buys his fruit you may inherit a lot of money some day!

3. Letter to the editor: "It is unfortunate that the House voted to provide so little in funding for the MX missile and I hope that Americans will write to their Congressmen voicing their disapproval. Soviet ICBMs outnumber ours and the Russians are several years ahead of us in developing space weapons systems. At this very moment you and I both are targets for some Russian missile. The MX will come up for funding again. Write!"

—*Miltonville Gazette*

★4. *"Don't risk letting a fatal accident rob your family of the home they love—on the average more than 250 Americans die each day because of accidents.* What would happen to your family's home if you were one of them? Your home is so much more than just a place to live. It's a community you've chosen carefully . . . a neighborhood . . . a school district . . . the way of life you and your family have come to know. And you'd want your family to continue sharing its familiar comforts, even if suddenly you were no longer there. . . . Now, as a Great Western mortgage customer, you can protect the home you love. . . . Just complete the Enrollment Form enclosed for you."

—Advertisement from Colonial Penn Life Insurance Company

5. You've made your mark and your scotch says it all. *Glen Haven Reserve.*

6. Dear Senator Jenkins,

I am writing to urge your support for higher salaries for state correctional facility guards. I am a clerical worker at Kingsford Prison, and I know whereof I speak. Guards work long hours, often giving up weekends, at a dangerous job. They cannot afford expensive houses, or even nice clothes. Things that other state employees take for granted, like orthodontia for their children and a second car, are not possibilities on their salaries, which, incidentally, have not been raised in five years. Their dedication deserves better.

Very truly yours, . . .

★7. In *Shelley vs. Kraemer,* 334 U.S.1 (1948), the "argument" was put before the Supreme Court that "state courts stand ready to enforce restrictive convenants excluding white persons from the ownership or occupancy of property covered by such agreements," and that therefore "enforcement of covenants excluding colored persons may not be deemed a denial of equal protection of the laws to the colored persons who are thereby affected." The court decided that "this contention does not bear scrutiny." In fact, the contention seems to be an example of what form of pseudoreasoning?

8. The suggestion was made in the spring of 1985 to replace the word *manpower* in the course description of Dartmouth's Business Administration 151, Management of Human Resources, because of the sexist connotation of the word. This brought delighted responses in the press.

Shouldn't they get rid of *management* in the course title, wrote someone, in favor of *personagement?* Shouldn't *human* in the title give way to *huperson,* asked another? Is the course open to *freshpersons,* a third wondered? In fact, is the course open to any person, the same individual queried? *Son* is a masculine word; therefore *person* itself is sexist.

9. "You going to take Jefferson for Geography 25?"

    "Yeah, I heard he's pretty good."

    "I had him last semester. He's really good. One thing, though, is that he spends a lot of time harping on ecology and the environment."

    "Yes, well my opinion is that most of that stuff is hooey. These environmental guys tell us the water's bad, the air's bad, the world's not fit for dogs. We can't let ourselves believe things're that bad or we'll go crazy with worry. It can't be true."

    "Well, maybe. Jefferson's class is still worth taking, though."

★10. There are very good reasons for the death penalty. First, it serves as a deterrent to those who would commit capital offenses. Second, it is just and fair punishment for the crime committed. Third, reliable opinion polls show that over seventy percent of all Americans favor it. If so many people favor it, it has to be right.

EXERCISE 6-12

This exercise, which presents an advertisement (see page 174) that appeared in *The Progressive* in December 1984 and January 1985, together with some examples of letters that the ad provoked, is more difficult than the preceding ones and may be best suited for class discussion.

For each of the following passages, (a) briefly state the main issue; (b) identify the feeling or sentiment, if any, that the speaker or writer is trying to express or elicit; and (c) state whether that feeling or sentiment, or any claim made in the effort to elicit it, is relevant to the main issue. In addition, (d) if the passage illustrates a type of pseudoreasoning that has a name, give the name. We have analyzed the ad and the first letter in the answers to this chapter.*

Letter 1

"I object to the advertisement 'Sponsored by the Tobacco Industry Labor/ Management Committee' that appeared on page 39 of your December issue.

"Do the tobacco workers believe we should all take up smoking and expose ourselves to the risk of lung cancer so that they can keep their jobs? What

---

The Progressive wishes us to make clear that it ran the ad because it does not believe in censorship: "Presumably, each of our irate correspondents had read the tobacco ad and had been left none the worse for reading it. Yet each apparently assumed that others could not be trusted to exercise such good judgment. Censors always assume that they are strong enough to handle material that others must be shielded from."

We're the tobacco industry, too.

In 1983, our brothers and sisters marched in Washington honoring the memory of Dr. Martin Luther King. We worked for passage of the Voting Rights Act. We marched in the Nation's Capital to support health care for the elderly. In 1981, we rallied in support of Social Security. We were part of the historic Solidarity Day March. And again and again, we have fought to save the Food Stamps program.

You may be surprised to know we also work for the tobacco industry.

We are proud members of the Bakery, Confectionery and Tobacco Workers International Union. And we care about the same things working people all over the country care about—jobs, equality, social justice, economic democracy, peace. We also care about the wages and benefits we have won for ourselves and our families while working in the tobacco industry.

We want you to know our industry is threatened—not by foreign competition or old-fashioned technology—but by well-meaning people who haven't stopped to consider how their actions might affect others.

Everyone knows there is a controversy over smoking. What everyone doesn't know . . . and should . . . is that attacks on the tobacco industry threaten the livelihoods of thousands of working Americans who have marched, worked, and struggled for causes we all believe in.

The tobacco industry creates jobs, which for many of us make the difference between poverty and dignity. It means a lot to us.

about the people who make nuclear weapons—should we risk nuclear war so *they* can keep their jobs?

"I am saddened to see *The Progressive* accept such an advertisement."

—V.P.A., Wilmette, Illinois

Letter 2

"Because of the use of tobacco, hundreds of thousands of Americans will die agonizing deaths. Anyone who traffics in and profits from this deadly drug—farmers, workers, executives, sellers, and even publications which take tobacco ads—has the blood of cancer victims on his hands.

"The tobacco and alcohol industries enjoy an undeserved tolerance in America because they are so well entrenched and wield enormous economic and political power. Yet the use and abuse of their products claim far more casualties than do illegal drugs. If we should be concerned about the loss of jobs of tobacco workers, should we not be equally concerned about the jobs of dealers, growers, and workers in marijuana, cocaine, and heroin?"

—R. K., Greeley, Colorado

Letter 3

"It is ironic that the regressive ad to bolster tobacco industry profits (and presumably jobs) appeared in the same issue of *The Progressive* as a well-deserved critique of the health delivery system in the United States. In effect, the ad asked all of us to reconsider our attitude toward smoking and not overreact to such trifles as the threat of lung cancer.

"To give the appeal added authenticity, the ad features a large picture representing the working class—a woman as well as black and white workers. . . . It's not surprising that the ad is sponsored by a 'Labor/Management Committee,' one of the shrewder coopting devices of capital.

"One wonders whether in the future *The Progressive* will carry ads advocating the need to build more nuclear missiles and power plants in the name of saving jobs."

—D. S., Jamaica, New York

Letter 4

"My first reaction to the tobacco industry ad was to say 'and the next ad will be from the workers who built and loaded the ovens at Belsen.' However, the ad does bring up a serious problem and some real contradictions. Any other industry that has killed as many people as the tobacco industry would have been closed down decades ago.

"People have always been forced by economic circumstances to work where they could. If the only game in town is an industry that kills people in wholesale lots, is it our obligation as socially oriented activists to protect the society as a whole?

"When major polluters are forced to change their operations, workers sometimes suffer. 'Jobs' are, in fact, used as an excuse to avoid correcting many environmental and work-hazard problems. Federal funds are spent to support activities such as tobacco-growing because of 'jobs.' This issue has been used by the polluters and their friends to attempt to divide the progressive forces; witness this ad.

"Instead of falling for these tactics, we should turn them around. We should insist that tobacco subsidies continue—but that they only be used to develop other means of economic activity in the affected areas, including retraining of all affected workers."

—L. O., Philadelphia, Pennsylvania

EXERCISE 6-13 (ESSAY)

Find an example of pseudoreasoning in a newspaper editorial or opinion magazine (substitute an example from an advertisement or a letter to the editor only as a last resort and only if your instructor permits it). Identify the issue and what side of the issue the writer supports. Explain why the passage you've chosen does not really support that position—that is, why it involves pseudoreasoning. If the writer's claims do support some other position (possibly on a different, related issue), describe what position they do support.

7 Pseudoreasoning II

There's a mighty big difference between good, sound reasons and reasons that sound good.

—Burton Hillis

Just as you probably recognized scare tactics and apple polishing in the preceding chapter, many of this next group of pseudoreasoning patterns are so common that their names frequently occur in popular literature (straw man, ad hominem, slippery slope, etc.). Patterns in this group are generally less dependent upon direct appeals to a person's feelings and emotions than those covered in Chapter 6, however.

A careful reader may notice that some types of pseudoreasoning actually fit the definition of "argument" given in Chapter 1. But they are best treated like their nonargument brethren (types like the horse laugh and apple polishing) because, with a little practice, they can be recognized for what they are without going through the kinds of argument analysis we'll take up in Part Two.

Keep in mind that a passage is not confined to one form of pseudoreasoning—it's possible to engage in two or more types at the same time. Some varieties are often found working together in pairs to mislead us into accepting or rejecting a claim when we have no business doing so.

Finally, in those cases where a type of pseudoreasoning can be turned into a form of legitimate reasoning, we'll point out what would be required to accomplish it.

177

Ad Hominem

Sometimes it's easy to confuse the merits of a claim (or theory or policy) with those of its source. We may be inclined to reject a claim, for example, if it comes from someone we disapprove of or don't like. In effect, we say:

I reject your claim because you are [*blank*].

We get an example of pseudoreasoning by replacing the "[blank]" with any term or phrase that might have a negative impact: "a liar," "ignorant," "a Republican," "a Democrat," "just saying that to get rich," and so on. Rare exceptions can occur, but it takes a peculiar kind of example to count as an exception. For instance: "I reject your claim because I know that you have been paid to lie about this matter."

The reason any such replacement of the blank produces pseudoreasoning is that a fact about the person making a claim is rarely grounds for rejecting the claim. You may remember from our discussion in Chapter 3 that we sometimes have reason to doubt the credibility of a source. When we have such doubts we should be careful before we *accept* a claim from that source, but the doubts are rarely grounds for *rejecting* the claim. When we reject a claim or urge others to reject it because it comes from a source we disapprove of or don't like, we commit the fallacy of **ad hominem.** (*Ad hominem* is Latin for "to the man," indicating that it's the person and not the subject matter that's being addressed.)

The proper response to a claim from a source whose credibility we doubt is to suspend judgment about it, or, in extreme cases, to ignore it. No matter what claim Ms. M. might make, we are rarely justified in rejecting it as false because of our knowledge or suspicions about Ms. M.

Things are different when Ms. M. supplies *reasons* for believing something—that is, if she gives an argument for her claim. The question of whether those reasons establish the claim—that is, whether the truth of the claim can be inferred from those reasons—is totally unaffected by her lack of credibility. No fact whatsoever about Ms. M. would constitute a reason for rejecting, discounting, objecting to, or even suspending judgment about the worth of her inference. Considerations as to a person's credibility are irrelevant to the question of whether her premises establish her conclusion.

There are several subspecies of ad hominem pseudoreasoning. The first, illustrated by the examples above, is the **personal attack.** We engage in it when we make abusive remarks about a person and use them as grounds for rejecting what that person says. (We are also guilty of this type of pseudoreasoning when we reject the claims of people whom we simply dislike, as indicated in our discussion of bias in Chapter 3.)

How many ad hominems have been committed in this conversation?

We get a slightly different wrinkle if, instead of saying abusive things about a person, we make reference to his circumstances, inferring that a claim he makes is false because somebody in his position could be expected to make such claims. Example:

> John says that we should reject what Father Hennesy says about the dangers of abortion because, "After all, he's a Catholic priest and priests are required to hold such views."

It may be true that Father Hennesy is a priest and that his views on abortion represent those of the Catholic church. That does not make his views false, however. John has given us an example of a "circumstantial" ad hominem. We'll include it in the personal attack category because of its close relationship to other examples in that category. As a matter of fact, a person often means to be abusive toward a speaker by referring to the speaker's circumstances—as when the latter is said to be a communist (or a conservative or a liberal).

A second major type of ad hominem is based on claims of inconsistency. When we say of a person that her claim is false because it's inconsistent with something else she has said or with her own behavior, we are guilty of a **pseudorefutation.** It is reasonable to expect people to avoid making claims

A Pseudorefutation?

According to a report in *Fate* magazine, the noted Philippine "psychic surgeon" Tony Agpaoa died recently, at the advanced age of 42. Agpaoa reportedly could pull "diseased" tissue from the body of patients without making an incision and without leaving any scar, although skeptics charged that he was merely practicing sleight of hand. Inexplicably, when Agpaoa became ill, he sought treatment from conventional doctors, and not from other "psychic surgeons."

—*The Skeptical Inquirer*

The Skeptical Inquirer obviously doesn't think much of "psychic surgery." Is it guilty of pseudoreasoning in the above passage? Why or why not?

A Typical Pseudorefutation

In the summmer of 1988 four teenagers broke into the backyard of journalist Carl Rowan. Rowan, who had written several articles in favor of gun control, shot one of the intruders in the wrist when he lunged at the journalist. Rowan said that he would be justified in using a gun as long as society is "awash in guns and drugs," but gun advocates felt otherwise. The National Rifle Association called Rowan hypocritical for opposing guns but owning one himself. Senator Steven Symms, R-Idaho, bought Rowan a membership in the NRA, and stated that Rowan's actions demonstrated the falseness of his antigun position.

But of course, his actions did no such thing. This is a pseudorefutation.

that conflict, of course, and, as we have seen, when one claim conflicts with another, they cannot both be true. But we cannot infer that it is *this* claim currently before us that is false. We must also allow people the opportunity to change their minds—sometimes we make claims that conflict with something we said earlier simply because we've learned that the earlier claim is false. To refuse to allow a change of mind is to require that we carry our earliest opinions to the grave.

An Irrelevant Blast at Marxism

An elaborate example of a pseudoreasoning personal attack appears in an article by Paul Johnson in *Commentary*. Mr. Johnson begins by endeavoring to establish that Karl Marx was personally anti-Semitic, citing a letter from Marx to Friedrich Engels and an anti-Semitic essay Marx had written entitled "On the Jewish Question." According to Johnson, the essay contained in embryonic form the essence of Marx's socialist theory. Thus, Johnson goes on to argue, Marx's socialism is but "an expanded and transmuted form of his earlier anti-Semitism."

So far, Johnson is not guilty of pseudoreasoning. He is offering his readers reasons for believing that Marx's socialist theory is an outgrowth of alleged anti-Semitism. However, Johnson goes further, into pseudoreasoning: "The origins of Marxism," he writes, "can never be wholly erased. Whatever disguises Marxism may take, it retains this stigma, like a mark of Cain."

Rejecting Marxism in this way, in "whatever disguise it may take" because of its alleged origins in "anti-Semitic conspiracy theory," is an example of what is sometimes called the **genetic fallacy** (attacking the origins or genesis of a view while ignoring the claims of the view itself). The source or origination of a theory, however objectionable that source might be, is logically unrelated to the question of whether the theory itself is acceptable. Marxism is a vast philosophy consisting of many doctrines together with supporting reasons. Such theories must stand or fall on their merits or lack thereof. If the author of this article believes he has turned up a flaw in Marxism because he has pointed out an evil in its origins, he has produced an irrelevant thesis.

Sometimes a person's behavior seems inconsistent with what the person says. For example, Mr. Wright makes claims about the merits of generosity, and he urges others to be generous. But his own behavior is that of a very stingy, ungenerous person. We might well accuse Mr. Wright of hypocrisy, but it would be pseudoreasoning to take his behavior as a reason for rejecting his claims about generosity. Another example: Let's say your doctor tells you that you should not use tobacco. We engage in pseudorefutation if we discount her advice because she smokes herself. Again: Her behavior is not a reason for rejecting her claims about tobacco. (She may be seriously addicted to tobacco and simply has been unable to quit, even though she knows that her health would benefit from quitting.)

The last version of this type of pseudoreasoning is the **genetic fallacy**, as illustrated in the box "An Irrelevant Blast at Marxism." As its name indicates, it is committed when the origins of a view are said to be a reason for rejecting the view as false.

It's nice to have this version available when "ad hominem" doesn't seem to fit the case. This can happen when something other than an individual is identified as the source of the rejected claim. For example, if we urge people to reject a policy just because it was put forth as part of the Republican (or Democratic) party platform, we commit a type of pseudoreasoning essentially like ad hominem, although we are not attacking a specific individual.

Selfish Rationalizing

Myers is a member of the Danville School Board, which is trying to determine whether to remodel a current public school or build a new one on property the school district already owns. The remodel would be less expensive, and Myers is not convinced the district can afford a new school. But he owns several building lots near the site of the proposed school, and these would greatly increase in value if it were built. After a restless night or two, Myers decides to vote for the construction of the new school. "The new facilities would be wonderful for the kids," he reasons, "and maybe we can find a buyer for the old property and offset much of the cost of construction."

It is conceivable that self-interest (or greed, if you prefer) is motivating our school board member. He has a purely selfish reason for voting for the new school: He hopes to profit from its proximity to his building lots. He does *not* have a reason for thinking that the sale of the old property will make the new school affordable. It is also not clear that remodeling the old school wouldn't provide equally "wonderful" facilities for the district's students. So, assuming that his vote was motivated by self-interest, Meyers is rationalizing. **Selfish**

rationalizing is the inventing of or focusing on a nonselfish secondary reason for accepting a claim in order to avoid feeling guilty about one's principal motive for accepting it when that motive is personal gain. The secondary reason is a pseudoreason.

Notice that hope for personal gain is not limited to financial gain. We can hope for anything. Thus, advertisements that promise health, good looks, thrilling experiences, clean dishes, pleasant breath, and restful sleep all appeal to someone's hopes. Further, there is nothing irrational about doing something, or buying some product, or supporting some political candidate or measure that offers to satisfy one's hopes. However, critical thinkers will not waste time or money trying to satisfy hopes that stand little chance of being satisfied, or buying products that afford little promise of fulfilling their hopes. In this context, it is pseudoreasoning, or rationalizing, to pretend that it is not your desire for something that induces you to take an action or to accept a claim, but some other, legitimate reason.

We should note that rationalizing selfish interests in this way is very common. Fortunately, not every decision a person makes that happens to benefit herself is made for the sake of that benefit. Sometimes, thank goodness, we do make conscientious decisions, and sometimes such decisions do, quite incidentally, yield benefits for us. It would be uncritical indeed for us to condemn automatically as a case of selfish rationalizing each decision for which a person received some benefit.

Burden of Proof

The requirement that a person produce evidence to support his position is sometimes called "the burden of proof." When an issue is in dispute, the burden of proof may be shared equally by the disputants, or it may fall more properly on one side than the other. The **burden of proof** type of pseudoreasoning occurs when this burden is misplaced. An example should help make this clear.

Some people believe in ghosts not because of any evidence that there *are* ghosts but because nobody has shown there are no such things. This is pseudoreasoning of the burden of proof type because it places the requirement of proving their position on the issue (the "burden") entirely on those who do not believe in ghosts.

Occasionally a person can get away with shifting the burden of proof from his side of an issue to his opponent's side by a simple remark. Notice:

> SEAN: I think we should invest more money in expanding the interstate highway system.

RUTH: I think that would be a mistake.

SEAN: How could anybody object to more highways?

With his last remark, Sean has attempted to put the burden of proof on Ruth. Such tactics can put one's opponent in a defensive position; Ruth has to show why we should *not* spend more on roads rather than Sean having to show why we *should* spend more.

How do we know where the burden of proof should properly be placed? In general, we might think that the burden of proof should be equally shared by those on different sides of an issue, and there are times when that is indeed the proper way to distribute it. But such equal sharing is not always appropriate. In most cases, what determines whether the burden of proof should fall more on those who advance a claim or more on those who object to it is the initial plausibility of the claim itself. A claim's initial plausibility is determined in turn by how it "fits" with our background knowledge. A claim that is consistent with our background knowledge has more initial plausibility than one that conflicts with it. The less initial plausibility a claim has, the greater the burden of proof that falls on one who advances the claim.

The preceding is a rule of thumb, of course, and not one that admits of precise application. However convenient it might be, we can't assess the specific degree of a claim's plausibility and then determine with precision just exactly how much evidence its advocates need to produce before we're willing to accept the claim. But, as a rule of thumb, it can keep us from setting the requirements unreasonably high for some claims and allowing others to slide by unchallenged even though they don't deserve to. Obviously, we should place a smaller burden of proof on one who says, for example, that cars with large engines get lower gas mileage than cars with small engines than on somebody who makes the

The Presumption of Innocence

We must point out that there are sometimes specific reasons why the burden of proof is placed entirely on one side. The obvious case in point is in criminal court, where it is the prosecution's job to prove guilt. The defense is not required to prove innocence; it must only try to keep the prosecution from succeeding in its attempt to prove guilt. We are, as we say, "innocent until proven guilty." As a matter of fact, it's possible that more trials might come to a correct conclusion (i.e., the guilty get convicted and the innocent be acquitted) if the burden of proof were equally shared between prosecution and defense. But we have wisely decided that, if we are to make a mistake, we would rather it be one of letting a guilty person go free than one of convicting an innocent person. Rather than a kind of pseudoreasoning, then, this lopsided placement of the burden of proof is how we guarantee a fundamental right: the presumption of innocence.

claim that Clyde's eighty-seven-year-old grandmother swam across Lake Michigan last winter.

In some cases, too, the burden of proof falls automatically on the person taking the affirmative side of the issue. If the issue is whether there is a tenth planet, then the burden is on the person who says there is. If the issue is whether there is a global warming trend, then the person who claims the affirmative must advance the proof. Yes, this method of determining the burden of proof may conflict with the principle of assigning it on the basis of the initial plausibility of the claim advanced. When there is conflict, generally the initial-plausibility principle wins out. If the issue is whether you will die someday, then the burden is on the person who takes the negative side and says that you will not, since the claim that you will not is most implausible.

Be alert when your inability to *disprove* a claim is said to show that you are mistaken in doubting the claim or in asserting that it is false. It doesn't, unless the burden was on you to disprove the claim. Your inability to disprove that there is extrasensory perception is no reason to think that you are mistaken in doubting that ESP exists. But psychics' repeated inability to disprove common sense skepticism about ESP *does* weaken *their* case.

Straw Man

We get a case of straw man pseudoreasoning when someone ignores an opponent's actual position (X) and presents in its place a distorted or misrepresented version of that position ("X"). A distorted version of the opposition's views is more easily attacked, much like a straw man is more easily knocked over than a real one. Thus:

> *X is false because "X" is false.*

Examples:

> Senator Peckingham says that we ought not deploy the MX missile. I disagree entirely. I cannot understand why he would want to leave us defenseless like that.

> Mr. and Mrs. Herrington are arguing about cleaning out their attic. "Why, we just went through all that old stuff last year," Mr. Herrington exclaims. "Do we have to clean it out every day?"
>   "There you go again," his wife retorts, "exaggerating as usual. Nobody said anything about doing it every day—it's just that you want to keep everything around forever, and that's ridiculous."

The Herringtons are each stating distorted versions of the other's position. Presumably Mrs. Herrington does not want to clean the attic out on a daily basis, nor is it likely that Mr. Herrington wants to keep every old thing around forever.

In the preceding example, the speaker has distorted the senator's position. Who said anything about leaving the country defenseless? Not the senator—*his* claim was only that we shouldn't deploy the MX.

Straw Man

> The campaign against strategic defense is heating up, and by the time President Reagan is inaugurated, the crockpot of opposition will be furiously boiling. A spectrum-spanning panoply of forces stands opposed to America's defending itself against megadeath. . . .
>
> The arms-control faithful. Surprise. Whatever its vices, this group can never be charged with inconsistency. It has consistently opposed both strategic modernization and strategic defense, believing religiously that a pact of mutual suicide between the superpowers is the surest guarantee against nuclear war. Nuclear weapons are evil, but a necessary evil; defending against nuclear weapons is evil, but unnecessary, and therefore more evil. This group, moreover, consistently displays an innocent trust in the most banal pronouncements on peace issuing from the Kremlin, while invariably distrusting its own government.
>
> —*National Review*, January 11, 1985

The position described is probably not held by any person in the entire country. It is doubtful that even absolute pacifists believe nuclear weapons are necessary but that defending against them is evil.

False Dilemma

The pattern of pseudoreasoning known as **false dilemma** looks like this:

> *"X is true because either X is true or Y is true, and Y isn't* [said where X and Y can both be false]."

Examples:

> CONGRESSMAN CLAGHORN: Guess we're going to have to cut back expenditures on social programs again this year.
> YOU: Why's that?
> CLAGHORN: Well, we either do that or live with this high deficit, and that's something we can't allow.

> DANIEL: Theresa and I both endorse this idea of allowing prayers in public schools, don't we, Theresa?
> THERESA: I never said any such thing!
> DANIEL: Shhhh! You're not an atheist, are you?

In the first example, Claghorn maintains that either we live with the high deficit or we cut social programs, and therefore, since we can't live with the high

Dealing with a Dilemma

Brutus is saying, in effect, "Either X, raise me, or Y, fire me, and you don't dare fire me, so therefore X. The boss, however, is subtly implying that he may be very happy to live with Y."

False Charge of False Dilemma

Recently Albert and Rose Ross of Buffalo, New York, in a letter to the editor of their local newspaper, charged those who advocate disarmament with offering the American people a false dilemma, the choice between all-out nuclear war and "total capitulation" to international communism. Now, the Rosses certainly are correct in saying that this is a false dilemma, since there is a good bit of middle ground between all-out nuclear war and total capitulation, including the Rosses' preferred option, nuclear preparedness. However, it is doubtful that many Americans who advocate disarmament would ever pose such a dilemma. Even an American pacifist who favored communism would not suggest *capitulating* to the Communists (the recommendation would be for *adopting* communism). In short, the Rosses' charge of false dilemma is in fact a straw man. The Rosses have presented a caricature of a disarmament advocate's position.

Sometimes, false charges of pseudoreasoning can themselves *be* pseudoreasoning.

deficit, we have to cut social programs. But this reasoning works only if cutting social programs is the *only* alternative to a high deficit. Of course, that is not the case (taxes might be raised, or military spending cut, for example).

In the other example, Daniel's "argument" amounts to this: Either you are an atheist or you endorse prayers in public schools; therefore, since you are not an atheist, you endorse the prayers. But a person does not have to be an atheist in order to feel unfavorable toward public-school prayer. The alternatives Daniel presents, in other words, could both be false. Theresa might not be an atheist and still not endorse school prayer.

The example Daniel provides us shows how this type of pseudoreasoning and the preceding one can work together: A straw man is often used as part of a false dilemma. If a person wants us to accept X, then he may not only ignore other alternatives besides Y, he may exaggerate or distort Y. In other words, he leaves only *one* "reasonable" alternative, because the only other one he gives us is really a straw man.

It might help in understanding false dilemmas to look quickly at a *real* dilemma. Consider: You know that the Smiths heat their house in the winter. You also know that the only heating options available in their location are gas and electricity. Under these circumstances, if you find out that they do *not* have electric heat, it must indeed be true that they have gas heat, because that's the only alternative remaining. We only get false dilemma pseudoreasoning when reasonable alternatives are ignored. In such cases, both X and Y may be false and some other alternative may be true.

Therefore, before you accept X because some alternative, Y, is false, make certain that X and Y cannot both be false. Look especially for some third alternative, some way of rejecting Y without having to accept X. Example:

DANIEL: Look, Theresa, you're going to have to make up your mind. Either you decide that you can afford this stereo, or you decide that you're going to do without music for a while.

Theresa could reject both of Daniel's alternatives (buying this stereo and going without music) because of some obvious third possibilities. One, she might find a less expensive stereo. Or, two, she might buy a part of this stereo now—just the turntable, amplifier, and speakers, say—and postpone until later purchase of the tape deck, equalizer, walnut-grain speaker stands, and the rest.

Slippery Slope

We've all heard people make claims of the sort,

If we let X happen, the first thing you know Y will be happening.

This is one form of the **slippery slope**. Such claims amount to pseudoreasoning when in fact there is no reason to think that X will lead to Y. Sometimes X and Y can be the same kind of thing, or can bear some kind of similarity to one another, but that doesn't mean that one will inevitably lead to the other.

Opponents of handgun control sometimes use a slippery slope argument, saying that, if laws are passed to register handguns, the next thing we know there will be laws to make owning any kind of gun illegal. This is pseudoreasoning if there is no reason to think that the first kind of law will make the second kind more likely. It's up to the person who offers the slippery slope claim to show *why* the first action will lead to the second.

It is also argued that one should not experiment with certain drugs because experimentation is apt to lead to serious addiction or dependence. In the case of drugs that are known to be addictive, there is no pseudoreasoning present— the likelihood of the progression is clear.

The other version of slippery slope occurs when someone claims we must continue a certain course of action simply because we have already begun that course. It was said during the Vietnam War that, because the United States had already sent troops to Vietnam, it was necessary to send more troops to support the first ones. Unless there is some reason supplied to show that the first step *must* lead to the others, this is pseudoreasoning. (Notice that it's easy to make a false dilemma out of this case as well; do you see how to do it?)

Sometimes we take the first step in a series, then we realize that it was a mistake. To insist on taking the remainder when we could admit our mistake and retreat is to fall prey to slippery slope pseudoreasoning. (If you insist on following one bad bet with another one, we'd like to invite you to a friendly poker game.)

Slippery slope pseudoreasoning is sometimes called "the camel's nose." That's because once you let the camel get its nose in the tent, there's no stopping the rest of it from coming in.

Recap

The types of pseudoreasoning we've covered in this chapter are not quite as dependent upon appeals to emotion as most of those covered in Chapter 6. Some of those listed below often resemble legitimate arguments, but none can give us a reason for accepting or rejecting a claim. Sometimes points raised in pseudoreasoning of these types call for a closer look: Is a dilemma a real one or a false one? Is what is claimed to be a slippery slope really slippery? That is, is the progression mentioned really inevitable?

These two chapters do not cover every possible kind of pseudoreasoning, but the ones we've discussed should help make you sensitive to the difference between considerations that are truly relevant to a conclusion and the emotional appeals, factual irrelevancies, and other devices that often take the place of good reasoning.

In this chapter we examined the following types of pseudoreasoning:

Ad hominem
    Personal attack
        Circumstantial ad hominem
    Pseudorefutation
    Genetic fallacy
Selfish rationalizing

Burden of proof
Straw man
False dilemma
Slippery slope

Exercises

EXERCISE 7-1

Identify any examples of pseudoreasoning in the following passages. Tell why you think there is pseudoreasoning present and identify which category they belong in, if they fit any of those we've described.

★1. What! So now you're telling me we should get a new car? I don't buy that at all. Didn't you claim just last month that there was nothing wrong with the Plymouth?

2. Letter to the editor: "The recent Supreme Court decision outlawing a moment of silence for prayer in public schools is scandalous. Evidently the American Civil Liberties Union and the other radical groups will not be satisfied until every last man, woman and child in the country is an atheist. I'm fed up."

—*Tri-County Observer*

3. Overheard: "I don't care how serious they appear; anybody who's raking in as much money as those television evangelists can't really care about being a minister for plain, ordinary people."

★4. CARLOS: Four A.M.? Do we really have to start that early? Couldn't we leave a little later and get more sleep?

JEANNNE: C'mon, don't hand me that! I know you! If you want to stay in bed till noon and then drag in there in the middle of the night, then go by yourself! If we want to get there at a reasonable hour, then we have to get going early and not spend the whole day sleeping.

5. I know a lot of people don't find anything wrong with voluntary euthanasia, where a patient is allowed to make a decision to die and that wish is carried out by a doctor or someone else. What will happen, though, is that if we allow voluntary euthanasia, before you know it we'll have the patient's relatives or the doctors making the decision that the patient should be "put out of his misery."

6. We should impeach the Attorney General. Despite the fact that there have been many allegations of unethical conduct on his part, he has not done anything to demonstrate his innocence.

★7. I know there were many fine candidates for the job, but I finally decided that, since my wife knows me well, she would be the best person to hire. It's an advantage to the company to have people in the office who are going to get along well.

8. Don't tell me I should wear my seat belt, for heaven's sake. I've seen you ride a motorcycle without a helmet!

9. People who own pit bulls show a lack of respect for their friends, their neighbors, and anybody else who might come in contact with their dogs. They probably care more about dogs than they care about people.

★10. When it comes to the issue of race relations, you're either part of the solution or you're part of the problem.

EXERCISE 7-2

Identify any examples of pseudoreasoning in the following passages. Tell why you think there is pseudoreasoning present and identify which category they belong in, if they fit any of those we've described.

★1. Despite all the studies and the public outcry, it's still true that nobody has ever actually *seen* cigarette smoking cause a cancer. All the anti-smoking people can do is talk about statistics.

2. There is only one way to prevent this country from becoming dominated by the illegal drug establishment like Colombia has in South America, and that's to make a tenfold increase in the funds we spend on drug enforcement and interdiction.

3. Overheard: "Hunting immoral? Why should I believe that coming from you? You fish, don't you?"

★4. During the Vietnam War, American involvement was occasionally "justified" on the grounds that, if we failed to stop Communist advances into South Vietnam, we would in effect be turning over the entire free world to the Communist threat. Similar remarks are sometimes heard today regarding Nicaragua: Either we oust the Marxist Sandinistas from Nicaragua, or the whole of Latin America will find itself under Communist rule. Is this pseudoreasoning? If so, which pattern is it?

5. Letter to the editor: "I strongly object to the proposed sale of alcoholic beverages at County Golf Course. The idea of allowing people to drink wherever and whenever they please is positively disgraceful and can only lead to more alcoholism and all the problems it produces—drunk driving, perverted parties, and who knows what else. I'm sure General Stuart, if he were alive today to see what has become of the land he deeded to the county, would disapprove strenuously."

—*Tehama County Tribune*

6. Letter to the editor: "Dukakis argues that the MX missile should not be funded. But the liberal governor from up north has no experience dealing with the Soviets. Also, if we disarm ourselves there will be nothing to prevent the Soviets from achieving their objective of world domination.

Remember, 'We will bury you!' To ground MX is to lie defenseless before naked Soviet might."

—*Carlton Falls News*

★7. Letter to the editor: "So now we find our local crusader-for-all-that-is-right, and I am referring to Councilman Benjamin Bostell, taking up arms against the local adult bookstore. Is this the same Mr. Bostell who owns the biggest liquor store in Chilton County? Well, maybe booze isn't the same as pornography, but they're the same sort of thing. C'mon, Mr. Bostell, aren't you a little like the pot calling the kettle black?"

—*Chilton County Register*

8. Letter to the editor: "Once again the *Courier* displays its taste for slanted journalism. Why do your editorials present only one point of view?

"I am referring specifically to the editorial of May 27, regarding the death penalty. So capital punishment makes you squirm a little. What else is new? Would you prefer to have murderers and assassins wandering around scot-free? How about quoting someone who has a different point of view from your own, for a change?"

—*Athens Courier*

9. Editorial comment: "Once again the strident voices of the lunatic left are heard, this time in protest of South African apartheid. Now, don't get us wrong. We are not defending the South African system of government. But isn't it curious that those who complained so bitterly over South Africa have nothing at all to say about the brutal occupation of Afghanistan by the Soviets?"

—*Tehama County Tribune*

★10. It's practically a certainty that the government is violating the law in the arms deals with Saudi Arabians. When a reporter asked officials to describe how they were complying with the law, he was told that details about the arms sales were classified.

EXERCISE 7-3

Go through a newspaper, news magazine, or opinion journal looking for examples of the pseudoreasoning types discussed in this chapter. Clip out, photocopy, or write down any good examples and bring them to class for discussion. Your instructor may ask you to explain in writing why you think the example contains pseudoreasoning.

EXERCISE 7-4

Watch one of the news/public affairs programs on television ("The MacNeil/Lehrer News Hour," "Nightline," "Face the Nation," "Firing Line," etc.) and make a note of any examples of pseudoreasoning that occur. Explain in writing why you think the examples contain pseudoreasoning.

EXERCISE 7-5

Identify any examples of pseudoreasoning in the following passages. Tell why you think there is pseudoreasoning present and identify which category they belong in, if they fit any category we've described.

★1. Letter to the editor: "I would like to express my feelings on the recent conflict between county supervisor Blanche Wilder and Murdock County Sheriff Al Peters over the county budget.

"I have listened to sheriffs' radio broadcasts. Many times there have been dangerous and life-threatening situations when the sheriff's deputies' quickest possible arrival time is 20 to 30 minutes. This is to me very frightening.

"Now supervisor Wilder wants to cut two officers from the Sheriff's Department. This proposal I find ridiculous. Does she really think that Sheriff Peters can run his department with no officers? How anyone can think that a county as large as Murdock can get by with no police is beyond me. I feel this proposal would be very detrimental to the safety and protection of this county's residents."

—Chino Reporter

2. Letter to the editor: "Andrea Keene's selective morality is once again showing through in her July 15 letter. This time she expresses her abhorrence of abortion. But how we see only what we choose to see! I wonder if any of the anti-abortionists have considered the widespread use of fertility drugs as the moral equivalent of abortion, and, if they have, why they haven't come out against them, too. The use of these drugs frequently results in multiple births, which leads to the death of one of the infants, often after an agonizing struggle for survival. According to the rules of the pro-lifers, isn't this murder?"

—North-State Record

3. In her column of February 5, 1985, Abigail Van Buren printed the letter of "I'd rather be a widow." The letter writer, a divorcée, complained about widows who said they had a hard time coping. Far better, she wrote, to be a widow than to be a divorcée, who are all "rejects" who have been "publicly dumped" and are avoided "like they have leprosy." Abby recognized the pseudoreasoning for what it was, though she did not call it by our name. What is our name for it?

★4. Letter to the editor: "I was amused by Reader Joseph J. Jiran's argument that Latin is best left out of today's curriculum and that computer languages develop students' mental discipline better. He writes, 'The study of Latin is best reserved for romantics, candidates for cloisters, and yuppies craving another trivial pursuit.' The same sentence without the Latinate words would read: 'The of is best for, for craving another.' The acronym yuppies is a hybrid, two-thirds Latin; therefore I am counting it as Latin."

—Time magazine

5. Letter to the editor: "Once again the Park Commission is considering closing North Park Drive for the sake of a few joggers and bicyclists. These so-called fitness enthusiasts would evidently have us give up to them for their own private use every last square inch of Walnut Grove. Then anytime someone wanted a picnic, he would have to park at the edge of the park and carry everything in—ice chests, chairs, maybe even grandma. I certainly hope the Commission keeps the entire park open for everyone to use."

6. "Some Christian—and other—groups are protesting against the placing, on federal property near the White House, of a set of plastic figurines representing a devout Jewish family in ancient Judaea. The protestors would of course deny that they are driven by any anti-Semitic motivation. Still, we wonder: Would they raise the same objections (of unconstitutionality, etc.) if the scene depicted a modern, secularized Gentile family?"

—*National Review*

★ 7. On January 30, 1985, the *Sacramento Bee,* in an editorial, attacked Secretary of Defense Weinberger's argument that cutting the defense budget would hurt the nation's economic recovery, because for every billion dollars cut, 35,000 jobs would be lost. The *Bee* observed that it was an "old Kremlin argument" that capitalists can sustain their economies only by manufacturing weapons and starting wars, but that even the Kremlin had given up that argument twenty-five years ago. Is this pseudoreasoning?

8. Letter to the editor: "I see the do-gooders are at it again. This time they want to force everyone to use seat belts, even those who don't want to. A mandatory seat-belt law is an outrage. Isn't it about time we said no to these people? It's either that or give up and let the state dictate everything we do. I, for one, prefer to keep my rights."

—*Miltonville Gazette*

9. Letter to the editor: "Maybe Georgia Senator Julian Bond is right in his recent comments on the plight of blacks in the United States. Maybe things really are as bad as he seems to want us to believe. But it's interesting that you don't see them lining up to leave the country, do you?"

★ 10. "In his August 1982 speech to the American Bar Association, Ronald Reagan defended his nominations to the Civil Rights Commission as follows: 'They don't worship at the altar of forced busing and mandatory quotas. They don't believe you can remedy past discrimination by mandating new discrimination. . . . But these fine Americans are under fire. My nominating them supposedly compromises the independence of the commission. Well, forgive me, but that's pure hogwash.' "

—James Nathan Miller, *Atlantic Monthly*

EXERCISE 7-6

Identify any examples of pseudoreasoning in the following passages. Tell why you think there is pseudoreasoning present and identify which category they belong in, if they fit any category we've described.

★1. "Cape Town, South Africa. Senator Edward Kennedy issued a sharply worded rebuttal after South Africa's foreign minister said Kennedy should be more concerned with the plight of American blacks than with South Africa's racial policies. The Massachusetts Democrat released a statement defending the status of blacks in America after Foreign Minister Botha criticized him Thursday in a statement broadcast on South African television. Botha said Kennedy should stay out of South African affairs and be more concerned with blacks in the United States. He contended that 17,500 black youngsters suffer from malnutrition in Kennedy's home state."

—Associated Press

2. Edgerly has devoted his life to helping others. In fact, some would say that he goes too far in this regard. When the bank mistakenly credited his account with an extra thousand dollars, he promptly donated all of it to a fund to help the blind, noting to himself that those people needed the money far more than the bank did. Is this selfish rationalizing? Discuss the issue with your instructor and the class.

3. MOE: The death penalty is an excellent deterrent for murder.
   JOE: What makes you think so?
   MOE: Because there's no evidence that it's *not* a deterrent.
   JOE: Well, states with capital punishment have higher murder rates than states that don't have it.
   MOE: Yes, but that's only because there are so many legal technicalities standing in the way of executions that convicted people hardly ever get executed. Remove those technicalities and the rate would be lower in those states.

★4. Overheard: The new sculpture in front of the municipal building by John Murrah is atrocious and unseemly, which is clear to anyone who hasn't forgotten Murrah's mouth in Vietnam right there along with Hayden and Fonda calling for the defeat of America. I say: Drill holes in it so it'll sink and throw it in Walnut Pond.

5. Overheard: Once we let these uptight guardians of morality have their way and start censoring *Playboy* and *Penthouse,* the next thing you know they'll be dictating everything we can read. We'll be in fine shape when they decide that *Webster's* should be pulled from the shelves.

6. It seems the biggest problem the nuclear industry has to deal with is not a poor safety record, but a lack of education of the public on nuclear power.

Thousands of people die each year from pollution generated by coal-fired plants. Yet to date, there has been no death directly caused by radiation at a commercial nuclear power plant in the United States. We have a clear choice: an old, death-dealing source of energy or a safe, clean one. Proven through the test of time, nuclear power is clearly the safest form of energy and the least detrimental to the environment. Yet it is perceived as unsafe and an environmental hazard.

★7. A high school teacher once told my class that if a police state ever arose in America, it would be because we freely handed away our civil rights in exchange for what we perceived would be security from the government. We are looking at just that in connection with the current drug crisis.

For almost 30 years we've seen increasing tolerance, legally and socially, of drug use. Now we are faced with the very end of America as we know it, if not from the drug problem, then from the proposed solutions to it.

First, it was urine tests. Officials said that the innocent have nothing to fear. Using that logic, why not allow unannounced police searches of our homes for stolen goods? After all, the innocent would have nothing to fear.

Now we're looking at the seizure of boats and other property when even traces of drugs are found. You'd better hope some drug-using guest doesn't drop the wrong thing in your home, car, or boat.

The only alternative to declaring real war on the real enemies—the Asian and South American drug families—is to wait for that knock on the door in the middle of the night.

8. "The Mayor's argument is that, because the developers' fee would reduce the number of building starts, ultimately the city would lose more money than it would gain through the fee. But I can't go along with that. Mayor Tower is a member of the Board of Realtors, and you know what *they* think of the fee."

9. Letter to the editor: Next week the philosopher Tom Regan will be in town again, peddling his animal rights theory. In case you've forgotten, Regan was here about three years ago arguing against using animals in scientific experimentation. As far as I could see then and can see now, neither Regan nor anyone else has managed to come up with a good reason why animals should not be experimented on. Emotional appeals and horror stories no doubt influence many, but they shouldn't. I've always wondered what Regan would say if his children needed medical treatment that was based on animal experiments.

★10. In response to former Chief of Staff Don Regan's revelation that Nancy Reagan sought the advice of an astrologer, the White House spokesman at the time, Marlin Fitzwater said, "Vindictiveness and revenge are not admirable qualities and are not worthy of comment."

EXERCISE 7-7

This exercise is more difficult. Examine each of the following passages for pseudoreasoning. Not every selection may contain such examples, and (as always) some of the examples may conform only loosely, or not at all, to the patterns we have discussed in the last two chapters. Explain in a sentence or two why the pseudoreasons are irrelevant to the point at issue.

★1. Letter to the editor: "It's the same old chant from the local left wing radicals. They explain over and over how terrific the Marxist governments of Cuba, Nicaragua, and the Soviet Union are and how the real bad guys are the officials of the United States Government.

 "It gets to be tiresome after a while—all these people can do is parrot the official line from Moscow. It might do their education some good if they happened to notice that the Soviets, of whom they're so fond, killed hundreds of civilians in Afghanistan in the weeks before they began withdrawing."

2. In midsummer, 1985, a TWA flight from Athens to Rome was hijacked by a group of Shiite Moslems who, after executing one of the American passengers, held the remaining thirty-nine Americans as hostages for some two weeks. During this time, a few letters to editors and columns in American newspapers appeared in which the actions of the kidnappers were "explained" as resulting from and reflecting earlier American and Israeli "terrorist" acts. Some of the acts so named were the random shelling of the hills around Beirut by the battleship *New Jersey* and the detention by Israel of more than seven hundred Lebanese prisoners in what many observers, among them the International Red Cross, considered a violation of the 1949 Geneva Conventions on the treatment of war prisoners.

 Are such explanations merely disguised versions of "two wrongs make a right"? Does it all depend on the author's intentions? How, in general, can one distinguish between a genuine psychological explanation that is supposed to elucidate some event and a case of two wrongs making a right?

3. Editorial comment: "Letters across the country are being returned to senders marked 'Insufficient Address' with greater frequency because the Postal Service officials in Washington have decided to enforce an old edict.

 "The edict says that letters must contain the complete address information for both the mailing address and the return address to be delivered promptly. The slightest deviation from these rules can mean an 'Insufficient Address' stamp and a return to the sender.

 "This has markings of a decision shaped by a Washington bureaucracy stripped of its common sense. The flexibility afforded by guidelines is far preferable to the rigidity of edicts. This approach, however, would mean an admission that someone outside Washington has intelligence, a point the Congress and the bureaucracy always seem to have difficulty accepting."

—Herald Telephone

★4. During the 1984 presidential campaign, Walter Mondale frequently attacked President Ronald Reagan's economic policies as having produced a huge deficit that could ultimately ruin the economy. Vice President Bush dismissed the charge as "the politics of doom and gloom." "These people will find a dark cloud everywhere," he said. Was this pseudoreasoning?

★5. "Louis Harris, one of the nation's most influential pollsters, readily admits he is in the polling business to 'have some impact with the movers and shakers of the world.' So poll questions are often worded to obtain answers that help legitimize the liberal Establishment's viewpoints."

—Conservative Digest

6. "At a White House meeting in February of 1983 with Washington, D.C., anchormen, Ronald Reagan was asked to comment on 'an apparent continuing perception among a number of black leaders that the White House continues to be, if not hostile, at least not welcome to black viewpoints.' President Reagan replied as follows: 'I'm aware of all that, and it's very disturbing to me, because anyone who knows my life story knows that long before there was a thing called the civil-rights movement, I was busy on that side. As a sports announcer, I didn't have any Willie Mays or Reggie Jacksons to talk about when I was broadcasting major league baseball. The opening line of the Spalding Baseball Guide said, 'Baseball is a game for Caucasian gentlemen.' And as a sports announcer I was one of a very small fraternity that used that job to editorialize against that ridiculous blocking of so many fine athletes and so many fine Americans from participating in what was called the great American game.' Reagan then went on to mention that his father refused to allow him to see *Birth of a Nation* because it was based on the Ku Klux Klan and once slept in a car during a blizzard rather than stay at a hotel that barred Jews. Reagan's 'closest teammate and buddy' was a black, he said."

—JAMES NATHAN MILLER, The Atlantic Monthly

7. Letter to the editor: "Now that officials in the administration are talking openly about overthrowing the Marxist government of Nicaragua, we can expect the usual litany of complaints from the liberal press about the rights of Nicaragua to self-determination, blah, blah, blah. I wonder if these people ever stop to think that the Sandinista government of Nicaragua is exporting revolution in Central America and is but one more link in the Soviet chain to enslave the world and overthrow *our* democratic form of government."

—Midfield Sentinel

8. Stop blaming the developers for the fact that our town is growing! If you want someone to blame, blame the university. It brings the new people here, not the developers. Kids come here from God knows where, and

lots of them like what they find and stick around. All the developers do is put roofs over those former students' heads.

★9. "Even though the Soviet Union denounces Reagan's Star Wars defense program, you can be certain that it will do its own research on space weapons. No matter how good the defense, in all probability each country will always be able to deliver some nuclear weapons. So neither of us need space-defense research; what we need is fewer nuclear weapons."

—Cascade News

10. The Soviet Union understands three things: military strength, military strength, and military strength. If we continue the course of military spending that we developed during the '80's, we will continue to have the success at the bargaining table that produced the INF treaty. On the other hand, we could choose to slack off on military spending and forget about coming to reasonable terms on arms limitations with the Russians. The proper course of action seems obvious.

EXERCISE 7-8 (ESSAY)

Write an essay in which you explore both sides of the issue: Is capital punishment for murder a case of "two wrongs make a right?"

PART TWO

Arguments

8 Understanding and Evaluating Arguments

Few persons care to study logic, because everybody conceives himself to be proficient enough in the art of reasoning already.

—CHARLES SANDERS PEIRCE

. . . All philosophy is logic.

—BERTRAND RUSSELL

Our central concern, when we try to think critically, is whether or not to accept a claim. Sometimes the reasons for accepting a claim are explicitly set forth; other times they are not. When they are not—when we are dealing with unsupported or nonargued claims—we have to determine for ourselves whether there are reasons for accepting them. In Part One we discussed unsupported claims. We turn now to claims for which reasons have been set forth: argued claims. Our concern in this part is determining when an argument is worth accepting and when it is not.

The Anatomy of Arguments

An argument consists of a **conclusion** (the claim that is argued for) and **premises** (the claims that provide the readers or hearers with reasons for believing the conclusion). Here are two examples of arguments:

[Premise] Every officer on the force has been certified, and [premise] nobody can be certified without scoring above 70 percent on the firing range. Therefore, [conclusion] every officer on the force must have scored above 70 percent on the firing range.

[Premise] Mr. Conners, the gentleman who lives on the corner, comes down this street on his morning walk every day, rain or shine. So [conclusion] something must have happened to him, since [premise] he has not shown up today.

Notice that sometimes the conclusion of one argument can serve as the premise of another:

Argument 1

[Premise] Every student who made 90 percent or better on the midterms has already been assigned a grade of A. [Premise] Since Margaret made 94 percent on her midterms, [conclusion] she already has her A.

Argument 2

[Premise] All those students who have been assigned A's are excused from the final exam. [Premise] Margaret got an A, so [conclusion] she is excused from the final.

The claim that Margaret has a grade of A is the conclusion in the first argument but a premise in the second.

Notice also that arguments can have unstated premises:

[Premise] You can't check books out of the library without an ID card. So [conclusion] Bill won't be able to check any books out.

The unstated premise must be "Bill has no ID card." We'll have more to say about unstated premises following.

Conclusion Indicators

The words in this list sometimes indicate that a conclusion is about to be given. (The three dots represent the claim that is the conclusion.)

Thus . . .	Consequently . . .
Therefore . . .	So . . .
Hence . . .	Accordingly . . .

But be careful. These words can be used in explanations as well as arguments. For example, "The wind blew at over fifty miles per hour last night; hence all the tree limbs on the lawn this morning" would ordinarily be used to explain why the tree limbs were on the lawn. "Bill had a family emergency yesterday; thus he was unable to be at the meeting" might be used as an argument, but it might also be used to explain why Bill was unable to be at the meeting. Fortunately, we usually have some idea at the outset what a speaker or writer is up to—that is, whether the person is arguing for a point, describing something, explaining, and so on.

Premise Indicators

Sometimes premise indicators will help you spot a premise. The following are some common ones. Notice that the three dots (which represent the claim that is the premise) sometimes come before the indicator, sometimes after.

. . . shows that   since . . .
. . . establishes that   because . . .
. . . implies that   for . . .

Notice that those indicators that come before the premise can be used in explanations as well as arguments. If you say, "My car won't start because the battery is dead" to someone who already accepts the claim that your car won't start, the statement is not an argument for believing that it won't start; it's an explanation of why it won't start.

Arguments can have unstated conclusions as well:

[Premise] Insurance rates are low wherever the local fire department has a good rating, and [premise] the fire department in East Biggs has a top rating.

The unstated conclusion is "East Biggs must have low insurance rates."

Notice finally that there is a difference between **independent premises** and **dependent premises** for a conclusion.

Are There Unstated Arguments?

An argument can contain unstated premises or unstated conclusions, but the argument itself cannot be *entirely* unstated. A masked bandit who waves you against a wall with a gun is not presenting you with an argument, though his actions certainly provide you with a good reason for doing what he wants you to do. That is, if you do not want to get shot, then *you* need to construct an argument in your own mind—and quickly, too—with the conclusion "I'd better move" and the premise "If I don't move, I may get my head blown off."

Although there are unstated premises and unstated conclusions, then, there is no such thing as an unstated argument. Neither can *all* the premises in an argument be unstated. The masked bandit who waves his gun at you and says, "Better move over against that wall," has said and done something that gives you a reason for moving, but has not presented you with an argument. It might be said that waving a gun around *implies* a premise (e.g., "If you don't move I'll shoot you"), but implication is a relationship that holds only between claims—that is, only a claim can imply a claim. The masked man has not implied a premise by waving his gun; rather, he has created a situation in which you have every reason to do his bidding.

[Premise] Raising the speed limit will wear out the highways faster. In addition, [premise] doing so will result in more highway deaths. Therefore, [conclusion] we should not raise the speed limit.

[Premise] Raising the speed limit will waste gas. [Premise] We don't have any gas to waste. Therefore, [conclusion] we should not raise the speed limit.

The first example gives two independent premises, or reasons, for not raising the speed limit (doing so would wear out the highways; doing so would waste lives). The premises are independent of one another because the falsity of one would not cancel the support the other provides for the conclusion.

But the premises in example 2 (raising the speed limit will waste gas; we don't have any gas to waste) are dependent upon one another. The falsity of either premise would automatically cancel the support the other provides for the conclusion that the speed limit should not be raised.

EXERCISE 8-1

Indicate which blanks would ordinarily contain premises and which would ordinarily contain conclusions.

★1. ____a____ , and ____b____ . Therefore, ____c____ .
★2. ____a____ . So, since ____b____ , ____c____ .
★3. ____a____ , because ____b____ .
★4. Since ____a____ and ____b____ , ____c____ .
★5. ____a____ . Consequently, ____b____ , since ____c____ and ____d____ .

EXERCISE 8-2

Identify the premises and conclusions in each of the following arguments.

★1. Since all Communists are Marxists, all Marxists are Communists.
 2. The Lakers almost couldn't beat the Jazz. They'll never get past Dallas.
 3. If the butler had done it, he could not have locked the screen door. Therefore, since the door was locked, we know that the butler was in the clear.
★4. That cat is used to dogs. Probably she won't be upset if you bring home a new dog for a pet.
 5. Hey, he can't be older than his mother's daughter's brother. His mother's daughter only has one brother.
 6. Moscone will never make it into the state police. They have a weight limit, and he's over it.
★7. Presbyterians are not fundamentalists, but all born-again Christians are. So no born-again Christians are Presbyterians.
 8. I guess he doesn't have a thing to do. Why else would he waste his time watching daytime TV?
 9. "There are more injuries in professional football today than there were

twenty years ago," he reasoned. "And if there are more injuries, then today's players suffer higher risks. And if they suffer higher risks, then they should be paid more. So I think today's players should be paid more," he concluded.

★10. Let's see . . . If we've got juice at the distributor the coil isn't defective and if the coil isn't defective then the problem is in the ignition switch. So the problem is in the ignition switch.

EXERCISE 8-3

Identify the premises and the conclusions in the following arguments.

★1. The darned engine pings every time we use the regular unleaded gasoline, but it doesn't do it with super. I'd bet that there is a difference in the octane ratings between the two in spite of what my mechanic says.

2. Kera, Sherry, and Bobby were all carded at JJ's, and they all look as though they're about 30. Chances are I'll be carded too.

3. Seventy percent of freshmen at Wharfton College come from wealthy families so probably about the same percentage of all Wharfton College students come from wealthy families.

★4. When blue jays are breeding they become very aggressive. So scrub jays, which are very similar to blue jays, may also be expected to be aggressive when they're breeding.

5. She wears the finest clothes, orders the most expensive dishes, and, when she goes on vacation, she stays at the best resorts. It's pretty safe to assume, then, that she'll be interested only in our top line. Start off by showing her the Ferraris.

6. According to *Nature,* today's thoroughbred racehorses do not run any faster than their grandparents did. But human Olympic runners are at least twenty percent faster than their counterparts of fifty years ago. Most likely racehorses have reached their physical limits but humans have not.

★7. It's easier to train dogs than cats. That means they're smarter than cats.

8. "Let me demonstrate the principle by means of logic," the teacher said, holding up a bucket. "If this bucket has a hole in it, then it will leak. But it doesn't leak. So obviously it doesn't have a hole in it."

9. I know there's a chance this guy might be different, but the last person we hired from Alamo Polytech was a rotten engineer and we had to fire him. So I'm afraid that this new candidate is somebody I just won't take a chance on.

★10. If she were still interested in me, she would have called, but she didn't.

EXERCISE 8-4

In any of the following arguments that have more than one premise, determine whether the premises provide dependent or independent reasons for the conclusion.

★1. Hey, you're overwatering your lawn. See? There are mushrooms growing around the base of that tree—a sure sign of overwatering. Also, look at all the worms on the ground. They come up when the earth is over-saturated.

2. "Will you drive me to the airport?" she asked. "Why should I do that?" he wanted to know. "Because I'll pay you twice what it takes for gas. Besides, you said you were my friend, didn't you?"

3. If you drive too fast, you're more likely to get a ticket, and the more likely you are to get a ticket, the more likely you are to have your insurance premiums raised. So, if you drive too fast, you are more likely to have your insurance premiums raised.

★4. If you drive too fast, you're more likely to get a ticket. You're also more likely to get into an accident. So you shouldn't drive too fast.

5. YOUNG TURK: If Jesse Jackson had been elected president, we'd be a lot happier.
   SKEPTIC: What, you think so?
   YOUNG TURK: Yes. If he were president, he'd have lowered taxes by now; then we'd have more money. And if we had more money, we'd have more to spend. And if we had more money to spend, we'd be a lot happier.

6. DANIEL: Where did that cat go, anyway?
   THERESA: I think she ran away. Look, her food hasn't been touched in two days. Neither has her water.

★7. There are several reasons why you should consider installing a solarium. First, you can still get a tax credit. Second, you can reduce your heating bill. Third, if you build it right, you can actually cool your house with it in the summer.

8. From a letter to the editor: "By trying to eliminate Charles Darwin from the curriculum, creationists are doing themselves a great disservice. When read carefully, Darwin's discoveries only support the thesis that species change, not that they evolve into new species. This is a thesis that most creationists can live with. When read carefully, Darwin actually supports the creationist point of view."

9. Editorial comment: "The Supreme Court's ruling that schools may have a moment of silence but not if it's designated for prayer is sound. Nothing stops someone from saying a silent prayer at school or anywhere else. Also, even though a moment of silence will encourage prayer, it will not favor any particular religion over any other. The ruling makes sense."

★10. We must paint the house now! Here are three good reasons: 1. If we don't then we'll have to paint it next summer. 2. If we have to paint it next summer, we'll have to cancel our trip. 3. It's too late to cancel the trip.

EXERCISE 8-5

In any of the following arguments that have more than one premise, determine whether the premises provide dependent or independent reasons for the conclusion.

★1. All mammals are warm-blooded creatures, and all whales are mammals. Therefore, all whales are warm-blooded creatures.

2. Jones won't plead guilty to a misdemeanor, and if he won't plead guilty, then he will be tried on a felony charge. Therefore, he will be tried on a felony charge.

3. John is taller than Bill, and Bill is taller than Margaret. Therefore, John is taller than Margaret.

★4. Rats that have been raised in enriched environments, where there are a variety of toys and puzzles, have brains that weigh more than rats raised in more barren environments. Therefore, the brains of humans will weigh more if they are placed in intellectually stimulating environments.

5. From a letter to the editor: "In James Kilpatrick's July 7 column it was stated that Scientology's 'tenets are at least as plausible as the tenets of Southern Baptists, Roman Catholics . . . and prayer book Episcopalians.' Mr. Kilpatrick seems to think that all religions are basically the same and fraudulent. This is false. If he would compare the beliefs of Christianity with the cults he would find them very different. Also, isn't there quite a big difference between Ron Hubbard, who called himself God, and Jesus Christ, who said 'Love your enemies, bless them that curse you, do good to them that hate you'?"

6. We've interviewed two hundred professional football players, and 60 percent of them favor expanding the season to twenty games. Therefore, 60 percent of all professional football players favor expanding the season to twenty games.

★7. Letter to the editor: "I was enraged to learn that the mayor now supports the initiative for the Glen Royale subdivision. Only last year he himself proclaimed 'strong opposition' to any further development in the river basin. Besides, Glen Royale will only add to congestion, pollution, and longer lines at the grocery store, not that the grocers will mind."

8. Exercise may help chronic male smokers kick the habit, says a study published today. The researchers, based at McDuff University, put thirty young male smokers on a three-month program of vigorous exercise. One year later only 14 percent of them still smoked, according to the report. An equivalent number of young male smokers who did not go through the exercise program were also checked after a year and it was found that 60 percent still smoked. Smokers in the exercise program began running three miles a day and gradually worked up to eight miles daily. They also spent five and a half hours each day in modestly vigorous exercise such as soccer, basketball, biking, and swimming.

9. Believe in God? Yes, of course I do. The universe couldn't have arisen

by chance, could it? Besides, I read the other day that more and more physicists believe in God, based on what they're finding out about the Big Bang and all that stuff.

★10. From an office memo: "I've got a good person for your opening in Accounting. Jesse Brown is his name, and he's as sharp as they come. Jesse has a solid background in bookkeeping, and he's good with computers. He's also reliable, and he'll project the right image. Best of all, he's a terrific golfer. As you might gather, I know him personally. He'll be contacting you later this week."

Deduction and Induction

Philosophers have traditionally distinguished between deductive arguments and inductive arguments. **Deductive arguments** are those whose premises are intended to provide absolutely *conclusive* reasons for accepting the conclusion. **Inductive arguments** are those whose premises are intended to provide *some* support, but *less than conclusive* support, for the conclusion.

Examples of Deductive Arguments
Suppose Bill argues either of the following:

1. Every Republican voted for the president's tax proposal. Senator Aardvark is a Republican. Consequently, he voted for the tax proposal.

2. If Gonzalez runs as a Democrat, he will lose the election. But if Gonzales loses, Smith will win. Therefore, if Gonzalez runs as a Democrat, Smith will win.

Now, granted, we can't read Bill's mind. So we cannot say for sure that he intended the premises of these arguments to provide absolutely conclusive reasons for accepting their conclusions. Nevertheless, it is very, very difficult to imagine that if we questioned him about the matter, he would maintain otherwise. It is difficult to picture his saying about (1) for example, "Well, even though every Republican voted for the president's tax proposal and even though Senator Aardvark is a Republican, it may still be that Aardvark did not vote for the proposal." *Of course* Bill thinks his premises conclusively establish his conclusion! So we can regard (1), and (2), too, as examples of deductive arguments.

Examples of Inductive Arguments
3. For the last twenty-three years, autumn has been the season of the least rainfall in San Francisco. Therefore, this coming autumn will be drier in San Francisco than any of the other seasons.

4. I have checked out half the floppy disks in this shipment, and everyone of them has been defective, so I think it's a safe bet that the whole shipment is defective.

In the case of (3) and (4), it is likely that Bill would regard his premises as providing something less than absolutely conclusive support for his conclusions. So (3) and (4) qualify as inductive arguments.

Now, in many real-life cases you just can't be certain whether an argument is deductive or inductive. Suppose, for example, that Bill says something like this:

In the 1970s all Jeeps were made by American Motors. I suppose that means that at that time American Motors manufactured only Jeeps.

Has Bill presented a deductive argument or an inductive argument? Well, does he suppose that his premise (All Jeeps used to be made by American Motors) provides an absolutely knock-down reason for accepting his conclusion (All American Motors cars used to be Jeeps)? Or does he intend that premise to provide some support, but less than conclusive support, for the conclusion? Without asking Bill it would be mere speculation for us to say what he is thinking.

But there is one thing we can say without speculating. We can say that

Impeccable Deductive Logic

I LOVE YOU

THEREFORE I AM A LOVER

ALL THE WORLD LOVES A LOVER

YOU ARE ALL THE WORLD TO ME

THEREFORE YOU LOVE ME

Do you see the mistake in this argument? Hint: See Chapter 2 on ambiguity.

Bill's premise at best provides only very weak support for his conclusion, and *if* Bill thinks that his premise provides absolutely conclusive support for the conclusion, then he is mistaken. The fact that at one time all Jeeps were made by American Motors does not mean that at that or any other time American Motors manufactured only Jeeps.

Fortunately, it is rarely necessary to say whether a real-life argument is deductive or inductive. What we should always try to do, however, is consider whether the given premises do provide absolutely conclusive support for the conclusion or whether they provide some lesser degree of support, if any.

An argument whose premises do provide absolutely conclusive support for their conclusion is said to be valid. In other words, a **valid argument** has this characteristic: On the assumption that the premises are true, it is *impossible* for the conclusion to be false. This is merely a very precise way of saying that the conclusion of a valid argument *absolutely follows* from the premises.

Bill's argument above about Jeeps is therefore invalid. Here's an example of a valid argument:

[Premise] Every philosopher is a good mechanic, and [premise] Francois is a philosopher. So, [conclusion] Francois is a good mechanic.

The argument is valid because the conclusion absolutely follows from the premises. That is, on the assumption that the premises are true, it would be quite impossible for the conclusion to be false.

Notice that, even though the argument is valid, it so happens the premises are *not* true. (Not every philosopher is a good mechanic, and take it from us, Francois is not a philosopher. He's one author's pet goldfish.) However, that the premises are not true does not affect the validity of the argument, because the conclusion absolutely follows from the premises. The argument is valid even though no claim in it happens to be true. So, remember, *to be valid, an argument need not have true premises.* All that is required is that the conclusion absolutely follow from the premises. Whether or not the premises are true is a separate issue.

A valid argument whose premises *are* true is called a **sound argument.** Since it is valid, the conclusion follows from the premises, so the conclusion must be true, too. Thus, in sound arguments all claims are true:

[Premise] Some pesticides are toxic for humans and [premise] anything that is toxic for humans is unsafe for most humans to consume. Therefore, [conclusion] some pesticides are unsafe for most humans to consume.

This is a sound argument: (1) it's valid, because the conclusion absolutely follows from the premises, and (2) its premises, and hence its conclusion, are true.

Now, if an argument is invalid, that doesn't necessarily mean that it's no good and ought to be dismissed out of hand. Here's an example:

[Premise] Frank Smith has washed hundreds of loads of clothes in his Twirlclean washing machine and never once has it given him problems. [Conclusion] Therefore, it won't give him a problem with the load he's now washing.

This argument is invalid, which is only to say that it's possible that the conclusion is false even assuming the premise to be true. But notice that, even though it's *possible* that the conclusion is false, it's *unlikely* that it is false.

An argument like this one is said to be relatively *strong*. More precisely, a **strong argument** has this distinguishing characteristic: On the assumption that the premises are true, its conclusion is *unlikely* to be false. Again, notice that the premises don't actually have to be true for the argument to be strong.

Arguments can be evaluated as stronger or weaker depending on how likely the premises show the conclusion to be. *Strong* and *weak* are not absolute

Reasoning Containing Both Deductive and Inductive Elements

In July 1977, Cathleen Crowell, age sixteen, accused Gary Dotson, twenty, of raping her in a Chicago suburb. Dotson was convicted of the rape and given a twenty-five- to fifty-year sentence. In March 1985, the alleged victim, now married and known as Cathleen Webb, told Illinois authorities that her accusation had been false. Eventually Governor James Thompson freed Dotson because the sentence "left a cloud over the Illinois justice system" and because he felt that Dotson had served enough time for the crime. He did not pardon Dotson, however. The entire episode attracted national attention. In one letter to the editor that we read, a reader expressed skepticism concerning Webb's recantation. Webb is undeniably a liar, he argued, because what she says now contradicts what she said then. Further, he continued, why did she wait so long to come forth? Why did the judge who presided over the original trial reject Webb's recantation after reviewing the evidence a second time? Why did even the governor say that he thought Webb had been raped and Dotson properly convicted? Thus, the letter writer concluded, it seemed likely that Webb was lying in her 1985 testimony when she said Dotson had not raped her.

Any given piece of real-life reasoning may easily contain both deductive and inductive elements, as does the letter writer's reasoning referred to here. His deductive argument was, in effect, this:

[Premise] Webb said X then but now says not-X, and [premise] anyone who does this was lying either then or now. Therefore, [conclusion] Webb was lying either then or now.

His inductive argument was, in effect, this:

[Premise] Webb waited a long time to say not-X, and [premise] the judge and the governor reviewed the case and thought Dotson had been properly convicted. Therefore, [conclusion] she was probably not lying when she originally accused Dotson.

terms, in other words. Had Frank's Twirlclean given him trouble every now and then, then his conclusion that it won't give him a problem with the load he's now washing would have been much less likely, and his argument much weaker.

Because an argument can be evaluated as stronger or weaker depending on how likely the premises show the conclusion to be, it is important to notice the degree of certainty or confidence with which the conclusion is set forth. A conclusion prefaced with the words *it is extremely likely that* . . . or *it is virtually certain that* . . . will require much more solid support from its premises than a conclusion prefaced with *it is possible that* . . . or *so it may well be that* . . .

Notice that *valid*, unlike *strong* and *weak* and *likely* and *probable,* is an absolute term. One argument is not relatively more valid than another. An argument is either valid or it is not, and that's that.

So, to summarize:

1. A valid argument has this defining characteristic: On the assumption that the premises are true, it is impossible that the conclusion is false.
2. A valid argument whose premises are all true is called a sound argument.
3. A strong argument has this defining characteristic: If the premises are assumed to be true, then its conclusion is unlikely to be false.

The best policy is to say that valid arguments are neither strong nor weak: They're just valid. It also is not automatically a telling criticism of an argument to pronounce it invalid. If you tell us our argument is invalid, you are merely pointing out that, even assuming that our premises are true, our conclusion is not *necessarily* true. But pointing that out won't bother us much *if* all we wished to establish was that, given our premises, our conclusion is *probably* true. In other words, if ours is an inductive argument, we won't care that it's invalid—all we want it to be is relatively strong.

EXERCISE 8-6

Fill in the blanks where called for and answer true or false where appropriate.

★1. The premises of _____ arguments are intended to provide absolutely conclusive reasons for accepting the conclusion.
2. Valid arguments are said to be strong or weak.
3. Invalid arguments are never strong.
★4. Sound arguments are _____ arguments whose premises are all _____ .
5. The premises of a valid argument are never false.
6. If a valid argument has a false conclusion, then not all its premises can be true.
★7. If a strong argument has a false conclusion, then not all its premises can be true.
8. A sound argument cannot have a false conclusion.

9. A true conclusion cannot be derived validly from false premises.

★10. *Strong* and *weak* are absolute terms.

EXERCISE 8-7

Go back to exercises 8-2 and 8-3 and discuss whether each argument presented is inductive or deductive. In the answer section at the back of the book, we have answered items 1, 4, 7, and 10 in each set.

EXERCISE 8-8

Go back to exercises 8-2 and 8-3 and determine which arguments are valid. In the answer section at the back of the book we have answered items 1, 4, 7, and 10 in each set.

EXERCISE 8-9

Given the premises, discuss whether the conclusion of each argument that follows is (a) true beyond a reasonable doubt, (b) probably true, (c) possibly true or possibly false, (d) probably false, or (e) false beyond a reasonable doubt. You should expect disagreement on these items, but the closer your answers are to your instructor's, the better. Our opinions on 1, 4, 7, and 10 are given at the back of the book.

★1. The sign on the parking meter says "Out of Order," so the meter isn't working.

2. The annual rainfall in California's north valley averages twenty-three inches. So the rainfall next year will be about twenty-three inches.

3. In the last two presidential races, the winner of the Iowa Republican primary has not captured the Republican nomination. Therefore the winner of the next Iowa Republican primary will not capture the Republican nomination.

★4. The New York steak, the Maine lobster, and the beef stroganoff at that restaurant are all exceptionally good. You can probably count on all the entrees being excellent.

5. You've never taken a course from Danielson, but three of your friends have and they hated the woman. Chances are that you'd hate her too if you took a course from her.

6. Since the graduates of Harvard, Yale, Princeton, and other Ivy League schools generally score higher on the Graduate Record Examination than students from North State, it follows that the Ivy League schools do more toward educating their students than North State does.

★7. Although Max bled profusely before he died, there was no blood on the ground where his body was found. Therefore, he was killed somewhere else and brought here after the murder.

8. When liquor was banned in 1920, hospitalizations for alcoholism and related diseases plummeted; in 1933, when Prohibition was repealed, alcohol-related illnesses rose sharply again. Legalization of cocaine, heroin, and marijuana would not curb abuse of these substances.

9. In every year in the 1980s except one either the Los Angeles Lakers or the Boston Celtics, or both, were in the National Basketball Association championship series. Therefore we may expect the same to be true in the 1990s.

★10. First, it seems clear that, even if there are occasional small dips in the consumption of petroleum, the general trend shows no sign of a real permanent decrease. Second, petroleum reserves are not being discovered as fast as petroleum is currently being consumed. From these two facts we can conclude that reserves will eventually be consumed and the world will have to do without oil.

Unstated Premises

As noted above, arguments can have unstated premises. Suppose a husband and wife are dining out, and she says to him: "It's getting very late, so we should call for the check." For this little argument to be valid, this principle must hold true: *"If it is getting very late, then we should call for the check."* The wife, no doubt, is assuming this principle (among many other things), and even if *she* is not assuming it, *we* must assume it if we are to credit her with a valid argument.

Most real-life arguments are like this argument in that some unstated proposition must be assumed for the argument to be valid. And it is useful to be able to specify what must be assumed for a given argument to be valid. What, for example, must be assumed for the following argument to be valid?

That dog is a pit bull, so it has strong jaw muscles.

What must be assumed, of course, is that all pit bulls have strong jaw muscles. In other words, the argument is valid if and only if it is true that all pit bulls have strong jaw muscles. Further, since it is questionable whether *all* pit bulls have strong jaw muscles, we see that the validity of this argument depends on a questionable assumption.

However, recall that an argument need not necessarily be valid to be a good argument. Invalid arguments may still be strong, that is, their premises may provide strong support, though less than absolutely conclusive support, for their conclusions. Let's therefore ask, is there an unstated premise that would make the pit bull argument a strong one? The answer is that if we plug into the argument the premise that *most* pit bulls have strong jaw muscles, which is certainly a reasonable premise, the result is quite a strong argument:

> That dog is a pit bull.
> [Unstated: Most pit bulls have strong jaw muscles.]
> Therefore, that dog has strong jaw muscles.

If you can spot what must be assumed for an argument to be valid and to be strong, you'll be in a much better position to evaluate it. If a plausible premise suffices to make the argument valid, then it is a very good argument. If no very plausible premise would make the argument valid, but some very plausible premise would make the argument strong, it's still a good argument, how good it is depending on how strong it is and how plausible the unstated premise is.

Let's consider another example:

> He's related to Edward Kennedy, so he's rich.

For the argument to be valid, one must assume that *everyone* related to Kennedy is rich, and that's not a very plausible assumption. For the argument to be strong, one must assume that *most* people related to Kennedy are rich, and while that assumption is a good bit more plausible than the first assumption, it still isn't very plausible. The most plausible relevant assumption is that *many* people related to Kennedy are rich, but with that assumption plugged into the argument, the argument is not particularly strong.

Want one more example?

> It's February, so the almond trees will bloom by the end of the month.

This argument is valid only if it is assumed that the almond trees *always* bloom by the end of February. Maybe that's true where you live, but it's not true where we live. Still, where we live it's true that the almond trees *almost always* bloom by the end of February, and with this assumption plugged into the argument, the argument turns out to be pretty strong.

EXERCISE 8-10

Discuss what must be assumed for each of the following arguments to be valid.

EXAMPLE: The fan needs oil. It's squeaking.

WHAT MUST BE ASSUMED: Whenever the fan is squeaking it needs oil.

* ★1. Jamal is well mannered, so he had a good upbringing.
  2. Bettina is pretty sharp, so she'll get a good grade in this course.
  3. It must have rained lately, because there are puddles everywhere.
* ★4. He'll drive recklessly only if he's upset, and he's not upset.
  5. Let's see . . . they have tons of leftovers, so their party could not have been very successful.

6. I think we can safely conclude that the battery is still in good condition. The lights are bright.

★7. Either the dog has fleas or its skin is dry. It's scratching a lot.

8. Melton was a good senator. He'd make an excellent president.

9. Gelonek doesn't own a gun. He's sure to be for gun control.

★10. The Carmel poet Robinson Jeffers is one of America's most outstanding poets. His work appears in many Sierra Club publications.

EXERCISE 8-11

Go back to exercise 8-10 and discuss what must be assumed for each argument to be strong. In the answer section at the back of the book we have answered items 1, 4, 7, and 10.

EXAMPLE: The fan needs oil. It's squeaking.

WHAT MUST BE ASSUMED: When the fan squeaks it usually needs oil.

EXERCISE 8-12

Discuss what must be assumed for each of the following arguments to be valid.

★1. Prices in that new store around the corner are going to be high, you can bet. All they sell are genuine leather goods.

2. I had a C going into the final exam; but I don't see how I can make less than a B for the course, because I managed an A on the final.

3. He's a good guitarist. He studied with Pepe Romero, you know.

★4. That plant is an ornamental fruit tree. It won't ever bear edible fruit.

5. The Federal Reserve Board will make sure that inflation doesn't reach 10 percent again. Its chair is an experienced hand at monetary policy.

6. Murphy doesn't stand a chance of getting elected in this county. His liberal position on most matters is well known.

★7. Washington Mayor Marion Barry has been a target of federal probes into alleged cocaine use; he cannot be a very effective mayor.

8. Half the people in the front row believe in God; therefore half the entire class believes in God.

9. Montezuma State students are all career-oriented. I say this because every Montezuma State student I ever met was career-oriented.

★10 Population studies show that smoking causes lung cancer; therefore, if you smoke, you will get lung cancer.

EXERCISE 8-13

Go back to exercise 8-12 and discuss what must be assumed for each argument to be strong. In the answer section at the back of the book we have answered items 1, 4, 7, and 10.

Techniques for Understanding Arguments

A good argument is one whose premises support the conclusion—in other words, an argument that is either valid or strong and whose premises are worth believing. So, to evaluate an argument, one must answer these two questions:

1. Are the premises acceptable?
2. Do the premises support the conclusion?

Remember, however, that evaluating arguments is only part of critical thinking. If the argument we are evaluating is a good argument for the conclusion, well and good. If it is not, then we must determine whether there are *other* reasons for accepting or rejecting the conclusion, reasons that are not mentioned in the argument at issue.

Before we can proceed with the evaluation of an argument, we have to understand it. Many arguments are difficult to understand because they are spoken, and thus go by so quickly that we cannot be sure of the conclusion and the premises. Others are difficult to understand because they have a complicated structure. Still others are difficult to understand because they are embedded in nonargumentative material consisting of background information, prejudicial coloring, illustrations, parenthetical remarks, digressions, subsidiary points, and other window dressing. And some arguments are difficult to understand because they are confused or because the reasons they contain are so poor that we are not sure whether to regard them as reasons.

To understand any argument, the first task is to find the conclusion—the main point or thesis of the passage. The next step is to locate the reasons that have been offered for the conclusion—that is, to find the premises. Next, we look for the reasons, if any, given for these premises. To proceed through these steps, you have to learn both to spot premises and conclusions when they occur in spoken and written passages, and to understand the interrelationships among these claims—that is, the structure of the argument.

Clarifying an Argument's Structure

Let's begin with how to understand the relationships among the argumentative claims, because this problem is sometimes easiest to solve. If you are dealing with written material that you are free to mark up, one useful technique is to number the premises and conclusions, and then use the numbers to lay bare the structure of the argument. Let's start with this argument as an example:

I don't think we should get Peter his own car. As a matter of fact, he is not responsible because he doesn't care for his things. And anyway, we don't have enough money for a car, since even now we have trouble making ends meet. Last week you yourself complained about our financial situation, and you never complain without really good reason.

We want to display the structure of this argument clearly. What we do is this: First, circle all premise and conclusion indicators. Thus:

I don't think we should get Peter his own car. As a matter of fact, he is not responsible (because) he doesn't care for his things. And anyway, we don't have enough money for a car, (since) even now we have trouble making ends meet. Last week you yourself complained about our financial situation, and you never complain without really good reason.

Next, bracket each premise and conclusion and number them consecutively as they appear in the argument. So what we now have is this:

① [I don't think we should get Peter his own car.] As a matter of fact, ② [he is.not responsible] because ③ [he doesn't care for his things.] And anyway, ④ [we don't have enough money for a car], since ⑤ [even now we have trouble making ends meet.] ⑥ [Last week you yourself complained about our financial situation], and ⑦ [you never complain without really good reason.]

And then we diagram the argument as follows: Using an arrow to mean "therefore" or "is intended as evidence [or as a reason or as a premise] for," the first three claims in the argument can be diagrammed as follows:

Now ⑥ and ⑦ together support ④; that is, they are *dependent* reasons for ④. To show that ⑥ and ⑦ are dependent reasons for ④, we simply draw a line under them, put a plus sign between them, and draw the arrow from the line to ④, like this:

Since ⑤ and ⑥ + ⑦ are independent reasons for ④, we can represent the relationship between them and ④ as follows:

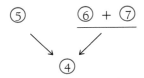

Finally, since ④ and ② are independent reasons for ①, the diagram of that entire argument is this:

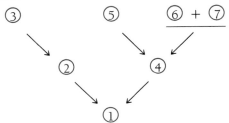

So, the conventions governing this approach to revealing argument structure are very simple: First, circle all premise- and conclusion-indicating words. Then, assuming you can identify the claims that function in the argument (a big assumption, as you will see before long), simply number them consecutively. Then display the structure of the argument using arrows for "therefore," and plus signs over a line to connect together two or more dependent premises.

Some claims, incidentally, may constitute reasons for more than one conclusion. For example:

① [Peter continues to be irresponsible.] ② [He certainly should not have his own car], and, as far as I am concerned, ③ [he can forget about that trip to Hawaii this winter, too.]

Structure:

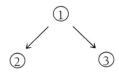

Of course, one might adopt other conventions for clarifying argument structure—for example, circling the main conclusion and drawing solid lines under supporting premises and wavy lines under the premises of subarguments. The technique we have described is simply one way of doing it; any of several others might work as well for you. However, *no* technique for revealing argument structure will work if you cannot spot the argumentative claims in the midst of a lot of background material.

Distinguishing Arguments from Window Dressing

We should point out that it is not always easy to isolate the argument in a speech or a written piece. Often, speakers and writers think that, because their main points are more or less clear to them, they will be equally apparent to their listeners or readers. But it doesn't always work that way.

If you are having trouble identifying a conclusion in what you hear or read, it *could* be because the passage is not an argument at all. Make sure that the passage in question is not a report, a description, an explanation, or something else altogether, rather than an argument. The key here is determining whether the speaker or writer is offering reasons intended to convince you of one or more of the claims made in the passage.

The problem could also be that the conclusion is left unstated. Sometimes it helps simply to put the argument aside and ask yourself, "What is this person trying to prove?" In any case, the first and essential step in understanding an argument is to spot the conclusion.

If you are having difficulty identifying the *premises,* consider the possibility that you have before you a case of nonargumentative persuasion (see Chapter 5). (You can't find premises in a piece of nonargumentative persuasion because there *are* no premises.) You have an advantage over many students in having learned about nonargumentative persuasion in Part One. By this time you should be getting pretty good at recognizing it.

Don't Forget Pseudoreasons

In Chapters 6 and 7 we saw that people will sometimes make statements in order to establish a claim when in reality their remarks have nothing to do with the claim. For example, "Margaret's qualifications are really quite good; after all, she'd be terribly hurt to think that you didn't think highly of them." Although Margaret's disappointment would no doubt be a reason for *something* (e.g., for keeping your views to yourself), it would not be a reason for altering your opinion of her qualifications. Her feelings are, in fact, thoroughly irrelevant to her qualifications. Extraneous material of all sorts can often be eliminated as argumentative material if you ask yourself simply, "Is this really relevant to the conclusion? Does this matter to what this person is trying to establish?" If you have worked through the exercises in Chapters 6 and 7, you have already had practice in spotting irrelevancies. If you haven't done these exercises, it would be useful to go back and do them now.

Evaluating Arguments

After you have come to understand an argument, it is time to evaluate it. You have to determine

1. Whether the premises are acceptable
2. Whether the premises support the conclusion

Are the Premises Acceptable?

Any premises for which reasons have been presented in the argument are the conclusions of subarguments and should be evaluated according to the principles in this chapter.

Unsupported premises should be evaluated in accordance with the guidelines and questions provided in Part One. Let us review these guidelines in summary fashion:

It is reasonable to accept an unsupported claim (in this case functioning as an unsupported premise) if the claim is an analytic truth or it comes from a credible source and does not conflict with what one has observed, one's background knowledge, or other creditable claims.

A premise that conflicts with what one has observed, or otherwise has reason to believe, should not be accepted unless there is very good reason for doing so.

A premise that conflicts with the claims of another credible source is also unacceptable unless the question of which source to believe has been resolved.

In addition, vague or ambiguous premises, and premises that are otherwise unclear, require clarification before acceptance. Clearly, any premise that is analytically false is unacceptable, and where two premises conflict with each other (see Chapter 3), the conflict must be resolved before either can function acceptably as a premise.

Some claims, most notably those that occur in certain kinds of explanations, should not necessarily be viewed as true or false in any straightforward sense. Such claims can be appraised in terms of the discussion in Chapter 4.

Do the Premises Support the Conclusion?

In other words, is the argument either (a) valid or (b) relatively strong? In the next three chapters we investigate this matter in some detail. In Chapter 9 we explain some of the most common valid and invalid deductive arguments, and in Chapters 10 and 11 we examine common types of inductive arguments.

Recap

An argument consists of a conclusion (the claim that is argued for) and premises (claims that provide reasons for believing the conclusion). Deductive arguments are those whose premises are intended to provide absolutely conclusive reasons for accepting the conclusion, whereas inductive arguments are those whose premises are intended to provide some support, but less than conclusive support, for the conclusion. Arguments are either valid or invalid; but invalid arguments may be, to varying degrees, strong or weak.

Before you can evaluate an argument, you must understand it. The all-important first step in understanding an argument is to find the conclusion. After that you must locate the reasons that have been offered in support of the conclusion (i.e., find the premises). One technique for clarifying the structure of a written argument, if you can identify the claims that function in the argument, is to number them consecutively as they are written and then use the numbers to lay out the structure of the argument as explained above.

After you have come to understand an argument, you can evaluate it by determining first whether the premises are acceptable and then whether the premises support the conclusion. In the next three chapters we examine common types of deductive and inductive arguments to give you a sense of when the premises of an argument do support its conclusion.

Additional Exercises

EXERCISE 8-14

Diagram the following "arguments," using the method explained in the text.

★ 1. ①, because ② and ③. [Assume that ② and ③ are dependent.]

 2. ① and ②; therefore ③. [Assume that ① and ② are independent.]

3. Since ①, ②; and since ③, ④. And since ② and ④, ⑤. [Assume that ② and ④ are independent.]

★4. ①; therefore ② and ③. But because ② and ③, ④. Consequently, ⑤. Therefore, ⑥. [Assume ② and ③ are independent.]

5. ①. ②. ③; therefore ④. ⑤, in view of ①. And ⑥, since ②. Therefore ⑦. [Assume ④, ⑤, and ⑥ are dependent.]

EXERCISE 8-15

Go back to exercises 8-2, 8-3, 8-4, and 8-5, and diagram the arguments using the method explained in the text. In the answer section at the back of the book we have answered items 1, 4, 7, and 10 for exercises 8-2 through 8-5.

EXERCISE 8-16

Diagram the arguments contained in the following passages, using the method explained in the text.

★1. Dear Jim,
Your distributor is the problem. Here's why. There's no current at the spark plugs. And if there's no current at the plugs, then either your alternator is shot or your distributor is defective. But if the problem was in the alternator, then your dash warning light would have been on. So, since the light isn't on, the problem must be in the distributor. Hope this helps.
Yours,
Benita Autocraft

2. The federal deficit must be reduced. It has contributed to inflation and it has hurt American exports.

3. It's high time professional boxing was outlawed. Boxing almost always leads to brain damage, and anything that does that ought to be done away with. Besides, it supports organized crime.

★4. They really ought to build a new airport. It would attract more business to the area, not to mention the fact that the old airport is overcrowded and dangerous.

5. Vote for Jackson? No way, Jose. He's too radical and he's too inexperienced, and his lack of experience would have made him a dangerous president.

EXERCISE 8-17

Diagram the arguments contained in the following passages, using the method explained in the text.

★1. Cottage cheese will help you to be slender, youthful, and more beautiful. Enjoy it often.

2. If you want to listen to loud music, do it when we are not at home. It bothers us, and we're your parents.

3. "Officials of the Pentagon have long complained that, as wasteful as their budget requests may be, members of Congress often worsen matters by piling on extra spending beneficial to their districts. There is a good chance, though, that there will be less of this boondoggling now that House Democrats have chosen Les Aspin, D-Wis., as chairman of the Armed Services Committee.

"A former systems analyst in the Defense Department under Robert McNamara, Aspin has an insider's knowledge of how the Pentagon operates and where the waste is likely to be. Nor is he likely to have much patience with fellow members' attempts to fatten the defense budget with pet weapons systems profitable to hometown contractors."

—*Brattleboro* (Vt.) *Reformer*

★4. From a letter to the editor: "The idea of a free press in America today is a joke. A small group of people, the nation's advertisers, control the media more effectively than if they owned it outright. Through fear of an advertising boycott they can dictate everything from programming to news report content. Politicians as well as editors shiver in their boots at the thought of such a boycott. This situation is intolerable and ought to be changed. I suggest we all listen to National Public Radio and public television."

5. "After two years in the pits, the American economy has just wrapped up its second straight year of high growth and low inflation—a happy combination that hasn't been achieved in this country since the early 1960s. But the nation can't afford to celebrate for very long, for we have floated out of recession on a sea of red ink, and if some changes aren't made soon, we are in danger of being drowned by it. There can be no doubt that the huge tax breaks and defense spending increases under the first Reagan administration drove the growth. They provided both supply-side incentives and a massive, old-fashioned fiscal stimulus to the economy. But they also produced record-breaking federal deficits, which helped produce high interest rates. And these must eventually take their toll."

—*Sacramento Bee*

6. "Does President Reagan really understand the seriousness of the farm-credit crisis? Is the farm debt relief bill he recently vetoed 'a multibillion-dollar blank check for farmers and bankers,' as charged? The answer to both questions is no.

"Farm organization officials claim the veto spells disaster for 'about 10 percent of our efficient, midrange farm operators who are hard-pressed to finance 1985 farming operations.'

"As Iowa Congressman Berkley Bedell and others have pointed out, the veto may actually increase the federal deficit. 'If large numbers of farms fail as expected, the entire economy will be devastated,' Bedell points out. 'Jobs will be lost, businesses will close and tax revenues to help reduce the deficit will be lost. We'll spend more money in the end trying to repair the damage.' "

—*The Messenger,* Fort Dodge, Iowa

★ 7. "Consumers ought to be concerned about the Federal Trade Commission's dropping a rule that supermarkets must actually have in stock the items they advertise for sale. While a staff analysis suggests costs of the rule outweigh the benefits to consumers, few shoppers want to return to the practices that lured them into stores only to find the advertised products they sought were not there.

"The staff study said the rule causes shoppers to pay $200 million to receive $125 million in benefits. The cost is a low estimate and the benefits a high estimate, according to the study.

"However, even those enormously big figures boil down to a few cents per shopper over a year's time. And the rule does say that when a grocer advertises a sale, the grocer must have sufficient supply of the sale items on hand to meet reasonable buyer demand."

—*The Oregonian*

8. "Richard Lugar's greatest attribute as the new chairman of the Senate Foreign Relations Committee is that he is not Jesse Helms. That alone is plenty of reason for any rational American to breathe a sigh of relief over his elevation to that job.

"Even now the Indiana senator's words and actions show that he will work to bring long-missing openness, bipartisanship and congressional independence to the conduct of U.S. foreign policy. By pressing the administration for policy changes in South Africa and Nicaragua, Lugar already has sent a message to the White House that the Republican Senate leadership expects to regain a significant voice. By scheduling a comprehensive committee review of American foreign policy, Lugar furthers the hope that the administration's major international initiatives will begin to undergo public, bipartisan scrutiny."

—*St. Petersburg* (Fla.) *Times*

9. From a letter to the editor: "Recently the California Highway Patrol stopped me at a drunk-drive checkpoint. Now, I don't like drunk drivers more than anyone else. I certainly see why the police find the checkpoint system effective. But I think our right to move about freely is much more important. If the checkpoint system continues, then next there will be checkpoints for drugs, seat belts, infant car seats, drivers' licenses. We will regret it later if we allow the system to continue."

★ 10. "Well located, sound real estate is the safest investment in the world. It is not going to disappear, as can the value of dollars put into savings accounts. Neither will real estate values be lost because of inflation. In fact, property values tend to increase at a pace at least equal to the rate of inflation. Most homes have appreciated at a rate greater than the inflation rate (due mainly to strong buyer demand and insufficient supply of newly constructed homes)."

—ROBERT BRUSS, *The Smart Investor's Guide to Real Estate*

11. "The constitutional guarantee of a speedy trial protects citizens from arbitrary government abuse, but it has at least one other benefit, too. It prevents crime.

"A recent Justice Department study found that more than a third of those with serious criminal records—meaning three or more felony convictions—are arrested for new offenses while free on bond awaiting federal court trial. You don't have to be a social scientist to suspect that the longer the delay, the greater the likelihood of further violations. In short, overburdened courts mean much more than justice delayed; they quite literally amount to the infliction of further injustice."

—Scripps Howard Newspapers

12. "There is a prevailing school of thought and growing body of opinion that one day historians will point to a certain television show and declare: This is what life was like in small-town America in the mid-20th century.

"We like to think those future historians will be right about *The Andy Griffith Show*. It had everything, and in rerun life still does: humor, wisdom, wholesomeness and good old red-blooded American entertainment.

"That's why we are so puzzled that a group of true-blue fans of the show want to rename some suitable North Carolina town Mayberry. The group believes there ought to be a real-live city in North Carolina called Mayberry, even though everybody already knows that Mayberry was modeled on Mount Airy, sort of, since that is Sheriff Taylor's, uh, Andy Griffith's hometown.

"No, far better that the group let the whole thing drop. For one thing, we don't know of anyplace—hamlet, village, town, or city—that could properly live up to the name of Mayberry. Perhaps the best place for Mayberry to exist is right where it is—untouched, unspoiled and unsullied by the modern world. Ain't that right, Ernest T. Bass?"

—*Greensboro* (N.C.) *News & Record*

★13. "There has been ample time now for debate to rage about the uses of HyperCard. Many users are already finding it a valuable tool for organizing their Macintosh work environments. I, seeing it as overkill for a Rolodex substitute (my paper Rolodex does the job just fine), initially thought it was more hype than substance. I still don't buy the official line. It's not a "software erector set," unless the software you have in mind falls within a pretty limited category. I haven't found it particularly easy to use, not for producing a functional finished product. I want it to do things it can't do (such as sort on more than two different fields), and it does things I don't want it to do (such as save changes automatically when I thought I was just experimenting)."

—HENRY BORTMAN, *MacUser*

14. Having your car washed at the carwash may be the best way to go, but there are some possible drawbacks. The International Carwashing Association (ICA) has fought back against charges that automatic car washes, in recycling wash water, actually dump the salt and dirt from one car onto the next. And that brushes and drag cloths hurt the finish. Perhaps there is some truth to these charges.

   The ICA sponsored tests that supposedly demonstrated that the average home car wash is harder on a car than an automatic wash. Maybe. But what's "the average" home car wash? And you can bet that the automatic carwashes in the test were in perfect working order.

   There is no way you or I can tell for certain if the filtration system and washing equipment at the automatic carwash are properly maintained. And even if they are, what happens if you follow some mud-caked pickup through the wash? Road dirt might still be caught in the bristles of the brushes or the strips of fabric that are dragged over your car.

   Here's my recommendation: Wash your own car.

15. Letter to the editor: "The worst disease of the 1990s will be AIDS, Acquired Immune Deficiency Syndrome.

   "AIDS has made facing surgery scary. In the last ten years several hundred Americans got AIDS from getting contaminated blood in surgery, and it is predicted that within a few years more hundreds of people will receive AIDS blood each year.

   "Shouldn't we be tested for AIDS before we give blood? As it is now, no one can feel safe receiving blood. Because of AIDS, people are giving blood to themselves so they will be safe if they have to have blood later. We need a very sensitive test to screen AIDS donors."

   —*North State Record*

★16.

Argument in Favor of Measure A

   "Measure A is consistent with the City's General Plan and City policies directing growth to the City's non-agricultural lands. A 'yes' vote on Measure A will affirm the wisdom of well-planned, orderly growth in the City of Chico by approving an amendment to the 1982 Rancho Arroyo Specific Plan. Measure A substantially reduces the amount of housing previously approved for Rancho Arroyo, increases the number of parks and amount of open space, and significantly enlarges and enhances Bidwell Park.

   "A 'yes' vote will accomplish the following: •Require the development to dedicate 130.8 acres of land to Bidwell Park •Require the developer to dedicate seven park sites •Create 53 acres of landscaped corridors and greenways •Preserve existing arroyos and protect sensitive plant habitats and other environmental features •Create junior high school and church sites •Plan a series of villages within which, even-

tually, a total of 2,927 residential dwelling units will be developed •Plan area which will provide onsite job opportunities and retail services . . .”
— County of Butte Sample Ballot, June 7, 1988

17.

Rebuttal to Argument in Favor of Measure A

“Villages? Can a project with 3,000 houses and 7,000 new residents really be regarded as a ‘village’? The Sacramento developers pushing the Rancho Arroyo project certainly have a way with words. We urge citizens of Chico to ignore their flowery language and vote no on Measure A.

“These out-of-town developers will have you believe that their project protects agricultural land. Hogwash! Chico’s Greenline protects valuable farmland. With the Greenline, there is enough land in the Chico area available for development to build 62,000 new homes . . .

“They claim that their park dedications will reduce use of our overcrowded Bidwell Park. Don’t you believe it! They want to attract 7,000 new residents to Chico by using Rancho Arroyo’s proximity to Bidwell Park to outsell other local housing projects.

“The developers imply that the Rancho Arroyo project will provide a much needed school site. In fact, the developers intend to sell the site to the school district, which will pay for the site with taxpayers’ money.

“Chico doesn’t need the Rancho Arroyo project. Vote no on Measure A.”
— County of Butte Sample Ballot, June 7, 1988

★18. Letter to the editor: “The gang war issue is very serious in our world because of guns and drugs. Jamaican police seized a cache of handguns, automatic rifles, and machine guns according to a recent issue of *Newsweek*. These guns were earmarked for gangs in the U.S. and for anyone else who wants to buy them. This was just one shipment and there are many others. Guns are easily available to all illegal people. Also, last week in Stockton at the opening of *Colors*, the movie on gang wars, a gang member was gunned down in front of the theater. There are many hundreds of gang killings each year in L.A. I think the police should do a better job of stopping these gangs from getting guns and killing innocent people.”

— *Miltonville Gazette*

19. Letter to the editor: “A relative of mine is a lawyer who recently represented a murderer who had already had a life sentence and broke out of prison and murdered someone else. I think this was a waste of the taxpayers’ money to try this man again. It won’t do any good. I think murderers should be executed.

“We are the most crime-ridden society in the world. Someone is murdered every 27 minutes in the U.S., and there is a rape every ten minutes and an armed robbery every 82 seconds. According to the FBI, there are 870,000 violent crimes a year, and you know the number is increasing.

"Also according to the FBI, only 10 percent of those arrested for the crimes committed are found guilty, and a large percentage are released on probation. These people are released so they can just go out and commit more crimes.

"Why are they released? In the end it is because there aren't enough prisons to house the guilty. The death sentence must be restored. This would create more room in prisons. It would also drastically reduce the number of murders. If a robber knew before he shot someone that if he was caught his own life would be taken, would he do it?

"These people deserve to die. They sacrificed their right to live when they murdered someone, maybe your mother. It's about time we stopped making it easy for criminals to kill people and get away with it."

—*Cascade News*

20. "There's no doubt that the U.S. Senate will ratify the U.S.–Soviet treaty on intermediate-range nuclear missiles. The few lonely Republican hardliners opposing it cannot prevail against the 90 senators who have rightly concluded that the treaty, which bans all medium-range nuclear missiles, including the Soviet SS-20s that have threatened Europe for a decade, is an advance for Western security and a triumph of American diplomacy.

"But unless the Senate votes an end to their dilatory tactics, Sen. Jesse Helms and his wrecking crew have it in their power to embarrass the president by delaying ratification of the treaty beyond next week's Moscow summit. A delay would not be a disastrous result, but it would be a needless source of friction at the summit.

"Since 1972, the United States has signed four major arms control agreements with the Soviets; it has yet to ratify a single one. If President Reagan cannot overcome the opposition of a handful of malcontents within his own party to win timely ratification of the INF Treaty, it will create clouds of doubt in Moscow about whether any American president can make his arms deals stick. As Secretary of State George Shultz says, the Senate must now 'show the world that the United States can come to closure.'

"The INF Treaty has been thoroughly examined by the Senate in hearings, troubling questions about verification have been ironed out in negotiations with the Soviets and treaty opponents have had a fair chance to make their case, however implausible and unconvincing. The debate is over; it's time to deliver a treaty for the president to take to Moscow."

—*Sacramento Bee*, May 25, 1988

EXERCISE 8-18 (ESSAY)

Decide whether each of the following claims should be accepted or rejected. Then, in an essay of no more than one page, present reasons for your decision. The instructor will call on members of the class to read essays; the rest of the class will identify the main conclusion and the premises.

1. It should not be illegal to possess marijuana.
2. Dogs are smarter than cats.
3. Humans have free will.
4. All college examinations should be open-book.
5. A national economy that requires perpetual growth cannot endure indefinitely.

EXERCISE 8-19 (ESSAY)

Write an essay in which you support a conclusion with two separate arguments, one inductive and one deductive.

9 *Common Patterns of Deductive Arguments*

A small number of extremely simple valid argument forms makes it possible to deal with a wide variety of deductive arguments—some of them very complex and subtle.

—WESLEY SALMON

The rest is deduction.

—SHERLOCK HOLMES

In this chapter we explain some of the most common patterns of valid and invalid deductive arguments. You will recall that deductive arguments are those whose premises are intended to provide absolutely conclusive reasons for accepting the conclusion. True, it is theoretically possible that someone whose argument follows one or another of these patterns may not intend his or her premises to provide absolutely conclusive reasons for accepting the conclusion, whatever it happens to be. But almost always when you encounter one of these patterns, the speaker or writer will regard the conclusion as absolutely following from the premises.

The patterns listed here are commonly encountered indeed. Strictly speaking, there are an infinite number of argument patterns, but a very small number do most of the work in everyday discourse, and those are the ones we concentrate on here.

Arguments and Argument Patterns _____

Let's look at a pair of arguments:

1. If John took the car tonight, then Leslie will have to walk to the movie theater. John did take the car. Therefore, Leslie will just have to walk to the movies.
2. If it rains tomorrow, the picnic will be canceled. It is going to rain tomorrow. Therefore, the picnic will be canceled.

A comparison of these two arguments shows that they have something in common—their structures are identical. We say that they share the same **argument pattern.** To illustrate the pattern, let's allow the letters P and Q to stand for the claims made in the first argument:

P = John takes (or took) the car tonight.
Q = Leslie will have to walk to the movies.

If we restate argument 1 using these two letters alone, it will look like this:

If P then Q.
P.
Therefore, Q.

Notice that the entire argument is represented by the letters that stand for the claims plus some "logical words"—*if, then,* and *therefore*. The letters that stand for the claims in this argument can actually stand for any claim whatsoever. We call the letters the **claim variables**, since what they stand for can vary.

Casting an argument into claim variables and logical words alone reveals its argument pattern. Notice that when the proper variables replace the proper claims, argument 2 reduces to exactly the same pattern as argument 1:

P = It will rain tomorrow.
Q = The picnic will be canceled.

The argument pattern for the argument is

If P then Q.
P.
Therefore, Q.

In most deductive arguments, and in all that we consider in this chapter, the argument pattern is the crucial factor in determining whether an argument is valid or invalid. If we discover that a given pattern is valid, *then every argument that has that pattern is a valid argument.* Since the two examples we have looked at share a pattern, and since that pattern turns out to be a valid one (as we show in the next section), *both* arguments 1 and 2 are valid.

Argument Patterns: Set One

Modus Ponens

The first valid argument pattern we'll look at is called **modus ponens**. This pattern, along with several others, has been around long enough and turns up often enough to have its own name. The two examples in the preceding section share the modus ponens pattern.

All arguments of this pattern contain a **conditional claim** as one premise (the "If . . . then . . ." claim in the examples). The "if . . ." portion is called the **antecedent** of the conditional, and the "then . . ." portion is called the **consequent.** Another premise affirms the "if . . ." portion, and the conclusion of the argument is the same as the "then . . ." portion. Let's look more closely at these separate components as they appear in their proper places within the modus ponens pattern:

A conditional claim (P stands for the antecedent of
the conditional, Q for the consequent) ⟶ If P then Q.
Affirmation of the antecedent (here we assert the
truth of the "if . . ." part of the first premise) ⟶ P.
The consequent of the first premise is the conclusion⟶ Therefore, Q.

How can we be confident that every argument with this pattern is valid? Stop and think: In order for a deductive argument to be valid, its conclusion cannot be false if its premises are true. Notice that it is simply impossible to have true premises and a false conclusion when the pattern is modus ponens. The second premise tells us P, and the first tells us "If P then Q." If both these premises are true, then it's impossible for the conclusion (Q) to be false.*

Here is another example:

If the rate of inflation continues at its present level, then the Federal Reserve Board will tighten the money supply. But there is nothing that will prevent the current rate of inflation from continuing. Therefore, the Fed will wind up tightening the supply of money.

We represent the claims in the argument thus:

P = The present rate of inflation will continue.
Q = The Federal Reserve Board will tighten the money supply.

*For a detailed account of the nature of "if-then" claims see Appendix 2.

And we get the modus ponens pattern by plugging in these letters for the claims:

> If P then Q.
> P.
> Therefore, Q.

Here's one last example before moving on:

> Farnsworth is clearly guilty of the crime. But if he is guilty, then Axelrod must have known about it all along. Therefore, Axelrod knew about it.

We first link the claim variables with the claims:

> P = Farnsworth is guilty of the crime.
> Q = Axelrod knew about it.

(We do not have to use these particular letters as our variables. We could have used F for the first claim and A for the second—there is nothing special about which letter stands for which claim. What *does* count is that we use the *same* letter for a claim wherever that claim appears in the argument.)

Now we can state the pattern of the argument:

> P.
> If P then Q.
> Therefore, Q.

Notice that in this example of modus ponens the order of the premises is reversed from that of previous examples. Here the conditional claim is the second one, and its antecedent is affirmed in the first premise. The order of the premises doesn't matter in the least; it's still a case of modus ponens and therefore valid. Given that Farnsworth is guilty, and given that *if* Farnsworth is guilty then Axelrod must have known about it, it must be true that Axelrod knew about it.

Affirming the Consequent

Now let's look at an argument pattern that somewhat resembles modus ponens but is *not* valid. The pattern is this:

> If P then Q.
> Q.
> Therefore, P.

In the modus ponens form, one of the premises affirms the antecedent of the other one, the latter being a conditional claim. In the current case, though, notice that the second premise affirms *not* the antecedent of the first premise but rather its consequent. This is a fallacious argument pattern, often referred to as **affirming the consequent.** However much the pattern resembles modus ponens, it is not valid. Here's an example of an argument of this pattern:

If Pinkerton voted in the last election, then he must be a citizen of the United States. And, as a matter of fact, he is a citizen of the United States. Therefore, Pinkerton voted in the last election.

By revealing the argument pattern of this example, we can identify the fallacy called affirming the consequent:

P = Pinkerton voted in the last election.
Q = Pinkerton is a citizen of the U.S.

When we replace the claims with these variables, we see the invalid form:

If P then Q.
Q.
Therefore, P.

Notice that it is entirely possible for both premises of this argument to be true while the conclusion is false. It is certainly true that if Pinkerton voted in the last election then he is a citizen, because only citizens are allowed to vote. And let's presume that it is true that Pinkerton is a citizen. Does it follow that he voted? Not at all. Lots of citizens are ineligible to vote (convicted felons, for example), and lots of citizens who are eligible don't bother to vote. So the information in the premises cannot guarantee the truth of this argument's conclusion.

What makes the invalidity of this argument pattern hard for some people to see is the fact that the antecedent of a conditional claim does not have to be true for the conditional claim itself to be true. In the preceding example, the claim "Pinkerton voted in the last election" can be false while the conditional in which it occurs remains perfectly true:

If Pinkerton voted in the last election, then he must be a citizen of the United States.

Don't Overlook Unstated Claims

Dear Editor:
Gasoline prices have dropped about three cents a gallon over the past ten months. Watch for fuel efficiency requirements to be rolled back and Detroit to trot out the gas hogs again.

—*Midfield Sentinel*

Remember that arguments are often presented with an unstated premise or conclusion. This letter can be analyzed as a case of modus ponens, with an unstated conditional premise. (If gasoline prices have dropped by about three cents a gallon over the past ten months, then federal fuel efficiency requirements will be rolled back and Detroit will trot out the gas hogs again.)

A conditional tells us what is or must be the case *provided that* the antecedent is true, not that the antecedent is *in fact* true. So, as the example shows, knowing that a conditional is true, and even that the consequent happens to be true as well, does not guarantee the truth of the antecedent, which in this argument pattern is the conclusion of the argument.

Here is another example of affirming the consequent:

> If the fuse has blown, then the lights will not be on. Sure enough, the lights are not on. So we must have a blown fuse.

Clearly invalid, right?

EXERCISE 9-1

Assign letters (claim variables) to claims in the arguments that follow, and then use the letters and the appropriate logical words to display the arguments' logical forms. Identify those arguments that have the valid modus ponens pattern and those that have the invalid pattern of affirming the consequent.

EXAMPLE: Jan's dog must be at least thirteen years old, and if it's that old it should be taken to the veterinarian at least twice a year. So Jan should take her dog to the vet at least twice each year.

ANSWER:

P = Jan's dog is at least thirteen years old.
Q = Jan's dog should be taken to the vet at least twice a year.
Argument pattern: P.
                      If P then Q.
          Therefore, Q.
Name of pattern: Modus ponens (valid)

1. If Baffin Island is larger than Sumatra, then two of the five largest islands in the world are in the Arctic Ocean. And Baffin Island, as it turns out, is about 2 percent larger than Sumatra. Therefore, the Arctic Ocean contains two of the world's five largest islands.

★2. Alexander will finish his book by tomorrow afternoon only if he is an accomplished speed reader. Fortunately for him, he is quite accomplished at speed reading. Therefore, he will get his book finished by tomorrow afternoon.

3. The alternator is not working properly if the ampmeter shows a negative reading. The current reading of the ampmeter is negative. So the alternator is not working properly.

★4. Fewer than 2 percent of the employees of New York City's Transit Authority are accountable to management. If such a small number of employees are accountable to the management of the organization, no improvement in the system's efficiency can be expected in the near future. So we cannot expect any such improvements any time soon.

5. If the danger of range fires is greater this year than last, then state and federal officials will hire a greater number of fire fighters to cope with the danger. Since more fire fighters are already being hired this year than were hired all last year, we can be sure that the danger of fires has increased this year.

Modus Tollens

Like modus ponens, the **modus tollens** argument pattern has one premise that is a conditional claim, but the other premise is the *denial* of the consequent of that conditional. The conclusion is the denial of the conditional's antecedent. Here is what it looks like:

> If P then Q.
> Not-Q.
> Therefore, not-P.

All arguments of this pattern are valid. Here's an example:

> If Jones made his payment on time, then he didn't owe finance charges. He did owe finance charges. So he did not make his payment on time.

In this argument:

> P = Jones made his payment on time.
> Q = He didn't owe finance charges.

Now note: Since Q = he did *not* owe finance charges, *Not-Q* = he *did* owe finance charges. Thus, the pattern of this argument really is modus tollens, even though at first it may not seem like it.

Here's why the conclusion of the argument absolutely follows from the premises: If Jones made his payment on time, then according to the first premise, he didn't owe finance charges. But the second premise tells us he *did* owe finance charges, which means that he *didn't* make his payment on time—and that's what the conclusion says.

Denying the Antecedent

Just as affirming the wrong part of a conditional premise produces an invalid look-alike for modus ponens, so does denying the wrong part, in this case the antecedent, produce an invalid counterpart to modus tollens. Here is the invalid argument pattern known as **denying the antecedent**:

> If P then Q.
> Not-P.
> Therefore, not-Q.

Notice: a conditional claim is false in only one case—where the antecedent is true and the consequent is false. Therefore, nothing follows about the consequent from a denial of the antecedent. That is, we can know the antecedent is false and still be unable to determine whether the consequent is true or false. Here's an example of this invalid pattern:

> If Bergdorf bought a Honda automobile, then he bought a Japanese car. But he didn't buy a Honda. Therefore, Bergdorf did not buy a Japanese car.

It does not follow that Bergdorf didn't buy a Japanese car from the facts that he would have bought a Japanese car *if* he had bought a Honda and that he did not in fact buy a Honda. Maybe he bought a Toyota. In that case both premises would remain true but the conclusion would be false—which would be impossible if the argument were valid.

Incidentally, when you set out to show that a given argument pattern is invalid, you need a certain amount of inventiveness. You have to invent a situation in which the premises of an argument of that pattern would be true and the conclusion false, and this requires creative as well as logical thinking. In the case above, imagining that Bergdorf bought a Toyota did the trick. This didn't require *much* creativity, because the argument is a simple one, but more complicated arguments sometimes require considerable creativity. The point is that logical thinking and creative thinking are not opposites—they work together and complement one another, and critical thinking includes both.

If P Then Q, and P Only If Q

Dear Editor:
If the president will lower taxes, then he must be prepared to make spending cuts. But he isn't prepared to do that. So he won't lower taxes.

Dear Editor:
The president will lower taxes only if he is prepared to make spending cuts. But he isn't prepared to do that. So he won't lower taxes.

Both these letters are instances of modus tollens. If you didn't see this, you may not have realized that the first claims in the arguments are equivalent. It may look at first like "P only if Q" says the same as "If Q then P," but it's a mistake to think so. "She can vote only if she is a citizen" is *not* equivalent to, "If she is a citizen then she can vote"; it's equivalent to, "If she can vote then she is a citizen."

Remember: P only if Q = If P then Q.

EXERCISE 9-2

Assign letters to the claims in the following arguments; then display the argument patterns and identify them as either modus tollens or denying the antecedent.

EXAMPLE: If no papers are filed in court, the suit cannot be prosecuted. But papers have been filed, so it must be that the prosecution of the case is going ahead.

ANSWER:

P = No papers are filed in court.
Q = The suit cannot be prosecuted.

Argument pattern: If P then Q.
                                   Not-P.
                   Therefore, not-Q.

Name of pattern: denying the antecedent (invalid)

1. If Jack Davis robbed the Central Pacific Express in 1870, then the authorities imprisoned the right person. But the authorities did not imprison the right person. Therefore, it must not have been Jack Davis who robbed the Central Pacific Express in 1870.
★2. If higher education were living up to its responsibilities, the five best-selling magazines on American campuses would not be *Cosmopolitan, People, Playboy, Glamour,* and *Vogue.* But those are exactly the magazines that sell best in the nation's college bookstores. Higher education, we can conclude, is failing in at least some of its responsibilities.
3. If the recent tax cuts had been self-financing, then there would have been no substantial increase in the federal deficit. But they turned out not to be self-financing. Therefore, there will be a substantial increase in the federal deficit.
★4. Broc Glover was considered sure to win if he had no bad luck in the early part of the race. But we've learned that he has had the bad luck to be involved in a crash right after the start, so we're expecting another driver to be the winner.
5. The public did not react favorably to the majority of policies recommended by Reagan during his second term. But if his electoral landslide in 1984 was a mandate for more conservative policies, the public would have reacted favorably to most of those he recommended after the election. Therefore the 1984 vote was not considered a mandate for more conservative policies.

Chain Argument

This valid pattern of deductive reasoning involves three conditional claims. It looks like this:

If P then Q.
If Q then R.
Therefore, if P then R.

Notice that, essentially, the premises lead us from P to R by means of the connecting claim, Q. The conclusion merely leaves out the connecting claim and goes straight from P to R based on the connection established in the premises. An example:

If the wind is up tomorrow, the sailing will be exciting. But if the sailing is exciting, Martha will not want to go. Therefore, if the wind is up tomorrow, Martha will not want to go sailing.

The only way the conclusion of this argument can be false is for one of the premises to be false, which means that the truth of both premises guarantees the truth of the conclusion. Thus, the argument is valid, as are all examples of the chain-argument pattern.

Reverse Chain Argument

This pattern is identical to the valid chain argument except that the conclusion is turned around—the antecedent and the consequent are reversed. The result is an invalid pattern. Here is what it looks like:

If P then Q.
If Q then R.
Therefore, if R then P.

And here is an example of this pattern:

If today is a federal holiday, then there will be no mail delivery. And if there

Chain Arguments with Many Links

Chain arguments are not limited to just two steps. The pattern

If A then B; if B then C; therefore if A then C

is the basic pattern, but it is also perfectly valid to reason through many such steps:

If A then B; if B then C; if C then D; and so on, all the way to if Y then Z; therefore, if A then Z.

If each link in the chain is a strong one—if, for example, A really does imply B, B implies C, and so forth—then the conclusion that A implies Z is established.

The ability to carry through long chains of reasoning is important, among other ways, in tracing out the consequences of our actions.

is no mail delivery, you will not receive your check today. Therefore, if you do not receive your check today, it's because it's a federal holiday.

Notice that there are many ways in which the premises of this argument can be true while the conclusion remains false. For example, the check might not have been mailed on time, it might have been lost in the mail, it might have been part of the loot in a mail robbery, or any number of other things. Once again, the point is that it is possible for the premises to be true and the conclusion false, and so we cannot depend on the truth of the premises to guarantee the truth of the conclusion.

EXERCISE 9-3

Assign letters to the claims in the following arguments and determine which of the arguments have the chain-argument pattern and which have the pattern of its invalid imposter, the reverse chain argument.

1. If Paul attends the ceremony, then so will Charles. And if Charles attends, he will take Susan. Therefore, if Paul attends the ceremony, Charles will take Susan.

★2. If the right amount of heat is applied to water at 212° F in a sealed container, then the pressure in the container will increase without any increase in the temperature. This follows from the facts that if the proper amount of heat is applied to water at 212° then steam at 212° is produced, and if steam at 212° is produced from water at the same temperature, the pressure in the container will increase without any increase in temperature.

3. Juniors are eligible to take the examination if seniors are, and if juniors can take it, then so can sophomores. So sophomores can take the exam if seniors can.

★4. If Boris is really a spy for the KGB, then he has been lying through his teeth about his business in this country. But we can expose his true occupation if he's been lying like that. So I'm confident that, if we can expose his true occupation we can show that he's really a KGB spy.

5. The commission will extend the bow-hunting season only if they cut back the rest of the primitive-arms season. Furthermore, if the commission is fair, then they will simply *have* to extend the bow-hunting season at least a few days. Consequently, the commission can be fair only if it cuts back the rest of the primitive-arms season.

EXERCISE 9-4

Assign letters to the claims in the following arguments and determine which pattern is exemplified by each argument. Note whether each argument is valid or invalid.

★1. If Charles did not pay his taxes, then he did not receive a refund. Thus, he did not pay his taxes, since he did not receive a refund.

2. If they wanted to go to the party, then they would have called by now. But they haven't, so they didn't.

3. If drugs are legalized, then quality will be monitored by the government. If quality is monitored by the government, then there will be fewer drug-caused deaths. Therefore, if drugs are legalized, then there will be fewer drug-caused deaths.

★ 4. If you are wealthy, then you are happy, and if you are happy, then you are smart. Therefore, if you are smart, then you are wealthy.

5. "You'll get an A in the class," she predicted.
"What makes you say that?" he asked.
"Because," she said, "If you get an A, then you're smart, and you *are* smart."

6. If Florin arrived home by eight, she received the call from her attorney. But she did not get home by eight, so she must have missed her attorney's call.

7. If I had passed the test for this class, and had turned in my homework, and had attended each day, and had shown up at my discussion group, then I would have passed this dumb class. But I didn't do any of those things. Guess I won't pass.

8. The acid rain problem will be cured, but only if the administration stops talking and starts acting. So far, however, all we've had from the president is words. Words are cheap. Action is what counts. The problem will not be remedied, at least not while this administration is in office.

★ 9. It seemed that at any time she might throw up her hands and exclaim about her good fortune. But she only did this, he noticed, when she could reasonably expect Charles to be present. Since she certainly wasn't proclaiming her good fortune now, he concluded that Charles would not make an appearance.

10. To build a larger muscle mass, it is sufficient to lift weights once every other day. Increased muscle mass, in turn, promotes a desire to lift more frequently. If you lift weights only once every other day, therefore, you will, paradoxically, find yourself wishing to lift more often.

Argument Patterns: Set Two

In this set of argument patterns we'll be discussing claims that relate classes of things (or, if you like, sets, categories, groups, flocks, or herds of things). For example, the claim "All sophomores are students" expresses a relationship between the class of sophomores and the class of students. Since we'll be dealing with classes, we'll make use of class variables—X, Y, and Z—not to be confused with claim variables, which we used in the preceding section. A **class variable** stands for a class of entities.

To identify argument patterns in this set, we need to determine what classes of things the claims in the arguments are about and then replace each class with its own class variable. In general, four kinds of claims relate two classes of things, and nearly every claim that states such a relationship can be rewritten in one of these forms:

All Xs are Ys.
No Xs are Ys.
Some Xs are Ys.
Some Xs are not Ys.

Obviously, most of the claims we make about classes are more complicated than those shown, but a remarkable number of our claims can be reduced to one of these forms without changing our intended meanings. For example, "Every X is a Y" is just another way of saying "All Xs are Ys." In some of the examples that follow, we'll see claims rewritten in one or another of these four standard forms.

Valid Conversions

A claim about two classes of things is said to have been converted when the places of the two classes have been switched. Converting a claim of the form "No Xs are Ys" results in "No Ys are Xs." "Some Xs are Ys" can be converted to "Some Ys are Xs."

Now, when some claims about classes of things are converted, the resulting claims are exact equivalents of the originals—that is, they have the same truth values under all circumstances; they say the same thing. In the list of standard form claims provided in the preceding section, two are equivalent to their converses. The first is the one that begins with *no*:

> *Every claim of the form "No Xs are Ys" is equivalent to its converse, "No Ys are Xs."*

Thus, "No employees of the corporation are members of the club" has the same meaning as "No members of the club are employees of the corporation." These two claims always have the same truth value.

> *Every claim of the form "Some Xs are Ys" is equivalent to its converse, "Some Ys are Xs."*

If it is true that some mammals are creatures that live in the sea, then it is equally true that some creatures that live in the sea are mammals. The two claims come to the same thing.

The two equivalents thus determined give us two new valid argument patterns. Each of the two is a one-premise pattern:

No Xs are Ys.
Therefore, no Ys are Xs.

Some Xs are Ys.
Therefore, some Ys are Xs.

It is simple to see the validity of arguments that fit these patterns. What is sometimes less simple is recognizing that many claims people make are really disguised versions of one of the two types of claim that appear in these arguments. For example, the claim "Rodents do not hibernate" means the same as the claim "no rodents are creatures that hibernate." This has the proper "No Xs are Ys" form and says the same thing as the original claim. When we put the original claim into this standard form, we can see that its converse, "No creatures that hibernate are rodents," follows from it.

Invalid Conversions

Claims of the following two forms are *not* equivalent to their converses:

1. All Xs are Ys.
2. Some Xs are not Ys.

Knowing that such claims are true does not allow us to draw any inference at all about their converses. For example, the claim

All Chevrolets are General Motors automobiles

is true, but its converse,

All General Motors automobiles are Chevrolets

is false. However, the claim

All creatures with hearts are creatures with lungs

is true and has the same form as the previous example, yet its converse is also true:

All creatures with lungs are creatures with hearts.

Hence the fact that a claim of the form "All Xs are Ys" is true does not allow us to determine anything about the truth of its converse, "All Ys are Xs." Remember,

From a claim of the form "All Xs are Ys," nothing follows about the truth value of its converse, "All Ys are Xs."

The same is true for claims of the form "Some Xs are not Ys." The converses of some such claims are true and those of others are false. Hence we cannot depend on any inference from such a claim to its converse. For example, the claim

Some undergraduates are not freshmen

is true, but its converse,

Some freshmen are not undergraduates

is false. But other examples of claims of this form may have true converses. For example,

Some freshmen are not women

is true, and so is its converse,

Some women are not freshmen.

Therefore, remember,

From a claim of the form "Some Xs are not Ys," nothing follows about the truth value of its converse, "Some Ys are not Xs."

EXERCISE 9-5

Each of the following claims may be rewritten in one of the standard forms. Do so. Remember, the standard forms are as follows:

All _____ are _____
No _____ are _____
Some _____ are _____
Some _____ are not _____

EXAMPLE: Bears are carnivorous: All bears are carnivorous.

★1. Only athletes play in the National Basketball Association.
  2. Not every criminal is a gambler.
  3. Exceptional employees are always rewarded.
★4. Few voters think critically.
  5. Many Democrats are conservative.
  6. Wherever there's smoke, there's fire.
★7. Mechanics make great lovers.
  8. The only people who vote are members.
  9. Angels aren't real.
★10. Richard Nixon was not impeached.

EXERCISE 9-6

Each of the following numbered claims is followed by two or more lettered claims. *First:* Rewrite each numbered claim in your head, putting it into one of the four standard forms. *Second:* Determine which of the lettered claims is the converse of the rewritten numbered claim (and hence is also the converse of the original numbered claim). *Last:* State whether or not the converse follows from the original numbered claim.

EXAMPLE: Not every cormorant can fly.
  (a) Some cormorants can fly.
  (b) Some creatures that can fly are not cormorants.
  (c) Some creatures that cannot fly are cormorants.

ANSWER: First, the original claim must be rewritten in standard form. After such rewriting, it says: "Some cormorants are not creatures that can fly." (Be careful in doing this part of the exercise—it's easy to change the meaning of the claim if you're not careful when you rewrite it.) It is clear that claim *b* is the converse of the rewritten original, and that these claims have a form ("Some Xs are not Ys") that does *not* imply their converses. So nothing follows about claim *b*.

  1. Everybody with a ticket will be admitted.
     (a) All people without tickets are people who will be admitted.
     (b) All people who will be admitted are people with tickets.
 ★2. None of the people with tickets will be kept waiting.
     (a) No people kept waiting are people who have tickets.
     (b) All people without tickets are people who will be kept waiting.
  3. Some of the most boring aquarium animals are *Limulus*.
     (a) All *Limulus* are boring aquarium animals.
     (b) Some *Limulus* are boring aquarium animals.
 ★4. Kids will be allowed to go on the ride only if they are tall enough to reach the bottom of the sign.
     (a) All kids tall enough to reach the bottom of the sign are kids who will be allowed to go on the ride.
     (b) Some kids who are allowed to go on the ride are kids who are tall enough to reach the bottom of the sign.
     (c) All kids who will be allowed to go on the ride are kids who are tall enough to reach the bottom of the sign.
  5. Some high-technology stocks have not been part of the recent rally in the stock market.
     (a) Some stocks that have been part of the recent rally in the stock market are not high-technology stocks.
     (b) Some high-technology stocks are stocks that have not been part of the recent rally in the stock market.
     (c) Some stocks that have not been part of the recent rally in the stock market are high-technology stocks.

Valid Syllogisms

Syllogisms are two-premise deductive arguments. However, the word is often reserved for certain two-premise arguments involving classes. We needn't go into any great detail about syllogisms in general, since we're only going to deal with four types of them, two valid and two invalid patterns. In our experience, these patterns turn up more often than other syllogistic patterns. (For a more detailed treatment of syllogisms, see Appendix 1.)

Let's look at the first valid syllogism pattern. Let X, Y, and Z stand for three classes of things.

Syllogism 1:

All Xs are Ys.
All Ys are Zs.
Therefore, all Xs are Zs.

Any argument of this form is valid; if the two premises are true, it is not possible for the conclusion to be anything but true. An example:

All Miami Dolphin home games are games that have sold out. All sold-out games are games that will be televised. Therefore, all Miami Dolphin home games are games that will be televised.

If the two premises are true, then it is not possible for the conclusion to be false. The same is true for any argument of the second syllogistic pattern:

Syllogism 2:

All Xs are Ys.
No Ys are Zs.
Therefore, no Xs are Zs.

No matter what classes of things Xs, Ys, and Zs might be, the premises of an argument of this form guarantee the truth of the conclusion. Notice that the second premise is a form that can be converted. Thus, this premise could just as easily have read "No Zs are Ys" and the argument would still be perfectly valid. Since the conclusion is of the same form, it too can be converted without changing the validity of the argument. All three of the following, then, are valid versions of this syllogistic pattern:

All Xs are Ys.	All Xs are Ys.	All Xs are Ys.
No Zs are Ys.	No Ys are Zs.	No Zs are Ys.
So, no Xs are Zs.	So, no Zs are Xs.	So, no Zs are Xs.

But if we were to convert the first premise, the one of the form "All Xs are Ys," we would no longer have a valid argument.

Invalid Syllogisms

The first invalid pattern we'll look at resembles the first valid pattern described above, but because one of the premises is converted, and because that premise is of a form that is not equivalent to its converse, it invalidates the argument pattern. Here is what it looks like:

Invalid Syllogism 1:

> All Xs are Ys.
> All Zs are Ys.
> Therefore, all Xs are Zs.

Notice that the second premise of this pattern is the converse of that in syllogism 1. Otherwise this form is identical to syllogism 1. But that invalid conversion is enough to make all the difference. Here is an example of an argument of this pattern, the invalidity of which is obvious:

> All dogs are mammals.
> All cats are mammals.
> Therefore, all dogs are cats.

Even though the premises of this argument are clearly true, the conclusion is just as clearly false. This demonstrates the invalidity of the argument pattern.

The last of the syllogistic argument patterns we'll consider looks a lot like syllogism 2, but it is different enough to be invalid. Here is what it looks like:

Invalid Syllogism 2:

> All Xs are Ys.
> No Zs are Xs.
> Therefore, no Ys are Zs.

Locke on the "Father" of Logic

. . . if syllogisms must be taken for the only proper instrument and means of knowledge; it will follow, that before Aristotle there was not one man that did or could know anything by reason; and that since the invention of syllogisms there is not one of ten thousand that doth.

—JOHN LOCKE

In the fourth century B.C., Aristotle invented the syllogism and he has often been called the father of logic as a result. Aristotle believed that every kind of logical inference could be reduced to syllogisms. He turned out to be wrong, but nevertheless a great many inferences *are* basically syllogistic. It was not until the nineteenth century that logic grew much beyond Aristotle's original conception, with the development and classification of new systems of inference. Basic among the nineteenth- and twentieth-century developments is the theory of truth-functional inferences, of which modus ponens, modus tollens, and the chain argument are examples.

Incidentally, Locke goes on to say that men did not and do not depend on Aristotle to be rational. Do you recognize the form of his argument?

It's modus tollens.

To demonstrate that this pattern of argument is invalid, we'll again plug in some class terms for our class variables. The argument we produce will have premises that are obviously true and a conclusion that is obviously false:

> All sophomores are undergraduates.
> No seniors are sophomores.
> So, no undergraduates are seniors.

Clearly, this conclusion does not follow from these premises, since it is false despite the truth of the premises. No argument of this form can be depended on to establish its conclusion no matter how trustworthy its premises may be.

Again, see Appendix 1 for a general account of the theory of the syllogism. We refer you there for further details about these and other forms of syllogisms.

EXERCISE 9-7

Put each of the following into the form of a syllogism, and then determine which of the four syllogistic forms or their variations discussed in the text the passage has. Note whether each is valid or invalid.

EXAMPLE: Everybody who is out after the curfew will be arrested. So, since nobody who gets arrested will be able to leave the country next week, nobody who is able to leave the country next week will be out after the curfew.

ANSWER: In its syllogistic form:

> All people out after the curfew are people who will be arrested.
> No people who are arrested are people able to leave the country next week.
> Therefore, no people able to leave the country next week are people out after the curfew.

PATTERN:

> All Xs are Ys.
> No Ys are Zs.
> Therefore, no Zs are Xs.

This is a version of valid syllogism #2, as may be seen if you convert the conclusion.

★1. All creationists are religious, and all fundamentalists are religious, so all creationists are fundamentalists.

2. Every sportscaster is an athlete, and no athlete is a college professor. Therefore, no sportscasters are college professors.

3. Anyone who voted for Dukakis favors expansion of medical services for the needy. So, the people who voted for Dukakis all favor higher taxes,

since anyone who wants to expand medical services must favor higher taxes.

★4. All cave dwellers lived before the invention of the radio, and no one alive today is a cave dweller. Thus, no person who lived before the invention of the radio is alive today.

5. Conservationists don't vote for Republicans, and all environmentalists are conservationists. Thus, environmentalists don't vote for Republicans. (Hint: Remember, the order of the premises can be reversed.)

6. Each philosopher is a skeptic, and no philosopher is a theologian. Therefore, no skeptic is a theologian. (Hint: Remember, you can convert some claims about classes.)

★7. Since all philosophers are skeptics, it follows that no theologian is a skeptic, since no philosophers are theologians. (Hint: Don't forget to convert, if necessary—and if permissible!)

8. Peddlers are salesmen, and confidence men are too. So, peddlers are confidence men.

9. Should drug addicts be treated as criminals? Well, addicts are all excluded from the class of decent people, yet all criminals belong to that class. Accordingly, no addicts are criminals.

★10. Critical thinkers recognize invalid syllogisms; therefore, critical thinkers are logicians, since logicians can spot invalid syllogisms, too.

EXERCISE 9-8

Put each of the following into the form of the syllogism, and then determine which syllogistic pattern each exemplifies. Note whether each is valid or invalid.

Caution: These exercises get increasingly difficult. Be prepared to spend some time on the last few items. Be challenged!

1. The Mohawk Indians are Algonquin and so are the Cheyenne. So the Mohawks are really just Cheyenne.

★2. All barbiturates are more dangerous than alcohol, and nothing that is more dangerous than alcohol ought to be sold over the counter. Therefore, no barbiturates ought to be sold over the counter.

3. All moas were Dinornithidae, and no moas exist anymore. So there aren't any more Dinornithidae. (Hint: Some claims may be converted.)

★4. Everybody on the district tax roll is a citizen, and all eligible voters are also citizens. So everybody on the district tax roll is an eligible voter.

5. "Only madmen would contemplate such a gamble [as launching a nuclear first strike]. Whatever else they may be, the leaders of the Soviet Union are not madmen. [Therefore, the leaders of the Soviet Union would not contemplate launching a nuclear first strike.]"
   —ROBERT S. McNAMARA and HANS A. BETHE, "Reducing the Risk of Nuclear War," in *The Atlantic Monthly*

★6. Any piece of software that is in the public domain may be copied without permission or fee. But that cannot be done in the case of software under copyright. So software under copyright must not be in the public domain.

7. Cases of "aesthetic surgery," which are all designed to make a patient look better, are classified in a category different from cases of reconstructive surgery. It must be, then, that reconstructive surgery is never designed to make a patient look better.

★8. Any country that will accept aid from the Soviet Union is a candidate for Russian subversion. So every country the United States fails to help is such a candidate, because if a country doesn't get help from us it's sure to get it from the Soviets. (Hint: Remember that the order of the premises doesn't matter.)

9. Stockholders' information about a company's worth must come from the managers of that company, but in a buy-out, the managers of the company are the very ones who are trying to buy the stock from the stockholders. So, ironically, in a buy-out situation, stockholders must get their information about how much a company is worth from the very people who are trying to buy their stock.

★10. Since 1973, when the U.S. Supreme Court decided *Miller v. California,* no work can be banned as obscene unless it contains sexual depictions that are "patently offensive" to "contemporary community standards" and unless the work as a whole possesses no "serious literary, artistic, political or scientific value." As loose as this standard may seem when compared to earlier tests of obscenity, the pornographic novels of "Madame Toulouse" (a pseudonym, of course) can still be banned. They would offend the contemporary standards of any community, and to claim any literary, artistic, political or scientific value for them would be a real joke.

Indirect Proof

A claim is proved indirectly by showing that its contradictory implies something false, absurd, or contradictory. The idea behind this type of proof becomes clear if you think for a moment about what a person actually means who says, "If Hart isn't a liberal, then I'm the King of England." The remark is actually just a way of saying that Hart is a liberal—by claiming, in effect, that the supposition that he is not a liberal is absurd. So, if we want to prove that a claim is *true* using this method, we begin with its *contradictory.* If we want to prove that P is true, we begin with not-P and show that *it* implies a false claim.

This proves that not-P is itself false, and hence that P is true. We can sketch the pattern this way:

not-P   (the contradictory of what we want to prove)

.
.

implies

.
.
.

_____Q_____   [where Q is an obviously false claim]

Therefore, not-P is false.
Therefore, its contradictory, P, is true.

The following example will show one way this pattern of reasoning can work. Let's say that Bill has saved up enough for a down payment on a new Mercedes-Benz and that his current budget will just cover the $500 per month payments. You want to prove to Bill that he cannot afford the car. So you begin with the assumption that he *can* afford it:

1. Bill can afford to own a new Mercedes.

Several claims (which make use of some made-up figures) follow from this initial claim:

2. Bill can afford payments of $500 per month.
3. Bill can afford insurance costs of $1,200 per year.
4. Bill can afford gasoline and tune-up costs of $1,000 per year.
5. Bill can afford some relatively expensive repair bills after the warranty period.

and, therefore,

6. Bill can afford about $685 per month in car expenses plus some relatively expensive repair bills after the warranty period.

Given Bill's budget, it is pretty clear that claim 6 is false. Bill budgeted enough for payments, but he did not think of all the related (but necessary) expenses—something many of us do when we want something bad enough. So, since claim 6 is false, and it followed from claim 1, claim 1 must be false too. The final conclusion of the argument is that the *contradictory* of 1 must be true: Bill can*not* afford to own a new Mercedes.

This pattern of reasoning is sometimes called **reductio ad absurdum** (reducing to an absurdity, or RAA, for short), because it involves showing that some claim implies a false, absurd, or contradictory result. Most versions are neither so informal as the remark about being the King of England that began this discussion nor so formal as the explicitly laid out version of the argument about Bill's automobile purchase—most examples that we run across in everyday affairs fall somewhere in between.

The ancient Greek philosopher Zeno (fourth–third century B.C.) is famous for his "proofs" that motion is impossible. One "proof" goes pretty much like this:

For anything to move, it must first go half the distance to where it is moving to. But before it can reach the halfway point, it must go half the distance to the halfway point. And before it can reach this new halfway point, it must go half the distance to it, and so on and so on. Thus, for anything to move, it must cover an infinite number of halfway points. But it is absurd to suppose that something can cover an infinite number of points in a finite time. Therefore, nothing can move.

As you can see, the argument is an example of RAA.

Two More RAAs

I. A simpler "proof" that motion is impossible (see preceding cartoon) has been attributed to Zeno:

Nothing can move, for if it did, it would have to move either in the place where it is or in the place where it is not. But for a thing to move in the place where it is, is for it not to move; and for it to move in a place where it is not is absurd, since nothing can be where it is not. Thus, motion is impossible.

The form of the argument is RAA, in which the supposition that motion is possible is said to lead to one or the other of two outcomes, both of which are equally absurd.

II. "Let's see if I've got this right. George Bush believes that abortion is murder, therefore it should be illegal. On the other hand, George Bush doesn't want criminal penalties for women who get abortions; he wants criminal penalties only for abortionists.

"In other words, it's OK for a woman to murder her baby, but it's not OK for someone to help her do it. Is that right? In other words, George Bush thinks it would be a good idea to pass legislation designed to force women to try to abort their own babies. Fabulous idea."

—JON CARROLL, *San Francisco Chronicle*

Begging the Question

To say that an argument begs the question is not to say that it fits any particular pattern of reasoning; rather, it's to say that the argument has a peculiar defect. **Begging the question** means smuggling the argument's conclusion into the premises. This can happen in more than one way: The conclusion can be stated as a premise more or less explicitly, or one or more of the premises may depend on the conclusion. In either case the person is *assuming* exactly what it is that needs to be *proved*. Here's a rather tired old example, but one that makes the point:

> God must exist, because the Scriptures state that He exists. The scriptures are correct because they are divinely inspired by God, and any divinely inspired writing must be true.

Notice that the conclusion, the claim that God must exist, is actually assumed by the premises. God can hardly be the inspiration of the Scriptures, after all, if He doesn't exist.

What can be confusing about question-begging arguments is that they are valid. If we include an argument's conclusion among its premises, then if the premises are true the conclusion must be true too. In a sense, then, the argument is not a bad one, in that its conclusion does indeed follow from its premises. And, in fact, one could make the point that *every* valid deductive argument must beg the question, since the conclusion of such an argument cannot contain more information than is given in its premises.

Our problem is how to distinguish between those valid deductive arguments that are really question begging and those that are not. This is no easy chore, for the distinction is not a clear one—there is simply no clear line between the two groups. Still, the problem is not really crucial, as we'll see.

There are two main points to be made about deciding whether an argument begs the question. First, the more obviously the conclusion restates a point made in the premises, the more likely we are to see the argument as question begging. The example above about the existence of God is a case in point: The premises of that argument *obviously* require that its conclusion be true, and hence the argument takes us nowhere. The second point follows closely on the first. If the conclusion is an obvious restatement of the premises, or if the latter rely on the truth of the conclusion in an obvious way, then any doubts we may have about the conclusion are immediately transferred to the premises. (Remember, if a deductive argument is valid, then its conclusion can be false only if at least one of its premises is false.) And if the premises are themselves dubious, then we are even more likely to find that the argument begs the question. Thus, a candidate for question begging is going to have these two features: (1) premises that inspire doubt, and (2) a conclusion that restates a point made in the premises or that is clearly assumed by the premises.

You might ask whether any argument that fits any of the valid patterns cataloged in this chapter doesn't beg the question. Doubtless many do. Whether a particular argument does beg the question depends, again, on how obvious it is that the conclusion is assumed in the premises. Since what is obvious to one may be less obvious to another, there is room for disagreement about any particular case.

The underlying issue about the question-begging nature of an argument is whether the argument leads anywhere. If the conclusion presents us with no point that was not already obvious from the premises, especially if the premises are themselves already subject to serious doubt, then a case can be built for question begging. To say that an argument begs the question, then, is really to say not that it is a bad argument, but that it gets us nowhere. As stated earlier, our task is to determine whether the premises of the argument are worth believing.

"Just Because"

QUESTION: Why should I be home by ten o'clock?
ANSWER: Because.
QUESTION: What makes you think *Rocky III* is a better movie than *Rocky I?*
ANSWER: Just because.

Have you ever heard a request for reasons answered with nothing more than *because?* Have you done it yourself? That's a case of begging the question. It amounts to supporting a conclusion, P, with a premise, also P. In the first example above, the *because* amounts to *You should be home by ten because you should be home by ten.* In the second example, it amounts to *Rocky III is better than Rocky I because Rocky III is better than Rocky I.* This is valid reasoning, true, but it is of no consequence whatsoever.

Begging the Question?

According to the Associated Press, when former CIA Director William Casey was released from Georgetown University Hospital where he had undergone brain surgery, a spokeswoman for the hospital was asked about his condition. Her reply: "He must have been in good condition. Otherwise, he would not have been released."

So Casey was released because he was in good condition. And we know he was in good condition because he was released.

Recap

Deductive arguments, both valid and invalid, take a great number of forms. Ten common, simple argument forms, half of them valid and half invalid, appear in this listing:

Valid Patterns	Invalid Patterns

Modus Ponens
    If P then Q.
    P.
Therefore, Q.

Affirming the Consequent
    If P then Q.
    Q.
Therefore, P.

Modus Tollens
    If P then Q.
    Not-Q.
Therefore, not-P.

Denying the Antecedent
    If P then Q.
    Not-P.
Therefore, not-Q.

Chain Argument
    If P then Q.
    If Q then R.
Therefore, if P then R.

Reverse Chain Argument
    If P then Q.
    If Q then R.
Therefore, if R then P.

Valid Conversions
1.   No Xs are Ys.
Therefore, no Ys are Xs.

Invalid Conversions
1.   All Xs are Ys.
Therefore, all Ys are Xs.

2.   Some Xs are Ys.
Therefore, some Ys are Xs.

2.   Some Xs are not Ys.
Therefore, some Ys are not Xs.

Valid Syllogisms

1.   All Xs are Ys.
    All Ys are Zs.
Therefore, all Xs are Zs.

Invalid Syllogisms

1.   All Xs are Ys.
    All Zs are Ys.
Therefore, all Xs are Zs.

2.   All Xs are Ys.
    No Ys are Zs.
Therefore, no Xs are Zs.

2.   All Xs are Ys.
    No Zs are Xs.
Therefore, no Ys are Zs.

Indirect proof, which makes use of the reductio ad absurdum method, establishes a claim by showing that its denial or negation implies a false, absurd, or self-contradictory claim. Begging the question is not a kind of argument, but a possible flaw in any valid deductive argument. It occurs whenever the conclusion of an argument is actually an obvious restatement of a premise or when one or more premises depend on the truth of the conclusion for *its* truth.

Additional Exercises

EXERCISE 9-9

Each of the following passages contains an argument that matches one of the argument patterns discussed in this chapter. As in previous exercises, isolate the argument by deleting any extraneous language; then identify the argument pattern and determine whether or not it is valid. Many of these exercises are challenging.

1. Evergreen trees can't be hardwood because they aren't deciduous. Hardwood trees are all deciduous.

★2. In this country, nothing counts except success on the job. And since traditional women's work has not counted as a "job," such work has not been properly appreciated.

3. From a letter to the editor: "The animal laboratories at the university would allow spot inspections if they were living up to the standards of the Animal Welfare Act. It seems clear that researchers are in violation of the law since they won't let anybody in there to see what's going on."

★4. There is incontrovertible proof that the Biblical account of the flood is a true story: If the flood didn't happen, it would have been absurd for Noah to have built an ark; hence the flood happened.

★5. From a letter to the editor: "Any project that gets taxpayers' money ought to be one that the taxpayers get some sort of benefit from, don't you think? So if the Federal Aviation Authority is going to pour millions in public funds into automated flight centers at all privately owned airports, then justice can only be served by forcing those airports to begin offering services to the public as well as their current wealthy patrons."

6. Whenever legislators have the power to raise taxes, they will always find problems that seem to require for their solution doing exactly that. This is an axiom, the proof of which is that the power to tax always generates the perception on the part of those who have that power that there exist various ills the remedy for which can only lie in increased governmental spending and hence higher taxes.

7. In order to satisfy the dairy interests of Alaska, including Senator Ted Stevens, the chair of the Appropriations Subcommittee on defense, the Air Force must turn down the bid from a Seattle dairy to supply milk

for one of the larger Air Force bases in Alaska. But turning down that bid will cost the taxpayers almost a quarter of a million dollars in annual milk costs for the base. The conclusion is as obvious as it is dumb: in order to satisfy Alaskan interests with political clout, the taxpayers have to shell out an extra two hundred grand.

★8. Every event has a cause other than itself, for if it did not, it would have caused itself, which is impossible.

9. HE: I believe everyone should be permitted to cheat.
   SHE: That's ridiculous.
   HE: Why?
   SHE: Assume that everyone were permitted to cheat. To say they are permitted to cheat means that it is all right for them to cheat. And if it's all right to cheat, then there's nothing wrong with cheating. But then, they wouldn't be cheating. So your suggestion is absurd.

★10. God, by definition, possesses all perfections. Existence, by definition, is a perfection. Therefore God, by definition, exists.

★11. The new dean at Stratford Business School initiated many new policies after taking office. All of the new policies emphasized employee and customer satisfaction. After a conversation with the new dean, an associate dean remarked that, since none of the policies of the old curriculum was among those initiated by the dean, he had to conclude, to his surprise, that none of the old curriculum emphasized employee and customer satisfaction.

12. So-called "junk bonds," high-risk corporate bonds, have turned out to be a good deal after all. If they weren't, their default rate, which was 1.5% of face value between 1974 and 1989 compared to .08% for corporate bonds overall, would outweigh their higher than normal yields— 2.6% higher than A-rated bonds. But, as it turns out, in the decade mentioned, the yields of the "junkers" have more than repaid the losses incurred by investors due to defaults.

★13. If Clint Eastwood had been right about the character he played in *A Fistful of Dollars* being too mercenary, he would never have made any of the "Dirty Harry" movies. That fact that the Dirty Harry movies were made, and have been resoundingly successful, proves that Eastwood's original worries about his character were mistaken.

14. Russell's theory had a chance of success only if it could escape from the paradox of inherence. But, in turn, it could escape from that paradox only if it contained a solution to the problem of asymmetrical relations. In the form in which Russell left it, the theory failed to solve the asymmetry problem, and the result was that, in the final analysis, it never really had a chance.

★15. If every government would initiate measures like those currently being put in place by Colombia, Europe, and the United States, we could virtually eliminate the drug problem. But such drug-producing countries as Peru and Bolivia do not have the will or the resources to emulate the countries that have clamped down. As a result, we can hope only for stabilization, not elimination, of the problem.

EXERCISE 9-10

Each of the following passages makes use of more than one pattern of argument. Isolate the argument by eliminating any language that is unnecessary to the argument, rewrite any claims that require it, and then identify and display the argument structure. Make sure you show how any subargument fits into the main pattern. Note: Take your time with these—they too are difficult. In fact, number 5 may be the hardest problem in the book. Have a good time with it.

EXAMPLE: If none of the animals in the lion house were originally from the wild, then the two tigers kept in the Asia compound are the only two big cats in the zoo that were donated by a foreign government. We're pretty sure the latter is the case, because, according to the records, none of the animals that came from the wild are currently kept in the lion house.

· Classes required for the argument, with appropriate letters assigned:

   L = animals kept in the lion house
   W = animals originally from the wild (i.e., animals not born in captivity)

· Claims required for the argument, with letters assigned:

   P = The two tigers in the Asia compound are the only two big cats donated by a foreign government.

· The structure of the argument:

If no L are W, then P.
<u>No W are L.</u>
Therefore, P.

We next include the structure of the subargument, however obvious it might be, since it is required to make the argument's validity clear:

	<u>No W are L.</u>
(step 1)	No L are W.

	<u>If no L are W, then P.</u>
(step 2)	P.

Step 1 is a valid conversion, and step 2 is a case of modus ponens. The argument as a whole, then, is valid.

1. If greater efficiency is to be had from our communication systems, then fiber optic technology will have to replace the current cable system. But if the current system is replaced by one employing fiber optics, then a great many communications workers are going to lose their jobs. So the

unhappy conclusion is that, if many communications workers are not to lose their jobs, we'll not achieve greater efficiency in communications.

★2. Nothing that has only a small chance of commercial success is worth years of dedicated effort. Therefore, none of these attempts at cashing in on Olympic medals to win commercial success is worth the years of effort it takes to be a medal winner. Look at Carl Lewis: He has not done well commercially despite four gold medals in the '84 Olympics, and if *he* can't do it, *any* such attempt to cash in on medals has a slim chance of succeeding.

3. Only large travel agencies can handle the travel business of major corporations, and the agencies that can handle corporate business are the ones that are going to survive the coming shakeout in the travel industry. Furthermore, if all the survivors are going to be large agencies, then we can expect to see a lot of mergers in the industry in the near future. So that's my prediction: We'll have a merger-happy travel industry for the next couple of years.

★4. The toy industry is going to help produce a generation of less thoughtful, more aggressive people, according to some psychologists. They argue that today's toys, like G.I. Joe, Go-Bots, Transformers, and the like, represent the world in black-and-white terms: There are good guys and bad guys and nothing in the middle. Aggressive individuals, including violent criminals, tend to see the world in exactly this way. It's a case of violence stemming from a superficial conception of the world.

5. Editorial comment: "If we're going to get excited about every case of an enlisted man turning out to have been selling information to the Russians, then we're going to have to believe that all the secrets sold in cases like the recent ones are dangerous to our national security in the hands of the Russians. But all of the material sold in all the recent cases has been classified 'secret' by our ridiculous classification system, and that category contains all the routine drivel of the operations of our security agencies, including newspaper clippings. It seems clear that it's a mistake to raise such cain every time some dope gets caught playing spy. We might be better off reviewing our classification system and our clearance procedures."

— *The Athens Courier*

EXERCISE 9-11 (ESSAY)

Consider the issue of whether the world must have been created by an intelligent being. (1) Write a short essay in support of either side of this issue. Include at least two arguments for your position that follow patterns described in this chapter. (2) Point out the patterns you used and symbolize the arguments.

10 Generalization and Related Inductive Reasoning

. . . all discovery of truths, not self-evident, consists of inductions, and the interpretations of inductions . . . all our knowledge, not intuitive, comes to us exclusively from that source.

—JOHN STUART MILL

General Claims

We treated claims extensively in Part One, but a few more specific remarks are called for here about general claims, since such claims function in important ways in the arguments discussed in this chapter. A **general claim** is a claim that refers to more than one member of. a class but not necessarily to every member of the class.

General claims are either universal or nonuniversal. If a single exception would serve to falsify a general claim, the claim is a **universal general claim**; otherwise it is **nonuniversal**. Here are some examples:

Universal General Claims

1. The club is off limits for all enlisted men.
2. Jimmy Carter never composed a string quartet.
3. Everyone present was overjoyed to hear the news.

Nonuniversal General Claims

1. Most senators do not favor a school-prayer amendment.
2. Eighty-nine percent of California voters regret having voted for Proposition 13, the survey shows.
3. Virtually every automobile manufactured in America comes off the production line with a major defect.

Some general claims that look universal at first may not be. For instance, someone who remarked, "Americans are crazy about hamburgers," *might* be making a universal claim but probably means only that many or most Americans are quite fond of hamburgers. If you replied to this remark by saying, "My uncle doesn't like hamburgers," your reply would probably not be taken as a refutation of the remark, since the latter was probably not intended to hold without exception.

Since general statements are about members of classes or groups of things, they refer to those members either collectively or individually (see Chapter 2 on grouping ambiguity). The claim "49 percent of voters under thirty voted for Dukakis" makes collective reference to voters under thirty—that is, it does not mean that 49 percent of each person voted for Dukakis. But the claim "everyone who voted in the primary is a registered Democrat" refers to the voters individually. As is plain, understanding a general claim requires knowing whether it is universal or nonuniversal and whether it refers collectively or individually to the members of a class or group.

Prescriptions, Decrees, Laws, and Definitions—An Important Class of General Claims

Each of the following is a universal general claim:

No child under the age of sixteen years may be placed in any State prison in company with adults convicted of crime, except in the presence of a proper official. (California law)

One must never employ one's rights so as to infringe upon the rights of others. (Moral prescription)

Anyone guilty of neglect of duty is said to be derelict. (Definition)

Entrance forbidden except to authorized personnel. (Decree)

The spontaneous flow of heat from hot to cold bodies is reversible only with the expenditure of mechanical or other nonthermal energy. (Physical law)

Work expands so as to fill the time available for its completion. (Parkinson's law)

Composition and Division

To think that what holds true of a group of things individually, automatically, and necessarily holds true of the same things collectively is to commit a mistake in reasoning known as the **fallacy of composition**. Here are two examples of this fallacy:

Lendl and Wilander are the two best tennis players in the world, so they'd make the best doubles team.

We don't spend *that* much on military salaries. After all, whoever heard of anyone getting rich in the Army? (We don't spend much on service personnel *individually*; therefore we don't spend much on them collectively.)

Conversely, to think that what holds true of a group of things collectively automatically holds true of the same things individually is to commit the error known as the **fallacy of division**:

The jury found with the plaintiff. Therefore, Smith, who sat on the jury, found with the plaintiff.

The Eastman School of Music has an outstanding international reputation; therefore, Vladimir Peronepky, who is on the faculty of Eastman, must have a good reputation.

When you are considering any general claim it is important to ask three questions.

1. *Is it clear what class is being generalized about?* If someone makes a general remark about "top government officials," "labor leaders," "young people," or "liberals," do you really know exactly what group of people is being referred to?

THE PROBLEM WE'LL TAKE UP TODAY IS ONE WE PHILOSOPHERS HAVE STUDIED FOR OVER TWO THOUSAND YEARS

YOU KNOW HE DOESN'T LOOK A DAY OVER TWO HUNDRED DOES HE?

2. *Is it clear what is being said about that class?* For instance, if someone asserts, "Most American businessmen resent the Treasury Department's tax proposal," it would be unclear precisely what "most American businessmen" actually thought of the proposal. There is a similar problem with "Seventy percent of those interviewed favored anti-abortion legislation." What, really, is it that those interviewed favored, and what does *favored* mean in this context?

3. *Is the general claim about something that can be known?* General statements about activities that people are secretive about—for instance, unorthodox sexual practices (or even orthodox ones), drug usage and other illegal activities, and secret military plans—are always suspect, since they could be sheer speculation.

Provided the general statement is clear, we can consider the strength of the argument on which it is based, if any, a matter we'll turn to shortly.

EXERCISE 10-1

Identify each of the following claims as *probably* a universal general claim or *probably* a nonuniversal general claim.

  ★1. Unpasteurized milk is dangerous to drink.
   2. In winter migratory birds fly south.
   3. Movie stars are rich and good looking.
  ★4. Whales are mammals.
   5. No one likes to be called a "yuppie" anymore.
   6. *Time* always outsells *Newsweek*.
  ★7. Antarctica is never hot.
   8. Giving in to terrorist demands is rarely, if ever, a good policy.
   9. Recessions are periods of reduced economic activity.
★10. A falling barometer is followed by rain.
 11. A barometer falls when atmospheric pressure is lowered.
★12. Since its sudden appearance in 1978, canine parvovirus has been of grave concern for pet owners.
 13. Overloaded household circuits are caused by the use of too many appliances at the same time.
 14. Mature walnut trees need a nitrogen fertilizer to keep them vigorous and productive.
★15. Concerned environmentalists never vote Republican.

EXERCISE 10-2

Evaluate the following general claims. You might keep in mind the three questions discussed in the text: (a) Is it clear what class is being generalized about? (b) Is it clear what is being said about that class? (c) Is the claim about something that can be known?

EXAMPLE: In my opinion, the Nicaraguan land reformers intend to play the Communist countries for suckers in order to raise the money they need to run their country.

ANSWER: (a) First, it may not be clear who the "Nicaraguan land reformers" are. (b) It certainly is not clear what is being said about them: What might one mean by "play the Communist countries for suckers"? (c) Finally, this claim is about the intentions of certain unnamed persons and as such should be considered speculative, though perhaps not completely unknowable.

★ 1. If your houseplants are turning yellow, you're either overwatering them or underwatering them.
  2. Those who are at risk for colorectal cancer should receive the appropriate medical examination at least once a year.
  3. The British soccer fan is a thug.
★ 4. Elephant seals are dumb, as seals go.
  5. Sixty-seven percent of adult American males believe there should be capital punishment for at least some crimes.
  6. Schools caught violating the NCAA rules will henceforth find their entire sport sidelined.
★ 7. The right-wing Republicans in the Senate have fouled up the Senate's advise-and-consent procedures.
  8. "Do women constitute a special political class with special interests of their own? Feminists of course believe they do."
                                                        —NORMAN PODHORETZ
  9. Enforcement of child support should be applied to both parents equally, regardless of gender.
★ 10. Magazines such as *Penthouse* and *Playboy* ought not be sold in clean, decent towns like ours.

Comparative General Claims

Reduces engine friction by up to 30 percent.

More than 20 percent more cargo space than any other truck in its class.

Quietest by far, according to independent laboratory tests.

Governor boasts, "Unemployment cut by half."

General claims that involve comparisons require special attention. Most especially, consider these questions:

1. *Are both terms of the comparison clear?* Such claims as "25 percent larger," "cut by over half," and "40 percent fewer," immediately demand the question "than what?" If no answer is clearly stated or implied, dismiss the comparison.

Sometimes, too, the comparative data needed to evaluate a general claim are not made clear, and then we cannot be certain of the significance of the claim. It may be interesting, for example, to learn the rate of violent murders in Melbourne County last year, but whether that rate is cause for alarm or celebration depends on how it compares with the rate for previous years. Another example: In his book *Losing Ground* (New York: Basic Books, 1984), Charles Murray claimed there was a seven-point drop in participation by black males in the labor force between 1969 and 1981. Well, both terms of *that* comparison are clear enough (1969 versus 1981). But Murray and others used this statistic to support the thesis that social programs stifle the incentive to work. What the critical reader would need to know is, how does Murray's statistic compare with data prior to 1969? Michael Harrington, writing in *The New Republic,* claimed that between 1955 and 1968 there had been an even larger drop (7.4 percent) in participation by black males in the labor force. Harrington cited comparative background data that, if true, entirely undercut Murray's thesis.

2. *Is the same standard of comparison used for both terms?* Check to be sure. A cited decline in the percentage of Americans living below the poverty level becomes less impressive when one learns that the poverty level has been raised.

It pays to be suspicious, too, when two or more comparisons are presented in different forms. Prior to the 1984 presidential election, Republicans boasted that under Ronald Reagan inflation had been cut by 60 percent, interest rates had been reduced by 35 percent, taxes had been reduced by 25 percent, and *seven million more people had found jobs.* You don't have to check the newspapers to know that the only reason the Republicans shifted from rates to absolute numbers in the last statistic was that the improvement in the unemployment rate—that is, the percentage of decrease in joblessness—had not been much to crow about.

3. *Are the items comparable?* Sure, the average income of people in X-land can be compared on paper with the average annual income of the citizens of the Federal Republic of Y, but just how meaningful is this comparison since, in X-land but not in Y, health, housing, and transportation costs are paid by the government? Be ever watchful for "apples-and-oranges comparisons." For example, don't place undue faith in a comparison between this April's retail business activity and last April's, if Easter fell in March in one year or the weather was especially cold.

One infamous case of comparing statistical apples with statistical oranges is reported by Darrell Huff in his classic book, *How to Lie with Statistics* (New York: Norton, 1954). Early in this century, the navy cited statistics showing the navy death rate during the Spanish-American War as only nine per thousand as compared with the sixteen per thousand death rate of civilians in New

York during that same period; the statistics were used by navy recruiters to show that it was safer to be in the navy, even during wartime, than out of it. But the comparison actually fails. The civilian population includes the ill, the elderly, and infants, all of whom have a higher death rate under any circumstances; the navy, on the other hand, is made up pretty much of healthy youths. If joining the navy will increase your life expectancy, this statistic doesn't show it.

4. *Are before/after changes genuine or due only to changes in reporting and recording practices?* For example, have cancer rates increased in the last century? Well, no doubt. But by how much is not known by *anyone,* since at least part of the increase is due to better diagnosis, reporting, and recording practices as well as to the fact that a higher percentage of people live to reach the prime cancer age.

5. *Is the range of comparison too broad or too vague to be meaningful?* "Delivers *up to* 25 percent more horsepower." "Reduced *by more than* one-third." "Saves *from* 15 *to* 45 percent." Just what *is* the range here? Remember that, as we discussed in Chapter 2, the amount of vagueness you can tolerate in a claim depends on your interests and purposes. Knowing that attic insulation will reduce your utility bill by 15 to 45 percent may be all it takes for you to know that you should insulate.

6. *Is the comparison itself too obscure to be meaningful?* "Have more fun in Arizona." "Gets clothes whiter than white." "Delivers more honest flavor." (In other words, have fun in Arizona. Gets clothes white. Can be tasted.) Be merciless in dismissing such vacuous claims.

7. *Is the comparison expressed as an average? If so, be sure that important details have not been omitted.* The average rainfall in Seattle is about the same as in Kansas City. But you'll spend more time in your galoshes in Seattle because it rains there twice as often. Central Valley Components, Inc., may report that average salaries of a majority of its employees over the past ten years have more than doubled, but that may not mean that CVC is a great place to work. Perhaps the increases were all due to converting the majority of employees, who worked half-time, to full-time and firing the rest. Comparisons that involve averages, *because* they involve averages, omit details that could be very important.

And, while we're on the subject of averages, it is important to note that there are different kinds of averages. Consider, for instance, the average annual paycheck at Central Valley Components, which happens to be $28,500. That may sound generous enough. But that average is the **mean** (total wages divided by the number of wage earners). The **median** wage, also an "average," which is the "halfway" figure (half the employees get more than the figure and half get less), is $15,000. Now, *this* average is not so impressive, at least from the perspective of a job-seeker. And the **mode**, also an average, the most common rate of pay, is only $10,000. So when someone quotes "the average pay" at CVC, which average is it? At CVC a couple of executives draw fat paychecks, so the mean is a lot higher than the other two figures.

"We Are Spending More

in poverty programs today than we were in 1981," said Dan Quayle in 1988. True, but *inflation-adjusted* funding of such programs declined. (Always take inflation into account in early/later dollar comparisons.)

In a class of things in which there are likely to be large or dramatic variations in whatever it is that is being measured, be cautious of figures about an unspecified "average."

EXERCISE 10-3

Criticize these comparisons, using the questions about comparisons discussed in the text as guides.

EXAMPLE: "You get much better service on Air Atlantic." Better than on what? (One term of the comparison is not clear.) In what way better? (The claim is much too vague to be of much use.)

★1. New improved Morning Muffins! Now with 20 percent more real dairy butter!
 2. "I would say our defense is five to ten times better than it was in the 1982 Superbowl."
 —Forty-Niner LAWRENCE ("DR. EVIL") PILLERS
 3. Major league ball players are much better than they were thirty years ago.

Percentages Versus Percentage Points

Be cautious when a comparison is expressed as a percentage—that is, X is such and such a percentage of Y. Suppose you are told that the frequency of X is, say, 60 percent higher than the frequency of Y. What does that tell you? By itself, hardly anything. An 80-percent frequency is 60 percent higher than a 50-percent frequency, and that's an absolute difference of thirty percentage points. But a 12-percent frequency is also 60 percent higher than an 8-percent frequency, and that's an absolute difference of only four percentage points.

Similarly, if my taxes are increased from 25 to 30 percent, that's an increase of five percentage points, which is unpleasant enough. It's also an increase of 20 percent, which sounds much worse, especially if it is called, as it often is, a "whopping" increase of 20 percent. If the inflation rate advances from 10 to 12 percent during a Democratic administration, the Democrats will describe it as an increase of only two percentage points. The Republicans, of course, will describe it as an increase of (a "whopping") 20 percent. Both are correct, but the Republican description makes the increase sound much more dramatic.

Playing with Before-and-After Percentages

If your taxes are cut by 30 percent, and then raised by 40 percent, they will be higher than they were originally, correct? Wrong. A 40-percent increase will bring them back to only 98 percent of what they were originally.

Moral: If before and after amounts are different, then the same percentages of each amount will not be identical. This is why it takes a 100-percent raise to restore a 50-percent cut. Thinking that it takes a 50-percent raise to restore a 50-percent cut is a variety of apples and oranges—cuts and raises are not comparable in this way.

★4. What an arid place to live. Why, they only had ten inches of rain here last year.

5. On the whole, the mood of the country is more conservative than it was in the sixties.

6. Which is better for a person, coffee or tea?

★7. The average GPA of graduating seniors at Wayward State is 3.25, as compared with 2.75 twenty years ago.

8. Women can tolerate more pain than men.

9. Try Duraglow with new sun-screening polymers. Reduces the harmful effect of sun on your car's finish by up to 50 percent.

★10. What a brilliant season! Attendance was up 25 percent over last year.

EXERCISE 10-4

Criticize these comparisons, using the questions discussed in the text as guides.

★1. You've got to be kidding. Stallone is much superior to Norris as an actor.

2. Blondes have more fun.

3. The average chimp is smarter than the average monkey.

★4. The average grade given by Professor Smith is a C. So is the average grade given by Professor Algers.

5. Crime is on the increase. It's up by 160 percent over last year.

6. Classical musicians, on the average, are far more talented than rock musicians.

★7. Long-distance swimming requires much more endurance than long-distance running.

8. "During the 1979 monitoring period, the amount of profanity on the networks increased by 45–47 percent over a comparable 1978 period. A clear trend toward hard profanity is evident."
   —DON WILDMON, founder of the National Federation for Decency

9. Married people are less likely to be victims of crime than single or divorced people, a new study shows.

★10. Which is more popular, the movie *Gone with the Wind* or Bing Crosby's version of the song "White Christmas"?

EXERCISE 10-5

Find two examples of faulty comparisons and read them to your class. Your instructor may ask other members of the class to criticize them.

Inductive Generalizations: From a Sample to a Class

It is reasonable to accept general claims that issue from credible sources, though this advice is subject to those qualifications discussed in Chapter 3. However, it is often important to consider the worthiness of any *argument* that is offered in support of a general claim. We call such arguments **generalizations.**

In the premises of an inductive generalization, a thing is said to be characteristic of a sample of a class or population of things. And in the conclusion the same thing is said to be a characteristic of the entire class (or most of it). We call the entire class or population the **target population** and the sample class the **sample.**

Example 1:

Premise: Every member of the Campaign for Economic Democracy that I've met so far has been a socialist.

Conclusion: Therefore, all members of the Campaign for Economic Democracy are socialists.

Example 2:

Premise: Seventy-two percent of the Presbyterians we have interviewed believe there should be an anti-abortion amendment to the Constitution.

Conclusion: Therefore, seventy-two percent of all Presbyterians believe there should be an anti-abortion amendment to the Constitution.

Keep these two examples in mind. We'll refer to them again.

For a truth about a sample to warrant a generalization to an entire class, the sample must be *representative* of the class. This means that, ideally, the sample must possess all the relevant features of the target population and that it should possess them in the same proportions as the target population. If, in the first example above, half the members of the Campaign for Economic Democracy are thirty or over and half are under thirty, then our sample is more representative if half of *its* members are thirty or over and half are under thirty. If the Presbyterians we interviewed in example 2 were all participants in a national right-to-life conclave, there is excellent reason to think that they might not be typical Presbyterians relative to the question of abortion amendments. So, remember:

No generalization based on an unrepresentative sample is trustworthy.

Unfortunately, if the issue is a very complicated one, we may not even be able to list all the features that are relevant, let alone know in what proportion they occur in our target population. In such cases we try to ensure the representativeness of our sample by relying on randomness. A **random sample** is one in which every individual in the population has an equal chance of being selected. Obtaining a truly random sample in an extremely heterogeneous, or diversified, population can be difficult indeed, and the techniques employed by statisticians to guarantee randomness are therefore sometimes quite sophisticated. So, when we are dealing with reports of technical studies, it is better to accept the opinions of experts than to try to evaluate the randomness of any sampling procedures on our own. Unfortunately, this is true even though the most conscientious scientific sampling procedures may not produce a truly representative sample.

Yet there are reasonably reliable common sense guidelines that we can employ in evaluating our own generalizing arguments and, for example, the less technical arguments that appear in daily conversations and newspapers. First, any general statements made in the argument should be clear with respect to the three questions discussed in the first section of this chapter. That is, we should be clear about our own generalizations and those of others: exactly what the sample and target populations are; precisely what characteristic is being attributed to the sample and target populations; and whether what is being claimed about the sample or target population is knowable.

Two additional points are important. First, to say that a sample is unrepresentative is to say that something important is true of the sample that is not true of the target population. Thus, it should diminish our confidence in a generalizing argument to discover that something is true of the sample that is not true of the target population. Likewise, the fewer such differences between sample and target population, the more confidence we should have in the generalization.

The Bias Bugbear

The operation of a poll comes down in the end to a running battle against sources of bias.

—DARRELL HUFF

It is doubtful that bias (nonrepresentativeness) can be completely eliminated even from surveys and polls that have properly randomized samples. For bias can be introduced by causes that are unknown, and by causes that, while known, cannot easily be controlled. The subject's desire to please the pollster, for example, is an obvious and well-known source of bias, but one that is quite difficult to eliminate completely.

Thus, for instance, if we learned that a smaller percentage of Presbyterians in the sample (example 2) attend church regularly than is the case for Presbyterians in general, our confidence in the generalization's conclusion should decrease.

Second, in general, and with one qualification discussed below, if there could be important differences between the sample and the target, as would be the case if the sample were not random and no precautions had been taken to ensure its representativeness, the more diversified the individuals in the sample, the more likely it is that the *sample* is representative, and the stronger would be the argument—that is, the more confidence we should have in the conclusion. Conversely, the less diversified the sample, the less representative it is apt to be, and the weaker the argument—that is, the less confidence we should have in the conclusion.

Thus, in example 1, the more diversified are the members of the Campaign for Economic Democracy I've met—provided, of course, that they are all socialists—the more likely it is that *all* CED members are socialists. On the other hand, though, if the CED members I've met are all graduate students with annual incomes less than $15,000, then I should have less confidence in the conclusion than if the sample included CED members from various walks of life with widely divergent incomes.

In summary, our confidence in an argument should be affected by the similarities and dissimilarities among the items in the sample, and between the sample and the target population. But now notice that the similarities and dissimilarities that affect the strength of the argument are *those we can reasonably suppose are relevant to the generalization at issue*. The argument about the CED is not strengthened by noting that the sample includes people who are diversified with respect to hair color, weight, last movie seen, or number of letters in first name. Nor would the argument be weakened if by some odd coincidence the people in the sample were highly uniform with respect to these characteristics. For, as far as we know, these characteristics are not relevant to the question of whether one is a socialist. It is often difficult to determine what characteristics are relevant to the generalization at issue, and the skimpier our background knowledge the more difficult it is.

Notice also that in some cases the strength of an argument is *not* weakened by the fact that the items in the sample are homogeneous—that is, very similar to one another. For example, we could safely generalize about the melting temperature of lead based on experiments done on two identical samples of pure lead (or even one, if our instruments were known to be accurate). But we could not safely generalize about the amount of lead that exists in the blood of New Yorkers on the basis of autopsies performed on two automobile mechanics who worked in the same garage in Brooklyn. The difference is that we already possess the information (in our background knowledge) that a given piece of chemically pure lead will be a thoroughly representative sample with respect to the question of the melting point of lead; likewise we know that

Dubious Generalization

"OF COURSE THE SUN'S GONNA COME UP! IT ALWAYS DOES, EVERY MORNING."

We're kidding. Excellent generalization. (If we couldn't depend on generalizations like this, none of us would be safe getting out of bed in the morning.)

two automobile mechanics could not possibly be a representative sample with respect to the question of the lead content in the bodies of New Yorkers.

Finally, observe that generalizations to nonspecific nonuniversal conclusions—for example, "*most* members of the CED are socialists" or "*a majority of* Presbyterians favor an anti-abortion amendment"—are safer than generalizations to an entire target population (for the simple reason that nonuniversal general statements are not so easily refuted, since a single counterinstance does not falsify them). However, a generalization from a sample to *some specific percentage* of the target population (e.g., "72 percent of Presbyterians favor an anti-abortion amendment") requires somewhat more extensive discussion.

Statistical Inductive Generalizations

A generalization from a sample to the conclusion that a certain *percentage* of the target population possesses a certain characteristic is what we shall call a

Faulty Reasoning with Statistics

statistical inductive generalization. Thus, example 2 in the preceding section, which states that 72 percent of all Presbyterians favor an anti-abortion amendment because 72 percent of the Presbyterians in a sample favor the amendment, is an inductive generalization of the statistical variety.

Now, the evaluation criteria that we have already discussed apply as well to statistical inductive generalizations as to other generalizations. But it is important to note that no inductive argument can possibly establish that some *precise* percentage of a target population has a given characteristic.

For example, knowing that 50 percent of a random sample of Chaplain University students favor tuition tax credits does *not* warrant the unqualified general conclusion that *exactly* 50 percent of all Chaplain University students favor tuition tax credits. What it warrants is a general conclusion to the effect that *approximately* 50 percent of all Chaplain University students favor tax credits. This is only common sense. Just consider: If you polled a random sample of students at your university and found that 50 percent of the sample favored tax credits, you wouldn't bet that *exactly* 50 percent of all the students at your university favored tax credits. A better bet would be that *about* 50 percent favored it. You'd want to leave yourself a little leeway on both sides of 50 percent, the size of which would depend on how large your random sample had been, and on how much money you had bet. The smaller your random sample, the more leeway you would want to allow yourself. Likewise, the more money you bet, the more leeway you would want to allow yourself.

Thus, if you found, for instance, that 50 percent of a random sample of *one hundred* students favored tax credits, you might be willing to bet, say, $5 that between *49 and 51 percent* of the total student population favored tax credits, but you certainly wouldn't bet $1,000. However, you might be quite willing to bet $1,000 that between *40 and 60 percent* of the total student population favored tax credits, based on your finding that 50 percent of a random sample of a hundred favored tax credits. On the other hand, if your random sample consisted of only ten students (rather than one hundred), you wouldn't risk a $1,000 bet unless you were given a lot of leeway. You would say, perhaps, "Well, based on my random sample of ten students, according to which 50 percent favored tax credits, I'll bet $1,000 that between 20 percent and 80 percent of all the students at this university favor tax credits. But if you want me to narrow down the range a bit, I'll have to reduce the size of my bet."

Thus, you can see that knowing that 50 percent of a random sample of Chaplain University students favor tax credits warrants not a conclusion that *exactly* 50 percent of all Chaplain University students favor tax credits, but rather a conclusion about a *range* or *interval* of probable percentages, a conclusion tht looks like this:

> Between about —— and —— percent of Chaplain University students favor tuition tax credits (where the first blank would be filled with some number below 50 and the second blank with a number the same distance above 50).

Now, it so happens that, given that one-half of a random sample of one hundred Chaplain University students favor tax credits, according to the mathematics of statistics there is a 95-percent probability that between 40 and 60 percent of Chaplain University students favor tax credits. Or, to put it somewhat differently, given that one-half of a random sample of one hundred Chaplain University students favor tax credits, it follows *at the 95-percent confidence level,* that 50 percent of Chaplain University students, *give or take 10 percentage points either way,* favor tuition tax credits. This ten-point spread either way is an **error margin**, or, as statisticians call it, a **confidence interval.** Its size depends on two things: the size of the random sample and the confidence level (the probability that the conclusion is correct, or, if you wish, the amount of money you'd be willing to bet). At a given confidence level, a larger random sample will produce a smaller error margin. At a given size of random sample, a higher confidence level will produce a larger error margin.

In everyday inductive reasoning we usually simply conclude, somewhat vaguely, that "most" so-and-sos are such-and-such, or that "chances are" if you're a so-and-so then you're a such-and-such. Rarely do we reason inductively to conclusions in which some specific percentage is mentioned. For the most part we leave statistical inductive generalizations to the pollsters, survey takers, and other statisticians. An exception occurs when we ourselves, reading the results of a poll taken of a sample population, extend those results to the entire population, as when we conclude that, because a poll taken by our local

Table 10-1 *Approximate Error Margins for Various Size Random Samples*

(95-percent level of confidence; observed percentage of characteristic in sample: 50)

Size of Sample	Error Margin (Confidence Interval)
10	0.20 to 0.80
25	0.28 to 0.72
50	0.36 to 0.64
100	0.40 to 0.60
250	0.44 to 0.56
500	0.46 to 0.54
1,000	0.47 to 0.53
1,500	0.48 to 0.52

SOURCE: Ronald N. Giere, *Understanding Scientific Reasoning* (New York: Holt, Rinehart and Winston, 1979), p. 213. Reprinted with permission.

newspaper indicates that 70 percent of the local people in a "random" survey favored such-and-such, about 70 percent of everyone in our community favors such-and-such. To make and evaluate such extensions from a sample to an entire population, we should have some idea of the error margins that are associated with random samples of various sizes. Table 10-1 shows the approximate error margins for samples of various sizes.

The table shows, for example, that if 50 percent of a random sample of ten so-and-sos are such-and-such, then there is a 95-percent probability that between 20 and 80 percent of all so-and-sos are such-and-such. If 50 percent of a random sample of twenty-five so-and-sos are such-and-such, then there is a 95 percent probability that between 28 and 72 percent of all so-and-sos are such-and-such. And so forth.

Notice that the figures in the table are all at the 95-percent level of confidence, which is the level at which many scientists are comfortable. In fact, if you are evaluating the report of a reputable statistical study and the confidence level is not specified, it is safe to assume that the confidence level of the study was at least 95 percent.

Of course, one can never be certain whether "informal" surveys of the sort conducted by hometown newspapers or the local Elks Club are based on samples that are truly random, so such surveys should be evaluated with an eye to the criteria discussed earlier in this section.

Finally, if you are considering reports of statistical studies done by others, it pays to be somewhat cautious of findings based on questionnaire samples, for it is frequently true that most questionnaire respondents are those who are *not* disinterested in the issue in question—that is, they are those who have an axe to grind one way or another. Thus, such samples are often nonrepresentative, even if the questionnaire was sent out randomly. And, as always, one should be cautious in accepting statistical generalizations about any issues concerning which people might be less than truthful, or about which they have been asked leading or biased questions. (Obviously, where the question asked was, "Do you think the murdering of innocent prebirth children should be unconstitutional?" it would be unwise to conclude that 72 percent of all Presbyterians believe there should be an anti-abortion amendment to the Constitution on the ground that 72 percent of a sample favor such an amendment.) Before accepting any claim that so-and-so favor or believe such-and-such, find out, if you can, what the question asked was, and evaluate it according to those principles of clarity and neutrality discussed in Chapters 2 and 5.

Sample Size

Some people believe that the larger the target population is the larger the sample must be for the inductive argument from the sample to the entire population to be a strong one. In fact, this is not true. What counts is not how

Sex, Cuddling, and the Ann Landers Survey

One inductive generalization that caused a tremendous hubbub was Ann Landers's finding in 1985 that 72 percent of the women in America would give up sex for a little tender cuddling.

The finding was based on the responses of more than ninety thousand readers to the question, directed to women, "Would you be content to be held close and treated tenderly, and forget about 'the act'?" Landers asked respondents to send a simple yes or no response on a postcard.

So what do you, dear critical thinker, conclude about American women from this? Very little, we trust. First, though Landers's sample was huge, there is no reason to suppose that it was representative. In fact, there is almost certainly reason to think that it was not. The people who went to the trouble of responding were likely to have strong feelings on the issue, and there is no way of telling in which direction this might have biased the sample. It is also quite probable that the sample included a higher percentage of women who had sexual problems, since women who do might have had more motivation to write in and express themselves. Indeed, one cannot even be sure that all, or even most, of the respondents were women. And even if they were, are the women who read Ann Landers representative of all women? Are even those who read newspapers representative?

Second, the question itself is troublesome. Those women who value cuddling and sex *equally* might be a bit unsure how to respond to the question, and those women who want *neither* cuddling *nor* sex from their husbands or lovers logically could not answer the question at all, given the way it was phrased. Finally, *saying* whether or not you would be content with something is sometimes quite different from actually being or not being content.

large the population is but whether the sample of that population is representative. This is true whether you are considering statistical or nonstatistical inductive generalizations. Thus, in Table 10-1, which shows error margins, no mention is made of the size of the target population. Nor, in our earlier example involving tax credits, was mention made of the size of the total enrollment of Chaplain University. To discover how cold a batch of beer is, a sip or two will suffice, whether the beer comes in a pint-size mug or in a half-gallon stein.

Another commonly held belief is "the larger the sample the better." There is *some* truth in this, we have shown. If the sample is random, the larger it is the more precise are the statistical conclusions that can be generalized from it. Further, as is only common sense, the more extensive is our experience with items of a given type the more confident we can be in our own generalizations about items of that type. The reason is that in cases where there could be important differences between our sample and the target class and no special steps have been taken to ensure that the sample is representative, the larger the sample, the smaller are the chances that the sample and target class will be dissimilar.

Summary

We can summarize the considerations discussed here about the strength of generalizing arguments in four questions. These questions pertain equally to any such argument, whether of the statistical or nonstatistical variety:

1. *Is it clear what the sample and target classes are and what characteristic is being attributed to each?*
2. *Is what is claimed about these classes knowable?*
3. *How different is the target from the sample?* (Remember, the more different the one is from the other, the weaker the argument, and the less different, the stronger the argument.)

Royko on Landers

Chicago Tribune columnist Mike Royko, whose wisdom we have sampled before, took an approach to criticizing the Landers survey that was rather different from ours. He simply parodied Landers with his own "Sex and Bowling Survey," in which he asked his readers this question: "Given a choice, men, would you rather be having sex with your wife or out bowling with your buddies?" (Results? Sixty-six percent of the men preferred sex, a finding that is no more generalizable than was Ann Landers's—which was Royko's point, we presume.) By the way, would you say that Royko has presented us with a case of the horse laugh (Chapter 6)?

4. *How diversified and how large is the sample?* (Remember, if there could be important differences between the sample and the target, as would be the case if no special steps were taken to ensure that the sample was representative, then the larger and more diversified the sample, the greater the likelihood that it was representative, and the stronger the argument.)

Finally, remember that though statistical generalizations to specific percentages are never warranted, generalizations based on random samples may be more or less precise depending on level of confidence and size of sample. Whether a sample is really random is difficult for the lay person to know; therefore, claims about randomness should be evaluated on the basis of the credibility of their sources.

Fallacies of Inductive Generalizations

To generalize about an entire class on the basis of a sample that is so small that it couldn't possibly be representative is called the **fallacy of hasty generalization.** To judge that all (or even many) welfare recipients are in reality wealthy because you know one who owns a Mercedes-Benz is to commit this fallacy.

To generalize about an entire class on the basis of a biased—that is, nonrepresentative—sample is to commit the **fallacy of biased generalization.** Obviously, there is some common ground between this fallacy and that of hasty generalization.

To ignore data that offer reasonable support for a general claim in favor of

Fear and Hope from Listerine

"98% of the people reading this ad have plaque," the ad warns in bold print. But fear not: "They can reduce it as much as 50% with Listerine."

"As much as," of course, is that vague range that we commented on earlier. But how did Listerine come up with such statistics? The ad explains the 50 percent reduction, in part (and in smaller print): "With a professional cleaning, regular brushing, and rinsing with Listerine twice a day, you can reduce plaque buildup up to 50% over brushing alone for better oral hygiene." Well, that must explain it. The Listerine users in the comparison also get the benefit of professional cleaning, so no wonder their plaque levels are reduced.

As for the 98-percent figure, it's probably true. But we'll bet Listerine didn't experiment with a random sample to arrive at it. Having plaque is a natural condition of anyone who eats. The only time a person's mouth might be entirely free of plaque is just after it's been cleaned professionally, if it is entirely free even then.

Incidentally, notice that the 98-percent statistic would not be reduced even if 100 percent of the people reading the ad used Listerine.

Unemployment? What Unemployment??

One of the more infamous examples in recent years of the fallacy of anecdotal evidence (or hasty generalization, take your pick) was Ronald Reagan's twice- or thrice-used technique of downplaying the unemployment statistics by waving a copy of the "Help Wanted" section of the want ads. Unemployment can't be that bad, is what, in effect, the president argued. Why, just look at all these employers right here in Washington searching for people to work for them.

an example or two that don't is to commit the **fallacy of anecdotal evidence**, really a subspecies of hasty generalization. For example, to dismiss the accumulated evidence that cigarette smokers have a shortened life expectancy because you know several smokers who have lived to a ripe old age is to commit this fallacy.

EXERCISE 10-6

Define the following concepts:

★1. Inductive generalization
 2. Target
 3. Sample
 4. Random sample
★5. Statistical inductive generalization

The Letter That Was a Photocopy of Itself

We recently received a chain letter we were supposed to photocopy and send off to twenty more people (without asking them for money!). According to the letter, "Constantine Diar [whoever he is] received the letter in 1983. A few days later he won a lottery prize of $2 million. Carlos Daddots, an office employee, received the letter and forgot it. He lost his job."

We hoped that whoever sent the letter to us did not do so because he or she believed these claims, for even if they are true, to conclude that everyone who follows the example of "Constantine Diar" will have good luck and everyone who follows the example of "Carlos Daddots" will have bad luck would be to generalize very hastily indeed. (This reasoning could also be analyzed as a case of post hoc—see Chapter 11).

Incidentally, the best line in the letter was the first: "This is a photocopy of a letter originally mailed from England that has been around the world nine times." Think of that. Apparently the *original itself* said, "This is a photocopy of a letter originally mailed from England that has been around the world nine times."

EXERCISE 10-7

"Every student I've met from Tulare State has believed in God. Therefore, most of the students from Tulare State believe in God."

★1. In this generalization what is the sample?
 2. What is the target?
 3. What characteristic is being attributed to the sample and target?
★4. Could it be known whether or not a given student had this characteristic?
 5. Suppose that Tulare State is (as the name implies) a state university, and has no admission requirement pertaining to religious beliefs. Suppose further that the students in the sample were all interviewed as they left a local church after Sunday services. Are these suppositions relevant to the confidence we should have in the argument? If the answer is "yes," how should they affect our confidence in the argument?
 6. Suppose that all the students interviewed were freshmen. Is this supposition relevant to the confidence one should have in the argument? If the answer is "yes," how should it affect our confidence in the argument?
★7. Suppose that all the students interviewed were on Tulare State's football team. Is this supposition relevant to the confidence one should have in the argument? If the answer is "yes," how should it affect our confidence in the argument?
 8. Suppose that the researchers selected all the students interviewed by picking every fiftieth name on an alphabetical list of students' names. Is this supposition relevant to the confidence we should have in the argument? If the answer is "yes," how should it affect our confidence in the conclusion?
 9. Suppose that the students interviewed all responded to a questionnaire published in the campus newspaper titled "Survey of Student Religious Beliefs." Is this supposition relevant to the confidence we should have in the argument? If the answer is "yes," how should it affect our confidence in the conclusion?
★10. Suppose that the students interviewed were selected at random from the Records Office's list of registered automobile owners. Is this supposition relevant to the confidence we should have in the argument? If the answer is "yes," how should it affect our confidence in the conclusion?

★EXERCISE 10-8

You want to find out what percentage of residents of your local community believe the sheriff's department is adequately staffed, so you conduct a survey. Name four characteristics of the sample that would bias the survey—that is, that would reduce our confidence that your findings applied to the community at large. For example, if the people in the sample were all interviewed in a local bar, that characteristic should diminish our confidence that your findings can be extended to the community in general. Try to come up with four other such biasing characteristics.

EXERCISE 10-9

Now name four characteristics of a sample that would increase our confidence that your findings applied to the community at large. For example, if the people surveyed belonged to a wide range of economic backgrounds, that would increase our confidence that your findings applied to the entire community.

EXERCISE 10-10

Now name four characteristics of your sample that would not affect our confidence one way or the other. In other words, name four characteristics that are irrelevant to the issue. We trust you need no further examples.

EXERCISE 10-11

Suppose that you are interested in finding out what percentage of people in your community lift weights. Name four characteristics of your sample that would decrease our confidence that your results were generalizable to the whole population, four that would increase our confidence, and four that would be irrelevant to whether your results would generalize.

EXERCISE 10-12

Suppose you want to determine what percentage of people in your state believe that gasoline taxes for road repairs should be increased. Name four characteristics of your sample that would decrease our confidence that your results were generalizable to the whole population, four that would increase our confidence, and four that would be irrelevant to whether your results would generalize.

EXERCISE 10-13

Smitty raises llamas. He also likes to gamble, but he will bet a large sum only if he thinks he has a sure thing, which he defines as at least a 95-percent chance of winning. On which of the following bets should he risk a large sum?

★1. A random sample of 250 delegates to the World Llama Lovers convention reveals that 30 percent believe that llamas should not be bred before age three. Should Smitty risk a large sum that 30 percent of all the delegates share this belief?

  2. Should he risk a large sum that *at least* 30 percent share this belief?
  3. That at least 22 percent share this belief?
★4. That no more than 37 percent share this belief?
  5. That no more than 33 percent share this belief?
  6. If the random sample were 100, rather than 250 (with 30 percent of the delegates believing that llamas should not be bred before age three), should he risk a large sum that 30 percent of all the delegates share this belief?
★7. That at least 35 percent share this belief?
  8. That at least 22 percent share this belief?
  9. That no more than 37 percent share this belief?
★10. That no more than 33 percent share this belief?

EXERCISE 10-14

Read the passage below and then answer the questions that follow.

> In the Sunrise University History Department students are invited to submit written evaluations of their instructors to the department's personnel committee, which uses those evaluations to help determine whether history instructors should be recommended for retention and promotion. In his three history classes Professor Ludlum has a total of 100 students. Six students turned in written evaluations of Professor Ludlum; four of these evaluations were negative and two were positive. Professor Hitchcock, who sits on the History Department Personnel Committee, argued against recommending Ludlum for promotion. "If a majority of the students who bothered to evaluate Ludlum find him lacking," he stated, "then it's clear to me that a majority of all his students find him lacking."

★1. What is the sample in Professor Hitchcock's reasoning?
  2. What is the target?
  3. What characteristic is Professor Hitchcock attributing to the sample and the target?
★4. Could it be known whether the individuals in the sample class and target class have that characteristic?
  5. Are there possibly important differences between the sample and the target that should reduce our confidence in Professor Hitchcock's conclusion?
  6. Does Professor Hitchcock have any information concerning the diversification of the sample?
★7. Is the sample random?
  8. How about the size of his sample? Is it large enough to help ensure that the sample and target classes won't be too dissimilar?
★9. Based on the analysis of Professor Hitchcock's reasoning that you have just completed in the foregoing questions, how strong is his reasoning?

EXERCISE 10-15

Identify any fallacies that are present in the following passages:

★1. From a letter to the editor: "I read with great interest the May 23 article on the study of atheists in federal prisons, according to which most of these atheists identify themselves as socialists, communists, or anarchists. That most atheists, along with all their other shortcomings, turn out to be political wackos surprises yours truly not one bit."

2. I ordered a packet of seeds from Hansen Seed Company last year, and only half of them germinated. I'll bet you only get half the plants you're expecting from the order you just sent them.

3. From a letter to the editor: "According to your June 4 editorial ('Seat Belt Laws a Must') statistics show overwhelmingly that you're safer wearing a seat belt. So much for statistics. I had a friend who died because he was wearing his seat belt. The investigator at his accident reported that if he had not been wearing his belt, he would have been thrown clear of the wreck. As it was, he burned to death because he was trapped in his seat."

★4. Drug abuse among professional athletes is a serious and widespread problem. Three players from a single team admitted last week that they had used cocaine.

5. Most Americans favor a national lottery to reduce the federal debt. In a poll taken in Las Vegas, more than 80 percent said they favored such a lottery.

6. Overheard: "All these studies that supposedly show that exercising is good for your health—what a bunch of hooey. What about that guy that wrote all those health books and died when he was jogging? Are you going to tell me he wouldn't take them all back if he could?"

★7. From a letter to the editor: "Throughout the country moviegoers are cheering Sylvester Stallone as Rambo, who singlehandedly conquers the Russian army to free a prisoner. So now we see what the current batch of films is all about: vengeance, hatred, and violence. Their message? The ends justify the means. No wonder we're in trouble."

8. From a letter to the editor: "In May 1984, members of the Animal Liberation Front stole several hours of videotapes of experiments done to animals at the University of Pennsylvania's Head Injury Clinical Research Center. According to reliable reports, one of the tapes shows baboons having their brains damaged by a piston device that smashed into their skulls with incredible force. The anesthetic given the baboons was allegedly insufficient to prevent serious pain. Given that this is what animal research is all about, Secretary of Health and Human Services Margaret Heckler acted quite properly in halting federal funding for the project. Federal funding for animal research ought to be halted, it seems to me, in the light of these atrocities."

9. "A majority of Ohio citizens consider the problem of air pollution critical. According to a survey taken in Cleveland, more than half the respondents identified air pollution as the most pressing of seven environmental issues, and as having either 'great' or 'very great' importance."

★10. Overheard: "You're not going to take a course from Harris, are you? I know at least three people who say he's terrible. All three flunked his course, as a matter of fact."

Inductive Analogical Arguments

Different writers characterize analogical arguments differently. We shall regard them as arguments in which something that is said to hold true of a sample of a certain class is also said to hold true of another member of the class. That is, we regard an analogical argument as having this form:

Premises: Such-and-such holds true for all (or most, or some specific percent) of a sample of a certain class of things, and item T is a member of that class.
Conclusion: Therefore, T also has that characteristic.

Example:

Premises: Over the past twenty years, I've owned three Volkswagens, all of which have been reliable and economical. I'll buy another Volkswagen.
Conclusion: It too will be reliable and economical.

This example closely resembles inductive generalizations (treated in the preceding section), which consist of generalizing from a sample to an entire class. The only difference is that in the example the generalization is from a sample of a class to *another individual* in the class rather than to the entire class. The *analogy* is between the three Volkswagens I have already owned and the Volkswagen I might buy, hereafter called the next Volkswagen.

Again, let's call the sample of the class for which something is said to hold true the *sample,* and let's call item T the *target.* Thus, in the example, the three Volkswagens I have owned are the sample, and T, the target, is the next Volkswagen.

Given the similarity between inductive analogical arguments and inductive generalizations, it is not surprising that our means of appraising the two kinds of arguments are essentially identical.

The first step in appraising an inductive analogical argument is to understand the analogy—that is, what the sample and the target are. You must also determine what characteristic is being attributed to the sample and the target, and whether what is being claimed about the sample or the target is actually knowable.

Beyond this, the greater the relevant differences between the items in the sample and the target, the weaker the argument will be. Conversely, the more the relevant similarities, the stronger the argument will be. (If the next Volkswagen is a Rabbit but the others were all beetles, I would have less confidence that the next VW will be reliable and economical then I would if the others were all Rabbits.)

Also, the more diversified the sample, the better the argument, assuming that important differences could exist between the sample and the target item. (The more diversified the sample, the more likely it is that the target item will be like at least some members of the sample class, which is why diversification in the sample strengthens the argument.) Conversely, the less diversification in the sample the weaker the argument will be.

Thus, for example, if my past Volkswagens were all buses, then I would have less confidence that the next VW would also be reliable and economical, *unless,* of course, the next VW were also a bus. (If it were a bus, the argument would be *stronger,* because the similarity between the target and the sample would be greater. If an increased similarity among the items in the sample results in an increased similarity between those items and the target, then the increased similarity *strengthens* the argument.) But if my sample were diversified, and I owned, say, a beetle, a bus, and a squareback, and all of these were reliable and economical, then I might feel reasonably confident that a VW of any sort would be reliable and economical.

Sample Size

As with inductive generalizations, what is important is that the sample in an analogical argument be similar to the target item, not that the sample be of a certain size. Reasoning analogically from the chemical properties of a single sample of pure uranium to another sample of pure uranium is as sound as generalizing from a single sample. To be sound, the analogical argument need not involve a sample of a particular size. If there could be important differences between the items in the sample and the target, we are entitled to feel more confidence in analogical reasoning that is based on a larger sample. If you've owned a dozen Volkswagens, all of which have been reliable and economical, you are entitled to feel even more confidence in the reliability and dependability of your next Volkswagen than if you had owned but three. The increase in confidence is essentially due to the fact that your having owned a dozen Volkswagens has decreased the likelihood that your next Volkswagen will be dissimilar to all the Volkswagens in your sample.

Finally, the larger the percentage of the sample that have the characteristic in question, the stronger will be the argument. In the example, 100 percent of

Congressman Goodloe Byron

Maryland Congressman Goodloe Byron, who reportedly ran twenty miles a day for ten years, died in 1978 at the age of forty-eight, while running. (That he died while running is perhaps unsurprising, as occasions on which he was not running must have been rare.) Byron had a brother who died in his thirties of heart disease and another brother who had a bypass operation in his thirties. Byron's father died of heart disease at forty. An examination of Byron's heart revealed that he too had severe atherosclerotic heart disease.

Analogical reasoning concerning medical conditions within the same family is very strong because of the important shared biological characteristics. Had Congressman Bryon reasoned analogically, he could have concluded with some confidence that he had a higher than normal risk of heart disease. Indeed, it is possible that Bryon ran so much precisely *because* he did reason analogically and thought he could avoid heart problems by exercising heavily. (Unfortunately for the congressman, only moderate exercise is recommended for those who already have heart disease.)

my Volkswagens have been reliable and economical, so I can be more confident that my next Volkswagen will be reliable and economical than I could if, say, only two of my three Volkswagens had been reliable and economical.

So, let's summarize with the questions that should be asked of any analogical argument:

1. *Is is clear what the sample class and the target item are and what is being attributed to each?*
2. *Is what is being claimed about the sample and target knowable?*
3. *How different is the target item from the sample items?* (The greater the differences are, the weaker the argument will be; the fewer the differences, the stronger the arguments.)
4. *How diversified and large is the sample?* (Assuming that the sample and target differ, the larger and more diversified the sample the better, as we have explained.)

Finally, with regard to analogical arguments, we should also consider:

5. *How large a percentage of the sample has the characteristic in question?* (The larger the better.)

EXERCISE 10-16

Having been wowed by the physical fitness ads on TV and in the magazines, Mike tries lifting weights. Everything goes well for the first couple of months,

Analogical Argument?

The instructor believes that public school teachers are terribly underpaid as compared with city garbage collectors, and illustrates the disparity between the salaries of each by comparing their salaries to a grape and a watermelon. He intends, of course, for the dramatic impact of the analogical illustration to convince others of his belief. But a vivid illustration of a belief is not an argument for adopting that belief, though it can be an attempt at nonargumentative persuasion, which it is in this case.

except that Mike notices he hurts his back every time he does a deadlift. He decides to strike deadlifting from his routine, figuring that the next time he tried the lift it would just hurt his back again.

⋆1. In this argument, what is the sample?

2. What is the target?

3. What characteristic is being attributed to the sample and target?

⋆4. Can what Mike believes about the sample and target be known?

⋆5. Are there any important differences between the sample and target?

⋆6. How diversified is the sample?

⋆7. How large is his sample?

8. Suppose Mike decides to try the deadlift again, but with less weight. Is this supposition relevant to the argument? If the answer is "yes," is the argument made stronger or weaker by the supposition?

9. Suppose Mike changes to a different gym. Is this supposition relevant? If the answer is "yes," is the argument strengthened or weakened by the supposition?

10. Suppose Mike has used a variety of different techniques and postures when deadlifting in the past, but all with the same painful result. Is this supposition relevant? If so, does it strengthen or weaken the argument?

EXERCISE 10-17

For the past four years, Clifford has gone on the Fourth of July hundred-mile bike ride sponsored by the Cyclamates, a local bicycle club. He has always become too exhausted to finish the entire hundred miles. Figuring that he's had enough, Clifford plans to do only the second half of the ride this year.

⋆1. In this argument, what is the sample?

⋆2. What is the target?

⋆3. What characteristic is attributed to the sample and target?

4. Is what is being claimed in the argument about the sample and target knowable?

5. Are there any important relevant differences between the sample and the target?

6. Is there relevant diversity in the sample?

⋆7. Suppose that all the previous rides had been through hill country and that this year's ride is on flat ground. Would this make Clifford's argument stronger or weaker? Why?

⋆8. Suppose that Clifford doesn't know where this year's ride will be held. Would his argument be stronger or weaker if all the previous rides had been in hill country?

⋆9. Suppose that Clifford doesn't know where this year's ride will be held. Would his argument be stronger or weaker if some of the rides had been in hilly country and some in flat country?

⋆10. Suppose Clifford has used a different bike in each of the previous rides. Would this make his argument stronger or weaker?

EXERCISE 10-18

On three occasions Kirk has tried to grow artichokes in his organic (no-chemicals) backyard garden, and each time his crop has been ruined by mildew. Billie prods him to try one more time, and he agrees to do so, though he secretly thinks the effort will be a waste of time, and that the mildew will win out again. Decide whether any of the following suppositions are relevant to the argument, and for each that is, determine whether it makes Kirk's argument stronger or weaker. Consider each supposition separately from the others. By the way, before you begin, be sure you know what Kirk's argument is.

★1. Suppose that this time Kirk is going to plant the artichokes in a new location.
2. Suppose that on the past three occasions Kirk planted his artichokes at different times during the growing season: One crop was started early, one in the middle of the growing season, and one late.
3. Suppose that in the past, one crop was started during a dry year, one during a wet year, and one during an average year.
★4. Suppose that this year's growing season has been predicted to be much warmer than usual.
5. Suppose that in the past only two of the three crops were ruined by mildew.
6. Suppose that this year Billie decides to plant marigolds near the artichokes.
★7. Suppose that this year there is supposed to be a solar eclipse.
8. Suppose that this year for the first time Kirk fertilizes with lawn clippings.
9. Suppose that this year Billie and Kirk have a large dog.
★10. Suppose that this year Kirk installs a drip irrigation system.

EXERCISE 10-19

"Everytime we've visited the Farallon Islands, and we've been there several different times and at different times of the year, it's been foggy and cold. So, when you visit there next week, dress warmly. It's bound to be cold and foggy." Evaluate this argument by answering the following questions:

★1. Is it clear what the sample and target are, and what characteristic is being attributed to both?
★2. Is what is claimed about the sample and target knowable?
3. Are there any important differences between the sampled items and the target?
★4. Are the size and diversification of the sample great enough to ensure that the sampled items and the target will not be too dissimilar?
5. What percentage of the sampled items have the characteristic in question? Does this factor help strengthen or weaken the argument?

EXERCISE 10-20

Evaluate each of the following arguments just as you did in the preceding exercise. These exercises are more difficult than the preceding ones and may be best suited to class discussion or short-essay answers.

1. Senator Cranston has been an excellent senator, so he would make an excellent president.

★2. Beatrice likes the representative from Tri-State Investments. He is polite, well informed, and kind. She decides, therefore, that he will not mislead her and agrees to purchase the life insurance policy he recommends.

3. The Barneses are travelling to Europe for a year and decide to find a student to house-sit for them. They settle on Homer because he is neat and tidy in his appearance. "If he takes such good care of his personal appearance," Mrs. Barnes thinks, "he's likely to take good care of our house, too."

4. In every one of the last six presidential elections, from 1968 to 1988, the Democratic Party has run a candidate that was more liberal than his Republican opponent. In five of those six elections, the Democrat has lost; the only exception was Jimmy Carter's win over Gerald Ford in 1976, and Carter only won with 50.1 percent of the popular vote. The Democrats' only hope in '92 is to run a conservative.

★5. Record company executive to record producer: "Look, I want this record done just the way you did their last hit. In fact, just take their last hit and rework it a bit; use different lyrics, but the same beat, the same backup, the same sound. It'll sell if the sound's the same."

6. A household that does not balance its budget is just asking for trouble. It's the same, therefore, with the federal government. Balance the federal budget, or watch out!

7. Mark is almost ready to throw the steak on the fire. While he's making the salad, he feeds his dog, Wilbur, a piece of the meat. A few minutes later he notices Wilbur has grown ill with a stomach problem of some sort. Mark decides he'd better not eat the steak.

★8. First it was cyclamates. They were taken out of soft drinks because they caused cancer. Then it was saccharin. It too was discovered to be carcinogenic. So I don't care what they call this new artificial sweetener. It'll probably be carcinogenic, too.

9. Oregon has a bottle-return law, just like the one proposed here in California, and the Oregon law works! It's cleaned up the highways, provided extra jobs. It will do the same here.

10. " . . . if a body and an environment were supposed [in which we might exist after our present body dies] . . . of a kind radically different from bodies of flesh and their material environment, then it is paradoxical to suppose that, under such drastically different conditions, a personality could remain the same as before. . . . To take a crude but telling analogy, it is past belief that, if the body of any one of us were suddenly changed

into that of a shark or an octopus and placed in the ocean, his personality could, for more than a very short time, if at all, recognizably survive so radical a change of environment."

—C. J. DUCASSE, *A Critical Examination of the Belief in a Life After Death*

Statistical Syllogisms

A **statistical syllogism** is an argument in which it is assumed that, because something is true of some percentage of a certain class of things, it is true of some specific member of that class. That is, statistical syllogisms have this form:

> Premises: Such-and-such is a characteristic of all (or most, or some specific percentage) of a certain class of things, and item T is a member of that class.
> Conclusion: Therefore, T also has that characteristic.

Here's an example:

> Premises: Most 1990 Jeeps are Cherokees, and Jones owns a 1990 Jeep.
> Conclusion: Therefore, Jones's Jeep is a Cherokee.

As the example shows, the only difference between a statistical syllogism and an analogical argument is that in an analogical argument the reasoning proceeds *from a sample*. In a statistical syllogism there is no sample.

Although in a statistical syllogism it must be clear what characteristic is being attributed to the class and individual in question, and although all such attributions must be of the sort that could be known to be true, the strength of a statistical syllogism depends primarily on the percentage of the class that has the characteristic in question. If 90 percent of 1990 Jeeps are Cherokees, then it's likelier that Jones's 1990 Jeep is a Cherokee than if only 51 percent of them are. (If 100 percent of 1990 Jeeps are Cherokees, then it would follow with deductive certainty that Jones's Jeep is a Cherokee.)

Note that where two statistical syllogisms draw *different* conclusions about the same target, we should have more confidence in the conclusion of the argument that more narrowly defines the class of things in question with respect to relevant characteristics. Compare the following argument with the first example of a statistical syllogism:

> Premises: Most 1990 Jeeps that cost more than $18,000 are Grand Wagoneers, and Jones owns a 1990 Jeep that costs more than $18,000.
> Conclusion: Therefore, Jones's Jeep is a Grand Wagoneer.

Clearly, given what we know about Jones and 1990 Jeeps, it's more likely that Jones owns a Grand Wagoneer than a Cherokee.

Appeals to Authority

When we accept someone's claim (see Chapter 3), we are in effect using a statistical syllogism. Our implicit reasoning is similar to one of the following patterns:

Example 1

Premises: Most observations made under good physical conditions by unbiased witnesses who are not distracted, emotionally upset, and so on (see Chapter 3) are accurate, and this observation is such an observation.
Conclusion: Therefore, this observation is accurate.

Example 2

Premises: Most claims made by unbiased experts relative to their subject of expertise, when their claims are not controversial among other experts in the subject, are reliable, and this claim is such a claim.
Conclusion: Therefore, this claim is reliable.

Example 3

Premises: Most claims made by Jones relative to this subject have turned out to be true, and this is a claim made by Jones relative to this subject matter.
Conclusion: Therefore, this claim is true.

Thus, we can understand why, logically, we should have less confidence in the claims made by some individuals than in those made by others. The percentage of claims that are correct is smaller for some individuals than for others. For example, *some* observations made by emotionally distressed persons under conditions of poor lighting may be correct, but the percentage of such observations that are correct is still relatively distant from 100 percent, as compared with observations made by those who are not emotionally upset and are not handicapped by poor physical conditions. Accordingly, the statistical syllogisms whose first premises refer to the observations of someone who is emotionally distressed, or whose observations are made under poorly illuminated conditions, are comparatively weak.

Similarly, the opinions expressed by experts in subjects outside their fields of expertise provide premises for only comparatively weak statistical syllogisms. Traditionally, one who tries to prove something about subject X by citing the opinion of an expert in nonrelated subject Y is therefore said to commit the fallacy of **appeal to illegitimate authority.** We may also regard as appeals to illegitimate authority attempts to prove claims by appealing to the say-so of *any* individuals whose circumstances make it unsafe to assume that most of what they say about the subject at hand is true. Thus, for instance, seeking to establish a claim by appealing to the eyewitness reports of someone who is mentally fatigued, say, or emotionally upset, or prejudiced, or deranged, or who frequently lies, and the like may all be regarded as appeals to illegitimate authority.

If you recall the discussion of ad hominem pseudoreasoning in Chapter 7, you may remember we said it is a mistake to reject a claim as false because of some fact about the person making the claim. To reject a claim on these grounds is usually the result of a weak statistical syllogism much like those underlying appeals to illegitimate authority. Unless "X" stands for something like "a pathological liar," the percentage of claims made by a person who is X

Ad Hominem?

Controversial Book on Morality Is Published by Prometheus

Prometheus is pleased to announce the June publication of *Telling Right From Wrong,* a book of moral philosophy. The author, Timothy J. Cooney, shocked the New York publishing world by forging a letter of endorsement in support of his book. The letter, purportedly written by well-known Harvard University professor Robert Nozick, was discovered to be a forgery shortly before Random House was to publish the book in late 1984. Random House subsequently dropped it from its list of forthcoming titles.

Jason Epstein, editorial director of Random House, said at the time, "It's a dilemma, because the book is absolutely brilliant and I had pretty much decided to publish it before Cooney sent me that so-called letter from Nozick. . . . But what does one do when confronted with a decision to publish a terribly important book whose author turns out to be flawed?"

Prometheus, long a leading publisher of philosophy, felt that *Telling Right From Wrong* was an exacting work of philosophy with much to recommend it. "The issue for us," said Paul Kurtz, editor

of Prometheus, "was the merit of the work itself. We read it independently and found it was an original book—thought provoking, controversial, even at times brilliant. It's a contribution to the field and deserves publication." Advance reviews have confirmed this evaluation. *Publisher's Weekly* hailed *Telling Right From Wrong* as "a fresh, sometimes profound approach to moral philosophy."

Cooney's innovative analysis illuminates our moral language and the assumptions underlying its use. He contends that much of our prescriptive language about such controversial issues as gambling, abortion, capital punishment, homosexuality, prostitution, divorce, freedom of speech, and pornography is devoid of moral content. These issues are really matters of politics or opinion rather than morality, claims Cooney. He finds that modern philosophers have overlooked the fact that what we call "good" or "bad" often reflects not moral judgment but the satisfaction or frustration of general, shared desires.

Ad hominem? Well, maybe, but probably not. Certainly not on the part of the Prometheus ad, which nicely distinguishes between the merits of Cooney's work and the merits of Cooney. But it would probably also be inaccurate to characterize Random House's rejection of Cooney's book as an *ad hominem.* Notice that Jason Epstein, editorial director of Random House, still regards the book as "brilliant." In other words, he is not rejecting the book as false, inaccurate, or flawed (if he did regard the work as flawed because the author forged a letter, then he would be guilty of an *ad hominem*). Rather, Epstein seems to have made an ethical decision, or perhaps a practical decision based on considerations about sales or the Random House image, not to publish the work of a "flawed" author.

that are false is relatively too distant from 100 percent for us to be confident that any such claim is false. And so ad hominem, like appeal to illegitimate authority, is a case of an implicit statistical syllogism gone wrong.

EXERCISE 10-21

Identify any instances of *ad hominem* or appeal to illegitimate authority in the following passages.

★1. SHE: We'd be better off to get a Zenith. I learned from their salesman that they have the best repair record of any make.

★2. HE: Yeah, sure. What other baloney did he feed you? Look, he *sells* Zeniths, for crying out loud. Of course he'd say they have the best record.

3. Overheard: "There's absolutely no point in asking a conservationist if toxics are contaminating Butte County wellwater. As a conservationist, of course he'll say they are."

4. Let's buy gold. The dollar's going to drop and the price of gold is going to rise. This I heard, and this I believe. It came from our doctor, and he's filthy rich.

★5. Overheard: "I've had it with *Doonesbury*. Some people claim it's a profound comment on society, blah, blah, blah. But the only reason the guy that writes it came back from his vacation was to attack Ronald Reagan. The only thing funny about it is that it's in our newspaper, which usually is pretty good."

6. From a letter to the editor: "The Secretary of Defense claims we cannot cut defense spending by so much as a jot. Right. What the generals want, the generals get. What the Secretary is, is just another lawyer. It's not what's right that matters, it's what you can get. No wonder his relations with Congress are so poor."

★7. . . . then there was the fellow who went out and bought a new $300 compressor for his home air conditioner because his friend, an automobile mechanic, told him he needed a new one. Turns out he didn't need a new compressor at all. It just shows you: If you have a problem with your car, take it to a mechanic. If you have a problem with your air conditioner, take it to someone who knows something about them.

8. From a letter to an editor: "It is a widely accepted view, which your readers seem to share, that zoning and zoning ordinances are good things that protect the rights of property owners, help promote uniform and controlled growth, and stimulate business and industry. Unfortunately, zoning is unconstitutional. Here I cite no less authority than the United States Constitution (Amendment XIV), and our own Pennsylvania Constitution (Article I, Section I). Read them sometime. You'll be surprised."

★9. Are you really going to believe her about librarians' salaries not being excessive? I'll have you know she herself is a librarian, or don't you think that matters?

★10. HE: Dr. Coder says it's just a noncancerous keratosis, I think he called it. Just a little scaly patch on my skin. Nothing to worry about.
SHE: Yes, well, he's not a skin specialist, either, so I wouldn't necessarily accept that. Better make an appointment with a dermatologist.

11. In one of the follow-up columns to her sex survey (see page 278) Ann Landers wrote, "Comments by Erica Jong, Andrew Greeley, Helen Gurley Brown, Gay Talese and Gloria Steinem showed insight and understanding. A few so-called sex experts who called the survey 'dangerous' demonstrated incredible ignorance and missed the point completely."

★12. In one of his columns, Mike Royko had a word or two to write about Sylvester Stallone, who, according to Royko, after completing the movie *Rambo: First Blood Part II*, explained that it was an attempt to secure some credit for Vietnam veterans. Royko quotes Stallone as saying, "The people who pushed the wrong button all took a powder. The vets got the raw deal and were left holding the bag. What Rambo is saying is that if they could fight again, it would be different."

Royko went on to observe that during the Vietnam War, when Stallone could have been a "real-life Rambo," he spent his time first at American College of Switzerland "teaching rich girls how to touch their toes" and then as a drama major at the University of Miami "improving his tan."

13. From a letter to the editor: "The *Bee* editorial headed 'The Murder of Innocents' deplored the motive behind the Air India tragedy by posing the following question: 'What possible reason could there be for killing 329 innocents, so many of them children . . . ?' The writer then urges Americans never to accept some 'maniacal logic' that offers an excuse for such a heinous crime.

"Below this editorial followed a second, which urged Governor Deukmejian to strike from a family-planning bill awaiting his signature a stipulation prohibiting state funding to any family-planning agency that provides abortions, or incentives or referrals to obtain them.

"What an incongruous position—to condemn the murder of 80 innocent children in a plane over the Atlantic, but to condone the murder of 4,000 children nationwide per day in the womb.

"Isn't this the very same 'maniacal logic' that permits constant slaughter under the guise of 'family planning,' a euphemistic term to obscure another form of 'murder of the innocents'?"

★14. Although I've not read much of Jean-Paul Sartre's existentialism, I'm pretty confident that its influence will be bad in the long run. I don't know how you could expect anything else, really. Maybe you weren't aware of it, but the philosophy of Martin Heidegger was the single biggest influence on Sartre, and Heidegger was a dues-paying member of the NSDAP (the Nazi Party) from 1933 until 1945.

15. From a letter to the editor: "Oregon Senator Mark Hatfield has been outspoken in urging the Senate not to give the president the power he

wants to veto individual items in spending bills passed by Congress. The line-item proposal seems like a good one to me, despite what the Hatfields and Kennedys and the other Senate liberals say about it. Hatfield is always out after the president. (I really for the life of me cannot understand why he calls himself a Republican.) I say listen to Senator Dan Evans of Washington, another Republican, one who favors the proposal. Evans is a former governor in a state that had the line-item veto. He says it works."

EXERCISE 10-22 (ESSAY)

Pretend that you are working for the city council of your town. One important issue before the council is what to do about limiting growth in the city, and you have been hired to design a survey to find out what members of the community think about growth. Write a proposal that you can submit to the council that will accomplish the job and that you can defend against possible objections from council members. Remember that "growth," pure and simple, is pretty vague. You'll want to refine the issue at the outset. Then determine how big a sample you'll need, how to select it, what questions to ask, and so on.

Recap

When encountering general claims it is important to consider these questions:

1. Is it clear what class is being generalized about?
2. Is it clear what is being said about that class?
3. Is what is being claimed knowable?

General claims that involve comparisons require special attention; in particular, it is wise to ask yourself these questions:

1. Are both terms of the comparison clear?
2. Is the same standard of comparison used for both terms?
3. Are the items comparable?
4. Are before/after changes genuine or due to changes in reporting and recording practices?
5. Is the range of comparison too broad or too vague to be meaningful?
6. Is the comparison itself too obscure to be meaningful?
7. If the comparison is expressed as an average, have important details been omitted?

With regard to arguments that involve general claims, you'll recall the three basic kinds. First, there are *inductive generalizations*, arguments that generalize from a sample of a class to the entire class, most of it, or some specific percentage of it. Second, there are *analogical arguments*, in which you reason that something true of a certain sample class must therefore be true of some other member of the class. And third, there are *statistical syllogisms*, in which you reason from a general claim about all or most of some specific percentage of a class to some individual member of that class.

In all three types of arguments it's important to be clear as to what class is being generalized about and what is being said about that class and any member of it that has been singled out for attention. And, of course, anything being claimed about these classes or individuals must be knowable.

Beyond these questions of clarification, you should consider the following questions.

About inductive generalizations:

How different is the target from the sample?
How large and diversified is the sample?

About analogical arguments:

How different is the target from the sample?
How large and diversified is the sample?
How large a percentage of the sample has the characteristic in question?

About statistical syllogisms:

How large a percentage of the class has the characteristic in question?

11 *Causal Arguments*

Everything that we believe ourselves to know about the physical world depends entirely upon the assumption that there are causal laws.

—BERTRAND RUSSELL

'Tis only causation, which produces such a connection, as to give us assurance from the existence or action of one object, that 'twas followed or preceded by any other existence or action.

—DAVID HUME

In brief, a causal claim is one that states, where X and Y are different phenomena, that X causes or caused Y, that X is *a* cause of Y, that X plays a causal role in producing Y, or that X is a causal factor in producing Y. We turn now to the arguments that are most commonly used to support such claims.

Causation Among Specific Events

Let's say your car has been running pretty well. Then you decide to tune it up. After that it misses and backfires. You reason that something you did during the tune-up caused the problem. Your conclusion is that one specific event, tuning up your car (X), is the cause of some other specific event, the car's missing and backfiring (Y).

There are several ways of reaching a conclusion about one specific occurrence causing some other specific occurrence. In this section we'll discuss the two most frequently employed types of arguments designed to reach such conclusions, and we'll also take notice of four frequently encountered varieties of fallacies in causal reasoning.

> *Type 1.* <u>*X is the difference*</u>: *X caused Y because the occurrence of X is the only relevant difference between this situation where Y occurred, and situations where Y did not occur.*

This is most likely the reasoning you would use to conclude that your tune-up caused your car's present problems. You probably reasoned that the only relevant difference between the current situation, in which your car misses and backfires (Y), and the situations in which Y did not occur, is the occurrence of X, your tune-up. Therefore, you conclude, your tune-up, X, caused the missing and backfiring, Y.

In order to employ this pattern of reasoning, we need at least two circumstances available for our consideration, one in which the effect, Y, occurs and one in which it does not occur. We compare these two situations with possible causes in mind, and, if X is present where Y occurred and absent where Y did not occur, then, according to this causal reasoning pattern, X is the cause of Y.

Cautionary note: Although this pattern of reasoning is quite reliable, it is so only if an important condition is met. We need to be reasonably sure that X is the *only* relevant difference between the situations where Y occurs and those where it does not. So, before accepting such an argument, it is prudent to consider other possible relevant differences between this situation and those in which Y did not occur. For example, are you certain that you didn't fill up with a new brand of gasoline just before you tuned up? Are you sure a sixteen-year-old didn't drive the car between the tune-up and your test drive?

Here is a variation on the same pattern of reasoning: Theresa and Daniel both dined at Le Bistro, and later Daniel became ill. Since the only thing that seemed to distinguish this evening from several in the past (on which Daniel did not become ill) was his having dinner at Le Bistro, Daniel concludes that the cause of his illness was something served at the restaurant. Further, Daniel now recalls that he and Theresa ordered the same items from the menu, except Daniel managed to find room for the special dessert. He concludes, then, that it was the dessert that caused his illness.

Daniel has twice applied the same pattern of reasoning, first to conclude that it was something he ate at the restaurant that caused his illness, and then to conclude that it was the dessert. The dessert caused his illness, he reasoned, because the only thing that distinguished his situation from Theresa's, who did not fall ill, was that he ate the dessert.

Another Goodloe Byron Note

"He did live longer than his brothers and sisters, though. I like to think that the running did him some good."

> —DR. WILLIAM ROBERTS, a cardiac researcher at the National Institutes of Health in Bethesda, Maryland, commenting on the death of Congressman Goodloe Byron (see Chapter 10)

This is an example of type 1 reasoning. In effect, it says, The only relevant thing that distinguished Byron's case, in which (relatively) long life occurred, from the cases of his brothers and father, who did not live so long, was that Byron was a runner. The problem with this argument is that it is very difficult to be sure that running was the only relevant difference between Byron and his brothers and father. (For all we know, he might have lived even longer had he not been a runner.)

Daniel's argument isn't as strong as your argument about your tune-up, because too many things could have distinguished Daniel's "situation" on this particular evening from those in which he didn't become ill; also, too many other things could have distinguished Daniel's case from Theresa's—there were, in other words, too many other possible causes besides the one he has managed to recall.

> *Type 2. <u>X is the common thread</u>: X caused Y because X is the only common factor in more than one occurrence of Y.*

An example: Theresa and Daniel both became ill after dining at Le Bistro. When recalling what they ate there, they remembered that they both had the salad and that it was the only item they both ordered. They concluded that the salad was the cause of their becoming ill.

To make use of this variety of causal reasoning we need more than one occurrence of the effect Y. With possible causes in mind, we inspect the situations where Y occurred and, if X is the only likely cause that is present in each case, then we may conclude that X is the cause of Y.

How strong such reasoning is depends largely on two questions: In this case, how likely is it that the salad (X) was the *only* relevant common factor preceding the pair's illnesses (Y), and how likely is it that the illnesses could have resulted from two independent causes? The salad they both ate may have been the only relevant factor in their *dinner*, but there may have been other relevant common factors aside from any problem with Le Bistro's menu. (Were they both exposed to a virus a week ago? Did they both overeat?) And we may not be able to rule out two quite independent causes for the two cases. (Could Theresa have lately begun taking a new medicine and Daniel have overeaten?)

Mixing the Patterns

Researchers did follow-up studies on twenty individuals who had been identified as carriers of the AIDS virus. After three years, it was discovered that fourteen of the carriers had developed AIDS and six still showed no symptoms of the disease.

New experimental techniques were used to isolate and analyze the virus in all of the patients with symptoms and in one of those with no symptoms. The results of the tests showed that the virus from the asymptomatic carrier was of a new strain with an altered p24 antigen. The researchers concluded that this difference in strain was the cause of the lack of symptoms in this patient.

In an attempt to confirm their hypothesis, the scientists analyzed the virus from the other five asymptomatic carriers. Sure enough, they too were infected with the virus that has an altered p24 antigen. Said one of the scientists, "This establishes with reasonable certainty that the cause of AIDS patients' failure to develop symptoms over time is that they carry a different strain of the virus than the one we're accustomed to finding in victims of the disease."

Notice that, in the first of these hypothetical experiments, when the researchers analyzed virus from seven symptomatic patients and one asymptomatic carrier, they used the "X is the difference" pattern of reasoning. The confirming experiment, when the remaining asymptomatic patients were checked, made use of the "common thread" pattern. These two patterns are often used this way—one is applied to check results first obtained by the other.

The two patterns can also be used simultaneously, as would have been the case had all twenty patients been checked at once, with the same conclusions drawn.

"Finding a common thread" in a variety of occurrences of some mysterious effect is often the key to isolating its cause. But it is good practice when evaluating reasoning of this variety to consider (1) whether there might be factors common to the occurrences of the effect other than the one first noticed, and (2) whether the simultaneous occurrences of the effects may have been coincidental effects of two different causes.

There are times when we might use one or the other of our causal reasoning patterns and, because we fail to take account of some relevant factor, we arrive at a mistaken conclusion. For example, we may notice that effect Y is constantly accompanied by possible cause X and conclude that X causes Y when, in fact, both X and Y are actually caused by some unconsidered factor, Z. When we fail to consider such a possible common cause, we commit the **fallacy of ignoring a common cause.** Say, for example, that (1) a drop in the rate of inflation causes both (2) a rise in the price of stocks and (3) an increase in retail sales. To conclude that (2) caused (3) because both happened in close proximity, without considering that both may have been caused by a third factor, such as (1), is to commit the fallacy of ignoring a common cause.

A reverse of this mistake is sometimes called the **fallacy of assuming a common cause.** It consists of automatically assuming that two conjoined events must have had the same underlying cause. An example would be to assume that an automobile's hard starting and its backfiring must be the result of the same underlying problem. In Chapter 4, we recounted the strange nocturnal events that troubled the sleep of one of the authors. You may recall that, for a while at least, he automatically assumed that all the events had the same cause. Thus, he committed the fallacy of assuming a common cause.

The moral is, don't unthinkingly assume that two conjoined occurrences have a common cause. But don't unthinkingly assume that they do not either.

Even after we have good reason to suspect a causal connection between X and Y, it is still possible to confuse the cause with the effect. Identifying the wrong occurrence as the cause has traditionally been called the **fallacy of reversed causation,** but this fallacy is fairly rare. Of two events, one of which causes the other, the earlier event cannot be the effect. Unfortunately, in some cases it is difficult, if not impossible, to determine which of two causally related occurrences began first. For example, the direction of certain ocean currents is thought to be causally related to the direction of certain winds as well as to the existence of certain atmospheric pressure cells, and in the right circumstances a change in one will produce a change in the others. But which changes are causes and which are effects is sometimes hard to say, and weather scientists do not necessarily agree on the subject. Theoretically, those who turn out to be incorrect could be said to have committed the fallacy of reversed causation,

Fast Food Will Cause What?

From one to six hours after an average fast-food meal of a cheeseburger, french fries, milkshake and dessert, the fat is digested and enters the blood stream in the form of millions of little butter balls. . . . All the cells, including red blood cells, are coated with a thin layer of fat. The fat acts as an adhesive, and the cells stick together, forming clumps and blocking small vessels of the brain. It causes you to lose some memory, concentration and the ability to do your best mental and physical work. It blocks vessels in the heart, causing chest pain called angina. It inhibits the ability of insulin to get sugar from the blood into the cells and can cause diabetes. It causes many kinds of cancers. . . .

—NATHAN PRITIKIN, diet and fitness author,
quoted in *Runner's World*

The problem here is that the results of (unspecified) studies about causal factors in populations (fatty diets as a cause of memory loss, angina, etc.) have been applied to a specific occurrence: eating a cheeseburger, french fries, etc. It's like saying that because smoking is known to cause lung cancer, if you smoke a pack of cigarettes you'll get lung cancer. (This pattern of reasoning can also be analyzed as a fallacy of division. See Chapter 10.)

but in this instance we vote for forgetting the fancy terminology in favor of saying that they turned out to be wrong.

The final fallacy of causal reasoning we'll discuss is not so rare as the preceding one, unfortunately. It is common enough to have earned the Latin name **post hoc, ergo propter hoc** (after this, therefore because of this), or simply "post hoc," for short. This fallacy is committed whenever we conclude that, because one event, X, preceded another, Y, X is the cause of Y. Here's an example:

> The rate of inflation dropped dramatically after Ronald Reagan's Economic Recovery Act went into effect. Therefore Reagan and the Recovery Act can be credited with bringing about this fortunate result.

Causal reasoning of the "post hoc" variety is completely unsound, and may be rejected more or less automatically. If you think back to the example we invented about your car's misfiring after a tune-up, it may seem to be a case of post hoc reasoning. Notice, however, that your reason was not simply that the misfiring began after the tune-up; you had reason to believe that the tune-up was the *only* thing that changed before the car began giving problems. Similarly, the following argument is not a case of post hoc: "The rate of inflation was high until Reagan's Economic Recovery Act was implemented; therefore, *since that act was the only relevant change made in the economic situation before the lowering of inflation,* it is what brought about that change." Adding the proviso that the Recovery Act was the only relevant economic change made prior to the decrease in the rate of inflation makes the difference. Such an addition converts a post hoc argument into an argument of type 1. The hard work, of course, lies in establishing the proviso.

Remember, post hoc reasoning alone is always unsound. If the argument can be made sound, it will have to be converted into another pattern.

The Case of Jim Fixx

On Friday, July 20, 1984, Jim Fixx, author of several best-selling books on the health benefits of running, died of a cardiac arrhythmia due to coronary artery disease. Throughout the country, post hoc reasoning occurred in the media and in conversation. Fixx died while running; *ergo* the running caused his death. Even more widely committed (though we are speculating) was the fallacy of anecdotal evidence (Chapter 10). Although there is a fairly impressive body of epidemiological evidence that exercise prolongs life by lowering the risk of heart disease, many runners and nonrunners (again, we speculate) were more influenced by the death of one man than by this accumulated body of evidence. A single headline-grabbing case, especially one with such ironical overtones, can often overcome a ton of methodically gathered evidence. (For all we know, Fixx might have died years earlier had he not been a runner.)

Another Post Hoc About Fitness

Australian Rolet de Castello had a heart attack at age fifty-two while he was out running (yes, another such case). During recuperation, he suffered another heart attack that disabled him for a year with angina. He then went on the Pritikin diet of 10 percent fat and less than 100 milligrams of cholesterol each day, and his angina lessened. Within two years after the first attack he ran his first marathon, and within eight years he had run twenty of them. Remarked Nathan Pritikin, whom we've mentioned before, "[de Castello's] case proves that running does not prevent heart disease, but proper diet, even after a heart attack, can return you to an active vigorous life" (quoted in *Runner's World*).

Or maybe he returned to a vigorous life in *spite* of the diet. De Castello's case proves only that after a heart attack one might be able to run marathons.

Summary

We've discussed two common patterns of reasoning that some specific occurrence causes some other specific occurrence, and we've considered questions that you should ask whenever you encounter them. Take this opportunity to make sure you understand both patterns and the related questions, and if you don't, go back and review the appropriate pages. Here is a brief summary of the relevant material.

1. *X is the difference.* (X caused Y because X is the only relevant difference between this situation, where Y occurred, and situations where Y did not occur.)

Common Thread

Post Hoc

Question: Is the suspected cause the only relevant factor that distinguishes the situation in which Y is present from situations in which it is not? (Only if it *is* is the reliability of the argument beyond all question.)

2. *X is the common thread.* (X caused Y because X is the only relevant common factor in more than one occurrence of Y.)

   Questions: Is X the only relevant common factor preceding the occurrences of Y? (Only if it *is* can the argument be considered reliable.) Did the occurrences of Y result from independent causes? (The argument is reliable only if this possibility has been eliminated.)

EXERCISE 11-1

The three times Grimsley has eaten at the Zig Zag Pizza house he has fallen ill. The first time he ate a large pizza and a side order of hot peppers; the second time he had the all-you-can-eat ravioli special and the hot peppers; and the third time he had the giant meatball sandwich and the hot peppers. Concluding that the hot peppers were the offending item, Grimsley determines never to order them again. Answer these questions:

★1. What causal claim is at issue in this passage?

★2. Describe the reasoning employed in terms of the patterns discussed in the text.

★3. What question or questions should be asked relative to this pattern of reasoning?

★4. Invent at least one plausible alternative explanation of the effect. (If you think no other explanation is plausible, explain why.) Let the questions you listed in response to item (3) guide you.

★5. If any of the fallacies we have discussed appear, name them.

★6. Does the argument seem to you to be a good one? Explain.

EXERCISE 11-2

Evaluate the following arguments by answering these questions:

(a) What causal claim is at issue in this passage?
(b) Describe the reasoning employed in terms of the patterns discussed in the text.
(c) What question or questions should be asked?
(d) Invent at least one plausible alternative explanation of the effect. (If you think no other explanation is plausible, explain why.) Let the questions you listed in response to item *c* guide you.
(e) If any of the fallacies we have discussed appear, name them.
(f) Does the argument seem to you to be a good one? Explain.

★1. Each Monday and Friday Hubert jogs up Skyline Road to the top of Thompson Peak. This Friday he doesn't have the stamina to go more than halfway up and can't figure out why. Finally he remembers that he went to sleep earlier than usual the previous night. "Aha," he thinks. "That's the problem. Too much sleep."

2. Mr. Mahlman has observed earthworms appearing on his lawn from time to time. Puzzled, he thinks about possible causes. "One day they're there," he says to his wife, "and the next day they're not. Sometimes they come out early, sometimes late, sometimes right in the middle of the day. I wonder what brings them out?" Mrs. Mahlman is not puzzled. "I've seen them, too," she says. "And if you were paying attention you'd notice that every time you see them it's just after you've been watering, or after a heavy rain. It's the water that brings them out."

3. Darn! I get in the left lane and the right lane goes faster. I get in the right lane and the left lane goes faster. The Great Traffic Controller in the Sky is out to get me!

★4. The only time in my entire life that I've had a backache was right after I tried lifting weights. I'll never do that again!

5. Since the cat won't eat, Mrs. Quinstartle searches her mind for a reason why. "Now, could it be that I haven't heard mice scratching around in the attic lately?" she thinks. "Yes, that's it!" she concludes.

6. Ten abnormally wet winters on the Pacific Coast have been preceded by El Niños, a periodic heating of the equatorial Pacific Ocean. El Niños, therefore, caused the wet winters.

7. Each time one of the burglaries occurred, observers have noticed a red Studebaker in the vicinity. The police, of course, want to find the driver

of the car, believing that he or she may have something to do with the crimes.

⋆8. Harold has spent his last three spring vacations in Florida, and each time he has come down with a cold a few days after arriving. Figuring that being cooped up in a car with his friends on the long nonstop drive down from Boston is exposing him to too many germs, Harold decides to stay home this spring. Since he doesn't get a cold, he concludes that his hypothesis was correct.

9. The clickety-click sound in Egmont's bike has to be due to something that revolves, and that leaves only the wheels and the pedals. Since the sound stops whenever Egmont coasts, the cause must be in the pedal mechanism.

10. Judith's contact lenses have been bothering her for the last three days. Since she has just started using some new brands of rinsing and disinfecting solution, she suspects that one of them is the cause of her problems. Thinking back, she remembers that the day after she let the lens soak in the new disinfecting solution an extra long time she was especially bothered by the lenses. So she concludes that it is the disinfecting solution that caused her problem.

EXERCISE 11-3

Evaluate the following arguments, identifying any reliable patterns they fit and any fallacies they contain.

1. Malvina's pulse rate has always been around 148 after her aerobics class. For the past two weeks, however, it has dropped to around 138, and she cannot figure out why until she remembers that about two weeks ago she stopped drinking coffee. "There's the reason," she decides.

2. Hong is puzzled by the smell of burning electrical wiring in the cab of his pickup. Figuring that the problem has to be in the windshield wiper motor, radio, air conditioner, heater, or lights, he remembers that the problem seems unrelated to the weather or time of day or night. He then concludes that the radio is the source of the problem, because it is the only thing that could be running at any time of the day or night, in any weather, any season.

⋆3. Violette is a strong Cowboys fan. Because of her work schedule, however, she has been able to watch their games only once this season, and that was the only time they lost. She resolved not to watch any more Dallas games even if she has the chance. "It's bad luck," she thinks.

⋆4. The Mount St. Helens eruptions have all been preceded by earthquakes. Evidently, therefore, the earthquakes caused the eruptions.

5. From a letter to the editor: "After the Supreme Court abolished prayers in public schools, our metropolitan public school systems became homes for hardened criminals, drug addicts, and sex offenders, places where decent students fear constantly for their lives. What has happened to today's youth? Ask the Supreme Court. They know—they did it."

★6. When Walton plays, the Clippers win 80 percent of the time. When he doesn't, they have the worst record in the league. Whatever limited success they've had this season, therefore, is due to him.

★7. On Monday, Mr. O'Toole came down with a cold. That afternoon Mrs. O'Toole caught it. Later that evening their daughter caught it, too.

8. Elroy had chest pains for about two months. Recently, though, when he had a cold, the pains stopped. However, soon after the cold was over, the pains returned. "Odd," he thought. "There seem to be just two possible explanations. Maybe *not* having a cold causes my chest pain. But that's absurd. So the pains must be due to something that I didn't have or wasn't doing when I had the cold." Thinking further, Elroy recalls that when he had a cold he temporarily stopped drinking coffee and refrained from working out every day with the over-forty basketball league. He then reasons that either the coffee or the basketball is the cause of his pains.

9. When he was twelve years old Sean Marsee, of Ada, Oklahoma, began dipping snuff, and by the time he entered high school he had developed an addiction that led him to consume up to ten cans of snuff each week. In 1983, in his senior year, Marsee developed a painful sore on his tongue that refused to heal and that turned out to be malignant. Neither extensive surgery nor radiation contained the cancer, and in February 1984, he died. Many believed the snuff caused his death.

10. "Terrorists are attacking NATO and U.S. military installations in Europe almost daily. The attacks are being made by disparate groups with various causes. Yet the groups seem well-coordinated, well-financed and well-equipped with sophisticated bombs.

   "The Kremlin wanted to keep its missiles in place but deny NATO the ability to respond in kind. . . . Having lost that struggle, the Soviets may be attempting to achieve the same ends by terrorist tactics. Without question, something or someone is guiding the terrorist tactics. When different groups in five nations begin attacking the same targets with a plentiful supply of explosives, that is more than a coincidence. When the attacks all serve the purposes of the Soviet Union, that is no coincidence either."

   —*Houston Chronicle*

Causation in Populations

Many causal claims do not apply in any straightforward way to individuals but rather apply to populations.* The claim, "drinking causes cancer of the mouth,"

*For our analysis of causal factors in populations we are indebted to Ronald N. Giere, *Understanding Scientific Reasoning*, pp. 175–181; 247–281.

for example, should not be interpreted as meaning that drinking will cause mouth cancer for any given individual, or even that drinking will cause mouth cancer for the majority of individuals. The claim is that drinking is a causal factor for mouth cancer. It is best understood as meaning that there would be more cases of mouth cancer if everyone drank than if no one did. And so it is with other claims about causation in populations. To say that X causes Y in population P is to say that there would be more cases of Y in population P if every member of P were exposed to X than if no member of P were exposed to X.

The evidence on which such claims may be soundly based comes principally from three kinds of studies, or "arguments."

Controlled Cause-to-Effect Experiments

In **controlled cause-to-effect experiments** a random sample of a target population is itself randomly divided into two groups: an experimental group, all of whose members are exposed to a suspected causal factor, C (e.g., exposure of the skin to nicotine), and a control group, whose members are all treated exactly as the members of the experimental group are except that they are not exposed to C. Both groups are then compared with respect to frequency of some effect, E (e.g., skin cancer). If the difference, d, in the frequency of E in the two groups is sufficiently large, then C may justifiably be said to cause E in the population.

This probably sounds complicated, but the principles involved are matters of common sense. You have two groups that are essentially alike except that the members of one group are exposed to the suspected causal agent. If the effect is then found to be sufficiently more frequent in that group, you conclude that the suspected causal agent does indeed cause the effect in question.

Familiarizing yourself with these concepts and abbreviations will help you understand cause-to-effect experiments:

Experimental Group—the sample of the target population whose members are all exposed to the suspected causal agent

Control group—the sample of the target population whose members are treated exactly as the members of the experimental group are except that they are not exposed to the suspected causal agent

C—the suspected causal agent

E—the effect whose cause is being investigated

d—the difference in the frequency of this effect in the experimental group and in the control group

Let us suppose that the frequency of the effect in the experimental group is found to be greater than in the control group. *How much greater* must the frequency of the effect in the experimental group be before we can say that the suspected causal agent actually is a causal factor? That is, how great must d be for us to believe that C is really a causal factor for E? After all, even if nicotine does *not* cause skin cancer, the frequency of skin cancer found in the experimental group *might* exceed the frequency found in the control group because of some chance occurrence.

Well, suppose that there are one hundred individuals in our experimental group and the same number in our control group, and suppose that d was greater than thirteen percentage points—that is, suppose the frequency of skin cancer in the experimental group exceeded the frequency in the control group by more than thirteen percentage points. Could that result be due merely to chance? Yes, but there is a 95 percent probability that it was *not* due to chance. If the frequency of skin cancer in the experimental group were to exceed the frequency in the control group by more than thirteen percentage points (given one hundred members in each group), then this finding would be *statistically significant at the 0.05 level,* which simply means that we could say with a 95 percent degree of confidence that nicotine is a cause of skin cancer. If we were content to speak with lesser confidence, or if our samples were larger, then the difference in the frequency of skin cancer between the experimental group and control group would not have to be as great to qualify as statistically significant.

Thus, saying that the difference in frequency of the effect between the experimental and control groups is *statistically significant* at some level (e.g., 0.05) simply means that it would be unreasonable to attribute this difference in frequency to chance. Just how unreasonable it would be depends on what level is cited. As noted in Chapter 10, if no level is cited, as in reports of controlled experiments that stipulate only that the findings are "significant," it is customary to assume that the results were significant at the 0.05 level, which simply means that the result could have arisen by chance in about five cases out of one hundred.

Media reports of controlled experiments usually state or clearly imply whether the difference in frequency of the effect found in the experimental and control groups is significant. However, if, as occasionally happens, there is a question as to whether the results are statistically significant (i.e., are unlikely to have arisen by chance), it is important not to assume uncritically or automatically:

1. That the sample is large enough to guarantee significance. A large sample is no guarantee that the difference (d) in the frequency of the effect as found in the experimental group and as found in the control group is statistically significant. (However, the larger the sample the smaller d need be—expressed as a difference in percentage points—to count as significant.) People are sometimes overly impressed by the mere size of a study.
2. That the difference in frequency is great enough to guarantee significance. The fact that there seems to be a pronounced difference in the frequency

of the effect as found in the experimental group and as found in the control group is no guarantee that the difference is statistically significant. If the sample size is small enough, it may not be. If there are fifty rats in an experimental group and fifty more in a control group, then even if the frequency of skin cancer found in the experimental group exceeds the frequency of skin cancer found in the control group by as much as eighteen percentage points, this finding would not be statistically significant (at the 0.05 level). Even if each group contained a thousand rats, the difference of frequency of three points would not qualify as significant. (And remember that a three-point difference can be referred to as a "whopping" 50 percent difference if it is the difference between six points and three points.) Unless you have some knowledge of statistics, it is probably best not to assume that findings are statistically significant unless it is clearly stated or implied that they are.

Nevertheless, it may be helpful to you to have some rough idea of when a difference in frequency of effect as found in the experimental and control groups may be said to be statistically significant at the 0.05 level. Table 11-1 provides some examples.

In other words, if there are ten individuals each in the randomly selected experimental and control groups, then, to be statistically significant at the 0.05 level, the difference between experimental and control group in frequency of the effect must exceed forty percentage points. If there are twenty-five people in each group, then d must exceed twenty-seven points to be statistically significant, and so forth.

Even if it is clear, in a controlled experiment, that d is significant, there are a few more considerations to keep in mind when reviewing reports of experimental findings. First, the results of controlled experiments are often extended analogically from the target population (e.g., rats) to another popu-

Table 11-1 *Approximate Statistically Significant d's at 0.05 Level*

Size of Random Sample	Approximate Figure that d Must Exceed to Be Statistically Significant (in Percentage Points)
10	40
25	27
50	19
100	13
250	8
500	6
1,000	4
1,500	3

lation (e.g., humans). Such analogical extensions should be evaluated in accordance with the criteria for analogical arguments discussed in the previous chapter. In particular, before accepting such extensions of the findings, you should consider carefully whether there are important relevant differences between the target population in the experiment and the population to which the results of the experiment are analogically extended.

Second, it is important in controlled experiments that the sample from which the experimental and control groups are formed be representative of the

Experimental Studies with Animals

Experimental results obtained on laboratory animals are often extended analogically to humans. Indeed, the ultimate reason for doing most tests on animals is to learn something that will benefit humans. However, such analogical extensions of the results of animal experiments are sometimes derided because of presumed differences between rats, say, or guinea pigs, and humans. But laboratory animals and humans are very similar with respect to fundamental biological processes—with some animals more suitable to study for some processes, other animals for other processes—and it is therefore most unwise routinely to discount the results of animal studies as automatically inapplicable to humans.

Animal experiments are also sometimes dismissed because the animals are often exposed to doses of agents that far exceed any to which humans are likely to be exposed. Thus, for instance, a famous Canadian study that proved that saccharine can cause cancer in laboratory rats was widely ridiculed because the animals were given a diet consisting of 7 percent saccharine, and for a human's diet to consist of 7 percent saccharine that person would have to drink perhaps hundreds of bottles of diet cola every day.

Still, it is not the amount of a substance that makes it carcinogenic. If a substance is not carcinogenic, then it will not cause cancer regardless of how much of it is consumed. The fact that heavy doses of a substance cause cancer in a population of two hundred rats is good evidence that *any amount* of the substance causes cancer in rats (remember the definition of causation in populations!). As far as we currently know, carcinogenic agents do not suddenly begin to cause cancer only at some threshold level. Reducing the amount of a carcinogenic substance to which an experimental group is exposed would, as far as we can now tell, merely reduce the frequency of cancer in that group. This means only that if a very small dosage of that substance were used in an experiment, a very large sample of animals would have to be used for the results to show up as significant. It is simply much easier and more economical to increase the size of the dosage than to increase the size of the sample. (Note that if a very small amount of a substance—equivalent, say, to the saccharine in a single bottle of diet cola—resulted in only *one* extra case of cancer in every ten thousand rats, that amount would also result in *twenty thousand* cases of cancer in a population of rats equal to the human population of the United States.)

The Cambridge Institute for Psychological Studies

As we've indicated, when we are evaluating causal arguments in populations, there are matters on which we must rely on the credibility of our sources (e.g., in randomness of selection, significance of findings). Research conducted by reputable scientists and published in authoritative journals is generally reliable with respect to statistical details. But watch out for research conducted by self-styled "experts." Any outfit can call itself the "Cambridge Institute for Psychological Studies," and "publish" its reports in its own "journal." The name of this particular fictitious institute may sound impressive, of course, because of the associations one makes with Cambridge. So be watchful. Organizations with prestigious-sounding place names (Princeton, Berkeley, Palo Alto, Bethesda, etc.), proper names (Fulbright, Columbia, etc.), or concepts (institute, academy, research, advanced studies) *could* consist of little more than a couple of university dropouts with a dubious theory and an axe to grind.

target population, and thus it is essential that the sample be taken at random. Further, since the experimental and control groups should be as similar as possible, it is important that the assignment of subjects to these groups also be a random process. In reputable scientific experiments it is safe to assume that randomization has been so employed, but one must be suspicious of informal "experiments" in which no mention of randomization is made.

Nonexperimental Cause-to-Effect Studies

A **nonexperimental cause-to-effect study** (or "argument") is another type of study designed to test whether something is a causal factor for a given effect. In this type of study, members of a target population (say, humans) who have not yet shown evidence of the suspected effect E (e.g., cancer of the colon) are divided into two groups that are alike in all respects except one. The difference is that members of one group, the experimental group, have all been exposed to the suspected cause C (fatty diets, for example), whereas the members of the other group, the control group, have not. Such studies differ from controlled experiments in that the members of the experimental group are not exposed to the suspected causal agent *by the investigators*. Eventually, however, just as in the controlled experiment, experimental and control groups are both compared with respect to the frequency of E. If the frequency in the experimental group exceeds the frequency in the control group by a statistically significant margin, we may conclude that C is the cause of E in the target population.

In reports of nonexperimental cause-to-effect studies, as in reports of controlled experiments, if it is not stated or clearly implied that the findings are significant, do not assume that they are merely because either (1) the samples are large, or (2) the difference in the frequency of the effect in absolute terms or percentages is striking.

Likewise, (3) if a causal relationship found to hold in the target population on the basis of such a study is extended analogically to other populations, you should evaluate this analogical extension very carefully, especially with respect to any relevant differences between the target population and the analogical population.

And, finally, (4) note the following important difference between controlled experiments and nonexperimental cause-to-effect studies: In a *controlled* experiment, the subjects are assigned to experimental and control groups by a random process, after which the experimental subjects are exposed to C. This randomization ensures that experimental and control groups will be alike save for the suspected causal agent that the experimental group is then exposed to. But in the nonexperimental study the experimental group (which is still so-called even though no experiment is performed) is composed of randomly selected individuals who have already been exposed to the suspected causal agent, or who say they were. And the individuals who have already been exposed to C (or who say they were) may differ from the rest of the target population in some respect in addition to having been exposed to C. For example, there is a positive correlation between having a fatty diet and drinking alcoholic beverages. Thus, an experimental group composed by random means from those in the general population who have fatty diets would include more than its fair share of drinkers. Consequently, the high rate of colon cancer observed in this experimental group might be due in part to the effects of drinking.

It is important, then, that the process by which the individuals in the general population "self-select" themselves (as to whether they have or have not been exposed to C) not be biased in any way related to the effect. In good studies any factors that might bias the experimental group are controlled by one means or another. Often, for example, the control group is not randomly selected, but rather is selected to match the experimental group for any other relevant factors. Thus, in a study that seeks to relate fatty diets to cancer of the colon, since drinking may be relevant to getting cancer of the colon, an experimenter will make certain that the same percentage of drinkers is found in the control group as in the experimental group.

Nonexperimental studies of the variety explained here and in the next section are *inherently* weaker than controlled experiments as arguments for causal claims. Since we do not have complete knowledge of what factors are causally related to what other factors, it is impossible to say for certain that all the possibly relevant variables in such studies have been controlled. It is good policy, when considering such studies, to try to imagine characteristics that those who have been exposed to the suspected causal agent might have, and contemplate whether any of these factors may be related to the effect. If you can think of any relevant variables that have not been controlled, you should have doubts about any causal claim that is made on the basis of such studies.

Responsible Studies Can Lead to Different Conclusions

Is caffeine good or bad for you? Reputable studies have associated it with heart disease, cancer, breast disease, and high blood pressure. Other reputable studies have indicated that it can lower blood pressure, does not cause heart or breast disease, and keeps cancer from spreading. Whom are we to believe? The jury is still out on the issue, and neither of the two conflicting sets of findings should be accepted until there is a reason (beyond wishful thinking) to accept one set over the other. In other words, one treats such apparently conflicting studies as one would treat other conflicting claims by experts—refer to Chapter 3 on assessing credibility.

Nonexperimental Effect-to-Cause Studies

A **nonexperimental effect-to-cause study** is a third type of study designed to test whether something is a causal factor for a given effect. In this type of study, the "experimental group," whose members already display the *effect* being investigated, E (e.g., cancer of the mouth), is compared with a control group none of whose members have E, and the frequency of the suspected cause, C (e.g., using chewing tobacco), is measured. If the frequency of C in the experimental group significantly exceeds its frequency in the control group, then C may be said to cause E in the target population.

Cautionary remarks (1) through (3) from the discussion of nonexperimental cause-to-effect studies apply equally to nonexperimental effect-to-cause studies. That is, if it isn't clear that the findings are significant, don't assume that they are merely because (1) the samples seem large or (2) the difference in the cause expressed in absolute terms seems striking; and (3) evaluate carefully analogical extensions of the results to other populations.

Notice further that (4) the subjects in the experimental group may differ in some important way (in addition to showing the effect) from the rest of the target population. Thus, for instance, former smokers are more likely than others to use chewing tobacco, and they are also more likely than others to get mouth cancer. If you sample randomly from a group of victims of mouth cancer, therefore, you are likely to produce more ex-smokers in your sample than occur in the general population. The result is that you are likely to discover more chewing-tobacco users in the sample, even if chewing tobacco plays no role whatsoever in causing cancer of the mouth. Any factor that might bias the experimental group in such studies should be controlled. If, in evaluating such a study, you can think of any factor that has not been controlled, you can regard the study as having failed to demonstrate causation.

Notice, finally, that (5) effect-to-cause studies show only the probable frequency of the cause, not the effect, and thus provide no grounds for esti-

Effect-to-Cause Studies and "X Is the Difference"

As discussed in the text, we often reason that one specific event, X, caused another, Y, because the only relevant factor that distinguishes cases in which Y occurred from cases in which it did not is the presence of X ("X is the difference"). You may have observed that the reasoning employed in nonexperimental effect-to-cause studies is similar. We reason that C is a causal factor for E because the only relevant factor that distinguishes a group in which E is present from one in which it is not is that in the former there is also an unexpectedly high incidence of the suspected causal factor, C.

Though the two patterns of reasoning are similar, they are probably best viewed as not identical. This position, however, is controversial.

mating the percentage of the target population that would be affected if everyone in it were exposed to the cause.

Recap

Many of the arguments used to support cause-and-effect claims fall into one of two categories: (1) those used to support claims about causation between specific events, and (2) those used to support claims about causal factors in populations.

1. Kinds of arguments for claims about causation between specific events:
   (a) "X is the difference"
   (b) "X is the common thread"
These patterns of reasoning and the questions we should consider when we encounter them were summarized in the text.
2. Kinds of arguments for claims about causal factors in populations:
   (a) Controlled cause-to-effect experiments
   (b) Nonexperimental cause-to-effect studies
   (c) Nonexperimental effect-to-cause studies

The basic idea in controlled cause-to-effect experiments is to subject an "experimental" sample of the target population to a suspected causal factor and then to determine whether the incidence of the effect is significantly more frequent in this experimental group than in a control group. If it is, then the suspicion about the causal factor has been confirmed (for that population).

In the nonexperimental cause-to-effect study, the members of the experimental group are not exposed to the suspected causal agent by the investigators; instead, exposure has resulted from the actions or circumstances of the individuals themselves. If the effect is then found to be significantly more frequent in this "self-selected" experimental group than in a control group, then the suspicion about the causal factor has been confirmed (for the population).

In the third type of study, an "experimental" group whose members display the *effect* is compared with a control group whose members do not display the effect. If the suspected cause is significantly more frequent in the experimental group, then the suspicion about the causal factor has been confirmed (for the population).

Findings that are not statistically significant do get reported, and those who have no training in statistics are sometimes tempted to conclude that, if the frequency of the effect as found in the experimental group exceeds that in the control group *by any amount,* then a causal relationship has been established. You know now that within certain limits chance can account for a difference in frequency. If you have no knowledge of statistics, you should not attempt to evaluate these studies on the basis of your subjective feelings about the size of the differences in frequency or the size of the samples. (Remember too, from Chapter 10, that differences in frequencies when reported as percentages rather than as percentage points can appear quite impressive.) In such matters as whether findings are statistically significant, if we have no knowledge of statistics, and sometimes even if we do, we must take the word of the investigator or the person who is reporting the investigation, and this involves estimating the credibility of these sources.

We also have to take the reporter's or investigator's word for it that randomization has occurred where necessary in controlled cause-to-effect experiments, and that attempts have been made to control for sources of bias in cause-to-effect and effect-to-cause studies. So here again we must be prepared to evaluate the credibility of our sources, using those principles discussed in Chapter 3. Of course, if we can think of any factors that are possibly related to the effect that we learn have not been controlled, we are entitled to be suspicious of the study.

It is important as well to consider carefully any claims made about the applicability of the findings to populations other than those involved in the investigation. Here we must rely on those principles discussed in Chapter 10 for appraising analogical arguments.

One final note. In this chapter we have been concerned with some of the patterns of reasoning by means of which people support causal claims. We again call your attention to the distinction between the claims themselves and the patterns of reasoning that are used to support them, and remind you to evaluate such claims, whether or not they have been supported on the basis of the reasoning treated in this chapter, by using the guidelines discussed in Chapter 4.

Additional Exercises

EXERCISE 11-4

Identify each of the following as (a) a claim about causation between specific occurrences, (b) a claim about causal factors in populations, or (c) neither of these.

★ 1. The hibiscus died while we were away. There must have been a frost.
  2. Carlos isn't as fast as he used to be; that's what old age will do.
  3. Kent's college education helped him get a high-paying job.
★ 4. The most frequently stolen utility vehicle is a 1988 Jeep Wrangler.
  5. Vitamin C prevents colds.
  6. The man who put this town on the map was Dr. Jaime Diaz.
★ 7. The high reading on the thermometer resulted from two causes: This thermometer was located lower to the ground than at other stations, and its shelter was too small, so the ventilation was inadequate.
  8. Oily smoke in the exhaust is often caused by worn rings.
  9. The initial tests indicate that caffeine has toxic effects in humans.
★ 10. Neonatal sepsis is usually fatal among newborns.
  11. WIN 51,711 halted development of paralysis in mice that had recently been infected with polio-2.
  12. A stuck hatch cover on *Spacelab* blocked a French ultraviolet camera from conducting a sky survey of celestial objects.
  13. An experimental drug has shown broad antiviral effects on a large number of the picornaviruses against which it has been tested.
★ 14. Investigation revealed the problem was a short-circuited power supply.
  15. Arteriovenous malformations—distortions of the capillaries connecting an arteriole and a small vein in the brain—can bleed, causing severe headaches, seizures, and even death.
  16. America has never been invaded because of all the guns that citizens own.
★ 17. According to two reports in the *New England Journal of Medicine*, oil from fish can prevent heart disease.
  18. The most important cause in the growing problem of illiteracy is television.
  19. "Raymond the Wolf passed away in his sleep one night from natural causes; his heart stopped beating when the three men who slipped into his bedroom stuck knives in it."
                                    —Jimmy Breslin, *The Gang That Couldn't Shoot Straight*
★ 20. The dramatic increases in atmospheric CO_2, produced by the burning

of fossil fuels, are warming the planet and will eventually alter the climate.

EXERCISE 11-5

Read this passage, which was adapted from the source indicated, and then answer the questions that follow.

> A report in the *New England Journal of Medicine* states that an experimental vaccine against chicken pox has been found effective in tests on nearly 1,000 children.
>
> The new vaccine uses a live but weakened form of the virus developed in Japan. Dr. Robert E. Weibel, of the Children's Hospital of Philadelphia, and others gave it to 468 healthy children, while a control group of 446 received a placebo. During a nine-month follow-up period, not a single case of chicken pox occurred in the vaccinated group, while 39 of the control group contracted the disease.
>
> —CHRISTINE RUSSELL, *Washington Post*, reprinted in the *Reader's Digest*

★1. What is the causal claim at issue?
★2. What is the target population?
★3. What type of investigation is it?
★4. Summarize the differences between the experimental and control groups, including size.
★5. What is the frequency of the effect in the experimental and control groups? (In nonexperimental effect-to-cause studies, what is the frequency of the cause in the experimental and control groups?)
★6. Does the report state or imply, or is there otherwise reason to believe, that the findings are (or are not) statistically significant?
★7. Are there any other important aspects of the study that are unreported, or is there any other notable weakness in the investigation?
★8. What causal claim, if any, does the report seem to support?

EXERCISE 11-6

Evaluate the following passages by answering each of the questions.
(a) What is the causal claim at issue?
(b) What is the target population?
(c) What type of investigation is it?
(d) Summarize the differences between the experimental and control groups, including size.
(e) What is the frequency of the effect in the experimental and control groups? (In nonexperimental effect-to-cause studies, what is the frequency of the cause in the experimental and control groups?)
(f) Does the report state or imply, or is there otherwise reason to believe, that the findings are (or are not) statistically significant?

(g) Are there any other important aspects of the study that are unreported, or is there any other notable weakness in the investigation?

(h) What causal claim, if any, does the report seem to support?

★1. Does jogging keep you healthy? Two independent researchers, interested in whether exercise prevents colds, interviewed twenty volunteers about the frequency with which they caught colds. The volunteers, none of whom exercised regularly, were then divided into two groups of ten, and one group participated in a six-month regimen of jogging three miles every other day. At the end of the six months the frequency of colds among the joggers was compared both with that of the nonjoggers (group A) and with that of the joggers prior to the experiment (group B). It was found that, as compared with the nonjoggers, the joggers had 25 percent fewer colds. The record of colds among the joggers also declined in comparison with their own record prior to the exercise program.

2. A major new study has found that taking an aspirin every other day cuts the risk of having a first heart attack nearly in half. The study, sponsored by the National Heart, Lung and Blood Institute, indicated that aspirin was so effective in reducing the risk of a heart attack that it was prematurely terminated so that all 22,071 participants, half of whom did not take aspirin, could benefit from the newly gained knowledge. The data will be published this Thursday in the *New England Journal of Medicine*. The editor of the journal called the study "a milestone in the continuing struggle" against heart attack.

In the fifty-seven-month study, whose participants were all male physicians, 104 of those who took aspirin had heart attacks, as compared with 189 heart attacks in those who took only a sugar pill. This means ordinary aspirin reduced the heart attack risk for healthy men by 47 percent. At least seven long-term studies of more than 11,000 heart attack victims have shown that one-half or one aspirin per day can reduce the risk of a second attack by up to 20 percent.

—Adapted from the *Los Angeles Times*

3. Although cigarette ads sometimes suggest that smoking is "macho," new studies indicate that smoking can increase the risk of impotence. In a study of 116 men with impotence caused by vascular problems, done at the University of Pretoria, South Africa, 108 were smokers. Two independent studies, one done by the Centre d'Etudes et de Recherches di l'Impuissance in Paris, and reported in the British medical journal *Lancet*, and the other done by Queen's University and Kingston General Hospital in Ontario, found that almost two-thirds of impotent men smoked.

To test whether smoking has an immediate effect on sexual response, a group of researchers from Southern Illinois and Florida State universities fitted 42 male smokers with a device that measures the speed of arousal. The men were divided into three groups, one group given high-nicotine cigarettes, one group cigarettes low in nicotine, and one group mints. After smoking one cigarette or eating a mint, each man was placed in a private room and shown a two-minute erotic film while his sexual response was monitored. Then he waited ten minutes, smoked two more cigarettes or ate another mint, and watched a different erotic film, again being monitored.

The results: Men who smoked high-nicotine cigarettes had slower arousal than those who smoked low-nicotine cigarettes or ate mints.

—Adapted from *Reader's Digest*

4. Scientists at the Lawrence Livermore National Laboratory in California report that they have isolated and cloned two human genes that control and repair defective and damaged cells. A biophysicist and a biologist at the laboratory inserted the cloned normal genes from human DNA into the genetically defective cells of Chinese hamsters. The human repair genes took over the cellular machinery of the hamsters and corrected their defects, the scientists said. Approximately two-thirds of the cells that received the cloned genes returned to normal, while only about one-tenth of 1 percent of similar, untreated cells achieved a normal condition. It is hoped that the research will eventually produce an effective treatment for radiation-damaged tissue in humans, according to a spokesman for the laboratory.

—The figures are hypothetical, invented to illustrate current studies at Lawrence Livermore Laboratories, as reported by David Perlman in the *San Francisco Chronicle*

★5. The Food and Drug Administration recently gave final approval to the use of alpha-interferon, a hormone produced by the human body, for treating genital warts, a contagious viral disease that is spread sexually and affects about 8 million people a year. The FDA said alpha-interferon, injected into the warts, cleared or substantially reduced the lesions in 66 percent of the 192 patients who participated in three studies of the drug. Eighteen percent of patients had a 50 percent to 74 percent reduction in their warts.

—From a report by United Press International

6. Anesthesiologists at Harvard Medical School have challenged the long-standing belief among physicians that newborn infants cannot feel pain. One study cited by the Harvard group showed that almost all circumcised infants exhibit changes in their behavior for more than 22 hours after circumcision.

Another study compared infants given an anesthetic before circumcision with those who were not. The researchers found that for at least two days after the operation, babies who got the anesthetic were more attentive and less irritable, had better motor responses, and had a greater ability to quiet themselves when disturbed.

The doctors concluded that, without anesthesia, such painful procedures may have "prolonged effects on the babies' neurological and social development."

—"Dr. Dean Edell's Medical Journal," reporting on an article in the *New England Journal of Medicine*

7. "A study published in the July 27 *Journal of the American Medical Association* indicates that taking androgen (a male sex hormone) in high doses for four weeks can have important effects on the high density lipoproteins (HDLs) in the blood, which are believed to protect against the clogging of vessels that supply the heart. Ben F. Hurley, an exercise physiologist from University of Maryland in College Park who conducted the study at Washington University, monitored the levels of HDL in the blood of sixteen healthy, well-conditioned men in their early thirties who were taking androgens as part of their training program with heavy weights. Prior to use of the hormone, all had normal levels of HDLs. After four weeks of self-prescribed and self-administered use of these steroids the levels dropped by about 60 percent.

"Hurley is cautious in interpreting the data. 'You can't say that low HDL levels mean that a specified person is going to have a heart attack at an earlier age. All you can say is that it increases their risk for heart disease.' "

—D. FRANKLIN, *Science News*

★8. "New studies reported in the *Journal of the American Medical Association* indicate that vasectomy is safe. A group headed by Frank Massey of UCLA paired 10,500 vasectomized men with a like number of men who had not had the operation. The average follow-up time was 7.9 years, and 2,300 pairs were followed for more than a decade. The researchers reported that, aside from inflammation in the testes, the incidence of diseases for vasectomized men was similar to that in their paired controls.

"A second study done under federal sponsorship at the Battelle Human Affairs Research Centers in Seattle compared heart disease in 1,400 vasectomized men and 3,600 men who had not had the operation. Over an average follow-up time of fifteen years, the incidence of heart diseases was the same among men in both groups."

—EDWARD EDELSON, *New York Daily News*; reprinted in the *Reader's Digest*

★9. "Canadian researchers led by D. G. Perrin of the department of pathology at the Hospital for Sick Children in Toronto have found an important biochemical difference in the bodies of children who died from sudden infant death syndrome (SIDS), compared with infants who died from other causes. According to the scientists, the research suggests that infants at high risk for SIDS may manufacture the brain chemical transmitter dopamine at abnormally high levels. Theoretically, if the results of the investigations are borne out, a child at risk might be treated with dopamine-blocking drugs as a preventive measure, but the scientists caution it is too early to consider doing that. 'Just because [dopamine] is abnormal does not necessarily mean it's a primary cause,' says Perrin. 'It may be a secondary cause [a result of some other abnormality].'

"Perrin and his colleagues examined the carotid bodies of 13 SIDS babies and five infants who died from other causes. All but two of the SIDS babies had dopamine levels far in excess of those in the controls.

"SIDS claims about ten thousand infants between two months and four months of age each year in the United States. All SIDS deaths involve the mysterious cessation of breathing during sleep."

—J. GREENBERG, *Science News*

★10. "A new study shows that the incidence of cancer tumors in rats exposed to high doses of X-rays dropped dramatically when the food intake of the rats was cut by more than half. Dr. Ludwik Gross of the Veterans Administration Medical Center noted that this study is the first to demonstrate that radiation-induced tumors can be prevented by restricting diet.

"The experimenters exposed a strain of laboratory rats to a dose of X-rays that produced tumors in 100 percent of the rats allowed to eat their fill—about five or six pellets of rat food a day.

"When the same dose of X-rays was given to rats limited to two pellets of food a day, only nine of 29 females and one of 15 males developed tumors, the researchers reported.

"The weight of the rats on the reduced diet fell by about one-half, but they remained healthy and outlived their counterparts who died of cancer, Gross said. He noted that the restricted diet also reduced the occurrence of benign tumors. There is no evidence that restriction of food intake will slow the growth of tumors that have already formed in animals, he said."

—PAUL RAEBURN, *Sacramento Bee*

★11. "Encephalitis, or sleeping sickness, has declined greatly in California during the past thirty years because more people are staying inside during prime mosquito-biting hours—7 P.M. to 10 P.M., researchers said. Paul M. Gahlinger of San Jose State University and William C. Reeves of the School of Public Health at UC Berkeley conducted the study. 'People who watch television on warm summer evenings with their air conditioners on are less likely to be exposed during the peak biting period of mosquitoes that carry encephalitis,' Reeves said.

"The researchers found that those counties in California's Central Valley with the highest television ownership had the lowest encephalitis rates for census years. Of 379 Kern County residents interviewed by telephone, 79 percent said they used their air conditioners every evening and 63 percent said they watched television four or more evenings a week during the summer.

"The percentage of residents who spend more time indoors now because of air conditioning than in 1950 more than doubled, from 26 percent to 54 percent, the researchers said."

—Associated Press, *Enterprise-Record* (Chico, California)

12. "Tests of a novel self-care program suggest it is possible to handle minor illnesses at home and help cut down on the staggering national medical bill. A 1,625-member health-maintenance organization called the Rhode Island Group Health association took part in the program. Randomly chosen members used selected medical self-care books and brochures,

backed up, in some cases, by a telephone hot line and a counseling session with a nurse, to care for their families. A control group of families had no special educational help. The result was a 17 percent drop in visits to a doctor's office by the self-care families—and corresponding savings in medical costs."

—WILLIAM HINES, *Reader's Digest*

13. "Pap-smear tests are so effective they have cut the incidence of cervical cancer two-thirds among women who had at least one screening in ten years, according to a Swedish study. The study, which followed 207,455 women for a decade, also found that the incidence of cervical cancer among those women who never had smears taken was two to four times higher than among those who had the tests.

"Study co-author Cecil Fox, of the National Cancer Institute, stated that he thinks 'this study laid to rest, once and for all, the question, "Are Pap smears effective in reducing cancer of the cervix?" '

"Sweden has a population registry that enabled researchers to follow all the women in the study without losing track of any. The women ranged in age from thirty to over seventy. 'It's the first time anyone has studied a population of women across the entire spectrum of a society,' Fox said."

—*Reader's Digest*

★14. "A study released last week indicates that Type A individuals, who are characteristically impatient, competitive, insecure and short-tempered, can halve their chances of having a heart attack by changing their behavior with the help of psychological counseling.

"In 1978, scientists at Mt. Zion Hospital and Medical Center in San Francisco and Stanford University School of Education began their study of 862 predominantly male heart attack victims. Of this number, 592 received group counseling to ease their Type A behavior and improve their self-esteem. After three years, only 7 percent had another heart attack, compared with 13 percent of a matched group of 270 subjects who received only cardiological advice. Among 328 men who continued with the counseling for the full three years, 79 percent reduced their Type A behavior. About half of the comparison group was similarly able to slow down and cope better with stress.

"This is the first evidence 'that a modification program aimed at Type A behavior actually helps to reduce coronary disease,' says Redford Williams of Duke University, an investigator of Type A behavior."

—*Science News*

15. "In a study reported in the current issue of the journal *Cancer,* doctors found that vaccines made of living cancer cells from a patient's colorectal tumor can slow or prevent the subsequent appearance of cancer elsewhere in the body. In the study, twenty patients with colorectal cancer were given the vaccine. Four of them have had recurrences in the two to four years they've been followed, but none have died. The vaccine is

not intended to prevent colorectal cancer, but only to block recurrences in patients who have already had colorectal tumors surgically removed.

"The study was conducted by Dr. Herbert C. Hoover, chief of surgical oncology at the State University of New York in Stony Brook. Dr. Hoover emphasized, 'We need further study. We don't want people to get the idea we've got a cure for cancer,' he said."

—Associated Press

EXERCISE 11-7 (ESSAY)

1. Let's say that you want to know whether picking corn a few days before the kernels are full-sized will make the corn taste sweeter. Design a study that will provide you with an answer. Be sure to indicate what kind of results you would need to get in order to reach this or that conclusion.

2. The task is the same as in item 1, but this time the issue is whether being stung by honeybees produces any immunity against honeybee toxin. (Can you—humanely—use the same type of study you would use for problem 1?)

12 *Moral Reasoning*

*. . . and so we shall hold ever to the upward way and pursue
righteousness with wisdom . . .*

—PLATO

I ought, or I ought not, constitute the whole of morality.
—CHARLES DARWIN

Althoug¹ the issues themselves may touch us more deeply than others do,
reasoning about matters of morality is basically no different from reasoning
about matters of other kinds. Arguments that occur in moral discourse do not
constitute a new species beyond the inductive and deductive types that we
have already discussed. They do have a feature that distinguishes them from
other arguments, however, in that they all contain value-expressing conclusions. We'll begin by distinguishing between claims that express values and
those that do not.

Descriptive and Prescriptive Claims

Descriptive claims simply state facts (or alleged facts, since they may be false);
they tell how things are, or were, or might be. **Prescriptive claims**, on the
other hand, state how things *ought* to be; they are claims that impute values

to actions, things, or situations. Prescriptive claims, then, are value-expressing claims. They are called prescriptive because, either explicitly or implicitly, they prescribe—that is, they state *what a person ought to do.* For example, the claim "Lying is wrong" attaches a value, a negative one, to lying, and in so doing it implicitly prescribes that we avoid lying. Sometimes the prescription simply approves an action, object, or event. If B is unlikely ever to be in A's circumstances, someone might still make a prescription for B by telling him that A's action was right, or that was indeed what A ought to have done. The prescription here is simply for B to approve of A's action.

This exhortation to approve of something is also present in prescriptive claims that express values other than moral values. Aesthetic and honorific values are also expressed by such claims. Compare these two claims:

1. This painting has more blue in it than red.
2. This is a beautiful painting.

Claim (1) is purely descriptive; it states an alleged fact about a painting. But claim (2) does something different—it attributes a value to the painting, an aesthetic value. (In brief, the aesthetic value of something is the measure of where it falls on the scale between beautiful and ugly.) By attributing an aesthetic value to the painting, a person is saying that it is worthy of appreciation and approval and hence that a person *ought* to appreciate and approve of it. (Notice that the *ought* in the preceding statement is an aesthetic, not a moral, *ought.*)

A third kind of value that people sometimes attribute to things is honorific. We often use the word *respect* to refer to such a value. We may honor our grandparents, for example, without making any moral judgment about them one way or another. We bestow honor for reasons that differ somewhat from those for which we morally approve of something. People's status may confer honor upon them; so may their accomplishments. The English honor their Queen; we all respect an Olympic medalist. But, once again, the value we attribute in bestowing honor is different from either moral or aesthetic value.

Having distinguished other kinds of values, we'll concentrate now on moral values, beginning with some remarks on the vocabularly used to express them.

Although other words and phrases can do the job, the words *should, ought, right,* and *wrong* are those most often used to express moral values. The word *should* carries a moral value in the prescriptive claim "you should keep your promises." But notice that "You should take up tennis; I think you would enjoy it," although prescriptive, contains a nonmoral use of *should.* Nothing in the claim implies a moral duty to take up tennis; the prescription to take it up is offered only to provide a potentially enjoyable experience for the person to whom the claim is addressed.

Nonmoral uses of such words as *should* and *ought* generally express what needs to be done or what could be done in order to accomplish a certain goal. If one has no need or interest in accomplishing that goal, then there may be no reason to follow the recommendation. To put it another way, we make use of the nonmoral senses of *should* and *ought* when we make claims of the sort "If you want X, then you should do Y," and "If X is your goal, then you ought to do Y." In neither case is a moral value being attached to the action Y or to the goal X; one does not necessarily have any moral duty to do Y to accomplish X.

The words *right* and *wrong* operate similarly—they have both moral and nonmoral senses. There is a wrong (but not necessarily immoral) way to do an arithmetic problem, just as there are (morally) wrong ways of treating other people.

It is the moral uses of these terms that concern us here, uses by which we do impute moral values and moral duties. If we say that A ought (morally) to do X, we mean to imply that A has a moral duty to do X. Similarly, we use the words *should* and *ought* here as they are used in moral discourse—to indicate that a moral value or duty is implied. If A should or ought to do X, when the use of *should* or *ought* is a moral one, then it follows that it is morally correct for A to do X (or morally wrong for him not to do X).

EXERCISE 12-1

Determine which of the following claims are descriptive and which are prescriptive.

★1. Martina's car runs terribly; she should get it tuned up.
2. Martina is endangering people's lives driving that car without decent brakes; she should either get them fixed or use a taxi.
3. Ms. Beeson ought not to have embezzled that money from the bank.
★4. If Ms. Beeson wanted to avoid being caught, she would not have embezzled so much money from the bank.
5. Using a sector-copying program is the wrong way to duplicate copyrighted programs.
6. Duplicating copyrighted programs is the wrong way to get your software.
★7. You ought to write your mother more often.
8. Violence is always wrong.
9. His answers are always wrong.
★10. Margaret should thank her parents for helping her through the rough time she's had.

EXERCISE 12-2

Identify which of the following claims express moral values, which express nonmoral values, and which do not express values at all.

★1. The carpenter did an excellent job of remodeling the kitchen.
2. Everybody should be as kind and generous as Janice.
3. The judge in this case is a very well informed person.

★4. The judge's decision was clearly the right one, since they all got just what they deserved.

5. The sketches we got back from the designer were awful.

6. Allison's necklace is very old.

★7. The Rosens' wedding ceremony was the loveliest one I've ever seen.

8. The last set of essays was much better written than the first set.

9. Jim ought to learn to take his hat off when he's in someone else's house.

★10. Pat won a free trip to Europe—she's the luckiest person I know.

Getting an Ought *from an* Is

It has been said that no claim about plain fact can imply a claim that attributes a moral value or a moral obligation—that is, one cannot legitimately infer what *ought (morally) to be* the case from a claim about what *is*. Using the terminology just explained, we can restate this position by saying that no prescriptive conclusion can follow from a set of purely descriptive premises. For example, consider the following argument:

1. Mr. Jones is a parent of an infant child. Therefore, Mr. Jones ought to contribute to his infant's support.

The premise of this argument states a (nonmoral) fact. But the conclusion is an *ought claim*—it asserts a moral obligation of Mr. Jones. Whether such an *"ought* claim" can ever follow from a factual claim has been a controversial question among philosophers, and it is not our intention to settle the matter here. What we will do is adopt a course between two extremes, but one that favors the position that *"ought* claims" do not follow *directly* from *"is* claims." Our strategy in evaluating arguments that have prescriptive claims for conclusions and no such claims among the stated premises will be to treat them as arguments with unstated premises, as discussed in Chapter 8.

We can turn example 1 into an argument that establishes a prescriptive conclusion by making explicit a premise that was unstated. We have added such a premise in brackets:

2. Mr. Jones is a parent of an infant child. [Parents ought to contribute to the support of their infant children.] Therefore, Mr. Jones ought to contribute to his infant child's support.

The result is a valid deductive argument. If both the premises are true, then the conclusion must be true too.

Now, in a real-life dispute about whether Mr. Jones has an obligation toward his child, an argument like example 2 is not likely to convince anyone that an obligation exists who isn't already inclined to believe the claim. The

Morality by Definition

mo ral´ı ty [ME *moralitee,* fr. MF *moralité,* fr. LL *moralitat-, moralitas,* fr. L *moralis* moral + *-tat-, -tas- -ty* . . .] **2b moralities** *pl*: particular moral principles or rules of conduct . . .

—*Webster's New International Dictionary,* 3rd ed.

Particular cases provide the motivation behind thinking about morality, but the heart of such thinking is always about general principles.

fact that the argument is valid, however, does help clarify matters. It means that, if we still have doubts about the conclusion, then there is something about at least one of the premises that bears examination. Thus, the focus of attention is moved from the original point of contention, Jones's obligation, to the required premise, "Parents ought to contribute to the support of their infant children." Without this premise, the conclusion will not follow; with it, the conclusion clearly does follow. So our interest shifts to that premise, and this is a step in the right direction, for it causes us to begin thinking in terms of moral principles (or general claims) rather than in terms of a particular case. Do *all* parents have an obligation to support their infant children? Are there circumstances under which there would be no such obligation? It is important to consider such questions apart from the case of Mr. Jones, for otherwise it would be too easy for the particulars of that case to prejudice our thinking.

We will return to the matter of why it is important, especially in matters of morality, to deal in general principles rather than particular cases. In the meantime, our concern lies in determining what premise needs to be added to a set of purely "factual" premises in order for a moral value-laden conclusion to follow.

Consider this example:

3. A promised to pay B five dollars today.
   So, A ought to pay B five dollars today.

It is perfectly natural to want to see this as a valid argument as it stands. But, in keeping with our strategy, we require that an "*ought* claim" be explicitly stated in the premises. In this case, what would you say is the missing premise? The most obvious way of putting it is "One ought to keep one's promises." If we add the required premise we get this:

4. A promised to pay B five dollars today. [One ought to keep one's promises.]
   A ought to pay B five dollars today.

If it seems to you that the second premise is not really necessary in order for the conclusion to follow, that is probably because you understand promise making as automatically involving a moral duty—a duty to keep whatever promise is made. This amounts to seeing the added premise as an analytic truth (see Chapter 2). If indeed it is analytically true that, if one promises to do X it follows that one ought to do X, then there is certainly no harm in bringing this analytic truth into the argument as an additional premise. (Any analytic truth is automatically an acceptable premise for any argument, though, in contrast to our present situation, such truths do not usually help much.) And, analytic or not, it is necessary that some connection be established between promising and having a duty in order for the conclusion of the argument to follow.

Another example:

> Thurlow was trying to kill crabgrass in his yard by spraying a powerful herbicide on it. He sprayed too close to his neighbor's yard, and some of the spray got on his neighbor's rose bush. A few days later, the rose bush was dead. Thurlow admits that, even though it was an accident, the death of the rose bush was attributable to his error.
>
> Therefore, Thurlow ought to compensate his neighbor for the rose bush.

Can you tell which premise is missing?

Although other formulations might do as well, something like this is called for:

> One ought to compensate others for harm done to them as a result of one's own actions.

Since Thurlow's actions caused harm to his neighbor's shrubbery, he has a duty to compensate for that harm. The conclusion now follows validly from the premises.

Again, the premise we have added has the form of a general moral principle; it speaks to *any* case that, like Thurlow's, involves harm under certain circumstances. In general, when there is no value expressed in the premises of an argument—that is, when there are no prescriptive premises—and when the

Deriving an Ought from an Is

The writer of the letter to a newspaper from which the following paragraph is taken derives a prescriptive claim from a descriptive one:

. . . Medical care, like food and shelter, is one of the basic necessities of life. That makes it wrong for our fancy, high-priced hospitals and clinics to deny medical care to people without insurance or other means of payment.

The writer's prescriptive conclusion is derived through the help of an unstated "*ought* claim": It is wrong to deny the basic necessities of life to people just because they cannot afford to pay for them.

argument's conclusion expresses a value or duty, our strategy is to presume an unstated premise and make it explicit. The premise will always be one that attributes a value to or imposes a duty on a type of action, object, situation, or person.

EXERCISE 12-3

For the conclusion to follow from the premise in each of the following passages, a moral principle (a general "*ought*" or "*should*" claim) is necessary as an extra premise. Supply the missing principle—one that will cover this and any similar cases.

EXAMPLE: Mrs. Montez's new refrigerator was delivered yesterday, and it stopped working today. She has followed the directions carefully but still can't make it work. The people she bought it from should either come out and make it work or replace it with another one.

PRINCIPLE: A person (or firm) should make certain that the things he (or it) sells are in proper working order.

1. After borrowing Morey's car, Leo had an accident and crumpled a fender. So Leo ought to pay whatever expenses were involved in getting Morey's car fixed.
★2. When Sarah bought the lawn mower from Jean, she promised to pay another fifty dollars on the first of the month. Since it's now the first, Sarah should pay Jean the money.
3. Harold is obligated to supply ten cords of firewood to the lodge by the beginning of October, since he signed a contract guaranteeing delivery of the wood·by that date.
★4. John has done something terribly wrong. He copied all of the equations on the take-home exam from Tony's paper and turned them in as his own.
5. Scotty's Mother is not only getting too old to take care of herself, she is unable to pay for proper care in a nursing home. Seems to me that Scotty should either take her in or otherwise make sure that she is taken care of properly.
6. Mr. Thomas ought to treat his pets better. He feeds them so little they look like they're starving to death.
★7. Mortimer did the right thing when he decided to start a regular deduction from his paycheck on behalf of the United Way.
8. Daniel was bad yesterday. He let only one of the two next-door neighbor children ride his new bike.
9. I think it's immoral the way Martin pushed his children into dangerous sports like football and motocross racing.
★10. It's true there are more voters in the northern part of the state. But that shouldn't allow the North to dictate to the South.

EXERCISE 12-4

For the conclusion to follow from the premise in each of the following passages, a moral principle (a general *ought* or *should* claim) is necessary as an extra premise. Supply the missing principle—one that will cover this and any similar cases. These passages require somewhat more subtlety than those in Exercise 12-3.

1. Dr. Shelby is getting away with charging outrageous fees because he is the only physician in town. He really ought to lower his rates so he won't be taking advantage of the isolation of the community.

★2. The computer programs we recently received are all "shareware"—they are accompanied by notices saying that anyone who keeps and uses the program should send a small fee to the author. I think it's only right that we send a check to two of the program authors, since we've started getting a lot of use out of two of the programs.

3. If the Simmonses don't begin teaching their son some discipline, he's going to grow up to be an irresponsible adult. That would amount to moral irresponsibility on the part of the Simmonses.

★4. Karen and Gina were roommates for about five months, and, as far as Gina knew, they had planned to room together until the end of the school term. But when Gina returned from a weekend at her parents', Karen had moved out. Since she couldn't find a new roommate on such short notice, Gina asked Karen to pay half the next month's rent, but Karen answered that she didn't owe the rent since she wasn't living there anymore. I think Karen should pay at least half of one month's rent, since Gina was led to believe Karen was going to be living there and paying half.

5. Look, Sam! There's been a bad accident up ahead. We really ought to stop and see if there's any way we can help.

A Principle of Morality and Reason

We begin this section by considering the idea of fair treatment. This will lead us to a principle that underlies not only our notion of fairness to other people but *any* decision about how we ought to view or act toward two or more different cases, whether they involve individual people and actions or general policies and situations. In fact, the principle we'll arrive at will turn out to be fundamental not just to matters of morality but to reason itself.

How do we decide what is fair? One approach to treating cases fairly would be to treat them all in exactly the same way. But of course this would be difficult, and, as a matter of fact, it would not produce fair treatment much of the time. For example, to treat an adult and a child in exactly the same way (providing them the same meals, assigning them the same chores, etc.) would be to treat one of them unfairly under most circumstances. We must be more subtle if we are to be fair. Still, *something* like equal, if not identical, treatment seems to lie near the heart of our usual notion of fairness.

By adopting the following principle, we can take into account both the belief that equality is important to fairness and the absurdity of requiring identical treatment for all:

Relevantly similar cases should be treated in relevantly similar ways.

The word *relevantly* allows for the subtlety required to handle complicated cases. Notice also that by referring to *relevant* similarities we make the principle general rather than tying it to particular cases. Once the relevantly similar features of a case are made clear, our conclusion holds for all cases with those features. Now let's see how the principle works.

Imagine that you are an employer and have a pool of applicants for a vacant position. After inspecting the applicants' qualifications and conducting interviews, it is time to make your decision. How do you rank the applicants in a fair manner? The important consideration is that you consider only *relevant* qualifications. If two candidates are equally qualified in a skill or ability that is relevant to the job, then they should to that extent receive equal rankings. Differences in ranking should result only from differences in qualifications in relevant skills, knowledge, or ability. Unfair treatment of applicants by potential employers consists in ranking them lower than others when they are equally able in relevant areas even though they might be different in irrelevant ways. For this reason it is crucial that you determine what abilities are relevant to the job at hand before you review the applicants and that you resolve to use those abilities as the criteria for selection.

Discrimination of every sort is based on a violation of the principle we're examining. Racial discrimination is largely a matter of treating an individual differently because of an irrelevant feature: his or her race. There are very few jobs indeed in which race will affect a person's performance. Aside from playing certain roles as an actor, we can't think of any. Much the same is true of discrimination against women: For every job in which gender is a relevant factor there are dozens in which it is completely irrelevant.

This sort of case comes to mind almost immediately when we think of justice or fairness. There are others where the same principle is at work, even if less obviously. When a person decides to make a will, for example, on the assumption that he wishes to apportion his estate to his heirs in as fair a fashion as he can, he must make use of our principle. He must decide whether there are relevant differences among his spouse, children, and other potential heirs and then assign his estate on those grounds. Are differences in age relevant? What about differences in current and prospective income? Is it relevant that one child has come to visit every Christmas and another always sends a card on birthdays?

Relevantly Similar Cases?

The claims on the left were used in defense of slavery during the nineteenth century; on the right they have been adapted to support a pro-abortion position. To what extent do the claims rest on truly relevant similarities, do you think?

Although they may have hearts and brains, and they may be human lives biologically, slaves are not *legal* persons. The Dred Scott decision by the U.S. Supreme Court has made this clear.	Although they may have hearts and brains, and they may be lives biologically, unborn babies are not *legal* persons. Our courts will soon make this clear.
Black people become *legal* persons only when they are set free. Before that time, we should not concern ourselves about them, because they have no legal rights.	Babies become *legal* persons only when they are born. Before that time, we should not concern ourselves about them because they have no legal rights.
If you think slavery is wrong, then nobody is forcing you to be a slave owner. But don't impose your morality on somebody else!	If you think abortion is wrong, then nobody is forcing you to have one. But don't impose your morality on somebody else!
People have the right to do what they want with their own property.	Women have the right to do what they want with their own bodies.

It is just as important to treat relevantly *different* cases *differently* as it is to treat relevantly similar cases similarly. If one child in the will-making example makes a very comfortable income and another works hard to get by as an elementary school teacher, this factor (other things being equal) may be a sufficient reason for leaving more to the second than to the first. (The well-off heir could be assigned the family heirloom rocking chair, perhaps.)

So far we have been discussing the *fairness* of treating similar cases similarly, and this can obscure the fact that it is *rational* to treat cases this way—and, we might add, irrational to treat them otherwise. Notice that, if we make decisions without properly emphasizing *relevant* similarities and differences, our decisions are based on *irrelevant* factors. And to make a decision on such a basis is tantamount to behaving irrationally. (Discrimination, then, is not only unfair, it is irrational.)

As a critical reader might note, it is worthwhile to point out the crucial importance of separating relevant differences and similarities from irrelevant ones. But the question remains: How do we determine what factors are more relevant than others? Unfortunately, there is no formula for making such de-

Professional Players' Privilege?

The use of cocaine by major-league baseball players has been so widespread in recent years that scores of players have been implicated in criminal investigations as users, purchasers and, sometimes, as sellers of the drug. However, the players generally have not been prosecuted, and in some cases law enforcement officials have taken unusual steps to protect the players' identities.

—MICHAEL GOODWIN and MURRAY CHASS, *New York Times*

Although this passage does not explicitly compare two cases or kinds of cases, such a comparison is clearly intended. What kind of case is the baseball-players' case being implicitly compared to? (If the case of an ordinary person who isn't famous came to mind, you'd be right.)

terminations, since the question of relevance rests on the particular circumstances of a given case. One hint we can offer, however, is that it sometimes helps to imagine what would be different about the central issue if the factor in question were different. In the case of employers about to interview applicants, they should ask themselves whether job performance will be affected one way or another if they hire a man or a woman for the job; further, they need to determine what the evidence is to that effect. The man making the will might ask himself what the inheritance would mean to the schoolteacher if the latter already had an income equivalent to that of the stockbroker. If it would make a difference, then that is a sign that the factor is a relevant one. Still, this is no more than a rule of thumb; your own common sense, carefully applied, will have to be your guide in such matters.

EXERCISE 12-5

Each numbered passage below describes two or more cases—actions, events, situations, etc.—and is followed by a list of factors. Determine which factors are relevant to the issue of similar treatment. State the issue clearly, and then explain which factors are relevant and which are not, giving the reasons for your decisions.

EXAMPLE: Bacharach owns a company with twenty employees. Every year each employee receives a Christmas bonus. This year, Bacharach decided to give an 8 percent bonus to all the employees who have been with the firm for five years or longer, and 5 percent to all those who have been with the firm for less than five years.

FACTORS: (a) Bacharach does not have enough money to give every employee an 8 percent bonus.

(b) The longer an employee has been with the firm, the greater is the likelihood that the employee is loyal to the company.

(c) An employee's productivity may not depend upon his or her length of time with the company.

(d) Some employees are the sole means of support in their families.

(e) Some employees make substantially more regular pay than others.

ISSUE: Should Bacharach give more money to employees with five years or greater service, or should he treat them all equally?

FACTORS: (a) This factor is not relevant. The issue is whether some employees should receive larger bonuses than others, and, if so, whether the amount should be based on years of service. Bacharach could combine all the money and divide it by the number of employees to make all bonuses equal.

(b) This issue is probably relevant. Is the bonus designed to reward loyalty or is it just a gesture of goodwill? If the latter, then company loyalty is less important.

(c) Probably relevant. Questions similar to those asked in item b apply here.

(d) Other things being equal, we think this should be a relevant consideration, especially since the bonus is given at Christmas.

(e) This may be relevant, but it can cut two ways: On one hand, an across-the-board bonus may seem small to an employee who already makes a relatively large salary; on the other hand, an 8 percent bonus for a high-salaried employee may cost as much as a 7 percent bonus for several lower-paid employees.

★1. Pop singer Jeffrey Winters and the legendary vaudeville dancer Claude McPherson both died last month. The city is doing a memorial service for Winters, but McPherson got no more than mention and a photo in the local papers.

FACTORS: (a) Winters was younger than McPherson.

(b) More residents knew of Winters than of McPherson.

(c) McPherson was a celebrity for much longer than Winters.

(d) McPherson's family donated the land for the Downtown Plaza Park.

(e) Winters was good friends with the mayor.

2. The city council has decided to fund two new downtown parking lots for automobiles, but several parking areas for bicycles will have to be removed in the process. "There are just more people who drive downtown than come on bikes," a spokesman for the council said. Bicyclists complained about the decision because there is already a shortage of places to park bicycles legally in the downtown area.

FACTORS: (a) More people drive downtown than ride bicycles.

(b) Bicycles cause less pollution than automobiles.

(c) More bicycles can be parked in a given space than autos.

(d) Bicycles are less expensive than cars.

(e) Only one or two people can travel on a bicycle.

3. Ordinarily, if an argument between two people at their place of work led to one striking another with a blunt instrument, and the victim of the blow required twenty-five stitches as a result, the person who struck the blow would be convicted of aggravated assault. But when an argument and assault occurred between two professional hockey players during a game in 1975, a trial led to a hung jury and eventual dismissal of the charges.

FACTORS: (a) The victim of the assault knew he was in a dangerous profession.

(b) Fighting occurs frequently among professional hockey players during games.

(c) The assault occurred in the penalty box, not on the ice while the two players were "in the heat of battle."

(d) Previous fights among hockey players have not resulted in charges or convictions of the participants.

(e) Fighting is not an official part of the game of hockey.

★4. It is hypocritical to express moral indignation against hunters unless the person expressing it is a vegetarian.

FACTORS: (a) Animal populations in the wild may multiply beyond what the food supply can support unless some are taken by hunters.

(b) Domestic beef, pork, foul, and the like are *raised* to be killed — they wouldn't exist to begin with if it weren't for their food value to humans.

(c) Hunting teaches people to kill, which can have brutalizing effects on the personality of the hunter.

(d) An animal is equally "innocent" whether it lives in the wild or in a feed lot.

(e) Less killing of animals is better than more killing, whatever the circumstances.

5. Automobiles kill more people every year than handguns — they should be outlawed if handguns should be outlawed.

FACTORS: (a) Except for a very small number of instances, automobile deaths are the result of accidents.

(b) Many states require registration of both handguns and automobiles.

(c) Both automobiles and handguns have harmless uses.

(d) Outlawing automobiles would bring most of the country's movement to a halt.

(e) Both automobiles and handguns are often involved in serious crimes.

EXERCISE 12-6

Each of the items below describes two situations, actions, or policies that have at least a superficial resemblance. Your job is to determine whether the two situations, etc., are sufficiently similar to warrant similar treatment. If different treatment is warranted, describe what difference there is between the cases that warrants it.

1. Marina is kind and compassionate to her pets, but she is noticeably cold and indifferent to the suffering of other people.
★2. Susan believes in euthanasia but not in abortion.
3. Jenkins shoplifted a record from a local record store. Hopper bought a record, took it home and tape-recorded it, and then brought it back for a refund, claiming the record was not to his liking.
★4. Federal tax policy allows white-collar managers to deduct the expenses of taking business associates to lunch. Blue-collar workers are not allowed to deduct such expenses as the cost of work clothes.
5. Professor Stein admits that he grades his freshman and sophomore classes harder than he does his upper-class students. He sets the average grade for the former at C, but he sets the average grade for the latter at B.
6. Newspapers today will publish advertisements that make smoking seem sophisticated, but they continue to censor advertisements that are sexually explicit.
7. George Bush denounced the government of Nicaragua and supported guerrillas who want to overthrow it, but he backed the government of El Salvador against the guerrillas who are fighting against it.
8. Joseph organized protests against the government's treatment of Indians but he has never done a thing to protest the Soviet suppression of Jews.
9. Darreaux, the attorney, knew that Johnson was guilty and Gould was innocent, yet he defended both of them with equal skill and enthusiasm.
★10. Woods got roaring drunk at a local bar and had no business driving a car. He was lucky to have made it home alive even though he did get stopped and ticketed by the police. Hearst also had too much to drink, and though he was not as bad off as Woods, he should have called a taxi. Unfortunately, Hearst struck and killed a pedestrian in a crosswalk on his way home. To make the story more ironic, Woods had roared through the same intersection against a red light about five minutes before—doing sixty miles an hour. Now Woods faces a Driving Under the Influence charge and Hearst faces that charge plus another for vehicular manslaughter.

Evaluating Moral Reasoning

In this section we consider and evaluate two reasons for and two against the claim that professional boxing should be outlawed. We make explicit any premises that are required by the arguments in which the reasons appear, and then evaluate the results. You might do your own evaluations before reading the ones supplied, and then compare your results with ours.

1. This is probably the most obvious reason for the claim that professional boxing should be outlawed—that professional boxing results in a high incidence of injury, especially brain damage, to its participants.

Let's set up an argument properly, with all unstated premises made explicit:

> Professional boxing results in a high incidence of serious injury to its participants.
>
> [Any sport or activity that results in a high incidence of serious injury to its participants should be outlawed.]
>
> Therefore, professional boxing should be outlawed.

Notice first what is accomplished by the addition of the required additional premise, given within brackets. Immediately our attention is called to the general claim that *any* sport with a certain feature ought to be dealt with in a certain way. Thus, we are led to think not just of *this* case but of any and all similar cases. We must be prepared to accept this general claim about all relevantly similar sports or activities or give up the argument and try again, for without this premise the argument fails to establish its conclusion.

Are we prepared to accept the general claim? If so, we must be ready to outlaw bullfighting, motor racing, and possibly several other sports that result in a high incidence of serious injury to their participants. In so deciding we are making use of the principle discussed in the preceding section: Relevantly similar cases should be treated in relevantly similar ways. In this case, we are obliged by this principle to treat bullfighting and motor racing just as we decide to treat boxing if we determine that they are similar in the relevant respects. And in this case being similar in the relevant respects means that the second premise applies to each activity. Boxing, bullfighting, and motor racing all result in a high incidence of serious injury to their participants, and this makes the three sports relevantly similar.

Discovering the consequences of the argument in question does not settle the main issue, of course. We may or may not be prepared to outlaw other activities that are like boxing in a relevantly similar way. But, if we were to outlaw boxing *on the grounds stated in this argument,* it would be irrational not to outlaw the other activities as well.

Even though we may not be entirely convinced by this argument, it's still quite a good one. It brings an important reason to bear on the issue: the fact that boxing can cause serious injuries. The more important this fact is to us, the more weight this argument will have. We'll return to this point soon. In the meantime, we'll consider other reasons for and against outlawing professional boxing, since complex issues like this one are seldom decided on the basis of one argument alone.

The second reason we'll consider is this:

2. Professional boxing pits human beings directly against one another, each with the object of doing the other harm.

Once again, the first thing to consider is the additional premise needed to relate this claim to the issue of whether boxing should be outlawed. The premise required is, of course, this:

> [All activities that pit human beings against each other with the object of doing each other harm should be outlawed.]

And together they yield this conclusion:

> Professsional boxing should be outlawed.

The reason given in this argument is somewhat different from that in the first in that it hinges more on the *object* of the sport than on its results. Let us consider. Is the first premise true? Is the object of boxing to do harm to an opponent? It is certainly very close to it, since it is hard to imagine trying to win a match while doing an opponent no damage. (We do not mean *permanent* damage, of course.) Second, are there other sports whose objects are similar enough to that of boxing to be included under the second premise? American football might qualify, since, for some players—defensive linemen, for example—the main goal is attacking other players. While it is true that there is no official gain to be had from damaging the opposition, there is certainly a practical gain to be had from sending the opposing quarterback to the sidelines for medical attention. And, equally to the point, it is notoriously true that the best defensive players are those who are willing and able to do as much violence to their opponents as the rules will allow.

Regardless of what activities we decide fall under the scope of the second premise, we are not likely to find this argument quite as convincing as the first. This is because we are not as likely to find the object or point of a sport as upsetting as we are its injurious consequences. We simply take the latter more seriously; they are more important to us. (A sport that pitted participants against one another but never resulted in real harm to them would probably bother very few of us.) So this argument is probably less convincing than the first; the reason on which it is based is less important to us than the reason on which the first argument is based.

The next reason we'll consider supports the other side of the issue:

3. Professional boxing supplies an outlet for some individuals who would otherwise behave violently under more dangerous circumstances and against innocent people.

This claim attempts to turn a consideration *for* the original judgment that boxing should be outlawed into one *against* that judgment. The premise required to accompany this one is this general claim:

> [No activities that supply an outlet for individuals who would otherwise behave violently should be outlawed.]

And together they yield this conclusion:

> Professional boxing should not be outlawed.

The first premise claims an advantage to society by controlling violence that would otherwise be uncontrolled. One problem with such a claim is that it is itself very difficult to support; we have no reason for believing that it is true. As far as we can tell, it is little more than speculation.

A problem with the second premise is that, if it justifies boxing, it might also justify any number of other violent activities. Might gladiatorial contests reduce the number of murders in society? Would they be justified even if they did?

In short, reason 3 and the argument in which it occurs are not very convincing. It is not clear at all that the reason itself is true, and the premise required to accompany it supports the legalization of activities we want to remain illegal.

Here's the fourth and last reason we'll consider:

4. If professional boxing were outlawed, the personal freedom of boxers to assume risks would be violated.

The additional premise required is this:

> [The personal freedom of professional boxers to assume risks should not be violated.]

And the conclusion, again, is

> Professional boxing should not be outlawed.

This argument brings up the important and sometimes complicated matter of a person's personal freedom. It is true that, in general, we accept the claim that restrictions on an individual's freedom require strong justification, since we place great value on such freedom. But we also limit the freedom of individuals when it conflicts with other things we value. We must then take stock of how weighty the reasons are for outlawing boxing, since, as this argument shows, making boxing illegal would conflict with this widely held value.

A proponent of this argument might support the reason given in the first premise with a further reason—namely, that the freedom to assume the risks of boxing is *especially* important to many boxers, since boxing may be one of the few ways they can escape impoverished backgrounds. This complicates the issue by tying it to another question of moral importance: Is it morally correct to close off an opportunity for some individuals by outlawing boxing without providing a substitute by means of which they may be able to achieve success?

We find reason 4 a better reason than 3 for the conclusion that boxing should not be outlawed. Individuals' freedom to pursue activities that involve risk is important, and it is not a matter of speculation as was reason 3. The supplemental argument in favor of 4 given in the preceding paragraph shows why the specific freedom to pursue boxing as a career is important to some individuals.

In sum, then, this fourth reason and the argument in which it appears provide substantial grounds for accepting the argument's conclusion. Whether these grounds are conclusive will depend upon the relative importance of the values involved on both sides.

A large number of arguments on either side of this issue remain untreated here, of course. We could no more hope to supply them all than we could hope to settle the entire question in these few pages. But we do want you to notice a few salient points that can be drawn from these discussions.

First, you might suspect that no single reason is likely to be thoroughly convincing on such an issue. But remember from Chapter 8 that several independent reasons can be brought to bear in support of a single conclusion, and, while no one of them may succeed in establishing that conclusion, the combination of several may be convincing.

Second, when the conclusions of two arguments conflict, and both arguments are valid, then we have to give up at least one premise of one of the arguments. Presuming that we have our facts straight, the premise we have to give up is ordinarily one that expresses values. But how do we decide which one it is to be? We give up the one that carries the least weight.

To say that one consideration carries more weight than another is simply to say that it is more important to us than the other. That boxing injures people is a weightier fact than that it strikes some people as barbaric, for example. Even if boxing were established as barbaric and if everybody agreed that there was something wrong with barbarism, these considerations would not necessarily be significant enough to warrant outlawing the sport. But the fact that boxing causes injuries could outweigh any reasons for the opposite conclusion on its own. A premise may support a conclusion, then, but still be of insufficient

Speaking (on the Air) of Boxing . . .

Syndicated sports writer Jim Murray once wrote of a television announcer who became especially excited while describing the gory details of a beating taken by boxer Jerry Quarry,

"Quarry is bleeding from the nose!" screamed the announcer, "He can't see out of his eye! . . . His lip is split! . . . He's a punching bag!"

Commented Murray, in italics: "What if he were blind altogether? Champagne all around? . . . Can you get me four tickets to a train wreck? . . . How would you like a nice set of recordings made at midnight at Gestapo headquarters?"

Murray's remarks, though hyperbolic, do give graphic illustration to a point from which another argument for outlawing can easily be made: Boxing encourages interest and excitement in the pain and suffering of others. To create an argument, we need only add the premise that activities that encourage such interest and excitement should be illegal.

importance to make us accept the conclusion if we have more important reasons for a conflicting one.

We have encountered questions of weight before. For example, in Chapter 3, we discussed the credibility of sources. There are times when we have to decide which among several conflicting sources is the most credible. What is different in the realm of values is that, at a fundamental level, there are no rules of thumb to guide us in making our decisions. Some values are simply more important to us than others, and when values come into conflict, we may have to override some in order to serve others. Values are not immutable; they change as a result of experience. But at a given moment, each of us has a store of them. When we have acquired and evaluated all the information we can about a decision and we have traced out the various consequences and implications of the alternatives, what counts is which values we consider most important.

Finally, it is clear that issues like the one treated here have a way of getting complicated. We can hardly guarantee that learning to evaluate arguments, to distinguish among different issues, to ignore irrelevancies—in short, to think critically—will make issues easier to decide. In fact, these abilities may make important issues more difficult to decide. But you are still wiser for having learned to deal with issues in as thorough and competent a manner as you can. It is better to understand the complexity of matters and to live with a bit of uncertainty than to falsely believe that you have all the answers, however much temporary comfort there may be in such an attitude.

Recap

Reasoning about morality is distinguished from reasoning about matters of fact only in that the former always involves claims that express moral values. Such claims constitute one variety of prescriptive claims. Prescriptive claims, which express values of one sort or another, are contrasted with purely descriptive claims, which state how things happen to be or might be. Certain phrases, especially words such as *ought, should, right,* and *wrong,* are used in such claims in their moral senses. When we make such claims we impute moral values and moral duties.

Our strategy does not allow getting a prescriptive conclusion directly from premises that are purely descriptive. An argument that has a value-expressing conclusion—that is, a moral argument—must have a value-expressing premise if the conclusion is to follow. Although such premises often remain unstated, we need to make them explicit to see whether the value as expressed in the conclusion really does belong there. Making the prescriptive premise explicit also calls our attention to the general moral principles that underlie our discussion, and attention to such principles can prevent our being swayed by the emotional details of particular cases. Further, since morality and reason both tell us that cases that are alike in all relevant respects should be treated in similar ways, evaluating a moral argument involves tracing the consequences of this general moral principle as they affect cases not mentioned in the specifics of the one at hand. We saw how this works in our discussion of arguments about whether professional boxing should be made illegal.

Sometimes values conflict, and when that happens we can avoid the paralysis of indecision only be determining which of our conflicting values is most important to us. Rules of thumb cannot be provided in such matters; we must finally decide on grounds of what counts more for us and what counts less. In effect we are thus deciding which principles we put first and which have to give way.

Is This Bad Reasoning?

During the 1988 presidential campaign, Republican supporters of George Bush frequently attacked Bush's opponent, Governor Michael Dukakis of Massachusetts, as being soft on crime. Their evidence was a Massachusetts program that allowed some felons to go home on weekend passes. Unfortunately for Dukakis, the Bush campaign focused on one of those felons who when on furlough had raped a woman and stabbed her companion. Bush said that Dukakis owed people an explanation of why he supported such an outrageous program, and Bush supporters portrayed Dukakis as one who coddles criminals.

Near the end of the campaign, columnist Mike Royko of the *Chicago Tribune* called attention to the fact that when Bush had been a congressman in Texas, he had helped raise funds to start a halfway house for ex-convicts in Houston. Interestingly enough, one of the parolees raped and murdered a minister's wife, Royko noted. Further, Royko said, when Ronald Reagan had been governor of California, he too had instituted a prison furlough system much like the one in Massachusetts. In fact, observed Royko, one criminal furloughed under the Reagan program had actually murdered a Los Angeles policeman, and two others had murdered a woman in Orange County.

Of course, the supporters of Bush who accused Dukakis of coddling criminals said not a word of criticism about Bush's supporting a halfway house program that led to one murder or about Reagan's supporting a prison furlough program that led to two more. Royko regarded this as gross inconsistency on the part of the Bush people.

Now, our question to you: Is Royko guilty of faulty ad hominem reasoning? What about "pseudorefutation" or "two wrongs" pseudoreasoning?

No, he isn't; not in this case. Royko's point is that the Dukakis case on the one side and the Bush-Reagan cases on the other are sufficiently similar to warrant equal appraisal. The Bush supporters, Royko is telling us, were treating similar cases in dissimilar manners. If the Bush-Reagan problems were not evidence that Bush or Reagan was soft on crime, then neither was Dukakis' furlough program evidence that Dukakis was soft on crime.

Additional Exercises

EXERCISE 12-7

Below are five claims about social policy and values (let's call them "principal claims"). Following each principal claim is a list of considerations for and against the position the claim represents. Examine each of the considerations in turn. To show how it bears on the issue, construct an argument that has the principal claim or its denial as a conclusion and the consideration in question as one of the premises. Here's an example of the procedure:

EXAMPLE:

Principal claim: Large computer data bases of information on the personal and financial matters of individuals ought not to be allowed.
Considerations:
(a) Large data bases of personal and financial information lead inevitably to the sharing of information about a person without that person's knowledge and consent.
(b) Without large data bases of personal and financial information, the current system of personal financial management would collapse.

ANSWER: Consideration (a) supports the principal claim. An argument based on it might look like this:

Large data bases of personal and financial information lead to sharing of that information without the individual's knowledge or consent.

Sharing of such information under those conditions amounts to an invasion of the individual's privacy.

Any such invasion of a person's privacy is wrong.

Therefore, large data bases of such information ought not to be allowed.

Consideration (b) supports the *denial* of the principal claim. An argument might be constructed something like this:

Large data bases on individuals are necessary to support the current system of personal financial management.

If the system of personal financial management were to collapse, people would not be able to buy homes, automobiles, and other such items.

It is wrong to prevent people from being able to purchase homes, automobiles, and other such items.

Therefore, we must allow data bases on individuals.

Although the conclusions of these arguments conflict, each brings an important point to bear on the issue.

Notice, incidentally, that by making the arguments clear and explicit, we can determine how to think further about the issue. Is there perhaps a way of reconciling our requirements about privacy with our desire to have a workable system of personal financial management? For example, are there perhaps kinds of data bases that are not invasive of privacy but that still allow our system of personal credit to work? Could safeguards ensure that a person would be consulted and would have to give permission before personal information was exchanged? Is it true that our current system of personal financial credit is the *only* system that will enable people to buy houses and cars? If such efforts to reconcile the two considerations fail, we may finally have to decide: Which is more important to us, privacy in our financial affairs or our ability to make large credit purchases? If the conflict remains unresolved, we must choose between these competing values.

1. It is right for the government to intervene and require medical treatment of newborns with serious medical problems as long as there is a reasonable chance that medical treatment will save or prolong the child's life.
   (a) Parents can be tempted to allow a newborn to die because of the trouble and expense of keeping it alive.
   (b) A child with serious and uncorrectable medical problems will lead a less-than-satisfactory life.
   (c) Personal decisions about family matters ought not be in the hands of the government.
   (d) Physicians' medical expertise does not give them the ability to give advice and counsel about whether a child should live or die.
   (e) A family should not be made to suffer because of an unhappy genetic accident.
★2. Advertising is a form of socially approved swindling—all advertisers should be held strictly accountable for claims made in advertising, and no advertising should be allowed that goes beyond the statement of provable facts.
   (a) Policing the advertising industry would require an enormous bureaucracy and would be an unacceptable burden on society.
   (b) Freedom to advertise is part of freedom of speech—as long as outright harmful lies are prohibited.
   (c) Millions of dollars a year are spent on goods and services that turn out not to satisfy their buyers.
   (d) People who sell products that do not live up to their advertising claims are engaged in a form of lying.
   (e) Advertising that plays on people's hopes and fears takes advantage of innocence and gullibility.
3. Employees who know of illegal or unscrupulous tactics on the part of their companies are duty bound to speak up—to blow the whistle.

(a) No firm can do business without the loyalty of its employees.

(b) Having knowledge of a practice that is wrong and doing nothing about it make a person an accomplice to that practice.

(c) Blowing the whistle on a firm that employs you is a form of ingratitude, and ingratitude is immoral.

(d) A reputation as a whistle-blower can ruin a person's employability and endanger the well-being of that individual's entire family.

(e) In the long run, shady business is bad business.

(f) Living with injustice and unfairness eventually causes people to lose their own sense of justice and fairness.

4. We should do away with the death penalty once and for all.

(a) Executing a person is simply a form of murder.

(b) People who commit murder have already given up their own right to live.

(c) The death penalty may be harsh, but it is the only solution society can afford for the problem of violent criminal offenders.

(d) A person who takes a life owes a life.

(e) The death penalty is an admission that we don't care enough to rehabilitate offenders.

(f) Some people, because of their personal circumstances, are more likely to receive the death penalty than others—it can never be administered fairly.

5. People have the right to die just as they have the right to live; euthanasia ought to be a viable choice for anybody.

(a) Deciding to die is an essentially private matter; it's nobody's business but the person's own.

(b) Euthanasia is moral only when the individual has made the decision deliberately and is of sound mind.

(c) Choosing to die is no more a person's right than choosing for somebody else to die.

(d) The morality of euthanasia depends upon whether the person is no longer capable of consciousness—the only acceptable cases are when the alternative is "vegetating," meaning that the decision is always in the hands of others.

EXERCISE 12-8 (ESSAY)

Below is a list of cases in which values come into conflict and on which arguments for various positions can be brought to bear. The issues may be discussed in class or given extended treatment in essays.

1. If a person discovers that all his long-distance telephone calls have been accidentally left off his monthly bill and he does nothing about it, choosing to pay the amount requested instead, is he guilty of stealing?

2. Patents for new ideas and inventions protect the rights of their discoverers or inventors but they also prevent the widespread dissemination and development of new ideas and inventions by making them the private and personal property of those who hold them.

3. As long as there are children in the world who are without proper food and medical care, it is immoral for anybody who has a comfortable life to fail to make a contribution to the welfare of those less fortunate.

4. People ought to be able to do whatever they want with their own property and resources even if this gives people with a large amount of money and property the right to have a disproportionate effect on the nature of a community.

5. When it comes to war, all the rules go out the window—there's no such thing as morality or immorality during wartime.

6. Food production is enhanced (and thus prices are affected) by the use of pesticides, but so is the poisoning of the land and the water.

7. Termination of a pregnancy at any time after conception involves the taking of a human life and is thus morally wrong.

8. Laws that require that people wear helmets while riding motorcycles are morally wrong, since they interfere with individuals' liberty while protecting them only from themselves.

9. When individuals believe that their country asks them to do something they believe is wrong, they have a moral obligation to disobey.

10. The only time censorship is morally justifiable is when it keeps potentially harmful material out of the hands of children.

Appendix 1
Categorical Logic

From the time of its inventor, Aristotle, until the nineteenth century, categorical logic was the only systematic logic. However, a host of refinements were made to the basic theory during this period of more than two thousand years. In these pages, we cover only the basics of the theory, but even this general overview will enable you to do a considerable amount of logic. Since logic is a skill, we have supplied exercises throughout the appendices to enable you both to practice and to check your comprehension of the material.

Categorical Claims. Categorical logic is based on **standard-form categorical claims.** A standard-form categorical claim is what results when you put words or phrases that name classes into the blanks of the following structures:

(A) All _____ are _____ .
    (*Example:* All Presbyterians are Christians.)
(E) No _____ are _____ .
    (*Example:* No Muslims are Christians.)
(I) Some _____ are _____ .
    (*Example:* Some Christians are Presbyterians.)
(O) Some _____ are not _____ .
    (*Example:* Some Christians are not Presbyterians.)

The phrases that go in the blanks are *terms;* the one that goes in the first blank is the *subject term* of the claim and the one that goes in the second blank is the *predicate term.* Thus, *Presbyterians* is the subject term of the first example above and the predicate term of the third and fourth examples. In our explanations we often use the letters S and P (for "subject" and "predicate") to stand for terms in categorical claims.

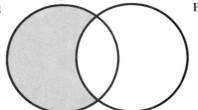

Figure 1.   A-claim: All S are P.

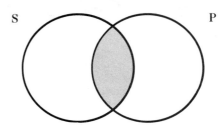

Figure 2.   E-claim: No S are P.

The letters in parentheses to the left of each type of claim are the traditional names of the types. (They come from the vowels in the Latin words for affirmative [A,I] and negative [E,O].) So the claim "All idolators are heathens" is an A-claim, as is any other claim of the form "All S are P." The same is true regarding the other letters and the other three kinds of claims.

Figures 1 through 4 show the four standard-form categorical claims represented by **Venn diagrams,** which are graphic illustrations of what the claims say. In the diagrams the circles represent the classes named by the terms; shaded areas represent areas that are empty, and areas containing Xs represent areas that are occupied.

Notice that in the diagram for the A-claim the area that would contain any members of the S class that were not members of the P class is shaded out—that is, it is empty. Thus, that diagram represents the claim "All S are P," since there is no S left that isn't P. Similarly, in the diagram for the E-claim, the area where S and P overlap is empty; any S that is also a P has been eliminated. Hence: No S are P.

We ordinarily use A- and E-type claims with the assumption that there exists at least one member of each class. Occasionally, however, we do not make that assumption, as when we say, "No unicorns are real creatures." Sets without any members require different handling, and, fortunately, they don't turn up often. In order to keep our treatment of categorical logic simple, therefore, we'll assume that all the classes we're discussing have members.

For our purposes in this appendix the word *some* means "at least one." So the third diagram represents the fact that at least one S is a P, and the X in

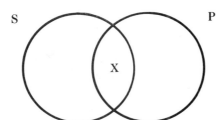

Figure 3.   I-claim: Some S are P.

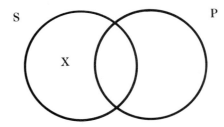

Figure 4.   O-claim: Some S are not P.

the area where the two classes overlap shows that at least one thing inhabits this area. Finally, the last diagram shows an X in the area of the S circle that is outside the P circle, representing the existence of at least one S that is not a P.

Although there are only four standard-form types of categorical claims, many other claims that are not exactly like any of these four can be rewritten or "translated" into one or another of them. For example, "Only athletes are long-distance runners" says "All long-distance runners are athletes." "Minors are not eligible" says "No minors are eligible people."

Make sure that you are entirely clear about what these four claims say and how the four diagrams work. This material is the foundation on which all of categorical logic, and thus the remainder of this appendix, is built.

EXERCISE A1-1

Rewrite each of the following claims as a standard-form categorical claim. Each rewritten claim should follow the exact form of an A-, E-, I-, or O-claim.

1. Every salamander is a lizard.
★ 2. Not every lizard is a salamander.
3. Not all lizards are salamanders.
★ 4. Only reptiles can be lizards.
5. Snakes are the only semiaquatic reptiles.
★ 6. Snakes are not the only semiaquatic reptiles.
7. Wherever there are snakes, there are frogs.
★ 8. There are frogs wherever there are snakes.
9. Whenever the frog population decreases, the snake population decreases.
★ 10. If something is a lizard, then it is a reptile.
11. Anything that qualifies as a frog qualifies as a reptile.
★ 12. The whale is not a fish.
13. Nobody arrived except the cheerleaders.
★ 14. Socrates is a Greek. (See answer section for a tip.)
15. The guy who held up the bank is my next-door neighbor.

The Square of Opposition. Two categorical claims *correspond* to each other if they have the same subject term and the same predicate term. So "All Methodists are Christians" corresponds to "Some Methodists are Christians," since in both claims *Methodists* is the subject term and *Christians* is the predicate term. Notice, though, that "Some Christians are not Methodists" does *not* correspond to either of the other two; it has the same terms but in different places.

We can now exhibit the logical relationships between corresponding A-, E-, I-, and O-claims. The **square of opposition**, in Figure 5, does this very concisely.

The A- and E-claims, across the top of the square from each other, are **contraries**—they can both be false but they cannot both be true.

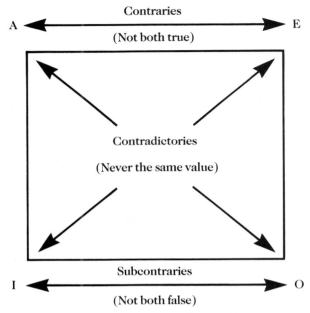

Figure 5.   The square of opposition.

The I- and O-claims, across the bottom of the square from each other, are **subcontraries**—they can both be true but they cannot both be false.

The A- and O-claims and the E- and I-claims, which are at opposite diagonal corners from each other, respectively, are **contradictories**—they never have the same truth values.

If we have the truth value of one categorical claim, we can often deduce everything there is to be found out about the other three corresponding claims by using the square of opposition. For instance, if we hear "All aluminum cans are recyclable items," we can immediately infer that its contradictory, "Some aluminum cans are not recyclable items," is false; the corresponding E-claim, "No aluminum cans are recyclable items," is also false, since it is the contrary of the original A-claim and cannot be true if the A-claim is true. The corresponding I-claim, "Some aluminum cans are recyclable items," must be true, because we just determined that *its* contradictory, the E-claim, is false.

However, we cannot always determine the truth values of the remaining three standard-form categorical claims. For example, if we begin by knowing only that the A-claim is false, all we can infer is the truth value (true) of the corresponding O-claim. Nothing follows about either the E or the I. Since the A and the E can both be false, knowing that the A is false does not tell us anything about the E—it can still be either true or false. And if the E-claim remains undetermined, then so must its contradictory, the I.

So here are the limits on what can be inferred from the square of opposition: Beginning with a *true* claim at the top of the square (either A or E), we can infer the truth values of all three of the remaining claims. The same is true if we begin with a *false* claim at the bottom of the square (either I or O): We can still deduce the truth values of the other three. But if we begin with a false claim at the top of the square or a true claim at the bottom, all we can determine is the truth value of the contradictory of the claim in hand.

EXERCISE A1-2

From the claim given, determine what the three corresponding standard-form categorical claims are. Then, assuming the truth value in parentheses for the given claim, determine the truth values of as many of the other three as you can.

  1. Some mice are short-tailed animals. (True)
★2. No drugs are completely harmless substances. (True)
  3. Some evergreens are not softwoods. (False)
★4. All gardens are laborious projects. (False)
  5. No Muslims are Methodists. (False)

Conversion. The E- and I-claims, but not the A and O, contain exactly the same information as their converses. You find the **converse** of a categorical claim by reversing the positions of the subject and predicate terms. Each member of the following pairs is the converse of the other:

(E) No Norwegians are Slavs.
     No Slavs are Norwegians.
(I) Some state capitals are large cities.
     Some large cities are state capitals.

Obversion. Every categorical claim, whether of the A, E, I, or O type, contains exactly the same information as its obverse. You find the **obverse** of a claim by (1) changing it into the form directly across the square from it (i.e., A changes to E and vice versa; I changes to O and vice versa) and (2) replacing the predicate term with its complementary term. A term is **complementary** to another term if it refers to everything the first term does not refer to. For example, *students* and *nonstudents* are complementary. Each member of the following pairs of claims is the obverse of the other:

(A) All Presbyterians are Christians.
     No Presbyterians are non-Christians.
(E) No fish are mammals.
     All fish are nonmammals.
(I) Some citizens are voters.
     Some citizens are not nonvoters.

(O) Some contestants are not winners.
     Some contestants are nonwinners.

Contraposition. A- and O-claims, but not E- and I-claims, contain exactly the same information as their contrapositives. You find the **contrapositive** of a categorical claim by (1) switching the places of the subject and predicate terms, just as in conversion, and (2) replacing both terms with complementary terms. Each of the following is the contrapositive of the other member of the pair:

(A) All Mongolians are Muslims.
     All non-Muslims are non-Mongolians.
(O) Some citizens are not voters.
     Some nonvoters are not noncitizens.

EXERCISE A1-3

For each of the following, find the claim that is described.

EXAMPLE: Find the contrary of the contrapositive of "All Greeks are Europeans." First, find the contrapositive of the original claim. It is "All non-Europeans are non-Greeks." Now, find the contrary of that. Going across the top of the square (from an A-claim to an E-claim), we get "No non-Europeans are non-Greeks."

1. Find the contradictory of the converse of "No clarinets are percussion instruments."
★2. Find the contradictory of the obverse of "Some encyclopedias are definitive works."
3. Find the contrapositive of the subcontrary of "Some Englishmen are Celts."
★4. Find the contrary of the contradictory of "Some sailboats are not sloops."
5. Find the obverse of the converse of "No sharks are freshwater fish."

EXERCISE A1-4

For each pair of claims, assume that the first has the truth value given in parentheses. Using the operations of conversion, obversion, and contraposition along with the square of opposition, decide whether the second claim is true, false, or remains undetermined.

EXAMPLE: (a) No aardvarks are nonmammals. (True)
         (b) Some aardvarks are not mammals.

Claim (a) can be obverted to "All aardvarks are mammals." Since all categorical claims are equivalent to their obverses, the truth of this claim follows from that of (a). Since this claim is the contradictory of claim (b), it follows that claim (b) must be false.

Note: If we had been unable to make the two claims correspond without performing an illegitimate operation (such as converting an A-claim), then the answer is automatically *undetermined*.

★1. (a) No mosquitoes are poisonous creatures. (True)
    (b) Some poisonous creatures are mosquitoes.
  2. (a) Some students are not ineligible candidates. (True)
    (b) No eligible candidates are students.
★3. (a) Some sound arguments are not invalid arguments. (True)
    (b) All valid arguments are unsound arguments.
  4. (a) Some residents are nonvoters. (False)
    (b) No voters are residents.
★5. (a) Some automobile plants are not productive factories. (True)
    (b) All unproductive factories are automobile plants.

Many of the following will have to be rewritten as standard-form categorical claims before they can be answered.

  6. (a) Most opera singers take voice lessons their whole lives. (True)
    (b) Some opera singers do not take voice lessons their whole lives.
  7. (a) The hero gets killed in some of Gary Brodnax's novels. (False)
    (b) The hero does not get killed in some of Gary Brodnax's novels.
  8. (a) None of the boxes in the last shipment are unopened. (True)
    (b) Some of the opened boxes are not boxes in the last shipment.
★9. (a) Not everybody who is enrolled in the class will get a grade. (True)
    (b) Some people who will not get a grade are enrolled in the class.
10. (a) Persimmons are always astringent when they have not been left to dry. (True)
    (b) Some persimmons that have been left to dry are not astringent.

Categorical Syllogisms. A **categorical syllogism** is a two-premise deductive argument whose every claim is a categorical claim and in which three terms each occur exactly twice in exactly two of the claims. Study the following example:

All Americans are consumers.

Some consumers are not Democrats.

Therefore, some Americans are not Democrats.

Notice that each of the three terms (*Americans, consumers,* and *Democrats*) occurs exactly twice in exactly two different claims. The terms of a syllogism are sometimes given the following labels:

Major term: the term that occurs as a predicate term of the syllogism's conclusion

Minor term: the term that occurs as the subject term of the syllogism's conclusion

Middle term: the term that occurs in both of the premises but not at all in the conclusion

The most frequently used symbols for these three terms are P for major term, S for minor term, and M for middle term. We use these symbols throughout to simplify the discussion.

The Venn Diagram Method of Testing for Validity. Diagramming a syllogism requires three overlapping circles, one representing each class named by a term in the argument. To be systematic, in our diagrams we put the minor term on the left, the major term on the right, and the middle term in the middle, but lowered a bit. We will diagram the following syllogism step by step:

No Republicans are collectivists.

All socialists are collectivists.

Therefore, no socialists are Republicans.

In this example, *socialists* is the minor term, *Republicans* is the major term, and *collectivists* is the middle term. See Figure 6 for the three circles required, labeled appropriately.

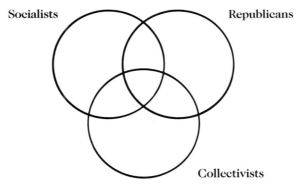

Figure 6.   Before either premise has been diagrammed.

We fill in this diagram by diagramming the premises of the argument just as we diagrammed the A-, E-, I-, and O-claims earlier. The premises in the above example are diagrammed like this: First: No Republicans are collectivists (Figure 7). Notice that in this figure we have shaded out the entire area where the Republican and collectivist circles overlap.

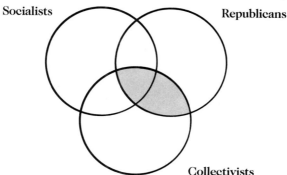

Figure 7.   One premise diagrammed.

Second: All socialists are collectivists (Figure 8). Since diagramming the premises resulted in the shading of the entire area where the socialist and Republican circles overlap, and since that is exactly what we would do to diagram the syllogism's conclusion, we can conclude that the syllogism is valid. In general, a syllogism is valid if and only if diagramming the premises automatically produces a correct diagram of the conclusion. (The one exception is discussed later in this appendix.)

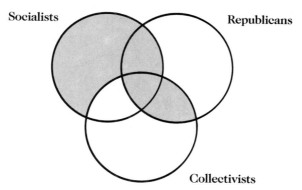

Figure 8.   Both premises diagrammed.

When one of the premises of a syllogism is an I or O, there can be a problem about where to put the required X. The following example presents such a problem (see Figure 9 for the diagram). Note in the diagram that we have numbered the different areas in order to refer to them easily.

Some S are not M.

All P are M.

Some S are not P.

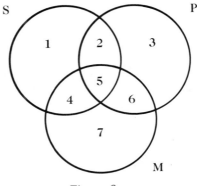

Figure 9

An X in either area 1 or area 2 of Figure 9 will make the claim "Some S are not M" true, since an inhabitant of either area is an S but not an M. How do we determine which area should get the X? In some cases, the decision can be made for us: *When one premise is an A or E and the other is an I or O, diagram the A or E premise first.* (Always shade before putting in Xs.) Refer to Figure 10 to see what happens with the current example when we follow this rule.

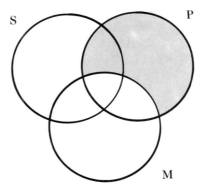

Figure 10

Once the A-claim has been diagrammed, there is no longer a choice about where to put the X—it has to go in area 1. Hence, the completed diagram for this argument looks like Figure 11. And from this diagram we can read the conclusion "Some S are not P," which tells us that the argument is valid.

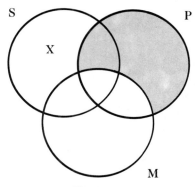

Figure 11

In some syllogisms the rule just explained does not help. For example:

All P are M.

Some S are M.

Some S are P.

A syllogism like this one still leaves us in doubt as to where to put the X even after we have diagrammed the A premise:

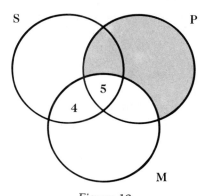

Figure 12

Should the X go in area 4 or 5? When such a question remains unresolved, here is the rule to follow: *An X that can go in either of two areas goes on the line separating the areas,* as in Figure 13.

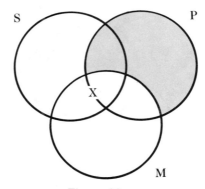

Figure 13

In essence, an X on a line says that it belongs in one or the other of the two areas, maybe both, but we don't know which. When the time comes to see whether the diagram yields the conclusion, we look to see whether there is an X *entirely* within the appropriate area. In the current example, we would need an X entirely within the area where S and P overlap; since there is no such X, the argument is invalid. An X *partly* within the appropriate area fails to establish the conclusion.

A last point before leaving Venn diagrams. When both premises of a syllogism are A- or E-claims and the conclusion is an I- or O-claim, diagramming the premises cannot possibly yield a diagram of the conclusion (because A- and E-claims produce only shading, and I- and O-claims require an X to be read from the diagram). In such a case, remember our assumption that every class we are dealing with has at least one member. This assumption justifies our looking at the diagram and determining whether any circle has all but one of its areas shaded out. *If any circle has only one area remaining unshaded, an X should be put in that area.* This is the case because any member of that class has to be in that remaining area. Sometimes placing the X in this way will enable us to read the conclusion, in which case the argument is valid (on the assumption that the relevant class is not empty), and sometimes it will not, in which case the argument is invalid, with or without any assumptions about classes having members.

EXERCISE A1-5

Use the diagram method to determine which of the following syllogisms are valid and which are invalid.

★1. No clothes made from cotton are clothes that won't shrink.
   All clothes that won't shrink are clothes that are too big in the store.
   No clothes that are too big in the store are clothes made from cotton.
2. All sound arguments are valid arguments.

   Some valid arguments are not interesting arguments.
   Some sound arguments are not interesting arguments.

3. All topologists are mathematicians.
   Some topologists are not statisticians.
   Some mathematicians are not statisticians.

★4. Every time Louis is tired he's edgy. He's edgy today, so he must be tired today.

5. Every voter is a citizen, but some citizens are not residents. Therefore, some voters are not residents.

6. All the dominant seventh chords are in the mixolydian mode, and no mixolydian chords use the major scale. So no chords that use the major scale are dominant sevenths.

★7. All halyards are lines that attach to sails. Painters do not attach to sails, so they must not be halyards.

8. Only systems with removable disks can give you unlimited storage capacity of a practical sort. Standard hard disks never have removable disks, so they can't give you practical, unlimited storage capacity.

9. All citizens are residents. So, since no noncitizens are voters, all voters must be residents.

★10. No citizens are nonresidents, and all voters are citizens. So all residents must be nonvoters.

EXERCISE A1-6

Put the following arguments in standard form (you may have to use the obversion, conversion, or contraposition operations to accomplish this); then determine whether the arguments are valid by means of diagrams.

★1. No blank disks contain any data, although some blank disks are formatted. Therefore, some formatted disks do not contain any data.

2. All ears of corn with white tassels are unripe, but some ears are ripe even though their kernels are not full-sized. Therefore, some ears with full-sized kernels are not ears with white tassels.

3. Prescription drugs should never be taken without a doctor's order. So no over-the-counter drugs are prescription drugs, because all over-the-counter drugs can be taken without a doctor's order.

★4. All tobacco products are damaging to people's health, but some of them are addictive substances. Some addictive substances, therefore, are damaging to people's health.

5. A few compact disk players use 4x sampling, so some of them must cost at least a hundred dollars, because you can't buy any machine with 4x sampling for less than a hundred dollars.

6. Everything that Pete won at the carnival must be junk. I know that Pete won everything that Bob won, and all the stuff that Bob won is junk.

★7. Only people who hold stock in the company may vote, so Mr. Hansen must not hold any stock in the company because I know he was not allowed to vote.

8. No off-road vehicles are allowed in the unimproved portion of the park, but some off-road vehicles are not four-wheel-drive. So some four-wheel-drive vehicles are allowed in the unimproved part of the park.

9. Some of the people affected by the new drainage tax are residents of the county, and many residents of the county are already paying the sewer tax. So it must be that some people paying the sewer tax are affected by the new drainage tax too.

★10. No argument with false premises is sound, but some of them are valid. So some unsound arguments must be valid.

The Rules Method of Testing for Validity. The diagram method of testing syllogisms for validity is intuitive, but there is a faster method that makes use of three simple rules. These rules are based on two ideas, the first of which has been mentioned already: affirmative and negative categorical claims. (Remember, the A- and I-claims are affirmative; the E- and O-claims are negative.) The other idea is that of *distribution*. When terms occur in categorical claims, they are either distributed or undistributed, which means only that the claim either says something about every member of the class the term names or it does not. Three of the standard-form claims distribute one or more of their terms. In Figure 14, the circled letters stand for distributed terms and the uncircled ones stand for undistributed terms. As the figure shows, the A-claim distributes its subject term, the O-claim distributes its predicate term, the E-claim distributes both, and the I-claim distributes neither.

> A-claim: All Ⓢ are P.
> E-claim: No Ⓢ are Ⓟ.
> I-claim: Some S are P.
> O-claim: Some S are not Ⓟ.

Figure 14. Distributed terms.

We can now state the three *rules of the syllogism*. A syllogism is valid if and only if all these conditions are met.

1. The number of negative claims in the premises must be the same as the number of negative claims in the conclusion. (Since the conclusion is always one claim, this implies that no valid syllogism has two negative premises.)
2. At least one premise must distribute the middle term.
3. Any term that is distributed in the conclusion of the syllogism must be distributed in its premises.

These rules are easy to remember and, with a bit of practice, you can use them to determine quickly whether a syllogism is valid.

Which of the rules is broken in this example?

All pianists are keyboard players.

Some keyboard players are not percussionists.

Some pianists are not percussionists.

The term *keyboard players* is the middle term, and it is undistributed in both premises. The first premise, an A-claim, does not distribute its predicate term; the second premise, an O-claim, does not distribute its subject term. So this syllogism breaks rule 2.

Another example:

No dogs up for adoption at the animal shelter are pedigreed dogs.

Some pedigreed dogs are expensive dogs.

Some dogs up for adoption at the animal shelter are expensive dogs.

This syllogism breaks rule 1, since it has a negative premise but no negative conclusion.

A last example:

No mercantilists are large landowners.

All mercantilists are creditors.

No creditors are large landowners.

The minor term, *creditors,* is distributed in the conclusion (since it's the subject term of an E-claim) but not in the premises (where it's the predicate term of an A-claim). So this syllogism breaks rule 3.

EXERCISE A1-7

Refer back to Exercise A1-6 and check the arguments for validity by using the rules of the syllogism. Note: Which rule is broken may depend on how you got the argument into standard form (e.g., by using operations on either a premise or on the conclusion). Answers to numbers 2, 5, 7, and 8 are given in the answer section.

EXERCISE A1-8

Apply the rules to the syllogisms in Exercise 9-7. (Answers to items 2, 4, 6, 8, and 10 are provided in the answer section at the end of the book.)

Appendix 2
Truth-Functional Logic

It was not until the late nineteenth and early twentieth centuries that **truth-functional logic** (known also as "propositional" or "sentential" logic) was systematized, which made its real power apparent. For purposes of this book, truth-functional logic is important mainly as a tool for analyzing and evaluating arguments. But it is also important in symbolic logic and the foundations of mathematics. We can think of its notions of true and false for claims analogically as on/off switches for electrical circuits, a concept that was the basis for the development of the modern digital computer.

Claim Variables. In the previous appendix we used capital letters to stand for terms in categorical claims. In this appendix, we'll use such letters to stand for claims. Our main interest is now in the way words like *not, and, or,* and so on affect claims and link them together to produce compound claims out of simpler ones. So don't confuse the Ps and Qs that appear in this appendix with the term variables that we used in Appendix 1.

Truth Tables. In truth-functional logic any given claim, P, is either true or false. The following little table, called a **truth table**, displays both possible truth values for P:

P
T
F

Whatever truth value the claim P might have, its *negation* (or contradictory), not-P—or, as we'll symbolize it, ~P—will have the other. Here is the truth table for negation:

P	~P
T	F
F	T

The left-hand column of this table sets out both possible truth values for P, and the right-hand column sets out the truth values for ~P based on P's values. This is a way of defining the negation sign, ~, in front of the P. The symbol means "change the truth value from T to F or from F to T, depending on P's values." Since T and F are opposites, P and ~P are negations of each other, although only one is preceded by the negation sign. In a moment we'll define other symbols by means of truth tables, so make sure you understand how this one works.

Since any given claim is either true or false, two claims, P and Q, must both be true, both be false, or have opposite truth values, for a total of four possible combinations. Here are the possibilities in truth-table form:

P	Q
T	T
T	F
F	T
F	F

A **conjunction** is a compound claim made from two simpler claims. *A conjunction is true if and only if both the simpler claims that make it up (its "conjuncts") are true.* We'll express the conjunction of P and Q by connecting them with an ampersand (&). The truth table for conjunctions looks like this:

P	Q	P & Q
T	T	T
T	F	F
F	T	F
F	F	F

P & Q is true in the first row only, where both P and Q are true. Notice that the "truth conditions" in this row match those required in the italicized remark above.

Here's another way to remember how conjunctions work: If either part of a conjunction is false, the conjunction itself is false. Notice finally that the word *and* is the closest representative in English to our ampersand symbol, but there are others that are correctly symbolized by the ampersand: *but* and *while,* for instance, as well as phrases like *even though.* So if we let P stand for "Parsons is in class" and Q stand for "Quincy is absent," then we should represent "Parsons is in class even though Quincy is absent" by P & Q. The reason, of course, is that the compound claim is true only in one case: where both parts are true. And that's all it takes to require an ampersand to represent the connecting word or phrase.

A **disjunction** is another compound claim made up of two simpler claims called "disjuncts." *A disjunction is false if and only if both its disjuncts are false.* We'll use the symbol v to represent disjunction when we symbolize claims— the closest word in English to this symbol is *or,* although none of our truth-functional symbols are *exactly* the same as their English counterparts, as we'll see later. The truth table for disjunctions is this:

P	Q	P v Q
T	T	T
T	F	T
F	T	T
F	F	F

Notice here that a disjunction is false only in the last row, where both of its disjuncts are false. In all other cases a disjunction is true.

The third kind of compound claim made from two simpler claims is the **conditional.** We'll use an arrow to symbolize conditionals: P → Q. The first claim in a conditional, the P in our symbolization, is the *antecedent,* the second—Q in this case—is the *consequent. A conditional claim is false if and only if its antecedent is true and its consequent is false.* The truth table for conditionals looks like this:

P	Q	P → Q
T	T	T
T	F	F
F	T	T
F	F	T

Only in the second row, where the antecedent P is true and the consequent Q is false does the conditional turn out to be false. In all other cases it is true. The closest English version of our arrow symbol is the expression *if . . . then . . .* The part following the word *if* is the antecedent and the part following *then* is the consequent. So *P → Q* says, roughly, "if P then Q."

Our truth-functional symbols can work in combination. Consider, for example, the claim *If Paula doesn't go to work, then Quincy will have to work a double shift.* We'll represent the two simple claims in the obvious way, as follows:

P = Paula goes to work.
Q = Quincy has to work a double shift.

And we can symbolize the entire claim like this:

~P → Q

Here is a truth table for this symbolization:

P	Q	~P	~P → Q
T	T	F	T
T	F	F	T
F	T	T	T
F	F	T	F

Notice that the symbolized claim ~P → Q is false in the *last* row of this table. That's because here and only here the antecedent, ~P, is true and its consequent, Q, is false. Notice that we work from the simplest parts to the most complex: The truth value of P in a given row determines the truth value of ~P, and that truth value in turn, along with the one for Q, determines the truth value of ~P → Q.

Another combination: "If Paula goes to work, then Quincy and Rogers will get a day off." This claim is symbolized this way:

P → (Q & R)

This symbolization requires parentheses in order to prevent confusion with (P → Q) & R, which symbolizes a different claim and has a different truth table. Our claim is a conditional with a conjunction for a consequent, whereas (P → Q) & R is a conjunction with a conditional as one of the conjuncts. The parentheses are what makes this clear.

You need to know several principles in order to produce the truth table for the symbolized claim P → (Q & R). First you have to know how to set up all the possible combinations of true and false for the three simple claims P, Q, and R. In claims with only one letter, there were two possibilities, T and F. In claims with two letters, there were four possibilities. *Every time we add another letter the number of possible combinations of T and F doubles, and so, therefore, does the number of rows in our truth table.* The formula for determining the number of rows in a truth table for a compound claim is $r = 2^n$, where r is the number of rows in the table and n is the number of letters in the symbolization. Since the claim we are interested in has three letters, our truth table will have eight rows, one for each possible combination of T and F for P, Q, and R. Here's how we do it:

P	Q	R
T	T	T
T	T	F
T	F	T
T	F	F
F	T	T
F	T	F
F	F	T
F	F	F

The systematic way to construct such a table is to alternate Ts and Fs in the right-hand column, then alternate *pairs* of Ts and *pairs* of Fs in the next column to the left, then sets of *four* Ts and sets of *four* Fs in the next, and so forth. The leftmost column will always wind up being half Ts and half Fs.

The second thing we have to know is that the truth value of a compound claim in any particular case (i.e., any row of its truth table) depends entirely upon the truth values of its parts, and if these parts are themselves compound, their truth values depend upon those of their parts, and so on until we get down to letters standing alone. The columns under the letters, which you have just learned to construct, will then tell us what we need to know. Let's build a truth table for $P \rightarrow (Q \& R)$ and see how this works.

P	Q	R	Q & R	P → (Q & R)
T	T	T	T	T
T	T	F	F	F
T	F	T	F	F
T	F	F	F	F
F	T	T	T	T
F	T	F	F	T
F	F	T	F	T
F	F	F	F	T

The three columns at the left, under P, Q, and R, are our *reference columns*, set up just as we discussed above. They determine what goes on in the rest of the table. From the second and third columns, under the Q and the R, we can fill in the column under (Q & R). Notice that this column contains a T only in the first and fifth rows, where both Q and R are true. Next, from the column under the P and the one under (Q & R), we can fill in the last column, which is the one for the entire symbolized claim. It contains Fs in only rows two, three, and four, which are the only ones where its antecedent is true and its consequent is false.

What our table gives us is a *truth-functional analysis* of our original claim. Such an analysis displays what truth value a compound claim has given the truth values of its simpler parts.

A final note before we turn to tips for symbolizing compound claims: Two claims are **truth-functionally equivalent** if they have exactly the same truth table—that is, if the Ts and Fs in the column under one claim are in the same arrangement as those in the column under the other. Generally speaking, when two claims are equivalent, one can be used in place of another—truth-functionally, they each imply the other.*

Symbolizing Compound Claims. Most of the things we can do with symbolized claims are pretty straightforward; that is, if you learn the techniques, you can apply them in a relatively clear-cut way. What's less clear-cut is how to get a claim symbolized in the first place. We'll cover a few tips for symbolization in this section, then give you a chance to practice with some exercises.

Remember, when you symbolize a claim you're displaying its truth-functional structure. The idea is to produce a version that will be truth-functionally equivalent to the original informal claim, that is, one that will be true under all the same circumstances as the original and false under all the same circumstances. Let's go through an example or two.

If and *only if*

(1) Quincy will get the day off if Paula goes to work.

Now, let's ask ourselves "What would it take to make this false?" We hope it's clear that this compound claim is false in case Paula goes to work but Quincy does not get the day off. Using P for "Paula goes to work" and Q for "Quincy gets the day off," the claim is false when P is true but Q is false. Now ask yourself, What symbolization is false under exactly these circumstances? (Look back at the truth tables for the connectives if you need to.) Notice that P → Q is false under just these conditions, and that is the correct symbolization of the claim.

One thing we can gather from this is that "if" introduces the antecedent of a conditional claim, even if it comes later in the sentence than the consequent. Remember, it's the logical words alone that determine the compound claim's structure, not the locations of its simpler parts.

Consider this one:

(2) Quincy will get the day off only if Paula goes to work.

---

*The exceptions to this remark are due to *nontruth*-functional nuances that claims sometimes have. Most compound claims of the form P & Q, for example, are interchangeable with what are called their commutations, Q & P. That is, it doesn't matter which conjunct comes first. (Note that this is also true of disjunctions but *not* of conditionals.) But at times *and* has more than a truth-functional meaning, and in such cases which conjunct comes first can make a difference. In "Daniel got on the train and bought his ticket," the word *and* would ordinarily mean "and then." So "Daniel bought his ticket and got on the train" turns out to be a different claim from the previous one; it says that he did the two things in a different order from that stated in the first claim. This temporal-ordering sense of *and* is part of the claim's occasional nontruthfunctional meaning.

If we think about what will make this false, what comes to mind? Notice that the claim says Quincy will get the day off only in one situation—where Paula goes to work. So the claim is false if he gets the day off *without* Paula's going to work. So the falsifying circumstances are Quincy's going to work (Q is true) and Paula's not going to work (P is false). The symbolization that turns out false in exactly that case is Q → P, and that's what we want for this one.

But what of our earlier rule that *if* introduces the antecedents of conditionals? Well, in this case, P is introduced by *only if* rather than *if* alone, and *only if* introduces the consequent of a conditional claim. Check yourself with this little exercise:

EXERCISE A2-1

Symbolize the following using the same claim variables as in the text above. (You can ignore differences in past, present, and future tense.)

★ 1. Paula will go to work if Quincy gets the day off.
★ 2. If Quincy gets the day off, Paula will go to work.
★ 3. Paula will go to work only if Quincy gets the day off.
★ 4. Only if Paula goes to work will Quincy get the day off.
★ 5. Quincy will get the day off if and only if Paula goes to work.

Number 5 introduced a new wrinkle, the phrase *if and only if*. Remembering our rules of thumb about how *if* and *only if* operate separately, it shouldn't surprise us that *if and only if* makes both antecedent and consequent out of the claim it introduces. We can make P both antecedent and consequent this way:

$$(P \rightarrow Q) \ \& \ (Q \rightarrow P)$$

We'll give some more tips on symbolization below, without such extensive commentary.

Either.   The word *either* tells us where a disjunction begins. It helps distinguish between *P and either Q or R* and *Either P and Q or R*. In the second, the disjunction begins at the beginning of the claim, so the first disjunct will be a conjunction, *P and Q*. The first claim is a conjunction. Without the word *either*, the claim would be ambiguous. (In fact, remembering Chapter 2, we know it's syntactically ambiguous.)

Unless.   If we were to symbolize the claim, *Paula will go to work unless Quincy gets the day off*, we might come up with

$$\sim Q \rightarrow P$$

This is correct, since the claim says the same as *If Quincy does not get the day off then Paula will go to work*. If you check to see which of our symbols (see pages 369–370) has exactly the same truth table as $\sim Q \rightarrow P$, it may surprise you. *Unless,* as it turns out, gives us another way of stating a disjunction.

Necessary and Sufficient Conditions. If X is a necessary condition for Y, then the truth of Y guarantees the truth of X, since we can't have Y without it. This amounts to saying that, if Y is present, then X must be present too. So a necessary condition appears as the consequent of a conditional claim.

If X is a sufficient condition for Y, then the truth of X is enough to guarantee that of Y. So a sufficient condition appears as the antecedent of a conditional. If X is claimed to be both necessary and sufficient for Y, then we make a conjunction of the two conditionals just as we did for *if and only if:* (P → Q) & (Q → P).

Now for some more practice.

EXERCISE A2-2

One test of your understanding of the truth-functional structure of a claim is your ability to symbolize it correctly. For each of the items below, let

P = Parsons objects
Q = Quincy turns the radio down
R = Rachel closes her door

and symbolize the claim using the symbols ~, &, v, and →.

EXAMPLE: If Parsons objects, then Quincy will turn the radio down but Rachel will not close her door.
SYMBOLIZATION: P → (Q & ~R)

Most of the difficult problems are answered in the answer section, but you should not consult it until you have come up with your own best attempt.

★1. If Parsons objects then Quincy will turn the radio down, and Rachel will close her door.
2. If Parsons objects, then Quincy will turn the radio down and Rachel will close her door.
3. If Parsons objects and Quincy turns the radio down then Rachel will close her door.
★4. If Parsons objects then if Quincy turns the radio down then Rachel will close her door.
5. Either Parsons objects or if Quincy turns the radio down then Rachel will close her door.
6. If either Parsons objects or Quincy turns the radio down then Rachel will close her door.
★7. If Parsons objects then either Quincy will turn the radio down or Rachel will close her door.
8. If Parsons objects then neither will Quincy turn the radio down nor will Rachel close her door.
9. If Parsons does not object then Quincy will turn the radio down.
★10. It is not the case that if Parsons objects then Quincy will turn the radio down.

11. Quincy will turn the radio down if Parsons objects.
12. Quincy will turn the radio down only if Parsons objects.
★13. Quincy will not turn the radio down unless Parsons objects.
14. Rachel will close her door unless Quincy turns the radio down.
15. Quincy will turn the radio down, but only if Parsons objects.

EXERCISE A2-3

Construct truth tables for the symbolizations you produced for Exercise A2-2. Determine whether any of them are truth-functionally equivalent to any others. (Answers to items 1, 4, and 10 are provided in the answer section at the end of the book.)

Truth-Functional Argument Patterns. Truth tables and other truth-functional methods provide us with another means of looking at and evaluating argument patterns. Let's consider a simple example. Let P and Q represent any two claims. Now look at the following argument:

P → Q
~P
Therefore, ~Q

We can construct a truth table for this argument by including a column for each premise and one for the conclusion. Here's what such a table looks like:

P	Q	~P	~Q	P → Q
T	T	F	F	T
T	F	F	T	F
F	T	T	F	T
F	F	T	T	T

The first two columns are reference columns, since they are for the letters that appear in the argument. The third and fifth columns appear under the two premises of the argument, and the fourth column is for the conclusion. Note that in the third row of the table both premises are true and the conclusion is false. This tells us that it is possible for the premises of this argument to be true while the conclusion is false, and thus that the argument is invalid. Since it doesn't matter what claims P and Q might be standing for, the same is true for *every* argument of this pattern. Here's an example of such an argument:

If the Forty-Niners beat Dallas, then the Rams will make the playoffs; but the Forty-Niners did not beat Dallas, so the Rams won't make the playoffs.

The first premise is a conditional, and the other premise is the negation of the antecedent of that conditional. The conclusion is the negation of the conditional's consequent. Thus this argument fits the pattern above and accordingly is invalid.

Here's an example of a slightly more complicated argument:

If Scarlet is guilty of the crime, then Ms. White must have left the back door unlocked and the colonel must have retired before ten o'clock. However, either Ms. White did not leave the back door unlocked or the colonel did not retire before ten. Therefore, Scarlet is not guilty of the crime.

Let's assign some letters to the simple claims so we can show this argument's pattern.

S = Scarlet is guilty of the crime.
W = Ms. White left the back door unlocked.
C = The colonel retired before ten o'clock.

Now we symbolize it to display this pattern:

S → (W & C)
~W v ~ C
_____
~S

Let's think our way through this argument. As you read, refer back to the symbolized version above. Notice that the first premise is a conditional, with *Scarlet is guilty of the crime* as antecedent and a conjunction as consequent. In order for that conjunction to be true, both "Ms. White left the back door unlocked" and "The colonel retired before ten o'clock" have to be true, as you'll recall from the truth table for conjunctions. Now look at the second premise. It is a disjunction that tells us *either* Ms. White did not leave the back door unlocked *or* the colonel did not retire before ten. But if either or both of those disjuncts are true, at least one of the claims in our earlier conjunction is false. So it cannot be that *both* parts of the conjunction are true. This means the conjunction symbolized by (W & C) must be false. And so the consequent of the first premise is false. How can the entire premise be true, in that case? The only way is for the antecedent to be false as well. And that means that the conclusion, "Scarlet is not guilty of the crime," must be true.

All of this reasoning (and considerably more that we don't require) is implicit in the following truth table for the argument:

S	W	C	~W	~C	~S	W & C	S → (W & C)	~W v ~C
T	T	T	F	F	F	T	T	F
T	T	F	F	T	F	F	F	T
T	F	T	T	F	F	F	F	T
T	F	F	T	T	F	F	F	T
F	T	T	F	F	T	T	T	F
F	T	F	F	T	T	F	T	T
F	F	T	T	F	T	F	T	T
F	F	F	T	T	T	F	T	T
1	2	3	4	5	6	7	8	9

We've numbered the columns at the bottom to make reference somewhat easier. The first three are our reference columns, numbers 8 and 9 are for the premises of the argument, and number 6 is for the argument's conclusion. The remainder—4, 5, and 7—are for parts of some of the other symbolized claims; they could be left out if we desired, but they make filling in columns 8 and 9 a bit easier.

Once the table is filled in, evaluating the argument is easy. Just look to see whether there is any row in which both premises are true and the conclusion is false. One such row is enough to demonstrate the invalidity of the argument. In the present case, we find that both premises are true only in the last three rows of the table. And in those rows the conclusion is also true. So there is no set of circumstances—no row of the table—in which both premises are true and the conclusion is false. Therefore, the argument is valid.

Now, even though filling out a complete truth table always produces the correct answer regarding a truth-functional argument's validity, it can be quite a tedious chore. Fortunately, there are shorter and more manageable ways of finding such an answer. The first we'll look at we'll call the *short truth table method*. Here's the idea behind it: Since, if an argument is invalid, there has to be at least one row in the argument's truth table where the premises are true and the conclusion is false, we'll look directly for such a row. Consider this symbolized argument:

$$P \rightarrow Q$$
$$\sim Q \rightarrow R$$
$$\overline{\sim P \rightarrow R}$$

We begin by looking at the conclusion. Since it's a conditional, it can only be made false one way, by making its antecedent true and its consequent false. So we do that, by making P false and R false.

Can we now make both premises true? Yes, as it turns out, by making Q true. This case,

P	Q	R
F	T	R

makes both premises true and the conclusion false and thus proves the argument invalid. What we've done is produce the relevant row of the truth table without bothering to produce all the rest. Had the argument been valid, we would not have been able to produce such a row. So here's the idea, once again: Try to assign Ts and Fs to the letters in the symbolization so that all premises come out true and the conclusion false. There may be more than one way to do it; any of them will do to prove the argument invalid. If it is impossible to make the premises and conclusion come out this way, the argument is valid.

EXERCISE A2-4

Construct truth tables to determine which of the following arguments are valid.

★1. Q v (Q → P)
    ~P
    ─────────
    ~Q

2. P → Q
    ~Q
    ─────────
    ~P

3. F v (Q → P)
    Q v ~P
    ─────────
    ~F

★4. P → (Q → R)
    P → Q
    ─────────
    R

5. P v (Q → R)
    Q & ~R
    ─────────
    ~P

6. (P → Q) v (R → Q)
    ~P → ~R
    ─────────────────
    Q

★7. (P & R) → Q
    ~Q
    ─────────
    ~P

8. P & (~Q → ~P)
    R → ~Q
    ─────────────
    ~R

9. (L v ~J)
    R → J
    ─────────
    L → R

10. ~F v (G & H)
    P → F
    ─────────────
    ~H → ~P

Deductions. Besides using truth tables, there is another method for evaluating the validity of an argument. If an argument is invalid, this method is not very useful for proving its invalidity, although it can provide some strong hints. The method is that of **deduction**; it involves actually deducing (or "deriving") the conclusion from the premises by means of a series of basic truth-functionally valid argument patterns and equivalences, or, as we call them here, truth-functional rules. How the system works will become clearer as we introduce the first few rules.

Group I Rules: Elementary Valid Argument Patterns

Rule 1: Modus Ponens (MP). Any argument of the pattern

$$P \rightarrow Q$$
$$\underline{P}$$
$$Q$$

is valid. That is, if you have a conditional among the premises, and the antecedent of that conditional occurs as another premise, then modus ponens says that the consequent of the conditional follows from those two premises. The claims involved do not have to be simple letters standing alone—it would have made no difference if, in place of P, we had had something more complicated, like (P v R), as long as that compound claim appeared everywhere that P appears in the pattern above.

If the consequent of the conditional is the conclusion of the argument, then the deduction is finished—the conclusion has been established. If it is not the conclusion of the argument you're working on, the consequent of the conditional can be listed just as if it were another premise to use in deducing the conclusion you're after. An example:

1. $P \rightarrow R$
2. $R \rightarrow S$
3. P   Therefore, S.

We've numbered the three premises of the argument and set its conclusion off to the side. (Hereafter we'll use a slash and three dots [/∴] in place of *therefore* to indicate what the conclusion is.) Now, notice that line 1 is a conditional, and line 3 is its antecedent. Modus ponens will allow us to write down the consequent of line 1 as a new line in our deduction:

4. R   1,3,MP

At the right we've noted the initials of the rule we used and the lines the rule required. These notes are called the *annotation* for the deduction. We can now make use of this new line in the deduction to get the conclusion we were originally after, namely S.

5. S   2,4,MP

Again, we used modus ponens, this time on lines 2 and 4. The same explanation as that for deriving line 4 from lines 1 and 3 applies here.

Rule 2: Modus Tollens (MT). The modus tollens pattern is this:

P → Q
~Q
___
~P

That is, if you have a conditional claim as one premise, and one of your other premises is the negation of the consequent of that conditional, you can write down the negation of the conditional's antecedent as a new line in your deduction. Here's a deduction that uses both of the first two rules:

1. (P & Q) → R
2. S
3. S → ~R   /∴~(P & Q)
4. ~R   2, 3, MP
5. ~(P & Q)   1, 4, MT

In this deduction we derived line 4 from lines 2 and 3 by modus ponens, and then 4 and 1 gave us line 5, which is what we were after, by modus tollens. The fact that the antecedent of line 1 is itself a compound claim, (P & Q), is not important; our line 5 is the antecedent of the conditional with a negation sign in front of it, and that's all that counts.

Rule 3: Chain Argument (CA).

P → Q
Q → R
___
P → R

This rule allows you to derive a conditional from two you already have, provided the antecedent of one of your conditionals is the same as the consequent of the other.

Rule 4: Simplification (SIM).

P & Q   P & Q
___   ___
P   Q

From any conjunction you can pull one conjunct out as a new line in your deduction.

Rule 5: Addition (ADD).

P   Q
___   ___
P v Q   P v Q

From any claim, any disjunction that has that claim as a disjunct may be derived.

Rule 6: Conjunction (CONJ).

> P
> Q
> ――
> P & Q

This rule allows you to put any two lines of a deduction together in the form of a conjunction.

Rule 7: Disjunctive Argument (DA).

> P v Q   P v Q
> ~P   ~Q
> ――   ――
> Q   P

From a disjunction and the negation of one disjunct, the other disjunct may be derived.

Rule 8: Constructive Dilemma (CD).

> P → Q
> R → S
> P v R
> ――――
> Q v S

The disjunction of the antecedents of any two conditionals allows the derivation of the disjunction of their consequents.

Rule 9: Destructive Dilemma (DD).

> P → Q
> R → S
> ~Q v ~S
> ―――――
> ~P v ~R

The disjunction of the negations of the consequents of two conditionals allows the derivation of the disjunction of the negations of their antecedents. (Refer to the pattern above as you read this and it will make a lot more sense.)

EXERCISE A2-5

For each of the following groups of symbolized claims, identify which of the Group I rules was used to derive the last line.

★1. P → (Q & R)
     (Q & R) → (S v T)
     P → (S v T)

★2. (P & S) v (T → R)
    ~(P & S)
    (T → R)

★3. P v (Q & R)
    (Q & R) → S
    P → T
    S v T

★4. (P v R) → Q
    ~Q
    ~(P v R)

★5. (Q → T) → S
    ~S v ~P
    R → P
    ~(Q → T) v ~R

Group II Rules: Truth-Functional Equivalences

A claim or part of a claim may be replaced by any claim or part of a claim to which it is equivalent by one of the following equivalence rules. Don't despair if this sounds complicated. The way such replacement works will become clear after a few examples.

There are a couple of differences between these rules on equivalences and the rules explained so far. First, these rules allow us to go two ways instead of one—from either claim to its equivalent. Second, these rules allow us to replace part of a claim with an equivalent part, rather than having to deal with entire lines of a deduction all at once. In the examples that follow the first few rules, watch for both of these differences.

We'll use a double arrow (↔) to indicate the equivalence of two claims.

Rule 10: Double Negation (DN).

P ↔ ~~P

This rule allows you to add or remove two negation signs in front of any claim, whether simple or compound. For example, this rule allows the derivation of either of the following from the other,

P → (Q v R)   P → ~~(Q v R)

since the rule guarantees that (Q v R) and its double negation, ~~(Q v R), are equivalent. This in turn guarantees that P → (Q v R) and P → ~~(Q v R) are equivalent, and hence that each implies the other.

Here's an example of DN at work:

1. P v ~(Q → R)
2. (Q → R)   /∴P

3. ~~(Q → R)   2, DN
4. P   1, 3, DA

Rule 11: Commutation (COM).

(P & Q) ↔ (Q & P)
(P v Q) ↔ (Q v P)

This rule simply allows any conjunction or disjunction to be "turned around," so that the conjuncts or disjuncts occur in reverse order.

Rule 12: Implication (IMPL). This rule allows us to change a conditional into a disjunction and vice versa.

(P → Q) ↔ (~P v Q)

Rule 13: Contraposition (CONTR). If this rule reminds you of the categorical operation of contraposition (see Appendix 1), that's because this rule is its truth-functional version.

(P → Q) ↔ (~Q → ~P)

This rule allows us to exchange the places of a conditional's antecedent and consequent, but only by putting on or taking off a negation sign in front of each.

Rule 14: DeMorgan's Laws (DEM).

~(P & Q) ↔ (~P v ~Q)
~(P v Q) ↔ (~P & ~Q)

Notice that when the negation sign is "moved inside" the parentheses, the & changes into a v or vice versa.

Rule 15: Exportation (EXP).

[P → (Q → R)] ↔ [(P & Q) → R]

Square brackets are used exactly as parentheses are.

Rule 16: Association (ASSOC).

[P & (Q & R)] ↔ [(P & Q) & R]
[P v (Q v R)] ↔ [(P v Q) v R]

Rule 17: Distribution (DIST).

[P & (Q v R)] ↔ [(P & Q) v (P & R)]
[P v (Q & R)] ↔ [(P v Q) & (P v R)]

Rule 18: Tautology (TAUT).

(P v P) ↔ P
(P & P) ↔ P

EXERCISE A2-6

The annotations that explain how each line was derived have been left off the following deductions. For each line, supply the rule used and the numbers of any earlier lines the rule requires.

★1. 1. P → Q   (Premise)
     2. R → S   (Premise)
     3. Q → ~S   (Premise)   /∴P→~R
     4. P → ~S
     5. ~S → ~R
     6. P → ~R

2.   1. ~P   (Premise)
     2. (Q → R) & (R → Q) (Premise)
     3. R v P   (Premise)   /∴Q
     4. R
     5. R → Q
     6. Q

3.   1. P → Q   (Premise)
     2. R → (~S v T)   (Premise)
     3. ~P → R   (Premise)   /∴(~Q & S) → T
     4. ~Q → ~P
     5. ~Q → R
     6. ~Q → (~S v T)
     7. ~Q → (S → T)
     8. (~Q & S) → T

★4. 1. (P & Q) → T   (Premise)
     2. P   (Premise)
     3. ~Q → ~P   (Premise)   /∴T
     4. P → Q
     5. Q
     6. (P & Q)
     7. T

5.   1. ~(S v R)   (Premise)
     2. P → S   (Premise)
     3. T → (P v R)   (Premise)   /∴~T
     4. ~S & ~R
     5. ~S

6. ~P
7. ~R
8. ~P & ~R
9. ~(P v R)
10. ~T

EXERCISE A2-7

Derive the indicated conclusions from the premises supplied.

★1. 1. P → R
     2. R → Q   /∴~P v Q

 2. 1. ~P v S
     2. ~T → ~S   /∴P → T

 3. 1. F → R
     2. L → S
     3. ~C
     4. (R & S) → C   /∴~F v ~L

★4. 1. P v (Q & R)
     2. (P v Q) → S   /∴S

 5. 1. (S & R) → P
     2. (R → P) → W
     3. S   /∴W

 6. 1. ~L → (~P → M)
     2. ~(P v L)   /∴M

★7. 1. (M v R) & P
     2. ~S → ~P
     3. S → ~M   /∴R

 8. 1. Q → L
     2. P → M
     3. R v P
     4. R → (Q & S)   /∴~M→L

 9. 1. Q → S
     2. P → (S & L)
     3. ~P → Q
     4. S → R   /∴R & S

★10. 1. P v (R & Q)
     2. R → ~P
     3. Q → T   /∴R→T

EXERCISE A2-8

Display the truth-functional form of the following arguments by symbolizing them; then use either the truth-table method, the short truth-table method, or the method of deduction to prove them valid or invalid. Use the letters provided.

EXAMPLE: If Maria does not go to the movies, then she will help Bob with his logic homework. Bob will fail the course unless Maria helps him with his logic homework. Therefore, if Maria goes to the movies, Bob will fail the course. (M, H, F)

SYMBOLIZATION: 1. ~M → H   (Premise)
                2. ~H → F   (Premise) /∴M→F

TRUTH TABLE:

M	H	F	~M	~H	~M → H	~H → F	M → F
T	T	T	F	F	T	T	T
T	T	F	F	F	T	T	F

We need to go only as far as the second row of the table, since both premises came out true and the conclusion comes out false in that row.

★1. If it's cold, Dale's motorcycle won't start. If Dale is not late for work, then his motorcycle must have started. Therefore, if it's cold, Dale is late for work. (C, S, L)

2. If profits depend on unsound environmental practices, then either the quality of the environment will deteriorate or profits will drop. Jobs will be plentiful only if profits do not drop. So, either jobs will not be plentiful or the quality of the environment will deteriorate. (U, Q, D, J)

3. The new road will not be built unless the planning commission approves the funds. But the planning commission's approval of the funds will come only if the environmental impact report is positive, and it can't be positive if the road will ruin Mill Creek. So, unless they find a way for the road not to ruin Mill Creek, it won't be built. (R, A, E, M)

★4. The message will not be understood unless the code is broken. The killer will not be caught if the message is not understood. Either the code will be broken or Holmes's plan will fail. But Holmes's plan will not fail if he is given enough time. Therefore, if Holmes is given enough time, the killer will be caught. (M, C, K, H, T)

5. If the senator votes against this bill, then he is opposed to penalties against tax evaders. Also, if the senator is a tax evader himself, then he is opposed to penalties against tax evaders. Therefore, if the senator votes against this bill, he is a tax evader himself. (V, O, T)

Appendix 3
Writing an
Argumentative Essay

Many times during your college career—and later, as well—you will have to sit down with a pen, pencil, or keyboard in hand and face the enemy: a blank piece of paper that has to be converted somehow into an essay. Although there are other kinds of writing you'll have to do from time to time, it is the argumentative essay that seems to cause students more trouble than any other variety. This appendix is designed to help you produce such essays by providing you with a program for getting organized, getting started, and getting done. What we can't do, naturally, is give you the gumption required to make you stop cleaning your room, sharpening pencils, and all the other things we do to avoid sitting down and starting to work. We're afraid you'll have to supply that yourself.

WHAT IS AN ARGUMENTATIVE ESSAY?

A piece of writing can be designed to accomplish any number of tasks. A narrative, for example, tells us what happened. It supplies us with information by describing a series of events (if it is factual) or it entertains us or makes us think about possibilities (if it is fanciful).

Argumentative essays may also supply factual information—most of them do—but their primary aim is to convince their readers of something, to settle an issue. Successful essays accomplish this by offering good arguments in favor of the side of the issue the author wishes the reader to accept. (See Chapter 1 for a discussion of *argument* and *issue*.)

Outside the classroom, we write argumentative essays all the time: letters of recommendation, proposals for change within a company, research papers, campaign literature, requests for funds for a civic project, and many letters to the editor of your local newspaper. While examples like these will vary in length, form, and style, at their hearts they are all designed to support positions on issues. Most of what follows will apply to any argumentative essay, but, with the bulk of our readers in mind, we'll concentrate primarily on the kinds of essays undergraduate students are asked to write in their courses.

You may be assigned an essay in which you are to defend a particular position on an issue. Or you may be given an issue and instructed to defend one side or another of it. Or you may have to identify an issue yourself and then choose the side you wish to defend. Whether the topic is of your choosing or your instructor's, you'll want to do the best job you can; even when you have to defend a position that you may not agree with, the practice you get will help make you a better writer in the long run.

GETTING STARTED

1. *Think about the issue.* Many students make the mistake of starting to write an essay well before they're ready to do so. You should reserve time not just for *writing* your essay but for *thinking* about it as well. If you begin writing before you have the issue thought out, you're likely to have to do a lot of starting over, or, even worse, you may wind up turning in a bad piece of work—or at least one that is well below your best.

So begin by thinking about the topic of your paper. (You should do this with a pencil in hand so that you can jot down ideas as you think of them. Don't worry too much about organization yet; that will come later. Think of this first stage as intellectual doodling.) Make certain you understand what the issue or issues are. Complicated subjects seldom boil down to a single, clear, concise issue. Rather, they tend to be messy, with the settlement of one issue sometimes difficult, impossible, or unnecessary unless certain others are settled first. Is the issue you're about to write on like this? Maybe you should refocus on a related issue that needs settling first. (Whether your town needs a new freeway—or sewer system or high school—may be important only if the town is going to grow substantially. Maybe the real issue is whether population growth should be controlled.) But it's also possible to write a *hypothetical* essay. We may not know whether we should accept claim X, but we could still argue that *if* we decide to accept X (maybe at a later time), *then* we should be prepared to accept some other claim, Y, as well. This can sometimes be a good strategy, especially when X is something we do not currently have enough data to make a judgment about.

Once you've settled on the issue, make certain you understand exactly what it is. If it isn't clear to you, it certainly won't be clear to your reader. And you certainly are not ready to begin writing.

After you've determined the issue you wish to discuss, think about what side you want to defend. You should consider all sides of the issue before you decide which one is the most defensible. It may be that your initial position will not turn out to be the best one. Each of us makes an occasional quick decision without taking the time to reason it out. And while we can sometimes get away with such tactics, it isn't the way to begin a piece of written work. So think through the position, at least in general terms, before you start to set things down on paper. You may decide that changing your mind and taking a different side is the most reasonable thing to do. Don't try to defend a lost cause just because it's the position that first appealed to you. Only the invincibly stubborn do that.

2. *Will your argument be affirmative or negative?* The kinds of positions that come most readily to mind are affirmative; that is, they offer a solution to a problem, they argue for a particular explanation for a phenomenon, they urge a particular course of action, and so on. But you should keep in mind that a perfectly good alternative is writing a *negative* paper, one designed to show that some solution, explanation, or course of action is mistaken. Essays that are critical of opposing positions are just as important as those that advance one's own position, and, as we'll see in a moment, most affirmative papers should contain at least some negative parts.

MAKING AN OUTLINE

3. *Why make an outline?* Very few people are so well organized and blessed with such good memories that they can go directly from thinking about a topic to writing a substantial essay about it. Most of us can benefit from making an outline first. If the essay is to be relatively short and about a relatively simple topic, then you may need an outline with only three or four items on it. Outlines are even more crucial for papers that are longer or that concern themselves with complex issues.

An outline will enable you to divide your labor up into parts, and this in turn can both produce a better essay and help you work on it more efficiently. While you're outlining, you don't have to be concerned with the actual words that will appear in the final product. You can concern yourself with just ideas and the structure you want your paper to have.

Later, when you're actually composing the language of the paper, you won't have to worry about what's coming next (it's already there in the outline); you can concentrate on putting together the sentences that will get the job done. And you will already have the structure of the essay down on paper. (A lack of structure, the main symptoms of which are straying from the topic at hand or never getting to the main point, is one of the most common failings of argumentative papers.) Simply sketching out an outline can be a great help in your thinking about your topic. Allow yourself enough time to do a good job. It will make the actual writing much, much easier.

4. *Why is your position on the issue the best one?* You probably didn't arrive at the position you've decided to defend (or decide to attack the position you're going to attack) just out of the blue. What are the reasons that support your position? In trying to answer this question, you're searching for premises to support your conclusion. Sort out the ones you come up with. Are they in-

dependent premises that give support for your conclusion "from different directions," as it were? Are they dependent—that is, do they work together to support your conclusion? (For a discussion of independent and dependent premises see Chapter 8.) Organize them into arguments in your outline. Here are a few things to think about when you're organizing your arguments:

- Do the premises you've identified really support your conclusion?
- Are they generally acceptable, or do you need separate arguments to support some of them?
- Are some simply too questionable to be of much use? A premise isn't very helpful if it's even more controversial than the conclusion it's supposed to support. But this doesn't mean that your premises have to be utterly bland, of course.
- Appeal to common ground when you can. Your premises may need support from other claims (which become premises in turn), and these claims may need some support themselves. But this process cannot go on forever. It's important that you try to identify claims your reader already probably accepts and show how they help support your position. For example, most people accept the claim that good schools are important. If such a fact can be brought to bear on your conclusion, so much the better.
- The other side of the previous point is that you should not belabor the obvious. Nobody likes axe murderers; don't waste time arguing that axe murder is unacceptable.
- Don't try to cover every point that has some remote relevance to your topic. You needn't say everything there is to say about a subject to write a good paper on it. And too many side issues can be distracting: *Don't get distracted from your main theme.*
- The preceding point goes for things like introductions as well as items that crop up along the way. The introduction to your paper should get right to the point; if the paper is only three pages long, you don't want to spend the first page and a half introducing your subject.
- Plan to spend most of your time and energy on points that your reader will find contentious or controversial. Be sure such claims are as well supported as you can make them. Can you think of one more argument for your most controversial claim? Do the premises that support it need just a bit more support themselves? These are questions you should ask at the outlining stage and again when you sit down to read over your first draft. If some of your reasons seem especially hard to defend, ask yourself why *you* believe them. Maybe you shouldn't.

5. *Use your sources wisely.* Don't expect your reader to accept a claim just because it comes from a source you consider to be an authority, especially if it's a claim about which experts disagree. (For a discussion of credibility of sources and expertise see Chapter 3.) Dr. J. may be an authority, but if other experts disagree with her on your subject, you should not let a citation of J. be your sole reason for advancing a claim.

6. *Anticipate objections and deal with them.* Unless your conclusions are already accepted by everybody familiar with your topic (in which case you probably should be writing about something else), there will be criticisms of your position. Try to think of what the most likely and most important ones will be, and say something about them. (For instance, if you're arguing that a new county jail should be built, someone is sure to claim that the county cannot afford to allocate sufficient funds to build one. You should anticipate such an objection and show either that the county already has the money available, that there are alternative sources of funds, or that there is some less important expenditure that could be cut back to make funds available for the jail.)

7. *Identify alternative views.* It is usually not enough to give reasons—even to *prove*—that your position is a reasonable one. There may be other positions on an issue that your reader would find equally reasonable. Say something about why such views are less attractive than yours. You should at least acknowledge the existence of alternative positions.

WRITING THE ESSAY

It must seem that you've already done most of the work you usually do when you write an essay, and all you've got for your trouble is an outline. Well, it's true that you have only an outline, but in fact a large part of your work is done. If you've done a good job of outlining, writing a draft of your paper should be easy. But that doesn't mean you should take it lightly, for the words you're now going to put on paper are the ones your reader will actually see. We have a couple more tips that we hope will help.

8. *Strive for clarity.* We can't emphasize this point too much. Have you ever heard of someone complaining that an essay was too clear? Of course not. One way you can get in trouble is with language that is vague or ambiguous. Another is by trying to write over your head. (This would be a good time to go back and read the first part of the section on complexity in Chapter 2.) Remember that almost nothing you say in your essay will be as clear to your reader as it is to you.

Unless you know or have been instructed otherwise, you should assume that your reader is an intelligent person but has no particular special knowledge of your subject. So give brief explanations of technical terms, and give examples where they would be helpful. The fact that you are writing for an instructor who probably already knows your subject does not mean that you should simply assume such knowledge. After all, your instructor wants to know whether *you* understand what you're writing about. So make sure you write a complete essay, not one with gaps you leave to your reader to fill in.

9. *Don't stray from your main theme.* We've said this before when talking about outlines, but it bears repeating. It's easy to wander off the subject and

wind up talking about something that turns out to be irrelevant. The fact that a related topic is interesting does not mean it's relevant to what you want to say. In fact, what you *avoid* saying can contribute almost as much to your essay as what you *do* say. Try to stick to the points you've made in your outline, although you should be ready to make changes if something new and important occurs to you.

10. *Watch for pseudoreasoning.* Pseudoreasoning, you should recall from the text (see Chapters 6 and 7), is not restricted to others. It can sneak into our own writing if we're not being careful, especially if we're writing about a subject we feel strongly about. If our reader spots a piece of pseudoreasoning in your paper—and she doesn't have to have had a critical thinking course to do that— that may be the part she remembers best.

An interesting twist on pseudoreasoning in student papers occurs when writers turn the subjectivist fallacy on themselves. "This has just been my opinion," they'll often say, usually toward the end of the essay. If a writer has done a good job, he has not given *just* his opinion. He's also given reasons in support of that opinion—he's provided arguments. So, if you've given good support for your conclusions, don't tell your reader that this is just your opinion, as if your position has no better chance of being correct than any other. That's giving away the store.

11. *Don't pad your paper.* In item 8, above, we encouraged you not to leave gaps in your paper; you want to do the most thorough job you can. But, like most things, this instruction can be carried too far. Most instructors can spot excess verbiage from a mile away, especially the sort that gets added in an attempt to make a paper seem more substantial than it really is. A good short paper is always better than a mediocre long paper. Give your subject all the room it deserves, but nothing extra. This goes not just for the body of the paper but for the introduction and conclusion as well. Nothing is quite so boring as an essay that begins, "In this paper I shall argue that . . ." and then goes on to itemize *everything* that's going to be said later. Such papers often make matters worse by saying, at the end, "In this paper I have argued that . . ." and repeating what has been said a *third* time. Such papers sound as though they're written to fit a formula. It's important to say at the outset what you're going to do, so that your reader has an idea of what to expect as she reads. But try to do it without using trite phrases and going on at great length. What you need to do is describe your primary thesis and maybe a few words about why it's important and what your approach will be. Then get on with the business of the essay.

12. *Look for help.* It's difficult to be a good critic of your own work. When you've written your first draft, read it over yourself, make any changes that seem required, then ask someone else to read it. A friend or roommate can supply valuable help with a minimum investment of time. When the time comes, you can supply the same service for him or her.

13. *Practice.* Writing is like every other skill: The more you do it the better at it you'll get. And the better at it you get, the more you'll enjoy doing it.

We said in Chapter 1 that critical thinking and good writing are very closely connected. And, however they might be connected in the learning process, it's at least true that your essays provide one of the best places for you to exhibit the critical thinking skills you've studied in this course.

ESSAY TOPICS

When you have to write an essay and can choose any subject you want, that's the one time you can't think of anything interesting to write about, right? To help at such times, we offer the following list of topics. You might choose to write directly on one of them, or you may find that some of them get you thinking about a related topic of your own invention.

1. Does an adopted child have a natural right to know who his or her natural parents are?
2. If your roommate's lover has invited you to have sex, should you inform your roommate?
3. If you believe it is wrong to hunt animals should you also believe that it is wrong to eat animals?
4. Should two different couples be permitted to trade babies if they want to?
5. Is there some characteristic that animals have (or do not have) that justifies using them in medical experiments that does not also justify using humans in the same kind of experiments?
6. Should there be no minimum drinking age?
7. Would it be wrong to execute a person picked at random if the outcome would be to end all possibility of nuclear war?
8. Does sexism exist in America?
9. Should there be capital punishment for first-degree murder?
10. Do people have psychic powers?
11. Is it ever right to commit adultery?
12. Which is better, for one innocent person to be punished for murder, or for ten murderers to go free?
13. Should contraceptives be made easily available to everyone under 16?
14. Should you inform your lover if you had one-time sex with someone else and there is no chance that your lover will find out about it?
15. Should pot be legalized?
16. Are there any situations in which it is right to hurt another human being physically?
17. Could there be situations in which it would be right for your university's administration to censor your student newspaper?
18. Is it right to terminate an engagement with someone because he or she has been in an accident and will be an invalid for life?
19. Should public nudity be legal?

20. Your roommate has bad breath, but is very sensitive. Should you inform him or her of the problem?
21. A woman's husband and her child have both ingested deadly mushrooms, and there is only enough antidote for her to save one of them. Should she save her husband's life?
22. Does God exist?
23. Is surrogate motherhood the same as baby selling?
24. Is it possible to remedy the problem of teenage drinking?
25. "If guns are outlawed, only outlaws will have guns"—a good argument against gun control?
26. Should women pose in the nude for sex magazines?
27. Is abortion a form of murder?
28. Is it worse for a species of large animals to be brought to extinction than a species of very small ones?

Note to instructor: Chapter 12 of *The Logical Accessory* contains several exercises that can be adapted for essay assignments.

Glossary

Ad hominem. A form of pseudoreasoning in which a claim or argument is rejected because of some fact about the author or source of the claim or argument.

Affirming the consequent. An argument consisting of a conditional claim as one premise, a claim that affirms the consequent of the conditional as a second premise, and a claim that affirms the antecedent of the conditional as the conclusion.

Ambiguous claim. A claim that could be interpreted in more than one way and whose meaning is not made clear by the context.

Analogical argument. An argument in which something that is said to hold true of a sample of a certain class is claimed also to hold true of another member of the class.

Analogy. A comparison of two or more objects, events, or other phenomena.

Analytic claim. A claim that is true or false by virtue of the meanings of the words that compose it.

Analytical definition. A definition that specifies (1) the type of thing the defined term applies to, and (2) the difference between that thing and other things of the same type.

Anecdotal evidence, fallacy of. A fallacy in which data that offer reasonable support for a general claim are ignored in favor of an example or two that do not.

Antecedent. *See* Conditional claim.

Appeal to belief. A pattern of pseudoreasoning: "X is true because everyone (lots of people, most societies, others, I, etc.) think that X is true."

Appeal to common practice. A pattern of pseudoreasoning that consists of trying to defend a wrong action by explaining that it is frequently carried out.

Appeal to the consequences of belief. This pattern of pseudoreasoning: "X is true (acceptable, reasonable, creditable, okay, etc.) because, if we didn't believe that X is true, then there would be unpleasant consequences."

Appeal to illegitimate authority. An attempt to prove a claim by appealing to the say-so of any individual whose circumstances make it unsafe to assume that he or she is believable about the subject at hand. *See* Illegitimate authority.

Appeal to pity. A pattern of pseudoreasoning in which someone tries to induce acceptance of a claim by eliciting compassion or pity.

Appeal to spite or indignation. A pattern of pseudoreasoning in which someone tries to induce acceptance of a claim by arousing spite or indignation.

Apple polishing. A pattern of pseudoreasoning in which flattery is disguised as a reason for accepting a claim.

Argument. A set of claims, one of which, known as the conclusion, is supposed to be supported by the rest, known as the reasons or premises.

Argument pattern. The structure of an argument. This structure is independent of the argument's content. Several arguments can have the same pattern (e.g., modus ponens) yet be about quite different subjects. Variables are used to stand for classes or claims in the display of an argument's pattern.

Assuming a common cause, fallacy of. Assuming without question that two conjoined events must have had the same underlying cause.

Background knowledge. The body of true and justified beliefs that consists of facts we learn from our own direct observations and facts we learn from others.

Bandwagon. *See* Peer pressure.

Begging the question. *See* Question-begging argument.

Biased generalization, fallacy of. A generalization about an entire class based on a biased sample.

Biased sample. A sample that is not representative.

Burden of proof. A form of pseudoreasoning in which the burden of proving a point is placed on the wrong side. One version occurs when a lack of evidence on one side is taken as evidence for the other side, in cases where the burden of proving the point rests on the latter side.

Categorical claim. Any standard-form categorical claim or any claim that means the same as some standard-form categorical claim. *See* Standard-form categorical claim.

Categorical logic. A system of logic based on the relations of inclusion and exclusion among classes ("categories"). This branch of logic specifies the logical relationships among claims that can be expressed in the forms "All Xs are Ys," "No Xs are Ys," "Some Xs are Ys," and "Some Xs are not Ys." Developed by Aristotle in the fourth century B.C., categorical logic is also known as Aristotelean or traditional logic.

Categorical syllogism. A two-premise deductive argument in which every claim is categorical and each of three terms appears in two of the claims—

e.g., all soldiers are martinets and no martinets are diplomats, so no soldiers are diplomats.

Causal explanation. *See* Physical explanation.

Causal factor. A causal factor for some specific effect is something that contributes to the effect. More precisely, in a given population, a thing is a causal factor for some specified effect if there would be more occurrences of the effect if every member of the population were exposed to the thing than if none were exposed to the thing. To say that C is a causal factor for E in population P, then, is to say that there would be more cases of E in population P if every member of P were exposed to C than if no member of P were exposed to C.

Chain argument. An argument consisting of three conditional claims, in which the antecedents of one premise and the conclusion are the same, the consequents of the other premise and the conclusion are the same, and the consequent of the first premise and the antecedent of the second premise are the same.

Claim. A statement that is either true or false.

Claim variable. A letter that stands for a claim.

Class variable. A letter that stands for a class of entities.

Common practice. A form of pseudoreasoning in which an action is defended by calling attention to the fact that the action is a common one (not to be confused with appeals for fair play).

Comparative general claim. A general claim that involves a comparison.

Complementary term. A term is complementary to another term if and only if it refers to everything that the first term does not refer to.

Composition, fallacy of. To think that what holds true of a group of things taken individually necessarily holds true of the same things taken collectively.

Conclusion. The claim in an argument that is argued for.

Conclusion indicator. A word or phrase that signals the occurrence of a conclusion.

Conditional claim. A claim that state-of-affairs A cannot hold without state-of-affairs B holding as well—e.g., "If A then B." The A-part of the claim is called the *antecedent;* the B-part is called the *consequent.*

Confidence interval. *See* Error margin.

Confidence level. *See* Statistical significance.

Conflicting claims. Two claims that cannot both be correct.

Conjunction. A compound claim made from two simpler claims. A conjunction is true if and only if both of the simpler claims that compose it are true.

Consequent. *See* Conditional claim.

Contextual vagueness. A term is contextually vague if it does not convey sufficient information for the context in which it is used. Example: "To get to the market, turn at the corner." (The word *turn* could mean turn left or turn right.)

Contradictory claims. Two claims that are exact opposites—that is, they could not both be true at the same time and could not both be false at the same time.

Contrapositive. The claim that results from switching the places of the subject and predicate terms in a claim and replacing both terms with complementary terms.

Contrary claims. Two claims that could not both be true at the same time but could both be false at the same time.

Control group. *See* Controlled cause-to-effect experiment.

Controlled cause-to-effect experiment. An experiment designed to test whether something is a causal factor for a given effect. Basically, in such an experiment two groups are essentially alike except that the members of one group, the *experimental group,* are exposed to the suspected causal factor, and the members of the other group, the *control group,* are not. If the effect is then found to occur significantly more frequently in the experimental group, the suspected causal agent is considered a causal factor for the effect.

Converse. The converse of a categorical claim is the claim that results from switching the places of the subject and predicate terms.

Conversion. A claim about two classes of things is converted when the words or phrases that designate the two classes have been switched.

Critical thinking. The careful and deliberate determination of whether to accept, reject, or suspend judgment about a claim.

Deduction (proof). A numbered sequence of truth-functional symbolizations, each member of which validly follows from earlier members by one of the truth-functional rules.

Deductive argument. An argument whose premises are intended to provide absolutely conclusive reasons for accepting the conclusion.

Definition by example. Defining a term by pointing to, naming, or describing one or more examples of something to which the term applies.

Definition by synonym. Defining a term by giving a word or phrase that means the same thing.

Denotation (denotative meaning). All those things to which a term correctly applies.

Denying the antecedent. An argument consisting of a conditional claim as one premise, a claim that denies the antecedent of the conditional as a second premise, and a claim that denies the consequent of the conditional as the conclusion.

Dependent premises. Premises that depend on one another as support for their conclusion. If the assumption that a premise is false cancels the support another provides for a conclusion, the premises are dependent.

Descriptive claim. A claim that states facts or alleged facts. Descriptive claims tell how things are, or how they were, or how they might be. Contrasted with prescriptive claims.

Disjunction. A compound claim made up of two simpler claims. A disjunction is false only if both of the simpler claims that make it up are false.

Division, fallacy of. To think that what holds true of a group of things taken collectively necessarily holds true of the same things taken individually.

Downplayer. An expression used to play down or diminish the importance of a claim.

Dysphemism. A word or phrase used to produce a negative effect on a reader's or listener's attitude about something, or to tone down the positive associations the thing may have.

Emotive force. The feelings, attitudes, or emotions a word or expression expresses or elicits.

Error margin. A range of possibilities; specifically, a range of percentage points within which the conclusion of a statistical inductive generalization falls, usually given as "plus or minus" a certain number of points.

Euphemism. An agreeable or inoffensive expression that is substituted for an expression that may offend the hearer or suggest something unpleasant.

Experimental group. *See* Controlled cause-to-effect experiment.

Expert. A person who, through training, education, or experience, has special knowledge or ability in a subject.

Explanation. A claim or set of claims intended to make another claim, object, event, or state of affairs intelligible.

Explanatory comparison. Comparisons that are used to explain.

Fallacy. An argument in which the reasons advanced for a claim fail to warrant acceptance of that claim.

False dilemma. This pattern of pseudoreasoning: "X is true because either X is true or Y is true, and Y isn't," said when X and Y could both be false.

Functional explanation. An explanation of an object or occurrence in terms of its function or purpose.

General claim. A claim that refers to more than one member of a class but not necessarily to every member of the class.

Generalization. An argument offered in support of a general claim.

Generalizing argument. *See* Generalization.

Genetic fallacy. The belief that a perceived defect or deficiency in the origin of a thing discredits the thing itself.

Gobbledygook. Gibberish or near gibberish.

Grouping ambiguity. A kind of semantical ambiguity in which it is unclear whether a claim refers to a group of things taken individually or collectively.

Hasty generalization, fallacy of. A generalization based on a sample too small to be representative.

Horse laugh. A pattern of pseudoreasoning in which ridicule is disguised as a reason for rejecting a claim.

Hyperbole. Extravagant overstatement.

Ignoring a common cause, fallacy of. Concluding that one of two conjoined events caused another without considering the possibility that both events may have resulted from a common cause.

Illegitimate authority. A person whose remarks on a given subject are not to be trusted as true. *See* Appeal to illegitimate authority.

Independent premises. Premises that do not depend on one another as support for the conclusion. If the assumption that a premise is false does not cancel the support another premise provides for a conclusion, the premises are independent.

Indirect proof. Proof of a claim by demonstrating that its negation is false, absurd, or self-contradictory.

Inductive analogical argument. *See* Analogical argument.

Inductive argument. An argument whose premises are intended to provide some support, but less than conclusive support, for the conclusion.

Inductive generalization. *See* Generalization.

Innuendo. An insinuation of something deprecatory.

Invalid argument. A deductive argument whose conclusion does not necessarily follow from the premises.

Loaded question. A question that rests on one or more unwarranted or unjustified assumptions.

Logic. The branch of philosophy concerned with whether the reasons presented for a claim, if those reasons were true, would justify accepting the claim.

Mean. A type of average. The arithmetic mean of a group of numbers is the number that results when their sum is divided by the number of members in the group.

Median. A type of average. In a group of numbers, as many numbers of the group are larger than the median as are smaller.

Mode. A type of average. In a group of numbers, the mode is the number occurring most frequently.

Modus ponens. An argument consisting of a conditional claim as one premise, a claim that affirms the antecedent of the conditional as a second premise, and a claim that affirms the consequent of the conditional as the conclusion.

Modus tollens. An argument consisting of a conditional claim as one premise, a claim that denies the consequent of the conditional as a second premise, and a claim that denies the antecedent of the conditional as the conclusion.

Moral argument. An argument whose conclusion is a moral prescriptive claim.

Negation. The contradictory of a particular claim.

Nonargumentative persuasion. An attempt to win acceptance for a claim that does not use argumentation.

Nonexperimental cause-to-effect study. A study designed to test whether something is a causal factor for a given effect. Such studies are similar to controlled cause-to-effect experiments except that the members of the experimental group are not exposed to the suspected causal agent by the investigators; instead, exposure has resulted from the actions or circumstances of the individuals themselves.

Nonexperimental effect-to-cause study. A study designed to test whether something is a causal factor for a given effect. Such studies are similar to nonexperimental cause-to-effect studies except that the members of the experimental group display *the effect,* as compared with a control group whose members do not display the effect. Finding that the suspected cause is significantly more frequent in the experimental group is reason for saying that the suspected causal agent is a causal factor in the population involved.

Nonuniversal general claim. A general claim that is not falsified by a few exceptions.

Obverse. The obverse of a categorical claim is that claim that is directly across from it in the square of opposition, with the predicate term changed to its complementary term.

Peer pressure. A pattern of pseudoreasoning in which you are in effect threatened with rejection by your friends, relatives, etc., if you don't accept a certain claim.

Personal attack. A pattern of pseudoreasoning in which we refuse to accept another's argument because there is something about the person we don't like or of which we disapprove. A form of ad hominem.

Persuasive comparison. A comparison used to express or influence attitudes or affect behavior.

Persuasive definition. A definition used to convey or evoke an attitude about the defined term and its denotation.

Persuasive explanation. An explanation intended to influence attitudes or affect behavior.

Physical explanation. An explanation that tells us how or why something happens in terms of the physical background of the event.

Post hoc, ergo propter hoc, fallacy of. Reasoning that X caused Y simply because Y occurred after X.

Precising definition. A definition that limits the applicability of a term whose usual meaning is too vague for the use in question.

Premise. The claim or claims in an argument that provide the reasons for believing the conclusion.

Premise indicator. A word or phrase that signals the occurrence of a premise.

Prescriptive claim. A claim that states how things ought to be. Prescriptive claims impute values to actions, things, or situations. Contrasted with descriptive claims.

Principal claim. The final conclusion of an argument.

Proof surrogate. An expression used to suggest that there is evidence or authority for a claim without actually saying that there is.

Proper vagueness. A term is properly vague if it does not have a precise definition—that is, if it admits of a large number of borderline cases. Examples: "rich," "bald."

Pseudoreason. A claim that is set forth as a reason for believing another claim but that is either logically irrelevant to the truth of the other claim or otherwise fails to provide reasonable support.

Pseudorebuttal. *See* Subjectivist fallacy.

Pseudorefutation. This pattern of pseudoreasoning: "I reject your claim because you act as if you think it is false," or "You can't make the claim now because you have in the past rejected it." A form of ad hominem.

Psychological explanation. An explanation of an occurrence in terms of someone's reasons or motives.

Question-begging argument. An argument whose conclusion restates a point made in the premises or clearly assumed by the premises. While technically valid, anyone who doubts the conclusion of a question-begging argument would have to doubt the premises, too.

Random sample. A sample of a population in which every individual has an equal chance of being selected.

Rationalizing. *See* Selfish rationalizing.

Reductio ad absurdum. *See* Indirect proof.

Reverse chain argument. An argument consisting of three conditional claims that is similar to a chain argument except that the antecedent and consequent of the conclusion have been switched.

Reversed causation, fallacy of. The mistaken belief that the cause of a cause-and-effect sequence of events is the effect.

Sample. That part of a class referred to in the premises of a generalizing argument.

Scare tactics. A pattern of pseudoreasoning in which someone says, in effect, "X is so because Y [where Y is a fact that, it is hoped, induces fear in the listener]."

Self-contradictory claim. A claim that is analytically false.

Selfish rationalizing. A pattern of pseudoreasoning in which you invent or focus on a nonselfish secondary reason for accepting a claim in order to avoid feeling guilty about your principal motive or reason for accepting it, which is for personal gain. The secondary reason is a pseudoreason.

Semantically ambiguous claim. An ambiguous claim whose ambiguity is due to the ambiguity of a word or phrase in the claim.

Sense. The set of characteristics a thing must have for a term to apply correctly to it.

Slanter. A linguistic device used to affect opinions, attitudes, or behavior without argumentation. Slanters rely heavily on the suggestive power of words and phrases to convey and evoke favorable and unfavorable images.

Slippery slope. A form of pseudoreasoning in which it is assumed that some event must inevitably follow from some other, but in which no argument is made for the inevitability.

Sound argument. A valid deductive argument whose premises are true.

Square of opposition. A table of the logical relationships between two categorical claims that have the same subject and predicate terms.

Standard-form categorical claim. Any claim that results from putting words or phrases that name classes in the blanks of one of the following structures: "All _____ are _____ "; "No _____ are _____ "; "Some _____ are _____ "; and "Some _____ are not _____ ."

Statistical inductive generalization. A generalization from a sample to the conclusion that a certain percentage of the target population possesses a certain characteristic.

Statistical significance. To say that some finding is statistically significant at a given *confidence level*—say, .05—is essentially to say that the finding could have arisen by chance in only about five cases out of one hundred.

Statistical syllogism. An argument in which it is reasoned that, because something is true of some percentage of a certain class of things, it is true of some specific member of that class.

Stereotype. An oversimplified generalization about the members of a class.

Straw man. Straw man pseudoreasoning occurs when someone ignores an opponent's actual position and presents in its place a distorted, exaggerated, or misrepresented version of that position.

Strong argument. An argument that has this characteristic: On the assumption that the premises are true, the conclusion is unlikely to be false.

Subjectivist fallacy. This pattern of pseudoreasoning: "Well, X may be true for you, but it isn't true for me," said with the intent of dismissing or rejecting X.

Syllogism. A deductive argument with two premises.

Syntactically ambiguous claim. An ambiguous claim whose ambiguity is due to the structure of the claim.

Target population. The population, or class, referred to in the conclusion of a generalizing argument.

Truth-functional equivalence. Two claims are truth-functionally equivalent if and only if they have exactly the same truth table.

Truth-functional logic. A system of logic that specifies the logical relationships among truth-functional claims—claims whose truth values depend solely upon the truth values of their simplest component parts. In particular, truth-functional logic deals with the logical functions of the terms *not, and, or, if . . . then,* etc.

Truth table. A table that lists all possible combinations of truth values for the claim variables in a symbolized claim or argument and then specifies the truth value of the claim or claims for each of those possible combinations.

Two wrongs make a right. This pattern of pseudoreasoning: "It's acceptable for A to do X to B, because B would do X to A," said where A's doing X to B is not necessary to prevent B's doing X to A.

Universal general claim. A general claim that admits no exception.

Vague claim. *See* Contextual vagueness; Proper vagueness.

Valid argument. An argument that has this characteristic: On the assumption that the premises are true, it is impossible for the conclusion to be false.

Venn diagram. A graphic means of representing a categorical claim or categorical syllogism by assigning classes to overlapping circles. Invented by English mathematician John Venn (1834–1923).

Weasler. An expression used to protect a claim from criticism by weakening it.

Wishful thinking. This pattern of pseudoreasoning: believing that something is true because you want it to be true (or believing that it is false because you don't want it to be true).

"X is the common thread." Reasoning that X caused Y because X is the only relevant common factor in more than one occurrence of Y.

"X is the difference." Reasoning that X caused Y because X is the only relevant difference between this situation, where Y occurred, and situations where Y did not occur.

Answers, Suggestions, and Tips for Starred Exercises

CHAPTER 1
What Is Critical Thinking?

EXERCISE 1-1

1. It's the careful and deliberate determination of whether to accept, reject, or suspend judgment about a claim.
3. No. There may be reasons for accepting the claim that have not yet been stated.
4. No. There may be reasons for rejecting the claim that have not yet been stated.
7. Purely informative language is most likely to be found where speakers or writers have an interest only in making sure that information is conveyed. Pure examples are relatively rare; encyclopedias provide about as good an example as there is.
8. Yes. Someone might persuade you to take a class in physics or automobile mechanics for exactly that reason.
9. Yes. One way to influence people's behavior is to lie to them. And if the behavior itself leads to no information, those influenced in this way wind up less informed than when they began.
10. Yes. For example, parents might try to convince their children to go to church to develop what the parents consider the proper attitude toward religion.
11. Yes. Someone might try to convince you that a certain book you both have read is a good book.
12. Absolutely. Have you ever heard remarks such as "You don't have to like it, just do it!"?
15. This is not as difficult as it might sound at this early stage. All you have to do is think of a reason why sixteen-year-olds should not be allowed to drink (e.g.,

because sixteen-year-olds do not have the maturity of judgment required to know when to stop). One reason will do. (It doesn't even have to be a good reason unless you want to produce a good argument.)

16. No

19. Yes, when there are no good reasons to act contrary to those feelings.

20. An argument addresses an issue; its conclusion answers the question implicit in the statement of the issue.

EXERCISE 1-2

1. To explain why he was unaware of the deal with the Iranians and the Contras. "I was not among those who discussed the Iran-Contra deal," expresses his thought more directly.

3. To give advice. This is pretty straightforward, although we think you could probably find better advice on the subject than this.

5. To instill an upbeat attitude toward Coke and to influence you to buy the product. "Coke is wonderful; buy it!" states the purpose more directly. Notice that the original version doesn't tell you *what* Coke is.

7. To discourage cheating. Although it is put in the form of a straightforward claim, it is actually a warning: "Don't cheat."

9. To complain about the media's treatment of conservatives as compared to its treatment of liberals. "Liberals get better treatment in the media than conservatives" states it succinctly.

11. To convince his listeners of his own importance in recent music. You might say he was bragging, except that we usually call such remarks bragging only if they are basically true. We seem to remember people dancing to the beat of popular music before Chubby Checker came onto the scene. (His remark sounds suspiciously like sour grapes, doesn't it?)

13. To encourage people to try Sterling cigarettes. "Buy Sterling" is the message. The comparison with Porsche, which has a strong image as a classy car, is designed to create a similarly strong image for Sterling.

15. To convey the idea that consumption of this product may reduce the risk of some kinds of cancer. The underlying message is, "Our cereal may help keep you from getting cancer." Such an approach plays on our fears, of course.

17. To defend his surgical practices. "I was merely trying to save the child, not enhance my reputation as a surgeon" is what he's saying, although the remark about babies dying gives the impression that he *had* to do something.

19. To justify not supporting programs to help such people. "We needn't worry about the homeless (or at least many of them)" conveys that message.

21. To amuse her listeners, we think. "I'm proud of how long this has lasted," would have done, but wouldn't have been as funny. If she's *seriously* proud of the longevity of her relationship, however, the remark may be even more amusing.

23. To complain. "I hate it that she won" is more direct. Do you suppose she would have cared about her opponent's father's wealth if *she* had won the tournament?

25. To amuse his audience and, probably, to make fun of the dozens of silly questions sportswriters ask athletes before important games. We can't think of a better way to put it.

EXERCISE 1-3

Selection 1
1. Claims a, b, and c are all unsupported claims. Claim d is supported by a, b, and c.
2. Claims a and b are both unsupported.
3. Claim a is supported by b and c, which are unsupported. The author's main purpose is to elicit the reader's support for EPA controls on lead in gasoline, claim d.

Selection 2
1. Claim a is supported by b, which is unsupported.
2. Claim a is supported by b, c, and d, which are all unsupported.
3. Claim a is supported by b and c, which are unsupported.
4. Claim a is unsupported; b is supported by a. With c, the writer is not making the claim in so many words, but does make it clear that he or she believes others should express their concern over the bookstore. The writer's main purpose is to motivate others to show their concern about the bookstore.

EXERCISE 1-4

1. The issue is whether you are better off buying a live Christmas tree than one that's been cut.
3. The issue is whether rice farmers should burn their fields.
7. The issue is whether the defeat of Bork's confirmation to the Supreme Court was healthy for our judicial system.
10. The issue is whether socialism is good for China.

EXERCISE 1-5

1. The main point of the essay is that Congress should give the FSLIC more money ("adequately capitalizing" it) with which to close up badly run savings & loans and pay off their depositors.
2. The reasons given are as follows:
   (a) Allowing badly run S&Ls to continue drives up the costs of healthy ones.
   (b) Merging badly run S&Ls with healthy ones (a major part of the present policy) increases future risks for the FSLIC.
   (c) Present policy protects badly managed S&Ls.
   (d) The second half of the second paragraph contains several claims that, taken together, support (a), above.

CHAPTER 2
Understanding Claims

EXERCISE 2-1

1. Syntactically ambiguous: Did the invitation *happen* yesterday or was the *movie* yesterday?
4. Syntactically ambiguous: Is "torture" an adjective modifying "victims," or is it a

verb with "victims" as direct object? (The difference could be important in determining how we think about therapists.)
7. Semantically ambiguous: Does "digital" have to do with fingers or with a kind of computer?
10. Syntactically ambiguous: Who did the mauling, the police or the coyotes?
13. Syntactically ambiguous: Is the assistant chaplain's suit against the *Dartmouth Review* or the professor of music?
16. Semantically ambiguous: Does "bring . . . to life" mean animate or deliver to the lives of customers?
19. Semantically ambiguous: "nothing is better" can mean either that, of the alternatives, none is better or that it's better to drink nothing at all than to drink this stuff.

EXERCISE 2-2

1. As a group
4. As a group
7. It's more likely that a person would mean to refer to the Giants as a group, but it's possible that he could be referring to the play of individuals.
10. As individuals
13. We find this one difficult but think a reference to a group makes a little more sense (individuals could not ordinarily stage invasions). Notice that there is no ambiguity in the claim; it's quite clear what is meant.

EXERCISE 2-3

1. In order of decreasing vagueness: (d), (e), (b), (c), (f), (a). Compare, say, (e) and (b). If Eli and Sarah made *plans* for the future, then they certainly *discussed* it. But just discussing it is more vague—they could do that with or without making plans.
4. In order of decreasing vagueness: (c), (d), (a), (b), (e)

EXERCISE 2-4

We find the most vague uses in claims 3, 6, 8, and 10.

EXERCISE 2-5

We find the most vague uses in claims 2, 3, 5, 6, and 7.

EXERCISE 2-6

Here are our comments on each of the italicized phrases:

(1) *administration officials* is pretty vague, but it's pretty standard language in press reports. Presumably the official in question is the DEA spokesman mentioned in the second sentence.
(2) *war on drugs* is a vague phrase, but it's a vague combination of events and policies that it refers to. We know what they're talking about.

(3) *turned the corner* is one of the two most vague, and possibly most misleading, of the items on the list. It *sounds* as though we can soon—or at least eventually—expect the country to be free of drug addiction, but this is not very likely, and we would probably find it difficult to get the spokesperson to commit himself to such a claim.

(4) *massive clean-up* is also vague enough to be misleading. Is Miami now relatively drug-free? Or does the speaker simply mean that this clean-up is "massive" compared to earlier clean-ups?

(5) *Miami area* is not too vague for this context.

(6) *twice as many arrests* is vague only if we have no idea and no way of finding out how many arrests were made the previous year.

EXERCISE 2-7

The first moral is that a word may mean something quite different from other words that it strongly resembles. The second moral is that it is not as bothersome as you thought to look words up in the dictionary, right? (You didn't think we were actually going to tell you what the words meant here in the back of the book, did you?)

EXERCISE 2-8

1. Mars
4. Any object you point to or name. But notice that, no matter what you point to, it will not be clear to an observer what qualifies that object as a *thing*. This word is much too general (i.e., vague) to be easily defined by example.
7. The New York Mets
10. The Red Cross. As an abstract noun (as in "Charity begins at home") this word is more difficult to define by example. You must point to or describe an act of generosity, sacrifice, and so on.
13. Injuring a puppy just for amusement
16. The class rankings of freshman, sophomore, junior, and senior
19. Number. What we said above about *thing* goes for this word too.

EXERCISE 2-9

1. Denotation
4. Denotation
7. Neither
10. Neither

EXERCISE 2-10

1. Synonym
4. Synonym
7. Analytical
10. Neither. This "definition" is offered just to praise motherhood.
13. This is closest to an analytical definition, but it tells "how to" rather than "what."

EXERCISE 2-11

1. Analytic truth. *Theft* is by definition a criminal activity.
4. Analytic truth
7. Analytic truth
10. Analytic, in one sense of *normal*, in which it means usual, standard, or ordinary. If *normal* were taken to mean something like *perfectly average* or *paradigmatic*, then this would not be analytic. In that case it wouldn't even be true, since few people are perfectly average.
13. In spite of recent speculation by some physicists that travel back into time may be possible, we believe that it isn't and hence that the claim is analytically true.

EXERCISE 2-16

1. Libra (Sept. 21–Oct. 30)
2. Cancer (June 21–July 20)
3. Taurus (April 21–May20)
4. Aries (March 21–April 20)
5. Scorpio (Oct. 21–Nov. 20)
6. Aquarius (Jan. 21–Feb. 20)
7. Sagittarius (Nov. 21–Dec. 20)
8. Pisces (Feb. 21–March 20)
9. Capricorn (Dec. 21–Jan. 20)
10. Gemini (May 21–June 20)
11. Virgo (Aug. 21–Sept. 20)
12. Leo (July 21–Aug. 20)

We hope you noticed how difficult it was to select the descriptions that fit you best. Is it clear why this task is difficult? Perhaps if you had known in advance which description was supposed to go with your birthdate it might have seemed more clearly applicable to you. It's easy to read yourself into a description if it is sufficiently vague.

EXERCISE 2-17

Our choices for the three most vague uses are 2, 5, and 9.

EXERCISE 2-18

1. Overturn
4. Clumsy
7. Pal
10. Tightwad

EXERCISE 2-19

1. Full-figured; fat
4. Showcase; show off
7. Imbiber; lush
10. Thinker; egghead

EXERCISE 2-20

1. An individual whose political philosophy is guided by the wisdom embodied in traditional institutions
4. An individual whose political philosophy is guided by ideas of democracy, reform, and progress

EXERCISE 2-21

1. A man who deals with women as objects for his own entertainment instead of as whole people
4. A person whose attention is given to meaningless intellectual puzzles and who knows little of the real world

EXERCISE 2-22

1. To explain a new phrase
4. To make fun of idealists (to invoke an attitude)
7. To eliminate ambiguity
10. To invoke an attitude about conservatives (and liberals too)
13. A persuasive definition, designed to expose hypocrisy in what people read and what they say they read
16. To explain an unfamiliar word
19. A humorous putdown of socialists

EXERCISE 2-23

1. Although U.S. government checks have been hole-punched, green, and printed on heavy paper since 1945, they will be replaced over the next three years, beginning next month, by lighter weight checks in pastel colors and decorated with drawings of the Statue of Liberty. Unlike the old, the new checks will be processed by equipment that reads symbols printed on the checks rather than patterns of holes. The new checks should be harder to counterfeit and cheaper to produce—the change is expected to save $6 million yearly.

CHAPTER 3
Evaluating Informative Claims

EXERCISE 3-1

1. Contraries
4. These do not conflict.
7. Contraries
10. Contraries

EXERCISE 3-2

1. Contraries, since some other day may be payday and both of these false. Notice that this rests on the assumption that there are not two paydays each week; if that

assumption is not true, then both Friday and Monday could be payday and hence both claims true—that is, not in conflict.

4. Contradictories
7. Contraries
10. We meant to puzzle you with this one. The two claims make a paradox: Look at either one. If it were true, it would be false; but if it were false, it would be true. The strangeness comes from the fact that the claims are "self-referential"—that is, they refer back to themselves. Such references can (obviously) cause trouble (or amusement).

EXERCISE 3-6

Poor physical conditions, impaired senses, faulty instruments, emotional upset, fatigue, distraction, bias, expectation, mental imbalance

EXERCISE 3-7

1. Credible; one's observations; one's background knowledge; other creditable claims
2. Our own observations
3. Our memories
4. Contradictories
5. Contraries; false

EXERCISE 3-9

2. This one is not too difficult. Unless *you* are a mechanic, the mechanic from the independent garage is clearly the most credible option. The salesperson, even if scrupulously honest, wants to make a sale, and probably will not have full knowledge of the car's condition. The former owner's mechanic may not list some problems in a car that should have been taken care of, though it is a good bet that any problems this person mentions are real ones. The former owner is not the best source either, because he or she may have neglected to mention certain problems to the used-car salesman and will be cautious in calling anyone's attention to them.
4. This one is a little tougher. Our view is that the most credible witness would be an experienced ice skater or ice-skating coach, with the nod going to the coach on the basis of more experience as a critical observer. In this instance, though, the Russian coach, however honest, is not disinterested and may be assumed to attach special importance to any faults he or she perceives or seems to perceive. Conclusion: We vote for the Canadian ice skater as the most credible of the choices listed. The least credible is probably Brian's mother, for reasons we presume are obvious. Of the two who remain, we'd listen to the ice hockey coach over the swimming coach, since ice skating has much more in common with hockey.

EXERCISE 3-10

1. The most credible choices are either the FDA or *Consumer Reports,* both of which investigate health claims of the sort in question with reasonable objectivity. The company that markets the product is the least credible source, since it is the most likely to be biased. The health food store owner may be knowledgeable, but there

is a good chance that his or her main source of information is the manufacturer of the product. Your local pharmacist can reasonably be regarded as credible, but he or she may not have access to as much information as the FDA or *CR.*

2. It would probably be a mistake to consider any of the individuals on this list as more expert than most of the others, although different kinds and different levels of bias are fairly predictable on the parts of the victim's father, the NRA representative, and possibly the police chief. The senator might be expected to have access to more data that are relevant to the issue, but that would not in itself make his or her credibility much greater than that of the others. The problem here is that we are dealing with a value judgment that depends very heavily upon an individual's point of view rather than his or her expertise. What is important to this question is less the credibility of the person who gives us an answer than the strength of the supporting argument, if any, that he or she provides (see Chapter 12).

3. While problem 2 hinges on a value judgment, this one calls for an interpretation of the original intent of a constitutional amendment. Here our choices would be either the Supreme Court justice or the constitutional historian, with a slight preference for the latter, since Supreme Court justices are concerned more with constitutional issues as they have been interpreted by other courts than with original intent. The NRA representative is paid to speak for a certain point of view and would be the least credible in our view. The senator and the U.S. president would fall somewhere in between: Both might reasonably be expected to be knowledgeable about constitutional issues, but much less so than our first two choices.

EXERCISE 3-11

1. Professor Fellowstone would possess the greatest degree of credibility and authority on topics d, f, h, and, compared with someone who had not lived in both places, i.

EXERCISE 3-13

1. CBS News does not have a history of sensationalist, irresponsible, or false reporting, and in general it may be taken as a reliable source of information. However, the claim in question is marked by a certain vagueness, especially in its employment of the terms *conspiracy* and *underreport* and the phrase *highest levels of American military intelligence.* Hence, further information would be required before one could ascertain precisely what the CBS charge amounted to. As it turns out, CBS was sued by General William Westmoreland, commander of American forces in Vietnam, for this broadcast, though he ultimately dropped the suit.

2. *Time,* too, has no history or reputation for sensationalist or irresponsible reporting, though it is notorious for mixing coloring material and opinion (usually middle-of-the-road) into its news reports. Here again the claim in question is vague, owing to the vagueness of the notion of sharing indirect responsibility. Thus, before accepting this claim the critical reader would want to find out what the specific complaint against Sharon was. Incidentally, the publication of this statement also resulted in a lawsuit; a jury found that the claim did indeed defame Sharon but that it was published "without malice" and therefore was not grounds for libel.

3. That the British manufacturer of Monopoly made the claim in question is very likely true—the Associated Press can be trusted to have reported that correctly.

That the maps, files, and so on were in fact smuggled to prisoners in Monopoly sets is also probably true, but one should not, on the basis of the manufacturer's reported word alone, regard this as certain.

4. Almost certainly true; this is the sort of claim about which an agency such as the Associated Press very seldom errs.

8. Since these claims are made by an individual who, as a staff writer for a reputable nontechnical science magazine, is probably well informed, and since they are printed in *Esquire,* a magazine that is not in general a suspicious source of information, and also since they coincide with our own observations that a person's features seem to become more pronounced with age, we'd be inclined to accept them. The claims are not, of course, particularly precise, and they are general statements not intended to apply to each individual person to the same degree. (Incidentally, we would be pleased to see a more authoritative source—for example, a professor of physiology writing in a science journal—pronounce them false.)

11. The author is unknown to us, but she is quoted in a college textbook published by a reputable publishing house and written by at least one reputable scientist (we have no information about the second author). The figures sound reasonable, but we would keep an open mind about them, since the authors of the text may not have checked them. Notice too that we do not know whether either author of the text is an expert *in this area.*

14. We don't know Jon Kennedy, but we'd assume that this magazine would be a reliable source of information about this sort of thing. We'd accept the claim.

CHAPTER 4
Explanations

EXERCISE 4-1

1. Argument. The conclusion is that the dog has fleas.
4. Explanation. The phenomenon explained is the worsening of water contamination.
7. Explanation. The phenomenon explained is your inability to sleep.
10. This is primarily an argument; it is designed to convince someone that, if they touch the pins, they may fry their computer's logic circuits. Notice that, in giving the argument, the author of this passage also explains *how* the circuits would get fried.
13. This is primarily an argument; its conclusion is the first claim of the passage. Like number 10, it also does some explaining of the phenomenon.

EXERCISE 4-2

2. General conditions and any relevant antecedent events, the latter in the form of causal chains.
6. Specification of relevant antecedent events (earlier links in the causal chain) and citation of a law of nature. The law of nature is more likely to be left unstated, since it is often common knowledge.
9. We generally hold that physical theories and laws admit fewer exceptions and are better confirmed than psychological theories and generalities.

13. Choose a thing, Y, that shares as many important features as possible with X and with which your audience has some familiarity. Then describe any important differences between X and Y.
15. The point of such a comparison is to produce as good a general conception of the unfamiliar item in the audience as possible. Sometimes this is easier if the comparison is general rather than precise and elaborately detailed. The detailed comparison may be more accurate but less effective in conveying the general idea.

EXERCISE 4-3

1. The fact that women open their mouths when they apply eye makeup is explained. This is a psychological explanation, assuming that women who open their mouths decide to do it in order to tighten the skin. It would not be unreasonable to call this functional as well; the function of the open mouth is to tighten the skin around the eyes, after all. (Remember: We're not deciding whether the explanations in this exercise are good ones.)
4. This is a functional explanation; the purpose of the black rubber is explained.
7. The scariness of Hitchcock's movies is explained. It's a psychological explanation.
10. The phenomenon explained is food poisoning symptoms. The explanation is causal (the presence of salmonella in milk, the failure of the pasteurization process at a Jewel plant to kill the bacteria).
13. The phenomenon explained is the youngster's contracting polio. The explanation is causal (the vaccination), but there's also a psychological element: If the FDA had not decided to approve the vaccine, he would not have been vaccinated and would not have come down with the disease.

EXERCISE 4-4

In the first and third paragraphs we find several psychological explanations for the drinking habits of the people surveyed. The second paragraph presents an interesting case: Psychological dependence could stand as either a psychological or a physical explanation of some people's drinking, depending upon the kind and depth of detail the explanation includes. It becomes a physical explanation if enough physical detail is given about *how* alcohol is psychologically addicting (such things as effects on the nervous system, for example). In the context in which it appears, however, and with no more information than that given, we can best characterize the explanation as psychological.

The fourth and fifth paragraphs give rudimentary physical explanations. The fourth explains certain cases of a variety of diseases; decreases in libido, fertility, and so on; and abnormal fetal development. The phenomenon explained in the fifth paragraph is the higher rate of fatal accidents among drivers who have been drinking.

If you cited an explanation for a change in personal attitudes about drinking in the final paragraph, you should reconsider. This is not an explanation at all but an argument. The change in attitudes is not an accepted claim that wants explaining; it is an assertion for which decreased sales in alcoholic beverages are offered as evidence.

EXERCISE 4-5

1. This explanation is full of problems. It is untestable, its relevance is questionable (we couldn't have predicted blue eyes from a previous incarnation unless we knew

more about the latter, but the explanation is too vague to do that), it contains unnecessary assumptions, and it conflicts with well-established theory about how we get our eye color. That's enough to do in nearly any explanation.

4. Reasonable explanation
7. Poor explanation: circular
10. Poor explanation: untestable (given the fact that subconscious desires are allowed), excessively vague, questionable relevance, conflict with well-established theory
13. Reasonable explanation
16. This one is a *justification*.

EXERCISE 4-7

1. On the information supplied alone, explanation B could be taken as slightly more likely, since it would explain both the extinctions and the wobbly orbits of the other two planets.
2. It would very nearly eliminate explanation A. Whichever explanation is going to work, it must account for the regular timing of the extinctions.
3. It would detract from explanation B (see answer 1).
4. Both would be considerably less likely.
5. Both would be somewhat less likely, although A might survive better than B. This is so because of the possibility that Nemesis might have a somewhat unstable orbit itself, accounting for *some* variations in the cycle of extinctions.

EXERCISE 4-8

1. At least three: poltergeists, RSPK, and trickery on Tina's part. The RSPK explanation has two versions, purposeful (Tina is controlling the "force") and nonpurposeful (Tina generates but does not consciously control the "force").
2. The writer seems to give the RSPK explanation and the natural explanation about equal weight. Notice that, if all supernatural explanations are discounted, this becomes a much less interesting story. The writer knows, of course, that stories about people who do *not* exhibit strange or supernatural powers are a dime a dozen, even if they describe teenagers under stress.
4. Hint: Does one require more unusual assumptions than the other?

CHAPTER 5
Nonargumentative Persuasion

EXERCISE 5-1

1. The second sentence is innuendo—the speaker implants the idea of Harriet's lying without actually accusing her of it.
4. The word *although* downplays the claim that ends at the comma; the remainder of the passage is a persuasive definition of *socialism*.
7. Innuendo: The speaker has said very little in Professor Lankirshim's behalf, even though he has made his remarks sound sympathetic. Notice how the word "necessarily" works in the second clause: Although the speaker claims that the pro-

fessor's work isn't necessarily going downhill, it's certainly left open whether it's in *fact* going downhill. The last sentence of the passage giveth ("He's still a fine teacher . . .") and then taketh away (". . . if the students . . . are to be believed"). The *if* part of the claim at least opens up doubts about Lankirshim's teaching by planting the notion that students may not be telling the whole truth about it. If you were Lankirshim and needed an endorsement, would this passage give you much pleasure?

10. The phrase *up to* in the first claim is a very important weasler. This driver may add seven miles per hour when compared with *some* other drivers, but it may add considerably less speed than that, or nothing at all, when compared with others. Using *up to* allows the writer of the ad to compare this driver with the worst of the competition rather than the best. The emphasis on the phrase *seven miles per hour* is itself a slanting device, even a form of hyperbole. It may make features of the product, if it really has them, seem more exciting than they actually are. The reference to university tests is a proof surrogate. What are you told about those tests? Nothing. Finally, notice that the tests, if legitimate, establish only that extra clubhead speed causes longer drives—not that this driver will produce either.

EXERCISE 5-2

1. "Did better than expected" implies that Robertson was not expected to do well: This is innuendo. "Chuckling" is used so often to describe babies that this almost qualifies as a persuasive comparison. In any case, it carries the suggestion that Robertson is good-natured, but empty-headed. "Going easy on the Bible-thumping" is more innuendo: It insinuates that Robertson in fact is a biblethumper. "He invoked his friend God" belittles Robertson's religious convictions; and "for all his attempts to seem normal, the Howdy Doody–faced evangelist" combines innuendo (it suggests that he isn't normal) with an outright insult. "One moment of transcendent lunacy"—this is a downplayer: It undermines the importance of Robertson's theory.

4. We find three slanters with a common theme in this passage. The words *fraud, scam,* and *bribed* are all hyperbolic and all have overtones of criminality that are not being literally asserted in the passage. There are ways of stating the points in which these words occur that do not make such insinuations. The word *rubber-stamped* is also a slanter; Congress may not have changed the president's request, but it does not follow that they did not consider it. *Rubber-stamped* carries with it not just approval, but the idea that they would have approved the request whatever it may have been for. The word *radical* adds little but extravagance to the point about escalation. How much does it take for an escalation to be *radical?* We do not think the phrase *brain drain* is a slanter. Its straightforward meaning seems to fit the case.

EXERCISE 5-3

2. "Michael Hawkins, an undersea explorer and filmmaker, uses a Zephyr 75 outboard engine from International Marine Corp. The engine runs smoothly and is powerful enough to move a boat faster than some larger engines."

4. "The Japanese attack on Pearl Harbor surprised and angered most Americans." (The word *sneak,* which has become closely associated with the attack on Pearl Harbor, is pure slant. It is rare that one country announces beforehand when and where it is about to attack another. The phrase *surprise attack* carries the same literal meaning and is neutral.)

6. "Our government learned thirty years ago that an aggressive strain of bees had escaped in South America and would eventually make their way to the United States. Some scientists have been working on breeding genes from unaggressive domestic bees into the aggressive strain, but the government has not funded their efforts. If the new bees do serious damage to United States agriculture, it will cost U.S. consumers."

8. "Daryn Kaiser speaks quietly and only after he has thought about what he is going to say. He reacts strongly against anyone who contradicts him."

EXERCISE 5-4

The main difference is that the author who weasels may want attention brought to the claim but a way out of it is challenged; the one who downplays wants to call attention away from a claim in the first place. The latter may even *hope* for a successful challenge to the downplayed claim.

EXERCISE 5-5

This one is easy: Persuasive definitions define, or appear to define; persuasive explanations explain, or appear to explain; and persuasive comparisons compare two things. All are phrased in emotive language, and all may make use of hyperbole.

EXERCISE 5-11

1. The first question is obviously loaded: It presumes that the major media have been wrong, but gives no evidence of it. The claim in the second sentence is somewhat hyperbolic (what does *profoundly* indicate?) and remains unsupported. *Elite* is hyperbole; *major* was used to say the same thing in the first sentence. In the last sentence, the clause *if they do not hate America first* is both weaseling and very strong innuendo. *Smug contempt* is hyperbole—what does it mean beyond "plain" contempt in this context? These claims are insinuated: The major media are frequently wrong; the people who control the major media probably hate America, or at least its traditional ideals.

5. If you fall for this writer's tactics, by the time you've read this far you will be tempted to dismiss Sheila Rule's report on Somalia no matter what it says. The passage insinuates that the information in the report was contributed by the U.S. ambassador or the C.I.A., and is going to be either meaningless drivel or will be heavily biased in favor of American "imperialist interests." Referring to American interests as "imperialist" in itself is to dismiss those interests as illegitimate, without any argument.

CHAPTER 6
Pseudoreasoning I

EXERCISE 6-1

1. Appeal to belief
4. Appeal to pity
7. Subjectivist fallacy
10. Appeal to indignation. There is also an example of straw man in the last sentence —
    we'll meet straw man in the next chapter.

EXERCISE 6-2

1. No
3. Yes. A popular automobile may have continued support from its maker, and this
   can be advantageous to the owner of such a car.
7. No. Notice, though, that our likes and dislikes seem to be influenced by the
   opinions of others, whether we want them to be or not.
10. It can be. Advertising a product as best-selling may create a feeling on the part of
    consumers that they will be out of step with the rest of society if they don't
    purchase the advertised product. (But within limits almost any product can be
    said to be popular or a best-seller, so the fact that such a claim is made is no
    reason for one to feel out of step by not purchasing the product.) Usually, however,
    the "best-seller" tag is intended to make us think that the product must be good
    because so many people cannot be wrong. In other words, such ads in effect are
    appeals to the "authority of the masses" or the "wisdom of society." However,
    unless you have some reason to believe (a) that the claims made in the ad about
    unusual popularity are *true,* and either (b) the buyers of the product have them-
    selves bought the product for some reason that applies in your case as well, or
    (c) you could indirectly benefit from the popularity of the item (popular cars, for
    instance, hold their resale value), then to buy a product on the basis of such
    advertising would be pseudoreasoning.

EXERCISE 6-3

1. Fear of embarrassing her parents
3. No
5. No

EXERCISE 6-4

1. Indignation or anger
3. No
5. Yes. Even if the facts alleged in the letter do warrant anger about some things the
   media do, they have no bearing on the issue at hand, which is whether the media's
   complaints about denied access are justified.

EXERCISE 6-5

1. Probably desires of becoming trim and fit
3. No

5. One person may *believe* that the ad has given a reason for preferring one exercise device over another and a second may not. The first would be guilty of pseudoreasoning, the second not. The *ad*, in any case, gives no reasons.

EXERCISE 6-6

1. Fear of having foul-smelling carpets
3. Anyone's carpet might have an unpleasant odor. The ad does not give you reason to think that you might be especially likely to have this problem.
5. No

EXERCISE 6-7

1. Fear of breaking down with no means of getting help
3. No
5. Anyone might break down. The salesman has said nothing to make you think that you might be especially likely to have this difficulty.

EXERCISE 6-8

1. Family tradition; loyalty
3. Yes, though it may not be a *good* reason for buying a Ford, it *is* a reason.
5. No

EXERCISE 6-9

1. *Issue:* Whether we should stop producing nuclear weapons
   Feeling or sentiment: Fear of nuclear war
   Relevant? Yes. The speaker thinks that continued production of nuclear weapons increases the chance of nuclear war; though this may *in fact* not be true, it *might* be true, so the speaker's concerns about the horrors of nuclear war are *relevant* to the issue. (However, whether the reason given for stopping production of nuclear weapons—i.e., that nuclear war would be awful—is a *good* reason, depends on how likely it is that continued nuclear-weapon production increases the chances of nuclear war. The strength of reasons is discussed in Part Two.)
4. *Issue:* Whether Ralph should be unconcerned about his wife and go play poker
   Feeling or sentiment: The speaker is flattering Ralph.
   Relevant? No
   Name: Apple polishing
7. *Issue:* Whether Conwell had overdone it in his sympathy for the captors
   Feeling or sentiment: Indignation at such sympathy, and, later in the passage, ridicule
   Relevant? No
   Name: Appeal to indignation, Horse Laugh
10. *Issue:* Whether God exists
    Feeling or sentiment: Desire for happiness, salvation, etc.
    Relevant? No
    Name: Appeal to consequences of belief

This is the way the answers go if we take the issue to be whether God exists, as indicated above. But the issue of whether a person is better off *believing* in God, whether or not God exists, produces different, and somewhat more controversial answers. Your instructor may wish to discuss this one in class.

EXERCISE 6-10

1. *Issue:* Whether one should vote no on 11
   Feeling or sentiment: Fear of sanitation problems and chemical sprays
   Relevant? Yes. These problems are relevant to the issue. The problem is therefore one of evaluating the likelihood that Proposition 11 will lead to these problems.
4. *Issue:* Whether George ought to accompany his friends to the river
   Feeling or sentiment: Embarrassment about studying instead of horsing around
   Relevant? No
   Name: Peer pressure
7. *Issue:* Whether the speaker's suggestion is worthwhile
   Feeling or sentiment: Vanity
   Relevant? No
   Name: Apple polishing
10. *Issue:* Whether college students should be allowed to vote on local issues
    Feeling or sentiment: Anger, indignation, outrage
    Relevant? Yes. That students don't have to live with the consequences of their votes is a reason for not allowing them to vote here. Whether that is a good reason is another matter. (One hopes the speaker isn't elderly, terminally ill, or likely to be transferred to another town.)

EXERCISE 6-11

1. *Issue:* Whether Mary Smith is the best candidate
   Feeling or sentiment: The chair is trying to elicit fear of getting a poor schedule.
   Relevant? No
   Name: Scare tactics
4. *Issue:* Whether one should purchase this company's mortgage insurance
   Feeling or sentiment: Fear of one's family losing its home on the reader's death
   Relevant? No, although it is relevant to the issue of whether to purchase *some* mortgage insurance.
7. *Issue:* Whether covenants excluding blacks are a denial of equal protection of the law
   Feeling or sentiment: A sense of fair play
   Relevant? No. The fact that state courts were willing to allow blacks to discriminate against whites in buying property does not justify allowing whites to discriminate against blacks. (This case reminds us of the famous remark about the law against sleeping under the bridge; it was said to be fair because it applied to rich and poor alike.)
   Name: Two wrongs make a right
10. *Issue:* Whether the death penalty is proper punishment
    Feeling or sentiment: There are three appeals in the three reasons: (1) to fear, indirectly, since successful deterrence keeps the amount of crime down, (2) to a sense of justice, and (3) to a desire not to go against the majority.

Relevant? (1) and (2) are relevant; (3) is not
Name: Appeal to belief (sentiment #3)

EXERCISE 6-12

Ad
Issue: Whether there should be "attacks" on the tobacco industry—that is, whether the industry should be regulated by restrictive policies
Feeling or sentiment: The ad attempts to elicit feelings of sympathy and compassion, and to awaken a desire for justice and fair play for tobacco industry workers.
Relevant? Yes. When considering what policies to adopt relative to an industry, the effect of policy on the workers is a relevant consideration, one that must be weighed. Whatever else has been said about the ad, it has not set forth considerations that are completely *irrelevant*. How much weight to attach to these considerations is, of course, an entirely different matter.

Letter #1
Issue: Whether *The Progressive* should run the ad
Feeling or sentiment: There is no neat way of categorizing the "appeal" made in this letter. One way of analyzing it would be as an attempt to elicit scorn at the ad by what might be called a straw-man horse laugh ("What do they think, that we should all take up smoking? Ha, ha, ha! Should we risk nuclear war so people can keep their jobs? Ho, ho, ho!").
Relevant? It is difficult to see any relevance in this letter to the issue of *whether* The Progressive *should run the ad.* That an ad warrants scorn is not a reason for not running it. Your instructor may analyze this letter differently.

CHAPTER 7
Pseudoreasoning II

EXERCISE 7-1

1. Pseudorefutation
4. Straw man
7. Selfish rationalizing
10. False dilemma

EXERCISE 7-2

1. Burden of proof
4. This is pseudoreasoning of the slippery slope variety unless reasons are given in support of the claim that Nicaragua will be followed by the other Latin American countries.
7. Pseudorefutation
10. Burden of proof

EXERCISE 7-5

1. Whether this is pseudoreasoning depends on whether there are currently only two officers in the department. If there are actually more, then the writer's claim about leaving the department with no officers is a straw man.
4. One way to look at this is as a rather complicated version of the horse laugh. The writer is saying that many English words derive from Latin, but his conclusion that everyone should study Latin doesn't follow, of course. (The same case could be made for Greek, and for other languages as well.)
7. The reference to the Kremlin's having given up the argument is a red herring. If the Kremlin has indeed given the argument up, it may have done so for reasons other than the fact that it's not a good argument. The passage does not fit any of our other categories neatly, although it rather resembles a reverse genetic fallacy: If X doesn't hold this position, then it's a bad position.
10. There are several things to notice about this passage. First, it involves some straw man pseudoreasoning (it's unlikely that opponents of the appointments require that appointees "worship at the altar of forced busing," etc.). Second, the claim about the appointees being "under fire" could be misleading in that a certain amount of criticism is surely expected in many such appointments (in which case Mr. Reagan's remark may be seen as a slanter or something similar to a straw man). Finally, it's interesting to notice that neither argument nor pseudoreasoning is given for the claim that the commission's independence is not compromised: "That's hogwash" is just another way of saying "It ain't so."

EXERCISE 7-6

1. Ad hominem: Pseudorefutation
4. Ad hominem: Personal attack
7. Slippery slope
10. Ad hominem: Personal attack

EXERCISE 7-7

1. This is basically an ad hominem. Presumably the main thesis is that "left wing radicals" are mistaken in praising Marxist governments and in criticizing the U.S. government. The claim at the end about Soviet wrongdoing is irrelevant to the issue of whether the U.S. government deserves criticism, but it's relevant to whether the Soviet government deserves criticism. We'd suspect straw man here as well—"all these people can do is parrot the official line from Moscow," and so on.
4. Yes—this is clearly pseudoreasoning. Bush's remark is irrelevant to Mondale's claim. This case does not fit one of our regular categories, but the general category of smokescreen will do.
5. The quoted remark from Harris is not relevant to the conclusion drawn in this passage, although we don't find one of our categories of pseudoreasoning in which the passage fits neatly, although ad hominem would not be a bad choice. Notice a possible ambiguity that may come into play: "Having an impact" might mean simply that Harris wants his work to be noticed by "movers and shakers" or that he wishes to sway people toward a certain political view. It's possible that he intended his remark the first way, but it's being taken in the second way in this passage.
9. We don't find any obvious pseudoreasoning in this passage.

CHAPTER 8
Understanding and Evaluating Arguments

EXERCISE 8-1

1. a. Premise
    b. Premise
    c. Conclusion
2. a. Premise
    b. Premise
    c. Conclusion
3. a. Conclusion
    b. Premise
4. a. Premise
    b. Premise
    c. Conclusion
5. a. Premise
    b. Conclusion
    c. Premise
    d. Premise

EXERCISE 8-2

1. Premise: All Communists are Marxists.
    Conclusion: All Marxists are Communists.
4. Premise: That cat is used to dogs.
    Conclusion: Probably she won't be upset if you bring home a new dog for a pet.
7. Premise: Presbyterians are not fundamentalists.
    Premise: All born-again Christians are fundamentalists.
    Conclusion: No born-again Christians are Presbyterians.
10. Premise: If we've got juice at the distributor the coil isn't defective.
    Premise: If the coil isn't defective then the problem is in the ignition switch.
    [Unstated premise: We've got juice at the distributor.]
    Conclusion: The problem is in the ignition switch.

EXERCISE 8-3

1. Conclusion: There is a difference in the octane ratings between the two grades of gasoline.
4. Conclusion: Scrub jays may be expected to be aggressive when they're breeding.
7. Conclusion: Dogs are smarter than cats.
10. Unstated conclusion: She is not still interested in me.

EXERCISE 8-4

1. Independent
4. Independent
7. Independent
10. Independent

EXERCISE 8-5

1. Dependent
4. Dependent; one premise is unstated: What's true for rats is probably true for humans.
7. Independent
10. Independent

EXERCISE 8-6

1. Deductive
4. Valid; True
7. False
10. False

EXERCISE 8-7

(Refer to Exercise 8-2)
1. Deductive—probably
4. Inductive
7. Deductive
10. Deductive

(Refer to Exercise 8-3)
1. Inductive
4. Inductive
7. With unstated premise such as "Being more easily trained is a *sure* sign of greater intelligence," the argument is deductive; with an unstated premise such as "Being more easily trained is a *good* sign of greater intelligence," the argument is inductive
10. Deductive

EXERCISE 8-8

(Refer to Exercise 8-2)
1. Invalid
4. Invalid
7. Valid
10. Valid

(Refer to Exercise 8-3)
1. Invalid
4. Invalid
7. If it's deductive as explained above, it's valid.
10. Valid

EXERCISE 8-9

1. Probably true; had "out of order" been written in pencil on the meter, we'd have a different opinion, since most of the meters in our town have those words scrawled on them.

4. Probably true; a restaurant that does a good job on these three different kinds of entrees will probably do a good job on the rest.

7. Probably true; it's possible that the killer cleaned up very thoroughly, but it's more likely that the body was brought from somewhere else.

10. True beyond a reasonable doubt; it may be that consumption will drop in the future or that discovery of new reserves will increase, but, as long as consumption at some level continues, *eventually* all the oil will be used up.

EXERCISE 8-10

1. Assumed premise: All well mannered people had a good upbringing.
4. Assumed conclusion: He will not drive recklessly.
7. Assumed premise: All dogs that scratch a lot have fleas or dry skin.
10. Assumed premise: Every poet whose work appears in many Sierra Club publications is one of America's outstanding poets.

EXERCISE 8-11

1. Assumed premise: Most people who are well mannered had a good upbringing.
4. Assumed conclusion: He will drive safely.
7. Assumed premise: Most dogs that scratch a lot have fleas or dry skin. (Or: When this dog scratches a lot, he usually has either fleas or dry skin.)
10. Assumed premise: Most poets whose work appears in many Sierra Club publications are among America's outstanding poets.

EXERCISE 8-12

1. Assumed premise: All stores that sell only genuine leather goods have high prices.
4. Assumed premise: No ornamental fruit trees bear edible fruit.
7. Assumed premise: Nobody who has been a target of federal probes into alleged cocaine use can be an effective mayor.
10. Assumed premise: If population studies show that smoking causes lung cancer, then all smokers will get lung cancer.

EXERCISE 8-13

1. Assumed premise: Most stores that sell only genuine leather goods have high prices.
4. Assumed premise: Few ornamental fruit trees bear edible fruit.
7. Assumed premise: Few people who have been targets of federal probes into alleged cocaine use can be effective mayors.
10. Assumed premise: If population studies show that smoking causes lung cancer, then most smokers will get lung cancer.

EXERCISE 8-14

1.

4.

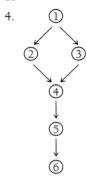

EXERCISE 8-15

(See Exercise 8-2)

1. ① All Communists are Marxists.
   ② All Marxists are Communists.

4. ① That cat is used to dogs.
   ② She won't be upset if you bring home a new dog for a pet.

7. ① Presbyterians are not fundamentalists.
   ② All born-again Christians are fundamentalists.
   ③ No born-again Christians are Presbyterians.

10. ① If we've got juice at the distributor the coil isn't defective.
    ② If the coil isn't defective then the problem is in the ignition switch.
    ③ The problem is in the ignition switch.

(See Exercise 8-3)

1. ① The engine pings every time we use the regular unleaded gasoline.
   ② The engine doesn't ping when we use super.
   ③ There is a difference in octane ratings between the two.

4. ① When blue jays are breeding they become very aggressive.
   ② Scrub jays are very similar to blue jays.
   ③ Scrub jays may be expected to be aggressive when breeding.

7. ① It's easier to train dogs than cats.
   ② Dogs are smarter than cats.

10. ① If she were still interested in me, she would have called.
    ② She didn't call.
    ③ [Unstated] She's not still interested in me.

(See Exercise 8-4)

1. ① You're overwatering your lawn.
   ② There are mushrooms growing around the base of the tree.
   ③ Mushrooms are a sure sign of overwatering.
   ④ There are worms on the ground.
   ⑤ Worms come up when the earth is oversaturated.

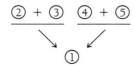

4. ① If you drive too fast, you're more likely to get a ticket.
   ② (If you drive too fast,) you're also more likely to get into an accident.
   ③ You shouldn't drive too fast.

7. ① You should consider installing a solarium.
   ② Installing a solarium can get you a tax credit.
   ③ Installing a solarium can reduce your heating bill.
   ④ Installing a solarium correctly can help you cool your house in the summer.

10. ① We must paint the house now.
    ② If we don't we'll have to paint it next summer.
    ③ If we have to paint it next summer, we'll have to cancel our trip.
    ④ It's too late to cancel our trip.

(See Exercise 8-5)

1. ① All mammals are warm-blooded creatures.
   ② All whales are mammals.
   ③ All whales are warm-blooded creatures.

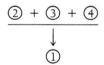

4. ① Rats that have been raised . . . have brains that weigh more. . . .
   ② The brains of humans will weigh more if they are placed in intellectually stimulating environments.

7. ① The mayor now supports the initiative for the Glen Royale subdivision.
② Last year the mayor proclaimed strong opposition to further development in the river basin.
③ Glen Royale will add to congestion.
④ Glen Royale will add to pollution.
⑤ Glen Royale will make the lines longer at the grocery.
⑥ [Unstated] The mayor should not support the Glen Royale subdivision.

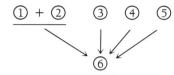

10. ① Jesse Brown is a good person for your opening in Accounting.
② He's sharp as they come.
③ He has a solid background in bookkeeping.
④ He's good with computers.
⑤ He's reliable.
⑥ He'll project the right image.
⑦ He's a terrific golfer.
⑧ I know him personally.

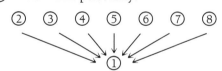

EXERCISE 8-16

1. ① Your distributor is the problem.
② There's no current at the spark plugs.
③ If there's no current at the plugs, then either your alternator is shot or your distributor is defective.
④ [Unstated] Either your alternator is shot or your distributor is defective.
⑤ If the problem was in the alternator, then your dash warning light would have been on.
⑥ The light isn't on.

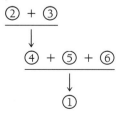

4. ① They really ought to build a new airport.
   ② It [a new airport] would attract more business to the area.
   ③ The old airport is overcrowded and dangerous.

Note: Claim number ③ could be divided into two separate claims, one about overcrowding and one about danger. This would be important if the overcrowding were clearly offered as a reason for the danger.

EXERCISE 8-17

1. ① Cottage cheese will help you to be slender.
   ② Cottage cheese will help you to be youthful.
   ③ Cottage cheese will help you to be more beautiful.
   ④ Enjoy cottage cheese often.

4. ① The idea of a free press in America is a joke.
   ② The nation's advertisers control the media.
   ③ Advertisers, through fear of boycott, can dictate programming.
   ④ Politicians and editors shiver at the thought of a boycott.
   ⑤ The situation is intolerable.
   ⑥ I suggest we all listen to NPR and public television.

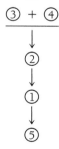

Note: The writer may see claim ① as the final conclusion and claim ⑤ as his comment upon it. Claim ⑥ is probably a comment on the results of the argument, although it too could be listed as a further conclusion.

7. ① Consumers ought to be concerned about the FTC's dropping the rule requiring markets to stock advertised items.

② Shoppers don't like being lured to stores and not finding advertised products.
③ The rule costs at least $200 million and produces no more than $125 million in benefits.
④ The figures boil down to a few cents per shopper over time.
⑤ The rule requires advertised sale items to be on hand in reasonable numbers.

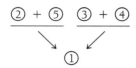

10. ① Well located, sound real estate is the safest investment in the world.
② Real estate is not going to disappear as can dollars in savings accounts.
③ Real estate values are not lost because of inflation.
④ Property values tend to increase at a pace at least equal to the rate of inflation.
⑤ Most homes have appreciated at a rate greater than the inflation rate . . .

13. ① HyperCard is overkill for a Rolodex substitute.
② HyperCard is not a "software erector set" unless the software you have in mind falls within a pretty limited category.
③ HyperCard is not particularly easy to use for producing a functional finished product.
④ I want it to do things it can't do (such as sort on more than two fields).
⑤ It does things I don't want it to do (such as save changes automatically).

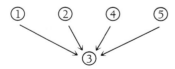

16. ① Measure A is consistent with the City's General Plan and city policies . . .
② A "yes" vote will affirm the wisdom of well-planned, orderly growth . . .
③ Measure A substantially reduces the amount of housing previously approved for Rancho Arroyo.
④ Measure A increases the number of parks and open space.

⑤ Measure A significantly enlarges and enhances Bidwell Park.

⑥ Approval of Measure A will require dedication of 130.8 acres to Bidwell Park.

⑦ Approval of Measure A will require the developer to dedicate seven park sites.

⑧ Approval of Measure A will create 53 acres of landscaped corridors and green-ways.

⑨ Approval of Measure A will preserve existing arroyos and protect sensitive plant habitats . . .

⑩ Approval of Measure A will create junior high school and church sites.

⑪ Approval of Measure A will plan villages with 2,927 dwellings.

⑫ Approval of Measure A will provide onsite job opportunities and retail services.

⑬ [Unstated conclusion:] You should vote for Measure A.

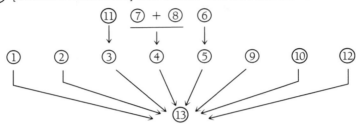

18. ① The gang war issue is very serious in our world because of guns and drugs.

② Jamaican police seized a cache of guns . . . , according to *Newsweek*.

③ These guns were earmarked for gangs in the U.S. and for anyone else who wants to buy them.

④ This was just one shipment and there are many others.

⑤ Guns are easily available to all illegal people.

⑥ A gang member was gunned down in front of a theater in Stockton that was showing *Colors*.

⑦ There are many hundreds of gang killings each year in L.A.

⑧ The police should do a better job of stopping these gangs from getting guns and killing innocent people.

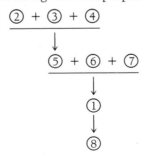

CHAPTER 9
Common Patterns of Deductive Arguments

EXERCISE 9-1

2.   P = Alexander will finish his book by tomorrow afternoon.
     Q = Alexander is an accomplished speed reader.
We'll do this one in two steps. First, let's put the letters in for the claims they represent:

   P only if Q.
   Q.
   Therefore, P.

The first premise, "P only if Q," is equivalent to "If P then Q," so we'll restate the argument with the claim recast:

   If P then Q.
   Q.
   Therefore, P.

This is a case of affirming the consequent and is invalid.

4.   P = Fewer than 2 percent of the employees of New York City's Transit Authority are accountable to management.
     Q = No improvement in efficiency of the system can be expected in the near future.

Pattern:

   P.
   If P then Q.
   Therefore, Q.

Modus ponens; valid

EXERCISE 9-2

2.   P = Higher education is living up to its responsibilities.
     Q = The five best-selling magazines on American campuses are *Cosmopolitan, People, Playboy, Glamour,* and *Vogue.*

Pattern:

   If P then not-Q.
   Q.
   Therefore, not-P.

Modus tollens; valid

Notice that this argument could have been symbolized with Q representing the claim "The five best-selling magazines on American campuses are *not Cosmopolitan,* etc.," in which case the Q and the not-Q would occupy each other's positions in the above pattern. All that is required to produce the modus tollens pattern is that the consequent of the conditional premise and the other premise deny each other; it doesn't matter which of them has the *not-* in it.

4.   P = Broc Glover will win the race.
     Q = Glover has had no bad luck in the early part of the race.

Pattern:
> If Q then P.
> Not-Q.
> Therefore, not-P.

Denying the antecedent; invalid

Notice that "P provided that Q" is usually equivalent to "P, if Q," and that this in turn is the same as "If Q then P."

EXERCISE 9-3

2.   P = The right amount of heat is applied to water at 212°F in a sealed container.
> Q = The pressure in the container increases without any increase in temperature.
> R = Steam at 212°F is produced.

Pattern:
> If P then R.
> If R then Q.
> Therefore, if P then Q.

Chain argument; valid

4.   P = Boris is a spy for the KGB.
> Q = Boris has been lying through his teeth about his business . . .
> R = We can expose his true occupation.

Pattern:
> If P then Q.
> If Q then R.
> Therefore, if R then P.

Reverse chain argument; invalid

EXERCISE 9-4

1.   P = Charles did not pay his taxes.
> Q = He did not receive a refund.

Pattern:
> If P then Q.
> Q.
> Therefore, P.

Affirming the consequent; invalid

4.   P = You are wealthy.
> Q = You are happy.
> R = You are smart.

Pattern:
> If P then Q.
> If Q then R.
> Therefore, if R then P.

Reverse chain argument; invalid

9.   P = She throws up her hands and exclaims about her good fortune.
> Q = Charles is present.

Pattern:
> If P then Q.
> Not-P.
> Therefore, not-Q.

Denying the antecedent; invalid

EXERCISE 9-5

1. All people who play in the National Basketball Association are athletes.
4. Some voters are not people who think critically.
7. This claim is ambiguous (see Chapter 2). It might mean either (a) Most mechanics are great lovers, or (b) All mechanics are great lovers. Note that (a) is not in standard form. When (a) is recast in standard form, it is: Some mechanics are great lovers.
10. In this claim, "Richard Nixon" denotes a class that has only one member, namely, Richard Nixon, and it says that no members of that class are members of the class of people who were impeached.

EXERCISE 9-6

For the following, the claims have been rewritten into standard forms for claims about two classes. Pay close attention to how this was done; often the rewriting is the only difficult part of such an exercise.

2. "No people with tickets are people who will be kept waiting."
   (a) No people kept waiting are people who have tickets.
   (b) All people without tickets are people who will be kept waiting.
   Claim *a* is the converse of the original claim and is equivalent to it.
4. "All kids allowed to go on the ride are kids tall enough to reach the bottom of the sign."
   (a) All kids tall enough to reach the bottom of the sign are kids allowed to go on the ride.
   (b) Some kids who are allowed to go on the ride are kids who are tall enough to reach the bottom of the sign.
   (c) All kids allowed to go on the ride are kids tall enough to reach the bottom of the sign.
   Claim *a* is the converse of the original and is *not* equivalent to it.

EXERCISE 9-7

1.   X = creationists
        Y = religious people
        Z = fundamentalists
   Pattern:
   > All Xs are Ys.
   > All Zs are Ys.
   > Therefore, all Xs are Zs.

   Invalid syllogism #1.

4.   X = cave dwellers
        Y = people who lived before the invention of the radio
        Z = people who are alive today
    Pattern:
        All Xs are Ys.
        No Zs are Xs.
        Therefore, no Ys are Zs.
    Invalid syllogism #2.

7.   X = philosophers
        Y = skeptics
        Z = theologians
    Pattern:
        All Xs are Ys.
        No Xs are Zs.
        Therefore, no Zs are Ys.
    Remember, a valid conversion of the second premise is: No Zs are Xs. And a valid conversion of the conclusion is: No Ys are Zs. Thus, this syllogism can be rewritten as follows:
        All Xs are Ys.
        No Zs are Xs.
        Therefore, no Ys are Zs.
    This is invalid syllogism #2.

10.   X = critical thinkers
        Y = recognizers of invalid syllogisms
        Z = logicians
    Pattern:
        All Xs are Ys.
        All Zs are Ys.
        Therefore, all Xs are Zs.
    Invalid syllogism #1.

EXERCISE 9-8

2.   X = barbiturates
        Y = substances that are more dangerous than alcohol
        Z = substances that ought to be sold over the counter
    Pattern:
        All Xs are Ys.
        No Ys are Zs.
        Therefore, no Xs are Zs.
    Valid syllogism

4.   X = people on the district tax roll
        Y = citizens
        Z = eligible voters
    Pattern:
        All Xs are Ys.
        All Zs are Ys.
        Therefore, all Xs are Zs.
    Invalid syllogism #1.

6.   X = pieces of software in the public domain
      Y = software that may be copied without permission or fee
      Z = software under copyright
   Pattern:
      All Xs are Ys.
      No Zs are Ys.
      Therefore, No Zs are Xs.
   This is one of the three variations of valid syllogism #2.

8.   X = countries the United States fails to help
      Y = countries that will accept aid from the Soviet Union
      Z = candidates for Russian subversion
   Pattern:
      All Ys are Zs.
      All Xs are Ys.
      Therefore, all Xs are Zs.
   Valid syllogism #1.
   The premises are in reverse order from that in which this pattern was introduced, but this fact is irrelevant to the validity of the pattern. We noticed this in the case of modus ponens earlier, and it is true for every pattern with more than one premise.

10.   X = the pornographic novels of "Madame Toulouse"
      Y = works with sexual depictions patently offensive to community standards and with no serious literary, artistic, political, or scientific value
      Z = works that can be banned as obscene after 1973
   Pattern:
      All Zs are Ys.
      All Xs are Ys.
      Therefore, all Xs are Zs.
   Invalid syllogism #1 (reverse the order of the premises to see this). Notice that in the original argument the first premise was stated more like "Nothing is a Z unless it is a Y." This is equivalent to "All Zs are Ys."

EXERCISE 9-9

2.   X = work that counts (i.e., is appreciated)
      Y = successful work "on the job"
      Z = traditional women's work
   Pattern:
      All Xs are Ys.
      No Zs are Ys.
      Therefore, no Zs are Xs.
   Valid syllogism #2 (a variation).

4.   P = The flood didn't happen.
      Q = It was absurd for Noah to have built an ark.
   Pattern:
      If P then Q
      (not-Q: this is an unstated premise)
      Therefore, not P.

Modus tollens; valid. However, the argument begs the question. It is intended to prove that the flood happened. But any person who has doubts about the flood will have exactly the same doubts about the unstated premise that it wasn't absurd for Noah to have built an ark.

Notice, too, that the argument could be analyzed as an RAA: We want to prove that the flood happened, and so we try to show that the contradictory position (that the flood did not happen) implies something obviously false, namely, that it was absurd for Noah to have built an ark. But this last claim is obviously false only to someone who accepts the Biblical account of the flood. Thus, even when it is analyzed as RAA the argument begs the question.

5. X = automated flight center projects at private airports
    Y = projects that get taxpayers' money
    Z = projects taxpayers should get some benefit from
    Pattern:
    All Ys are Zs.
    All Xs are Ys.
    Therefore, all Xs are Zs.
    Valid syllogism #1 (with premises reversed).

8. This famous argument could be analyzed as modus tollens, but usually it is analyzed as RAA: We want to prove that every event is caused by something other than itself, so we assume the contradictory position, and discover that this contradictory position implies an impossibility.

10. Y = perfections
     Z = attributes or characteristics of God
     X = existence (in other words, Z denotes a class that has only one thing in it, namely, existence)
     Pattern:
     All Ys are Zs.
     All Xs are Ys.
     Therefore, all Xs are Zs.
     Valid syllogism #1, with premises reversed.

11. X = new policies initiated by the dean
     Z = policies that emphasize employees and customer satisfaction
     Y = policies of the old curriculum
     Pattern:
     All Xs are Zs.
     No Ys are Xs.
     Therefore, all Ys are Zs.
     Invalid syllogism #2.

13. P = Eastwood was right about the character he played in *A Fistful of Dollars* being too mercenary.
     Q = He would never have made any of the "Dirty Harry" movies.
     Pattern:
     If P then Q.
     Not-Q.
     Therefore, not-P.
     Valid; modus tollens.

15.   P = All governments initiate drug-enforcement policies like those of Co-
            lombia, Europe, and the United States.
        Q = We could virtually eliminate the drug problem.
    Pattern:
        If P then Q.
        Not-P.
        Therefore, not-Q.
    Denying the antecedent; invalid
    The formulator of this argument *might* have meant to make the first premise say
    "We can eliminate the drug problem *only if* every country initiates policies . . .
    etc.," which would be "If Q then P," and would make the argument valid. It pays
    to be very careful when stating arguments—the author of this one might have had
    a valid argument in mind but simply misstated it.

EXERCISE 9-10

2. Classes:
        X = attempts to turn Olympic gold medals into commercial success
        Y = things that have only a small chance at commercial success
        Z = things worth years of dedicated effort
    Other claims:
        P = Carl Lewis's attempt to cash in on his four medals has not been com-
            mercially successful.
    Pattern:
        No Ys are Zs.
        P.
        If P, then all Xs are Ys.
        Therefore, no Xs are Zs.
    The second and third premises make a subargument (modus ponens), and the
    conclusion of that argument combines with the first premise to yield the conclusion
    from a valid syllogism. Here's the pattern with the subargument laid out fully:

P.	(original premise)
If P, then all Xs are Ys.	(original premise)
All Xs are Ys.	(modus ponens, from first two)
No Ys are Zs.	(original premise)
No Xs are Zs.	(conclusion of valid syllogism #2)

4. This argument requires some careful recasting to reveal its pattern:
    Classes:
        X = kids who are influenced by today's toys
        Y = people with a superficial conception of the world (or who see things in
            simple black and white)
        Z = aggressive people
    Other claims:
        P = If all kids who are influenced by today's toys are people with a superficial
            conception of the world, then toy manufacturers are causing the current
            generation to be aggressive people.
    Pattern:
        All Xs are Ys.

> All Zs are Ys.
> If all Xs are Zs, then P.
> Therefore, P.

What is required to establish the conclusion of this argument is a syllogism of the sort

> All Xs are Ys.
> All Zs are Ys.
> Therefore, all Xs are Zs.

If this were valid, the conclusion of the syllogism would combine with the last premise and, by modus ponens, produce P. But the syllogism required is not valid. Hence the argument fails.

In this version, we have interpreted the argument's premises in the strongest way in order to try to produce a deductive argument. Although we cannot isolate a valid deductive argument in the passage, there may be enough information in the passage to produce an inductive argument of at least modest merit. You might give it a thought after you've studied inductive arguments in the next chapter.

CHAPTER 10
Generalization and Related Inductive Reasoning

EXERCISE 10-1

1. Universal
4. Universal
7. Universal (probably)
10. Nonuniversal
12. Nonuniversal
15. This claim could be either universal or nonuniversal, depending on whether the speaker would accept a single exception as falsifying the claim. Of course, the same thing could be said of all the claims in the exercise, but in many the probable meaning of the speaker is a bit clearer.

EXERCISE 10-2

1. (a) It is reasonably clear what class is being generalized about.
   (b) The concepts *overwatering* and *underwatering* are rather too vague to be of much use to houseplant owners. The claim is made even more vague by saying that you might be overwatering *or* underwatering. *Turning yellow* is a little vague, but probably not too vague for most purposes.
   (c) If the concepts of over- and underwatering were spelled out more concretely, then you should be able to tell whether or not you're doing one or the other for plants that are turning yellow.
4. (a) Yes, the class is clearly enough specified.
   (b) What it means to say that they are "dumb, as seals go" is very obscure.
   (c) This all depends on what meaning is given to *dumb, as seals go.*
7. (a) The class is not clearly specified. One person's idea of what a right-winger is may be quite different from that of the next. (There are, of course, references

to senators that are even more unclear—for example, one might have said, "Some senators . . .")

(b) What these senators did is so unclear as to be virtually unintelligible.

(c) It is doubtful that you could know whether this claim were true, unless the charge against the senators was made much clearer.

10. (a) The class of magazines is not very clearly specified (it's about as unclear as *right-wing Republicans*).

(b) It is pretty clear what is being said about this class of things. What counts as a "clean and decent town like ours" is not really very clear, but the speaker probably means simply that such magazines ought not be sold in this town.

(c) Whether claims about what "ought" to be done can be known is controversial. Some philosophers argue that they cannot be known, at least in the way other claims are known. We'll talk more about "ought" claims in Chapter 12.

EXERCISE 10-3

1. Twenty percent more than what? (One might wonder what "real dairy" butter is, but it's no doubt safe to assume that it's just plain old butter.)

4. Fine, but how much rain did they have the year before? How much usually?

7. Okay, but don't jump to the conclusion that the seniors now are better: Maybe the teachers are easier graders.

10. In the absence of absolute figures, this claim does not provide any information about how good attendance was (or about how brilliant the season was).

EXERCISE 10-4

1. Superior? In what way? More realistic character portrayal? Better expression of emotion? Probably the claim means only, "I like Stallone more than Norris."

4. Fine, but don't infer that they both grade the same. Maybe Smith gives 10 percent each As and Fs, 20 percent each Bs and Ds, and 40 percent Cs, while Jones gives everyone a C. Who do you think is the more discriminating grader, given *this* breakdown?

7. Well, first of all, what is *long-distance?* Second, and more important, how is endurance measured? People do debate such issues, but the best way to begin a debate on this point would be by spelling out what you mean by *requiring more endurance*.

10. Apples and oranges. How can the popularity of a movie be compared with the popularity of a song?

EXERCISE 10-6

1. An inductive argument in the premises of which something is asserted to characterize a sampling of a class, and in the conclusion of which the same thing is said to characterize the entire class (or most of it).

5. A generalizing argument in the premises of which something is claimed to characterize a sampling of a class and in the conclusion of which the same thing is said to characterize a certain percentage of the target class.

EXERCISE 10-7

1. Students I've met from Tulare State.
4. Yes, assuming that a person's reports on his or her beliefs can inform us as to those beliefs.
7. The question is whether Tulare's football players are atypical with respect to belief in God. They could well be. The supposition weakens the argument.
10. Here again the question is whether car ownership renders the sample atypical with respect to belief or disbelief in God. It might not. For example, it's possible that all or almost all Tulare State students own cars. Then again, it might. Belief in God does vary with economic status, and car ownership does too.

EXERCISE 10-8

It could bias the findings if, for example, most of those surveyed (a) were of some single economic status, (b) were at a local gun show, (c) were public school teachers, or (d) were public servants.

EXERCISE 10-13

1. No
4. Yes
7. No
10. No

EXERCISE 10-14

1. The six students who turned in written evaluations
4. Yes. They could all be asked what their opinion of Ludlum is.
7. No
9. It's not very good. The sample is very small, given that it's not random, and very likely to be unrepresentative: The students who bothered to write have relatively strong feelings about Ludlum one way or the other, and there is no reason to think that the spread of their opinion will reflect the spread among Ludlum's students in general.

EXERCISE 10-15

1. Biased generalization
4. Hasty generalization
7. Hasty generalization
10. Biased generalization

EXERCISE 10-16

1. The past occasions on which Mike has done a deadlift
4. Yes
5. There *could* be important differences: Mike may have been using an improper technique in the past, and if he now uses a different technique he might not hurt his back. However, there are no important differences of which we have been made aware.

6. We have no information on this.
7. We have no information on this item, either.

EXERCISE 10-17

1. The four rides Clifford has taken with the Cyclamates
2. The ride he is considering taking with them this year
3. That he will become too exhausted to finish the entire ride
7. Weaker, since there is a relevant difference (flatter ground) between the target and the sample
8. Weaker, since we would have no diversity in the sample with respect to an unknown property of the target
9. Stronger, since we would have diversity in the sample with respect to an unknown property of the target
10. Stronger, since we would have diversity in the sample with respect to an unknown property of the target

EXERCISE 10-18

1. Relevant, weaker
4. Relevant, weaker
7. Irrelevant
10. Relevant, weaker

EXERCISE 10-19

1. Yes. The sample consists of our past visits, the target is your visit next week, and the characteristic being attributed to the visits is that they have been cold and foggy.
2. Yes. Whether a visit could have this characteristic is something that could be known.
4. Yes. We are especially impressed by the diversity of the sample. The past visits have occurred during different seasons. This fact strengthens the argument.

EXERCISE 10-20

2. Beatrice, we must presume, is reasoning analogically from unspecified past experience with other people. She is, in effect, reasoning that many of the people she's met who are polite, well informed, and kind (and these people are her sample) have also been honest, and that it follows therefore that the Tri-State rep (the target, another polite, well-informed, kind person) will be honest, too. Whether a person possesses such qualities can, of course, be known.

    The most important potential difference between the sample and the target is that the target is an investment salesman. We say "potential difference" because Beatrice's sample *might* consist of investment—or other—salesmen.

    As for the size and diversification of the sample, assuming that Beatrice has had a normal range of contact with people, her sample must be regarded as quite large, and highly diversified. This diversification helps overcome the weakness brought into the reasoning by the fact that the target is an investment salesman. Again, assuming that Beatrice has had normal contacts with others, most of the people in her sample who have been polite, well informed, and kind have probably also been honest, though undoubtedly some have not. Neither we nor Beatrice could specify an exact percentage, of course.

5. In this argument the speaker is reasoning analogically from past experience with other hit records. He's doubtlessly noticed that successors to hit records that imitate the hit turn out to sell very well. So his reasoning is, in effect, this: Many of the imitative follow-ups to hit records turn out to be successful; therefore, if we make this follow-up imitative, it will turn out to be successful, too. *Imitative* is, of course, a vague concept, but producers and record-company executives (and you and we as well) know well enough when a follow-up to a hit has a similar "sound." It is certainly knowable, too, whether a record sells well.

   There are no important differences between the sample and the target of which we, who have overheard the executive's remark, can be aware. The record about to be processed could be a follow-up to a very unusual-sounding hit, in which case an imitation might be too obvious for record consumers. Or perhaps the original hit was very long (so that people had their fill of that sound). But it is mere speculation on our part as to whether such differences exist.

   The size and diversification of the sample are no doubt quite large, as you don't ordinarily become a record-company executive without considerable experience in this area. As for the percentage of imitative follow-ups that become hits, this is a matter about which we could not conjecture, but it is worth noticing that even if only a small percentage of such records sell well, then it makes good business sense to produce them.

8. The most important thing to notice about this argument is that the relevant similarities and differences between the sample (cyclamates, saccharin) and the target (the newest artificial sweetener) all have to do with the chemical natures of these substances. Thus, unless you are a chemist or have some technical knowledge in this area, you couldn't reasonably conclude it likely that the latest sweetener is carcinogenic.

EXERCISE 10-21

1. We would classify this as an appeal to an illegitimate authority, hereafter abbreviated AIA. It is always risky to accept at face value salespeople's word about the merits of their products, even though they risk legal action if they make certain kinds of false statements. We think a critical thinker would need to get independent confirmation about this salesman's claim.

2. On the other hand, it would be an ad hominem (AH) to assert that the salesperson's claim was false simply because he was an illegitimate authority. However, it's not clear, in question 2, that the speaker is rejecting the claim as false: He may just be emphatically stating what we did above, in question 1. So let's call this a *possible AH.*

5. AH

7. The question here is this: Is an auto mechanic a reasonable authority on home air conditioning? Some auto mechanics do seem to have a knack for mechanical things, and there are some mechanical aspects to air conditioning, but we wouldn't buy a new compressor just because a mechanic said we needed one unless we could establish that he was knowledgeable about air conditioning. We'd say the fellow who bought the compressor was guilty of AIA.

9. This we'd call a *probable AH*. It's probable, though not certain, that the speaker is telling us to *disbelieve* the librarian's claim. (The speaker *may* be telling us just to suspend judgment on the claim, and if he or she is, then that's not an AH.)

10. No fallacies. Given that Dr. Coder is not a dermatologist, would it be an AIA to accept his diagnosis of this skin problem? We are inclined to think not. On the other hand, since the stakes are pretty high when you're dealing with something that may be life-threatening, you'd not be unreasonable to seek the opinion of a skin specialist. What would be unreasonable is to reject Dr. Coder's claim as false, on the grounds that skin is not his specialty. The second speaker comes close to doing that, but does not actually do so.

12. This isn't just an AH, in our opinion. Royko seems to be saying that Stallone isn't much of an authority on Vietnam since he wasn't there, and he obviously doesn't think much of Stallone's character and/or values.

14. This is an AH, since the speaker wishes to reject Sartre's views. This kind of AH, in case you don't remember from Chapter 7, is often called the "genetic fallacy."

CHAPTER 11
Causal Arguments

EXERCISE 11-1

1. Hot peppers at the Zig Zag pizza house have caused Grimsley's illness.
2. X is the common thread.
3. Is X the only relevant common factor preceding the occurrences of Y? Did the occurrences of Y result from independent causes?
4. The cause of Grimsley's problem is that he overate.
5. None do.
6. It's not bad, provided, of course, that Grimsley is taking into account the two questions asked above. Personally, we'd watch for other common factors, such as overeating or the heavy seasonings that might be found in each thing Grimsley ate. Too much grease would be another cause to consider—you know Zig Zag: It's not *real* Italian cooking.

EXERCISE 11-2

1. (a) Too much sleep is responsible for Hubert's physical incapacity.
   (b) X is the difference.
   (c) Is the suspected cause the only relevant factor that distinguishes this situation from those in which the effect is not present?
   (d) Hubert is coming down with a cold.
   (e) Post hoc.
   (f) No. There are far too many other things that might distinguish this situation from others in which he made it to the top of the hill.
4. (a) Lifting weights caused the backache.
   (b) X is the difference.
   (c) Is the suspected cause the only relevant factor that distinguishes this situation from those in which the effect is not present?

(d) Lifting something else improperly, bending over oddly, sleeping in an unusual position. But if it is true that this is the speaker's only backache, and that she's seen at least a little of life, then chances are that at one time or another she has lifted things, bent over, and slept in just about every conceivable way, and has done so without getting a backache.

(e) and (f). This might be a case of post hoc, ergo propter hoc, but having considered whether something else might have resulted in the backache, and having not had much luck in finding another plausible possible cause, we'd say that this argument is fairly decent.

8. (a) Being cooped up with his friends on the drive down from Boston has caused his colds.

(b) and (c). The argument involves two patterns of reasoning. First, Harold suspected that being cooped up with his friends is what caused his colds because that seemed to be the common thread. (He should therefore consider whether there were any other relevant common factors, and whether the colds resulted from independent causes.) Second, Harold uses "X is the difference." He stays at home, and thus reasons to himself, "The only difference between this situation in which I didn't get a cold and those situations in which I did was that this time I wasn't cooped up with my friends; therefore, I didn't get a cold because I wasn't cooped up with them; i.e., they gave me the colds." (Concerning this part of his reasoning, he should have considered whether being cooped up with his friends was the only relevant difference between this spring and last spring.)

(d) He might have caught the colds from different people while under way, or, even more likely, given the multitudes of college students who go to Florida in the spring, he could have caught the colds from someone after he arrived.

(e) None do.

(f) Harold's reasoning is not very good, and we doubt that you would have overlooked the possibilities that Harold overlooked for alternative explanations of his colds.

EXERCISE 11-3

(We've given our answers in the same (a), (b), (c) . . . format as was used in Exercise 11-2.)

3. (a) Violette caused the Cowboys to lose by watching them on TV.

(b) X is the difference.

(c) Was Violette's watching the Cowboys the only relevant thing that distinguished the occasion on which they lost from the occasions on which they won?

(d) This may have been the first time this season they played a superior team.

(e) X is the difference. If you thought that this argument was a case of post hoc, ergo propter hoc (she watched the Cowboys and they lost; therefore her watching them caused them to lose), you weren't far off. We called it a case of "X is the difference" because this wasn't the first game of the season: They had played other games, and this situation (in which they lost) was identical to the others except for one thing: Violette watched them on television. However, other writers might call this post hoc, and post hoc is a fallacy. The important point, in any case, is stated in answer (c).

(f) This is poor reasoning. It is remarkable that we have actually heard people make this argument. But when you think about it, this is the kind of reasoning that underlies most superstitious beliefs.

4. (a) The earthquakes caused the eruptions.

(b) The speaker here is assuming that the prior earthquakes are a common thread in the eruptions.

(c) Were the earthquakes the only relevant common factor preceding the eruptions? Could the eruptions have resulted from independent causes so that it was just coincidence that each one was also preceded by an earthquake?

(d) Eruptions and earthquakes were both the result of some more fundamental geological cause—for example, that involving the movement of continental plates.

(e) We would check with a geologist to see whether the earthquakes and eruptions were both the results of a common cause. If they were, then the fallacy would be ignoring a common cause.

(f) This isn't a very good argument. One should be open to the possibility of a common cause in cases like this, where it is very possible that one may exist.

6. (a) Walton's playing is the cause of whatever success the Clippers have had this season.

(b) Two patterns of reasoning are involved. First, Walton's playing is the common thread in occasions in which they win. Second, Walton's playing is the difference between occasions on which they win and those on which they lose.

(c) For the first pattern of reasoning, ask whether Walton's playing is the only relevant common factor in their winning and whether the occasions on which they won might not have resulted from independent causes. For the second pattern, consider whether Walton's playing is the only factor that differentiates the games that the Clippers win from those they lose.

(d) Other explanations are conceivable, but unlikely.

(e) None do.

(f) Strong argument.

7. (a) Mr. O'Toole gave his wife and daughter his cold.

(b) O'Toole's cold is the difference. The idea here is that the only difference between this occasion, on which Mrs. O'Toole and her daughter caught a cold, and other occasions on which they were healthy, was Mr. O'Toole's cold. Therefore his cold was the cause of their colds.

(c) Is Mr. O'Toole's cold the only thing that could have caused his daughter's and wife's colds?

(d) The wife and daughter caught their colds from someone else.

(e) This really is a case of post hoc because O'Toole's cold is almost certainly not a relevant difference. We know it is not relevant because we know that colds do not spread that quickly; at least, one doesn't begin to display symptoms so soon after encountering the virus. If we did not have that knowledge, then this would not be a bad argument, in our opinion.

EXERCISE 11-4

1. (a)
4. (c)
7. (a)

10. (b), but the claim is vague
14. (a)
17. (b)
20. (a)

EXERCISE 11-5

1. An experimental vaccine prevents chicken pox.
2. Target population: children
3. Type of investigation: controlled cause-to-effect experiment
4. The 468 children in the experimental group received the vaccine; the 446 in the control group did not.
5. One hundred percent of the experimental group had the effect (i.e., no chicken pox); 91 percent of the control group had the effect (407/446).
6. Yes. Given the credibility of the investigation, the claim "an experimental vaccine has been found effective" implies that the finding is statistically significant. Also, given the size of the samples and the difference in frequencies, you could conclude from what you have read in this chapter that the difference was statistically significant at .05.
7. Yes. Efforts taken to ensure that there were no important differences between control and experimental groups were not reported. But we'd assume, given the nature of the study and the credentials of the investigators, that the groups did not differ in any important way.
8. The experimental vaccine tested has been shown in this study to be effective in preventing chicken pox for at least nine months.

EXERCISE 11-6

1. (a) Exercise prevents colds.
   (b) Target population: humans
   (c) Type of investigation: controlled cause-to-effect experiment
   (d) The experimental group consisted of 10. There are two control groups, each with 10. The first, group A, consisted of the other ten nonexercising volunteers. The second, group B, consisted of the experimental group prior to the jogging program.
   (e) The experimental group had 25 percent fewer colds than control group A. Members of the experimental group also had fewer colds than the members of group B.
   (f) There are no reasons to assume that these findings are statistically significant. We know nothing about the researchers or their affiliations, and we know nothing about the publication in which their research was reported. Hence, we cannot take it on faith that the results are statistically significant.
   (g) We don't know anything about the gender or age or health or anything else about the volunteers. We also don't know anything about the process by which the volunteers were divided into two groups, so we don't know whether group B and control group A were alike in all relevant respects. Given no information about the researchers, we cannot assume selection into two groups was random.

(h) Jogging may reduce the frequency of colds. Then again it may not. This study wouldn't induce us to take up jogging.

5. (a) Injection of alpha-interferon into genital warts reduces or eliminates them.
   (b) Target population: the 8 million individuals who suffer from the warts.
   (c) This is an experimental cause-to-effect experiment, although the report does not identify a specific control group.
   (d) The experimental group consisted of 192 patients. The control group, we must presume, consisted of other, unidentified individuals who have been diagnosed as suffering from the warts. The size of the latter group cannot be determined from the information given.
   (e) Sixty-six percent of the experimental group showed clearing or reduction of the warts. We can probably assume that the warts do not ordinarily clear or reduce without treatment (a good report would have mentioned whether this is the case). If this is true, then the difference in frequency is very substantial indeed: sixty-six percent versus zero percent.
   (f) Yes. Even if there is a modest amount of spontaneous clearing or reduction of genital warts among untreated patients, sixty-six percent is surely a significantly greater improvement among the treated patients.
   (g) Had the reporter not omitted the usual rate of spontaneous reduction of the warts (as indicated in (e), above), we could determine the value of the treatment with greater confidence.
   (h) The claim at issue seems to be supported by the study.

8. *First Study*
   (a) Vasectomies don't cause disease.
   (b) Target population: adult male humans
   (c) Type of investigation: nonexperimental cause-to-effect study
   (d) The matched control and experimental groups consisted of 10,500 men; members of the experimental group were all vasectomized.
   (e) The frequency of the effect in the groups was "similar."
   (f) The report claims that the frequency of effect (disease) in the groups was "similar," so it is safe to assume, given the sources, that no statistically significant d was found.
   (g) The characteristics for which the pairs were matched is unreported.
   (h) The study strongly supports the claim that vasectomies don't cause disease, for at least about ten years.

   Second Study
   (a) Vasectomies don't cause heart disease.
   (b) Target population: adult male humans
   (c) Type of investigation: nonexperimental cause-to-effect study
   (d) The experimental group consisted of 1,400 vasectomized men. The control consisted of 3,600 men who had not had the operation.
   (e) The frequency of heart disease was "the same."
   (f) Yes, for the same reasons as given for the first study
   (g) Yes. Steps taken to ensure the similarity of the control and experimental groups were not mentioned. This is probably only a failure in the report, however.
   (h) Vasectomies probably do not cause heart disease in the first fifteen years after the operation.

9. (a) An abnormally high level of dopamine is a causal factor in SIDS.
   (b) Target population: human infants '
   (c) Type of investigation: nonexperimental effect-to-cause study
   (d) The experimental group consisted of thirteen infants deceased from SIDS. The control group consisted of five infants who died from other causes.
   (e) Eleven out of thirteen (85 percent) of the experimental group had dopamine levels "far in excess" of those of the controls.
   (f) Not really. It's not clear how the dopamine levels were quantified. Certainly the words of the investigator suggest caution.
   (g) Yes, the report does not state what steps were taken, if any, to match the subjects in the experimental group for other factors that might be relevant. The investigator's claim that dopamine could be a secondary cause indicates he thinks that there may be other important medical factors involved that cause both SIDS and the high dopamine levels.
   (h) What you should accept is the cautious claim of the investigator that a high dopamine level *may* be a cause of SIDS but may also be a secondary cause— that is, it and SIDS may both be the effect of some other cause.

10. (a) Radiation-induced tumors are prevented by dietary restrictions in rats exposed to high doses of X-rays.
   (b) Target population: rats
   (c) Type of investigation: controlled cause-to-effect experiment
   (d) The control group contained an unspecified number of rats that had been subjected to X-rays sufficient to produce tumors in all of them. The experimental group consisted of forty-four rats given the same dose of X-rays. The experimental rats were limited to two pellets of food a day; the control group rats were allowed to eat their fill.
   (e) None of the control-group rats had the effect (i.e., all the rats had tumors). Thirty-five out of forty-four experimental-group rats had the effect (i.e., no tumors). Thus, the frequency of the effect in the experimental group (35/44 = 80 percent) exceeded the frequency in the control group (0.00) by eighty percentage points.
   (f) The investigator is reported as saying that the study "demonstrates" that radiation-induced tumors can be prevented by restricting diet. The clear implication is, thus, that the results are statistically significant.
   (g) Yes. Neither the size of the control group nor attempts to randomize selection is mentioned. But this is clearly a reputable scientific investigation, so we'd assume that there are no breakdowns in the experimental design at these points.
   (h) The study strongly supports claim a.

11. (a) Encephalitis has declined in California during the past thirty years because more people are staying inside from 7 P.M. to 10 P.M. with their air conditioners on, watching television.
   (b) Target population: residents of California's Central Valley
   (c)-(f) By the time you reach this question, you should spot some confusion either in the investigation or in the report of the investigation. To establish a causal relationship between staying indoors and not getting encephalitis you would have to show that there would be fewer cases of the disease if everyone stayed indoors than if no one did. But you could establish a *correlation* between

staying indoors and not getting encephalitis merely by showing that the encephalitis rate was lower among those who stayed inside than among those who didn't, and this is apparently what the investigation attempted to do. However, that even this simple correlation was shown by the investigation is not clear from the report, because, according to the report, television *ownership* was compared with the encephalitis rate, not indoors television usership. Further, the statistics quoted—that 79 percent of the interviewed Kern County residents said they used their air conditioners every evening and that 63 percent said they watched television four or more evenings a week during the summer—are entirely unhelpful to the question of whether the encephalitis rate is related to either television ownership or television use. Finally, the last sentence of the report is totally incoherent. It makes no sense to talk of comparing the percentage of residents who spent more time indoors now with the percentage who spent more time indoors in 1950. (More time indoors than when?)

(g) Yes. No information is provided about actual encephalitis rates or about earlier usage of air conditioning and television. Further, staying at home, watching TV, and using the air conditioner, three different activities, seem to be treated interchangeably and confusingly here. We don't really know what is being measured or against what. Given the investigators, who are associated with reputable institutions, our suspicion is that the report may be more to blame for the various confusions than the study.

(h) As reported, the study supports only the statistic about television and air conditioner use among telephone owners in Kern County.

14. (a) A behavior modification program aimed at Type A individuals prevents heart attacks.

(b) Target population: Type A individuals

(c) Type of investigation: experimental cause-to-effect study

(d) The experimental group consisted of 592 out of 862 predominantly male heart attack victims; members of the group were given group counseling to ease Type A behavior. (Evidently all 592 were deemed Type A persons.) The matched control groups consisted of 270 subjects who received only cardiological advice.

(e) After three years, 7 percent of the experimental group had another heart attack, as compared with 13 percent of the control group.

(f) The material in this chapter suggests that the finding is probably statistically significant (at 0.05 level), given the size of the groups and the percentages involved.

(g) The report is unclear as to whether all subjects were of Type A, though perhaps this may be assumed, and it is also unclear as to what variables were matched. But, more important, details about how long counseling lasted are missing, and these could be important, since the report implies that continuation of the program was voluntary. Also, there seems to be confusion about what the investigators were researching—the relationship between the program and heart attack rate, between an actual behavioral modification and heart attack rate, between counseling and behavioral modification, or some combination or interplay of these.

(h) The conclusion the study supports (as reported here) is that Type A individuals who have had one heart attack can significantly reduce their chances of a second heart attack by participating (for some unspecified amount of time) in whatever kind of counseling program was conducted in the experiment.

CHAPTER 12
Moral Reasoning

EXERCISE 12-1

1. Prescriptive
4. Descriptive
7. Prescriptive
10. Prescriptive

EXERCISE 12-2

1. Nonmoral value
4. Moral value
7. Nonmoral value
10. No value

EXERCISE 12-3

2. People ought to keep their promises.
4. People ought not to claim credit for the work of others.
7. Actions that support charities are morally right.
10. A majority ought not be allowed to dictate to a minority.

EXERCISE 12-4

2. It is morally correct to compensate others whose work you voluntarily benefit from.
4. When one person acts to produce reasonable expectations on the part of another, and then the first unexpectedly leaves the other at a disadvantage, it is morally right for the first to compensate the second.

EXERCISE 12-5

1. *Issue:* Should the city memorialize McPherson to the same extent it does Winters?
   Factors:
   (a) Irrelevant. The city has no reason to celebrate either party's age.
   (b) Relevant. Such services are more for the living than the deceased, and thus there is a need for a larger service for the one whom more people knew. Notice that this is different from saying that one deceased *deserved* a larger service.
   (c) Irrelevant, or of very little relevance
   (d) Relevant. A substantial service would show gratitude toward the deceased and his family.
   (e) Irrelevant
4. *Issue:* Is hunting animals less justifiable than eating meat of purposely killed animals?
   Factors:

(a) Relevant. This factor brings up the issues of whether death by natural causes is to be preferred, and whether natural selection helps the population more than "hunter selection."

(b) Irrelevant, in our view. The animals did not decide that a short life was better than none at all, if it makes sense to speak of their having such choices. This factor could be controversial.

(c) Relevant, if true. This is a different kind of factor. Do slaughterhouses brutalize people (their employees), even if a smaller number of them?

(d) We do not see the relevance of this, since we are not sure of what a "non-innocent" animal would be.

(e) Relevant. More animals are commercially killed for food than as a result of hunting. This factor is linked to (b), and could be controversial as well.

EXERCISE 12-6

2. Clearly, the most obvious similarity between the subjects of Susan's views is that both euthanasia and abortion constitute taking the life of organisms that do not deserve to die. (This distinguishes both practices from, say, capital punishment.) Is this similarity significant enough to warrant Susan's treating them the same? From the other side, we can add that both euthanasia and abortion also prevent emotional and financial drains on people other than the subject. This too weighs for treating them the same, although it favors both rather than counts against both.

   We can think of a couple of factors that help to distinguish between the two practices. First, euthanasia often involves a choice by the subject. This is relevant, of course, only in instances where the death is indeed voluntary. In many things it does make a critical difference whether people request something or have it done to them without their consent. For such cases, this may make enough difference to justify Susan's different views on the two subjects.

   Second, it is controversial whether a fetus counts as a full-fledged human being. If one counts it as something less than such a human, this weighs on Susan's behalf. It would be necessary to have arguments to back up this claim about fetuses, of course. It would not be honest to count a fetus as less than a human *just so* one could then abort it.

4. An important similarity is that both candidates for tax deductions are necessary to their respective parties. Workers need work clothes, just the same as managers sometimes find lunches a necessary part of doing business with clients. This factor establishes an important similarity.

   What about the claim, sometimes made by the IRS, that work clothes can be worn for nonwork purposes? If this applied to one case but not the other, it would establish a relevant difference that might warrant different treatment at tax time. But notice that eating lunch benefits managers whether they talk business at the table or not. And proof that the work clothes are *not* used beyond the work place is analogous to proof that business *is* discussed over lunch—if both were given, the two cases match with respect to this factor.

   In short, we can find no relevant factor that is significant to warrant different treatment or the two possible deductibles. Maybe the IRS can help us out on this one.

10. Whether Hearst should be charged with and punished for a more serious crime than Woods depends, once again, on whether the differences between the two cases warrant such different treatment. The obvious difference is that Hearst caused a death and that Woods did not. This, in most of the courts in the land, would be enough to justify different treatment. But this doesn't mean there isn't more to be said. For example:

Woods was even more drunk than Hearst. This is relevant in that he probably produced a greater *risk* of hurting someone than Hearst did. To the extent that we punish people for creating dangerous or risky situations, this should make us consider punishing Woods at least as seriously as Hearst. The actual harm caused in Hearst's case looks a lot like plain bad luck when compared to Woods. Unless we're willing to admit that we'll punish people for having bad luck, this makes Hearst's punishment seem too severe or Woods' punishment seem too light.

One consideration that seems to run against the last point above is that nearly everything we do involves a certain amount of risk; luck is something we just have to live with in every aspect of life. We don't think this is relevant: The fact that luck plays a role in many activities is not a reason for letting it determine who is punished and for what.

So, although the law may have its reasons for being harder on Hearst, we find that punishing him more than Woods on the basis of their different luck is unwarranted.

EXERCISE 12-7

We supply here the premise needed to complete the argument. In some cases the principle claims given in the exercise should be rewritten to remove some of the slanted language.

2. (a) *Premise:* No industry should be policed if doing so would require a large bureaucracy and put an unacceptable burden on society.
   (b) *Premise:* No activity should be policed if the freedom to practice that activity is part of the freedom of speech and it does not involve outright harmful lies.
   (c) *Premise:* Any industry that helps cause the purchase of millions of dollars of goods or services that do not satisfy their purchasers ought to be policed.
   (d) *Premise:* Occupations that involve a form of lying should be policed.
   (e) *Premise:* Occupations that take advantage of people's innocence and gullibility should be policed.

EXERCISE 12-8

These issues can legitimately range so widely that any discussion we supplied may serve more to stifle than to help. We leave guidance up to your instructor.

APPENDIX 1
Categorical Logic

EXERCISE A1-1

2. Some lizards are not salamanders.

4. All lizards are reptiles.
6. Some semiaquatic reptiles are not snakes.
8. All places where there are snakes are places where there are frogs.
10. All lizards are reptiles.
12. No whales are fish.
14. Socrates is a Greek. Note: Claims like this are about single individuals. The way to handle them is as A- or E-claims. This one can be treated as "All people who are identical with Socrates are Greeks." Since only Socrates is identical with Socrates, we have turned the claim into one about a class with exactly one member: Socrates.

EXERCISE A1-2

2. All drugs are completely harmless substances. (False)
   Some drugs are completely harmless substances. (False)
   Some drugs are not completely harmless substances. (True)
4. No gardens are laborious projects. (Undetermined)
   Some gardens are laborious projects. (Undetermined)
   Some gardens are not laborious projects. (True)

EXERCISE A1-3

2. All encyclopedias are nondefinitive works.
4. No sailboats are sloops.

EXERCISE A1-4

1. False. Since (a) is a true E-claim, its converse, *No poisonous creatures are mosquitoes* is true, which is the contradictory of (b).
3. False. Begin by obverting both claims. This produces
   (a) Some sound arguments are valid arguments. (True)
   (b) No valid arguments are sound arguments.
   Then convert either of these. They now correspond to one another. From a true I-claim we can infer the falsity of the corresponding E-claim.
5. Undetermined. Obvert claim (a), then convert it. The results are
   (a) Some nonproductive factories are automobile plants. (True)
   (b) All nonproductive factories are automobile plants.
   These correspond, but nothing can be inferred about an A-claim from the corresponding true I-claim.
9. True. First, put the two claims into standard form:
   (a) Some people who are enrolled in the class are not people who will get grades.
   (b) Some people who will not get grades are people who are enrolled in the class.
   Then, if we obvert claim (a) and convert claim (b), we get
   (a) Some people who are enrolled in the class are people who will not get grades.

(b) Some people who are enrolled in the class are people who will not get grades.

We now see that (a) and (b) turn out to be the same claim. So, if the first is true, so is the second.

EXERCISE A1-5

1. Invalid:

   No C are non-S.
   All non-S are B.
   No B are C.

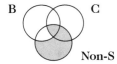

4. Invalid:

   All T are E.
   All T-T are E.
   All T-T are T.

   (T = times Louis is tired, etc.)
   (T-T = times identical with today)

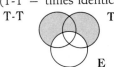

7. Valid:

   All H are S.
   No P are S.
   No P are H.

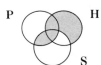

10. Invalid:

    All C are R.
    All V are C.
    No R are V.

    (Note: There is more than one way to turn this into standard form. Instead of turning nonresidents into residents, you can do the opposite.)

EXERCISE A1-6

1. No blank disks are disks that contain data.

   Some blank disks are formatted disks.

   Some formatted disks are not disks that contain data.

   Valid: Formatted disks   Disks that contain data

   Blank disks

4. All tobacco products are substances damaging to people's health.
   <u>Some tobacco products are addictive substances.</u>

   Some addictive substances are substances damaging to people's health.

   Valid: Addictive   Substances damaging to
              substances   people's health

                                      Tobacco products

7. All people who may vote are stockholders in the company.
   <u>Mr. Hansen is not a person who may vote.</u>

   Mr. Hansen is not a stockholder in the company.

   Invalid: Mr. Hansen   Stockholders in
                                       the company

                                       People who may vote

   Note: Remember that claims with individuals as subject terms are treated as A or E claims. (See A1-7, #7.)

10. After converting, then obverting the conclusion:

    No arguments with false premises are sound arguments.
    <u>Some arguments with false premises are valid arguments.</u>

    Some valid arguments are not sound arguments.

    Valid: Valid   Sound arguments
                  arguments

                                     Arguments with
                                     false premises

EXERCISE A1-7

2. After obverting both premises, we get:
   No ears with white tassels are ripe ears.
   <u>Some ripe ears are not ears with full-sized kernels.</u>
   Some ears with full-sized kernels are not ears with white tassels.

   Invalid: breaks rule 1

5. After obverting the second premise:
   Some compact disk players are machines with 4x sampling.
   <u>All machines with 4x sampling are machines that cost at least $100.</u>
   Some compact disk players are machines that cost at least $100.

   Valid

7. All people who may vote are people with stock.
   <u>No [people identical with Mr. Hansen] are people who may vote.</u>
   No [people identical with Mr. Hansen] are people with stock.

   Invalid: breaks rule 3 (major term)

8. No off-road vehicles are vehicles allowed in the unimproved portion of the park.
   <u>Some off-road vehicles are not four-wheel-drive vehicles.</u>
   Some four-wheel-drive vehicles are allowed in the unimproved portion of the park.

   Invalid: breaks rule 1

EXERCISE A1-8

 2. Valid; breaks no rule
 4. Invalid; breaks rule 3
 6. Invalid; breaks rule 3
 8. Invalid; breaks rule 2
10. Invalid; breaks rule 2

APPENDIX 2
Truth-Functional Logic

EXERCISE A2-1

1. Q → P
2. Q → P
3. P → Q
4. Q → P
5. (Q → P) & (P → Q)

EXERCISE A2-2

 1. (P → Q) & R
 4. P → (Q → R)
 7. P → (Q v R)
10. ~(P → Q)
13. ~Q v P

EXERCISE A2-3

1. P	Q	R	(P → Q)	(P → Q) & R
T	T	T	T	T
T	T	F	T	F
T	F	T	F	F
T	F	F	F	F
F	T	T	T	T
F	T	F	T	F
F	F	T	T	T
F	F	F	T	F

4.

P	Q	R	Q → R	P → (Q → R)
T	T	T	T	T
T	T	F	F	F
T	F	T	T	T
T	F	F	T	T
F	T	T	T	T
F	T	F	F	T
F	F	T	T	T
F	F	F	T	T

10.

P	Q	P → Q	~(P → Q)
T	T	T	F
T	F	F	T
F	T	T	F
F	F	T	F

EXERCISE A2-4

1. Invalid:

P	Q	~P	~Q	Q → P	Q v (Q → P)
T	T	F	F	T	T
T	F	F	T	T	T
F	T	T	F	F	T
F	F	T	T	T	T

(Row 3)

4. Invalid:

P	Q	R	P → Q	Q → R	P → (Q → R)
T	T	T	T	T	T
T	T	F	T	F	F
T	F	T	F	T	T
T	F	F	F	T	T
F	T	T	T	T	T
F	T	F	T	F	T
F	F	T	T	T	T
F	F	F	T	T	T

(Rows 6 and 8)

7. Invalid:

P	Q	R	~Q	P & R	(P & R) → Q	~P
T	T	T	F	T	T	F
T	T	F	F	F	T	F
T	F	T	T	T	F	F
T	F	F	T	F	T	F
F	T	T	F	F	T	T
F	T	F	F	F	T	T
F	F	T	T	F	T	T
F	F	F	T	F	T	T

(Row 4)

EXERCISE A2-5

1. Chain argument
2. Disjunctive argument
3. Constructive dilemma
4. Modus tollens
5. Destructive dilemma

EXERCISE A2-6

1.

Line number	Annotation
4.	1, 3, CA
5.	2, CONTR
6.	4, 5 CA

4.

Line number	Annotation
4.	3, CONTR
5.	2, 4, MP
6.	2, 5, CONJ
7.	1, 6, MP

EXERCISE A2-7

1.
1. P → R   (Premise)
2. R → Q   (Premise) /∴~P v Q
3. P → Q   1, 2, CA
4. ~P v Q   3, IMPL

4.
1. P v (Q & R)   (Premise)
2. (P v Q) → S   (Premise) /∴S
3. (P v Q) & (P v R)   1, DIST
4. P v Q   3, SIM
5. S   2, 4, MP

7.
1. (M v R) & P   (Premise)
2. ~S → ~P   (Premise)
3. S → ~M   (Premise) /∴R
4. P   1, SIM
5. P → S   2, CONTR
6. S   4, 5, MP
7. ~M   3, 6, MP
8. M v R   1, SIM
9. R   7, 8, DA

10.
1. P v (R & Q)   (Premise)
2. R → ~P   (Premise)
3. Q → T   (Premise) /∴R→T
4. (P v R) & (P v Q)   1, DIST
5. P v Q   4, SIM
6. P → ~R   2, CONTR
7. ~R v T   3, 5, 6, CD
8. R → T   7, IMPL

EXERCISE A2-8

1. 1. C → ~S   (Premise)
   2. ~L → S   (Premise) /∴C→L
   3. ~S → ~~L   2, CONT
   4. ~S → L   3, DN
   5. C → L   1, 4, CA

The deduction demonstrates that the argument is valid.

4.

M	C	K	H	T	(~C → ~M)	(~M → ~K)	(C v H)	(T → ~H)	(T → K)
T	T	T	T	T	T	T	T	F	T
T	T	T	T	F	T	T	T	T	T
T	T	T	F	T	T	T	T	T	T
T	T	T	F	F	T	T	T	T	T
T	T	F	T	T	T	T	T	F	F
T	T	F	T	F	T	T	T	T	T
T	T	F	F	T	T	T	T	T	F

In the seventh row, all the premises are true and the conclusion is false; hence the argument is invalid. (To save space, we've included only columns for reference, for the premises, and for the conclusion.)

Index

Addition (as rule of deduction), 381
Ad hominem, 178–181
  circumstantial, 179
Advertising, 137–140
Ambiguity, 21
  grouping, 23
  semantical, 22
  syntactical, 22
Analogical arguments. *See* Arguments, analogical
Analogies. *See* Comparisons, explanatory
Analytic definitions. *See* Definitions
Anecdotal evidence, fallacy of, 281
Antecedent (of a conditional claim), 234, 370
  denial of, 238–239
Apple polishing, 158–159
Argumentative essays, 388
Arguments, 8, 202
  deductive, 209–213
  diagrams for, 218–221
  and explanations, 83–85
  inductive, 209–213, 271–280
    analogical, 286–288
    statistical, 274–279
  and issues, 10
  patterns of, 232, 233
    truth-functional, 376–378
  sound, 211
  strong, 212
  structure of, 218–221
  unstated, 203
  valid, 211

Association (as rule of deduction), 384
Assumptions
  behind questions, 119
  hidden, 3
  unnecessary (in explanations), 99
Averages, 268–269

Background knowledge, 65–66
Bandwagon, 157–158
Begging the question, 255–256
Belief
  appeal to, 150–152
  appeal to consequences of, 152–153
Bias
  in inductive arguments, 272
  of sources, 77–79
  See also Sample, representativeness of
Biased generalization, fallacy of, 280
Burden of proof, 182–184

Causal agent, 311
Causal arguments
  about populations, 310–318
  about specific events, 300–306
Causal chains, 87
Causal explanations. *See* Explanations, causal
Cause-to-effect experiments, 311–315
Chain argument, 240, 381
Claims, 3
  ambiguous. *See* ambiguity
  analytically true, 38–39

Claims (*cont.*)
  categorical, 353
  causal, 300
  comparative general, 266–268
  conflicting, 59
  descriptive and prescriptive, 328–329
  general, 262
  spoken, 47–49
  universal general, 262
  vague, 27–28
  variables for. *See* Variables
Clarity
  and complexity, 40
  obstacles to, 21
Classes
  claims about, 243
  variables for. *See* Variables
Common cause
  consideration of (in explanations), 100
  fallacy of assuming a, 303
Common practice, 163
Common thread causal reasoning, 302–303
Commutation (as rule of deduction), 384
Comparative general claims. *See* Claims,
    comparative
Comparisons
  explanatory, 101–103
  persuasive, 126, 128
Complementary term (in categorical claims),
    357
Complexity, 40–43
Complicated language. *See* Complexity
Composition, fallacy of, 264
Compound claims, symbolization of, 373
Conclusions, 8, 202–205
  indicators, 204
  and issues, 10
  unstated, 236
Conditional claim, 234, 370
Confidence interval. *See* Error margin
Confidence level (of an inductive argument),
    276
Conflicting claims. *See* Claims
Conjunction, 369
  as rule of deduction, 382
Consequent (of a conditional claim), 234, 370
  affirming the, 235–236
Consistency (of explanations with well-
    established theories), 100
Contradictories, 59, 355
  See also Negation
Contraposition
  of categorical claims, 359
  as rule of deduction, 384

Contraries, 59, 355
Control group
  in cause-to-effect experiments, 311
Conversion (of categorical claims), 357
  invalid, 245–246
  valid, 244–245
Credibility, 67
  of observers, 73
Critical thinking
  defined, 3
  distinguished from logic, 5–6
  purposes behind, 6–8
  supported and unsupported, 8–9
  and writing, 12

Deception, 118
Deduction (truth-functional), 379
    See also Arguments, deductive
Definitions, 32–34
  analytic, 35
  by example, 34
  persuasive, 35, 126
  precising, 35
  stipulative, 35
  by synonym, 34–35
DeMorgan's laws (as rule of deduction), 384
Denotation. *See* Meaning
Dependent premises. *See* Premises,
    dependent
Dictionaries, 31
Dilemma
  constructive (as rule of deduction), 382
  destructive (as rule of deduction), 382
  false. *See* False dilemma
Disjunction, 370
Disjunctive argument (as rule of deduction),
    382
Distribution
  as rule of deduction, 384
  of terms in categorical claims, 366
Division, fallacy of, 164
Double negation (as rule of deduction), 383
Downplayers, 122
Dysphemisms, 117

Emotionally charged language. *See* Emotive
    force
Emotive force, 33
Error margin, 276
Essay topics (list), 394
Euphemisms, 117–118
Exaggeration. *See* Hyperbole, Straw man

Example, definition by. *See* Definitions
Experimental group
  in cause-to-effect experiments, 311
Expertise, 67–69
Explanations, 83
  and arguments, 83–85
  causal, 87–92
  functional, 94–95
  and justifications, 85–86
  persuasive, 126
  psychological, 92–94
Explanatory power, 98
Exportation (as rule of deduction), 384

Fallacy, 146
  of assuming a common cause. *See*
    Common cause
  of biased generalization. *See* Biased
    generalization
  of hasty generalization, 280
  genetic, 180–181
  of reversed causation. *See* Reversed
    causation
  subjectivist, 148
False dilemma, 186–188
Fear. *See* Scare tactics
Feelings
  and advertising, 138
  and pseudoreasoning, 154
  as supply reasons, 9
Frequency (of effect or suspected cause in
    causal arguments), 311
Functional explanations. *See* Explanations,
    functional

General claims. *See* Claims, general
Generalizations
  fallacies of, 280
  inductive, 271–274
  statistical, 274–281
Genetic fallacy, 180–181
Gobbledygook, 44
Government publications, 75

Hasty generalization, fallacy of, 280
Horse laugh, 159–160
Hyperbole, 124
Hypocrisy (and pseudorefutations), 181

Implication (as rule of deduction), 384
Independent premises. *See* Premises,
    independent

Indignation. *See* Spite or indignation, appeal
    to
Induction. *See* Arguments, inductive
Information tailoring, 132
Innuendo, 119
Irrelevance, of pseudoreasons, 146–147
Issues, 10

Laws of nature (and explanations), 91
Loaded questions, 119
Logic
  categorical, 353
  distinguished from critical thinking, 5–6
  truth-functional, 368
Loyalty, appeal to, 158

Mean. *See* Averages
Meaning
  denotative, 32
  sense, 32
Median. *See* Averages
Mode. *See* Averages
Modus ponens, 234–235, 380
Modus tollens, 238, 381
Moral values (expressed in claims), 329

Necessary and sufficient conditions, 375
Negation, 369
News media, 75, 132–136
Nicknames, 124
Nonargumentative persuasion, 116
Noncircularity (of explanations), 96
Nonexperimental cause-to-effect studies. *See*
    Causal arguments about populations
Nonexperimental effect-to-cause studies. *See*
    Causal arguments about populations

Objectivity
  and credibility, 71–72
  of truth, 149
Observations, conflicts with, 61
Obversion (of categorical claims), 357–358
Only if . . . (and *if . . . then . . .*), 239, 373
Ought—getting an *ought* from an *is*, 331–334
Outlining, 390

Peer pressure, 157–158
Percentages
  before and after, 270
  and percentage points, 269

Personal attack, 178–179
Persuasion. *See* Nonargumentative persuasion
Persuasive definitions. *See* Definitions
Physical explanations. *See* Explanations, causal
Pity, appeal to, 155–156
Population
  causation in. *See* Causation
  target. *See* Target
Post hoc (ergo propter hoc) fallacy, 305–306
Precising definitions. *See* Definitions
Predicate term. *See* Terms of categorical claims
Premises, 8, 202–205
  acceptability of, 222
  dependent and independent, 204–205, 219–220
  indicators, 204, 220
  unstated, 215–216, 236
Principal claim, 8
Proof
  indirect, 252–254
  surrogates, 123
  See also Burden of proof
Pseudoexplanations, 100
Pseudoreasoning, 146–148, 177, 393
  varieties of. *See* Ad hominem; Apple polishing; Belief, appeal to; Belief, appeal to the consequences of; Burden of proof; Common practice; False dilemma; Horse laugh; Loyalty, appeal to; Peer pressure; Personal attack; Pity, appeal to; Pseudorefutation; Rationalizing (selfish); Scare tactics; Slippery slope; Spite or indignation, appeal to; Straw man; Subjectivist fallacy; Two wrongs make a right; Wishful thinking
Pseudoreasons, 147, 221
Pseudorefutation, 179–180
Psychological explanations. *See* Explanations, psychological
Psychological inducements. *See* Pseudoreasoning
Psychological theories, 93

Question-begging. *See* Begging the question

RAA. *See* Reductio ad absurdum
Randomness. *See* Sample, random selection of
Rationalizing. *See* Selfish rationalizing

Reasons (for accepting claims), 3
Re-created "news," 133
Red herring, 147–148
Reductio ad absurdum, 253–254
Reference works, 74
Relevance (of explanations), 97
Relevantly similar cases (and relevantly similar treatment), 335–338
Reliability (of explanations), 98
Representativeness. *See* Sample
Reverse chain argument, 241–242
Reversed causation, fallacy of, 304
Ridicule. *See* Horse laugh
Rules of the syllogism, 366

Sample, 271
  in cause-to-effect experiments, 311–313
  random selection of, 272
  representativeness of, 271–273
  size of, 278, 287
Scare tactics, 154–155
Selfish rationalizing, 181–182
Sensationalism in the news, 135
Sense. *See* Meaning
Similarities (between samples and targets). *See* Sample, representativeness of
Simplification (as rule of deduction), 381
Slanters, 117
Slippery slope, 188
Smokescreens, 147
Soundness (of arguments). *See* Arguments, strong
Specific events
  causation in. *See* Causation
  explanations of, 91
Spite or indignation, appeal to, 161–162
Spoken claims. *See* Claims
Square of opposition, 355–357
Standard form categorical claims, 353
Standards of comparison, 267
Statistical generalizations
  See Arguments, statistical inductive
Statistical significance (in causal arguments about populations), 312–313
Stereotypes, 123
Stipulative definitions. *See* Definitions
Straw man, 184–185
Strength (of arguments). *See* Arguments, strong
Subarguments, 220
Subcontraries, 356
Subject term. *See* Terms of categorical claims
Subjectivist fallacy, 148–149

Syllogisms, 160, 247, 359–360
  valid, 247–248
  invalid, 248–249
Symbolization (of truth-functional claims), 369–375
Synonyms
  definition by. *See* Definitions

Target (population), 271
Tautology (as rule of deduction), 384
Television
  and advertising, 137–138
  and news, 135–136
Terms (of categorical claims), 353
Testability (of explanations), 96
Truth-functional equivalences, 383
Truth-functional logic. *See* Logic
Truth tables, 368
  testing validity by, 376–378
Two wrongs make a right, 162–163

Universal claims. *See* Claims, universal

Vagueness, 27
  contextual, 27
  in explanations, 97
  proper, 27
Validity (of arguments). *See* Arguments, valid
Value-expressing claims. *See* Claims, descriptive and prescriptive
Vanity, appeal to, 159
Variables
  claim, 233, 369
  class, 243, 353
Venn diagrams, 354
  testing syllogisms by, 360–364

Weaslers, 120
Wishful thinking, 146, 153
Words
  ambiguous, 22
  unfamiliar, 31–32
Writing
  and critical thinking, 12, 388–394
Wyrob, P., 469